Definitive
XSL-FO

ISBN 0-13-140374-5

94999

9 780131 403741

The Charles F. Goldfarb Definitive XML Series

Titles in this series are produced using XML, SGML, and/or XSL. XSL-FO documents are rendered into PDF by the XEP Rendering Engine from RenderX: www.renderx.com

About the Series Author

Charles F. Goldfarb is the father of XML technology. He invented SGML, the Standard Generalized Markup Language on which both XML and HTML are based. You can find him on the Web at: www.xmlbooks.com

About the Series Logo

The rebus is an ancient literary tradition, dating from 16th century Picardy, and is especially appropriate to a series involving fine distinctions between markup and text, metadata and data. The logo is a rebus incorporating the series name within a stylized XML comment declaration.

Definitive
XSL-FO

G. Ken Holman

PRENTICE HALL
Professional Technical Reference
Upper Saddle River, NJ 07458
www.phptr.com

A Cataloging-in-Publication Data record for this book can be obtained from the Library of Congress.

Editorial/Production Supervisor: *Faye Gemmellaro*
Editor in Chief: *Mark L. Taub*
Editorial Assistant: *Noreen Regina*
Marketing Manager: *Chanda Leary-Coutu*
Manufacturing Manager: *Alexis R. Heydt-Long*
Manufacturing Buyer: *Maura Zaldivar*
Cover Design: *Anthony Gemmellaro*
Cover Design Director: *Jerry Votta*
Book Design: *Dmitry Kirsanov*

Opinions expressed in this book are those of the Author and are not necessarily those of the Publisher or Series Editor.

Series logo by Dmitry Kirsanov and Charles F. Goldfarb, © 2002 Charles F. Goldfarb.

Prentice Hall books are widely used by corporations and government agencies for training, marketing, and resale.

For more information regarding corporate and government bulk discounts, contact:

Corporate and Government Sales: (800) 382–3419 or corpsales@pearsontechgroup.com

Printed in the United States of America

10 9 8 7 6 5 4 3 2 1

ISBN: 0–13–140374–5

Pearson Education LTD.
Pearson Education Australia PTY, Limited
Pearson Education Singapore, Pte. Ltd.
Pearson Education North Asia Ltd.
Pearson Education Canada, Ltd.
Pearson Educación de Mexico, S.A. de C.V.
Pearson Education—Japan
Pearson Education Malaysia, Ptd. Ltd.

With my love
to my parents Julie and Ted.

Overview

Contents

Chapter 7 Static content and page geometry sequencing 187

Contents

Contents

Foreword

Samuel Wesley said it best, back in 1700:

"Style is the dress of thought."

In other words, if you want to communicate your data well, you need to dress it in a style that will be accepted and understood by your intended audience.

For centuries, the needed styles have been achieved by means of sophisticated formatting and page-oriented navigational tools. The popular Web-based presentation technologies, such as HTML and CSS, can't do this job. But the alternatives, until recently, have all been proprietary.

Now the W3C's Extensible Stylesheet Language Formatting Objects (XSL-FO) Recommendation offers a standard XML vocabulary for describing almost any print-like style.

If you've worked with XPath and XSLT, you know the power of XSL to transform a document. XSL-FO is the rest of the XSL standard. It lets you style the rendition of your data with the meticulous control needed to accommodate the cultural expectations of different readers and the constraints of their environments.

G. Ken Holman is the perfect author to teach the powerful capabilities of XSL-FO. He founded the OASIS XSLT/XPath Conformance Committee and was a member of the W3C group that developed XML.

No one has taught the subject more. For his consulting firm, Crane Softwrights, Ken teaches XSL personally throughout the world and on Web-casts, and indirectly though the licensing of training courses.

Ken has developed a unique list-based style for writing about XSL that eliminates the problems that normal prose can introduce. Web Techniques said "Holman's outline style is surprisingly easy to read. I'd like to see other authors adopt his approach."

Canadian designer Dmitry Kirsanov created a book design that fully supports Ken's writing style. The design has been realized through XSL-FO stylesheets developed by Alina Kirsanova.

The result is Definitive XSL-FO. It will help you dress your thoughts in style, by mastering the power of XSL Formatting Objects.

Charles F. Goldfarb
Saratoga, CA
March 2003

Preface

We often take the printed form of information for granted.

Yet how many of us are satisfied with the printing functionality of a web browser? How often have you found the paginated result of printing a lengthy web document as easy to navigate as the electronic original?

Navigating a paginated document is very different from navigating a web page, and browser-based navigation mechanisms, understandably, will not work on printed output. How would we follow a printed hyperlink when the visible clickable content hides the underlying hyperlink target address?

When we produce a paginated presentation of our XML information, we necessarily must offer to the consumers of our documents a set of navigation tools different from those available on our web pages. These navigational aids have been honed since bound books have been used: headers, footers, page numbers, and page number citations are some of the constructs we use to find our way around a collection of fixed-sized folios of information.

Layout and typesetting controls give us the power to express our information on pages in a visually pleasing and perhaps meaningful way using a set of familiar typesetting conventions. Vendors of printing and publishing software have offered proprietary solutions implementing their choices of controls and aspects of layout using their semantics for paginated production. We may have been reluctant to use these proprietary tools for fear of locking ourselves into a technology not supported, or not supported well, by any other application.

Layout standards

Many aspects of layout are, in fact, adopted in the Web community; they are applicable for electronic displays and described in Recommendations such as Cascading Style Sheets (CSS). This Recommendation defines presentation semantics in areas such as font, margin, and color properties. Paginating marked up information is also not something new. The Document Style Semantics and Specification Language (DSSSL), the international standard on which XSL-FO is based, was used originally with SGML documents and therefore works unchanged with XML documents.

Accepting that HTML and CSS are suitable and sufficient for browser-oriented rendering of information, the W3C set out to define a collection of pagination semantics for print-oriented rendering. Along with paper results, these pagination semantics are equally suitable for an electronic display of fixed-size folios of information, e.g. in page-turner browsers or Portable Document Format (PDF) readers.

The Extensible Stylesheet Language (XSL), also known colloquially in our community as the Extensible Stylesheet Language Formatting Objects (XSL-FO), combines the heritage of CSS and DSSSL in a well-thought-out and robust specification of formatting semantics for paginating information.

The Recommendation itself is a rigorous, lengthy, and involved technical specification of the processes and operations performed by a formatting engine to effect paginated results consistent with other formatting engines acting on the same inputs. Well-written for its intended purpose and useful as a reference, the document remains out of reach for many people who just want to write XSL-FO stylesheets and print their marked-up information.

About this book

Definitive XSL-FO is written for the beginning XSL-FO stylesheet writer, not the XSL-FO engine implementer.

Background and overview information sets the stage for the stylesheet writer to comprehend why this XML vocabulary exists. Important terminology is explained and the names of key concepts are highlighted. The components of the vocabulary are grouped in discussions focused on functional areas. Examples illustrate each of the formatting objects.

It covers all the formatting objects of XSL-FO and summarizes their properties. This book assumes no prior knowledge of XSL-FO.

Simple things can be done simply in XSL-FO. The objective of this book is to help you get started producing high-quality layouts quickly. For esoteric requirements, the complete text of the XSL 1.0 Recommendation in all of its agonizing (but necessary) detail is required, so it is referenced section by section from the body of this book. Thus the reader with special requirements can delve into the nuance and finely-grained functionality not needed by most users.

Note that neither the Recommendation itself nor this book attempt to teach facets of typography and attractive or appropriate layout style, but only the formatting semantics, the implementation of those semantics, and the nuances of control available to the stylesheet writer and implemented by a stylesheet formatting tool. XSL-FO is a very powerful language with which we can possibly create very ugly or very beautiful pages from our XML-based information.

Typographical and navigation conventions

This book adopts a number of typographical conventions to assist in the navigation of the content.

- Section references to the Recommendation are in italics and parentheses,
  - e.g.: *(6.10.2)*.
- At times, Recommendation section references are paired with a page number from this book,
  - e.g.: *(7.18.1*; 368).
- Construct references are typeset as follows.

- Formatting objects and properties are in monospaced font,
  - e.g.: `basic-link`,
  - e.g.: `baseline-shift`.
- Data types are in monospaced slanted font face,
  - e.g.: *`angle`*.
- URL references are in monospaced font,
  - e.g.: `http://www.w3.org/TR/2001/REC-xsl-20011015/xslspec.html`.

Acknowledgements

The W3C XSL Working Group has done it again — after creating the XSLT and XPath Recommendations in 1999, they produced the XSL Formatting Objects Recommendation in October 2001. Many thanks to the co-chairs Sharon Adler and Steve Zilles for leading the team to create a powerful and usable specification of formatting semantics and the XML vocabulary we can now use to express how we need to paginate our information.

The team at Prentice Hall PTR has also done it again for me — after publishing *Definitive XSLT and XPath* (ISBN 0–13–065196–6) in December 1999, they produced this book for the companion Recommendation. Thank you, Mark Taub, for managing another of my projects through the process.

Thanks again to Dmitry Kirsanov and Alina Kirsanova for their editing, graphic layout, and production of the final result using XSL technology.

Thanks again also to Roman Kagarlitsky and the team at RenderX for the generous use of their XEP tool to render the book to PDF according to Alina's stylesheets.

And finally thanks as always to Charles Goldfarb for his continual encouragement and direction, giving me the confidence to bring another one of my training material works to the commercial publishing market.

G. Ken Holman
Kars, Ontario, Canada
March 2003

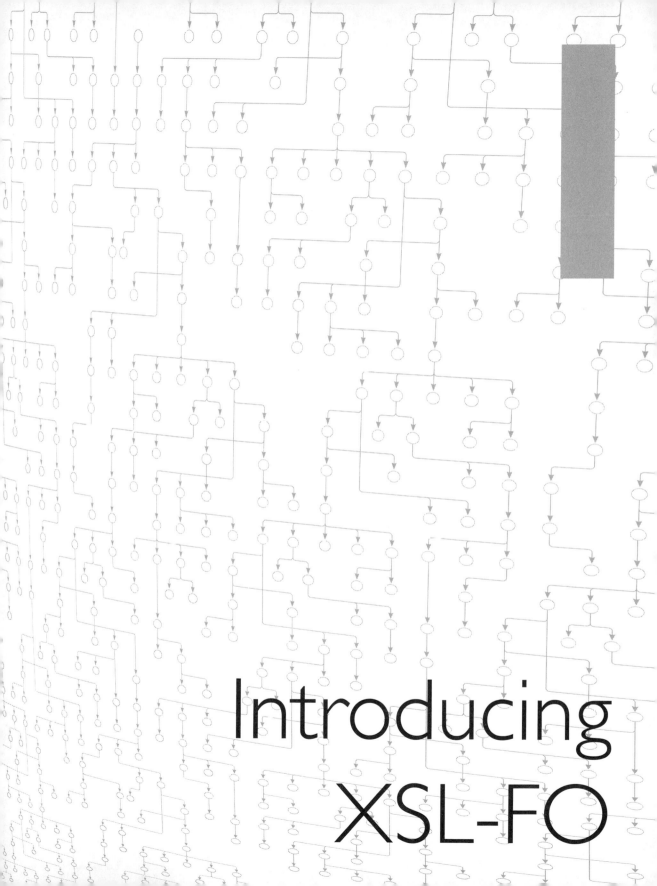

Introducing
XSL-FO

Introducing XSL-FO

Information that is presented in a browser window on the screen must be presented very differently in printed form. Fixed-size folios or pages necessarily require different navigation methods compared to the dynamic tools we use to navigate through a long selection of information in a browser. In the past, this has required our organizations to maintain two versions of the information: one for use in a variable-width, effectively infinite-length browser window, and the other for the printed page.

Perhaps we authored the information directly in the HyperText Markup Language (HTML) for use on the screen and then took the very same information into either a word processing application or publishing tool to produce the hardcopy version. Both these approaches are very presentation-oriented in that we need to capture our information twice, using the different constructs designed for these tools to format the appearance for the two reading audiences. Our maintenance effort for keeping the information up-to-date is doubled.

Consider the need to present training information to two audiences, one online and the other in printed form. The HTML presentation of a snippet of some training material in a web browser could look as in Figure 1–1 where an entire module is rendered as a single web page and the content shown is found somewhere in the middle of the page. Note the use of hyperlinks on the page in three of the bullets, the middle hyperlink having the focus as reflected in the status bar at the bottom of the window. When viewing the screen, the reader does not need to know where a hyperlink is terminated, or even whether it is terminated somewhere on the same page, because the act of interacting with the hyperlink dynamically moves the reader to the target address.

The markup used for the hyperlinks in Example 1–1 captures the presentation of this information using the anchor vocabulary of the web browser (HTML) to express how the information is rendered on the screen.

Note on lines 14 and 15, in the markup for the highlighted hyperlink, how the title of the section referenced by the anchor is part of the anchor itself. The same duplication of information would be necessary in a word processing document. When authoring a complete corpus of training material, the maintenance of all such references can be a nightmare, as any change in a title must be reflected everywhere the title is used.

Think about how this web page would be printed. If you had a color printer, you would recognize the presence of the hyperlink and how that underscored text is different from the argument to the function documented at the top of the window. This fragment is only a small part of a

Figure 1–1 Training information in an HTML window

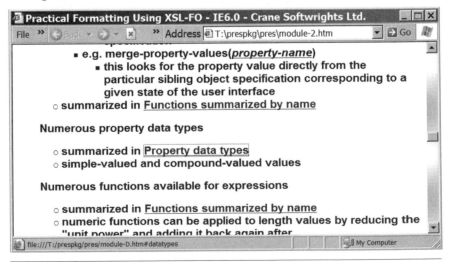

Example 1–1   An example of HTML markup

```
Line 01      <li>e.g. merge-property-values(<u><i>property-name</i></u>)
     02        <ul>
     03          <li>this looks for the property value directly from the
     04    particular sibling object specification corresponding to a given
     05    state of the user interface </li>
     06        </ul>
     07      </li>
     08    </ul>
     09    <li>summarized in <a href="module-B.htm#funcname">Functions
     10    summarized by name</a></li>
     11    </ul>
     12    <p>Numerous property data types</p>
     13    <ul>
     14    <li>summarized in <a href="module-D.htm#datatypes">Property
     15    data types</a></li>
     16    <li>simple-valued and compound-valued values</li>
     17    </ul>
     18    <p>Numerous functions available for expressions</p>
     19    <ul>
     20    <li>summarized in <a href="module-B.htm#funcname">Functions
     21    summarized by name</a></li>
     22    <li>numeric functions can be applied to length values by
     23    reducing the "unit power" and adding it back again after</li>
```

rendering of the module of training material, so the entire module would probably span dozens of pages. It would be very frustrating to know there is a link on your printed page to somewhere in your document, and not be able to quickly traverse it.

An Extensible Markup Language (XML) document is fundamentally different from an HTML document or a word processing document in that we can author our information in any vocabulary of element types and attributes that describes the data but not the presentation of that data. For this example, we could choose to create a hyperlink in our training material using a simple empty reference element without any "clickable text" in the actual authored markup, as shown in Example 1–2.

Note that the same hyperlink, on line 15 in XML markup, is an empty ref element. At the time the hyperlink is authored, the need to reference a particular location is all that is captured in the idref attribute, without any indication of how the hyperlink is presented to the user. Through indirection, the displayed text for presenting the hyperlink can be derived

Example I–2   An example of XML markup

```
Line 01   <course>
     02     <title>Practical Formatting Using XSL-FO</title>
     03
     04     <module id="basic">
     05       <title>Basic concepts of XSL-FO</title>
     06       <lesson id="vocab">
     07         <title>Formatting object XML vocabulary</title>
     08         <frame id="propexp">
     09           <title>Property value expressions</title>
     10           ...
     11             <point>summarized in <ref idref="funcname"/></point>
     12           </points>
     13           <para>Numerous property data types</para>
     14           <points>
     15             <point>summarized in <ref idref="datatypes"/></point>
     16             <point>simple-valued and compound-valued values</point>
     17           </points>
     18           <para>Numerous functions available for expressions</para>
     19           <points>
     20             <point>summarized in <ref idref="funcname"/></point>
     21           ...
     22         </frame>
     23       </lesson>
     24     </module>
     25     ...
     26         <frame id="funcname">
     27           <title>Functions summarized by name</title>
     28           ...
     29         </frame>
     30         ...
     31         <frame id="datatypes">
     32           <title>Property data types</title>
     33           ...
     34         </frame>
     35     ...
     36   </course>
```

at production time from the title child element of the hyperlink's target element on line 32. We get the same presentation, but if any changes are made to any of the titles, all references to these titles will be properly presented. The W3C has developed the Extensible Stylesheet Language Transformations (XSLT) Recommendation to do such rearranging of instances of XML information into instances of other vocabularies.

While the basic presentation of the material in both screen and paper formats is similar, the navigation tools need to be different when the presentation is designed for the paper medium. The browser environment can be recreated by transforming the XML vocabulary into the HTML vocabulary, creating the a anchor elements for the hyperlinks. The paper medium needs to support semantics not found in HTML, such as page numbers and page number citations, in order to allow the reader to properly traverse the hyperlinks in a collection of pages.

The Extensible Stylesheet Language Formatting Objects (XSL-FO) that is described in this book defines an XML vocabulary representing such pagination semantics. This is a powerful vocabulary for producing high quality printable output as a collection of fixed-sized pages. The page layout shown in Figure 1–2 is produced using the XSL-FO vocabulary for the presentation. The frame is presented on its own page and it contains references to frame elements elsewhere in the publication.

Just as XSLT is used to produce HTML from the XML of the training material, XSLT can be used in this example to transform the XML instance into an instance of the XSL-FO vocabulary. An XSL-FO formatting tool interprets the instance of XSL-FO to render page images. Note, below the middle of the page, how the hyperlink is presented as both the title of the referenced frame and the page number on which that frame is found. Note also that the current page number and the total page count are shown on the right of the page footer. The reader is now equipped to traverse the hyperlink in a way not possible when simply printing the HTML.

For producers of XML-based web services, XSL-FO is a way to meet the needs of the users who are unsatisfied with, or unwilling to accept, screen renderings and difficult to use printed browser pages. XSL-FO makes it possible to produce on demand lengthy information in a paginated form.

For web designers, XSL-FO allows printable versions of web pages to be made available to site visitors as downloadable print files, generated from the same source of information from which the HTML pages are generated. Some web sites even mimic print-like multiple pages to create more ad views per document, but such elaboration often confuses the printed output from the browser, thus necessitating making a paginated version available.

Just as we learned the HTML vocabulary to be able to control the presentation of our information in a web browser, we will learn the XSL-FO vocabulary to be able to control the layout and presentation of our information in a printable form. We will learn the new semantics, such as page number citations, and the ways to represent them in XSL-FO for the formatter to give us the results we need.

Figure 1–2   Training information in a printable page

Practical Formatting Using XSL-FO

Property value expressions
Chapter 2 - Basic concepts of XSL-FO
Section 3 - Formatting object XML vocabulary

A property's value can be the evaluation of an expression

- may include fixed values
    - e.g. `space-before="20pt div 2"`
- may include contextually-sensitive values
    - e.g. `space-before="from-parent(font-size) div 2"`
- same operators as in XPath 1.0
- includes same operands as in XPath 1.0
- includes length values as operands that are not allowed in XPath 1.0
- expressions influenced by the font size evaluate the font size before evaluating any other components of the expression

Core function library defined for property expressions

- functions with access to property values of the current node
    - e.g. `inherited-property-value(`*`property-name`*`)`
        - this obtains a value that may be specified on the current node or may be inherited from the closest ancestral node that specifies the value
- functions with access to property values of other nodes
    - e.g. `from-parent(`*`property-name`*`)`
        - this looks for the property value directly from the parent object specification
    - e.g. `merge-property-values(`*`property-name`*`)`
        - this looks for the property value directly from the particular sibling object specification corresponding to a given state of the user interface
- summarized in Functions summarized by name (page 307)

Numerous property data types

- summarized in Property data types (page 327)
- simple-valued and compound-valued values

Numerous functions available for expressions

- summarized in Functions summarized by name (page 307)
- numeric functions can be applied to length values by reducing the "unit power" and adding it back again after
    - a length has a unit power of 1, while a number has a unit value of zero
    - e.g. `round()` takes a number argument and not a length argument
    - can use: `round(` *`length-value`* `div 1.0cm ) * 1.0cm`

Third Edition - 2002-09-05 - ISBN 1-894049-10-1

Copyright © Crane Softwrights Ltd.   Information subject to restrictive legend on first page.   *Page 41 of 405*

2

XSL-FO
in context

2 XSL-FO in context

The first step in learning the W3C's Extensible Stylesheet Language Formatting Objects (XSL-FO) 1.0 Recommendation is to understand the context of this technology in light of other Extensible Markup Language (XML) Recommendations and markup standards. The XSL-FO XML vocabulary is used to express the desired formatting semantics that have a rich heritage from both the Document Style Semantics and Specification Language (DSSSL) and Cascading Style Sheets (CSS), as well as the integral Extensible Stylesheet Language Transformations (XSLT) Recommendation.

Extensible Markup Language (XML). We use XML to express information hierarchically in a sequence of characters according to a vocabulary of element types and their attributes. Using various Recommendations and other industry standards, we can formally describe the makeup and constraints of an XML vocabulary in different ways to validate the content against our desired document model.

Document Style Semantics and Specification Language (DSSSL). The International Organization for Standardization (ISO) standardized in DSSSL a collection of style semantics for formatting paginated information. DSSSL also includes a specification language for the transformation of Standard Generalized Markup Language (SGML) documents of any vocabulary, and implementations have since been modified to support the styling of XML documents of any vocabulary. This standard introduced the concept of a flow object tree comprising objects and properties reflecting the internationalized semantics of paginated output.

Cascading Style Sheets (CSS). Initially created for rendering HTML documents in browsers, CSS formatting properties can ornament the document tree described by a sequence of markup following that specific SGML vocabulary. CSS was later revised to describe the ornamentation of XML documents so that CSS-aware browsers can render the information found in a decorated document tree described by any XML vocabulary. Browsers recognizing these properties can render the contents of the tree according to the semantics of the formatting model governing the property interpretation.

Extensible Stylesheet Language family (XSLT/XSL/XSL-FO). Two vocabularies specified in separate W3C Recommendations provide for the two distinct styling processes of transforming and rendering XML instances.

The Extensible Stylesheet Language Transformations (XSLT) is a templating vocabulary used to describe how a processor creates a transformed hierarchical result from an instance of XML information.

The Extensible Stylesheet Language Formatting Objects (XSL-FO) is a pagination markup language whose vocabulary captures the semantics of formatting information for paginated presentation. Formally named Extensible Stylesheet Language (XSL), this Recommendation normatively incorporates the entire XSLT Recommendation by reference and, historically, these two used to be defined together in a single W3C draft Recommendation.

While XSLT is designed primarily for the kinds of transformation required for using XSL, it can also be used to meet arbitrary transformation requirements.

2.1 **The XML family of Recommendations**

2.1.1 Extensible Markup Language (XML)

To maintain text-based information in a hierarchical structure, the Extensible Markup Language (XML) describes a class of data objects called

"XML documents" and partially describes the behavior of computer programs that process these objects:

- `http://www.w3.org/TR/REC-xml`

A Recommendation fulfilling two objectives for information representation. We use XML to capture our information in a markup language defined by a vocabulary of elements and attributes described by a document model. We can presume a vocabulary informally using only XML-defined constraints, or we can formally declare the grammar, or model, of the vocabulary so that we may validate that our information adheres to our additional constraints. This vocabulary represents the labels and the granularity of the concepts we use for the expression of our information.

Nothing in XML is related to presentation or rendition. When we present documents visually or aurally, we are rendering the content according to the presentation semantics our stylesheets confer on the content. Nothing inherent in XML is related to presentation or rendition; it is entirely up to other standards to define presentation semantics and the syntax with which to engage them, and to presentation software to interpret these vocabularies and implement the semantics associated with the presentation vocabularies.

The vocabulary of elements and attributes used in an instance can be validated. An XML document is considered well-formed when it adheres to the constraints defined by the XML Recommendation. A set of user-defined constraints on the allowed elements, attributes, and text of the vocabulary can be specified at a grammar level by a declarative document model, or implemented at a semantic level by the application processing the information in the instance.

A grammar or document model can specify structural validation for the nesting and order of elements, their use of attributes, and the use of text. Certain aspects of content can be lexically validated and checked for referential integrity. A distinct process, separate from the applications acting on the information, can analyze an XML document against the formalized user-defined constraints of the document model expressed in an XML 1.0 Document Type Definition (DTD). Recently other validation mechanisms became available, including RELAX-NG, Schematron, W3C's XML Schema and the upcoming Document Schema Definition Language (DSDL — ISO/IEC 19757).

When the constraints cannot be defined with the expressiveness of a document model technology, an application can algorithmically validate an XML document by interpreting the semantics associated with the labels used in the structure of the document. Information "means" exactly what an application processing the information wants it to mean. Thus, an application can analyze the structure and content of an XML document for appropriateness to the application's purpose. It can test conditions or constraints that cannot be expressed in a formal document model syntax. It can algorithmically determine validity to support requirements that are not easily expressed declaratively.

Consider the simple well-formed XML instance `purc.xml` in Example 2–1.

Example 2–1   A well-formed XML purchase order instance

```
Line 01   <?xml version="1.0"?>
     02   <purchase>
     03     <customer db="cust123"/>
     04     <product db="prod345">
     05       <amount>23.45</amount>
     06     </product>
     07   </purchase>
```

The constructs in Example 2–1 represent purchasing information only because we recognize the names and assume they reflect the concepts that we understand. If we misunderstand the names used, yet believe we understand them correctly, we can "process" the information using our assumed semantics without invalidating the information as presented to us.

In the same way, we can feed this information to any XML-based application and the application can act on the names it has been programmed to recognize, thus interpreting the semantics of the information in the only way it knows. This may not, however, be the semantics assumed by the author of the document.

Indeed it is a common misconception that our document models somehow formally describe the semantics of our information. In fact, they only describe the vocabulary with which we identify components of our information. All we can use a document model for is validating that the structure and content of a character stream conforms to the constraints described using the features and limitations of the expression of the model description. XML 1.0 describes the Document Type Definition (DTD) expression of the grammar of an XML vocabulary. Other approaches mentioned before offer different benefits and limitations compared to using a DTD, and are candidates for validating the contents of XML documents. In all these cases the semantics represented by the vocabulary are defined in prose comments or supplemental documents.

The semantics of our information are formally described (i.e. interpreted) by the applications we use to process our documents, because a document only means what our applications think it means, by the processes they employ against our information by following the corresponding labels it finds therein.

XML vocabularies can be translated to an application's specific vocabulary. If our documents are composed in the same structure we wish to use for presentation, we can choose to decorate our structures with recognized formatting properties if that is sufficient to the presentation environment. If an alternative structure is needed, either in the same vocabulary or a vocabulary specific to the presentation technology, then we must rearrange and/or transform documents from our vocabulary into the presentation vocabulary.

In practice, it is far more beneficial in the long run to design your document structures according to your business practices and your plans for creating and maintaining your information. You should not be designing your models according to how you plan to present your information, as you may have many different ways you wish to do the presentation, both current and unexpected in the future. Through transformation, you can rearrange any information you create and maintain it in the order you wish to present. It may be difficult to accommodate business practices and information access requirements if you lock your information into a single presentation.

Markup-based rendering agents are programmed to recognize vocabularies geared for the presentation of information. These vocabularies may be purely attribute-based, as is true for Cascading Style Sheets (CSS). Other vocabularies are comprised of both elements and attributes, as is true for the HyperText Markup Language (HTML) and the Scalable Vector Graphics (SVG). When we want our information to be rendered by one of these agents, we must understand the presentation semantics implemented by the rendering agents.

To present our information, we are in effect interpreting the semantics of our vocabularies and choosing to represent our information packaged into the semantics of a rendering device. We must, therefore, transform instances of our vocabularies into instances of the rendering vocabularies in order for the rendering agents to present our information the way we wish. For example, we can transform our XML vocabularies into a combination of HTML and CSS vocabularies to render our XML documents in a wide range of web browsers that may, or may not, support CSS stylesheets. Those browsers recognizing CSS will make use of CSS presentation semantics, while browsers not recognizing CSS will use the accepted presentation semantics inferred by convention for the HTML vocabulary.

Namespaces distinguish constructs from different vocabularies. Properly identifying constructs in the information through their labels is essential to implementing the semantics of our data in our applications. A rigorous method of identifying constructs in XML information uses namespaces by prefixing element-type names with lengthy URI reference strings governed by ownership through domain name registration.

Such URI prefixes are included in names by associating a namespace prefix with the URI reference string and then using that prefix in the markup of the document to identify the names of element types and attributes.

But, again, these names are merely labels. The use of namespaces provides a more powerful labeling mechanism by employing names that incorporate the essence of ownership through the domain names of URI references. When we model our vocabularies, we must decide if we are going to use simple non-namespace-based naming conventions or namespace-based naming conventions, and accommodate the presence of the namespace URI in our applications if necessary.

An application can, therefore, be rigorous in recognizing namespace-based names to which it applies the assumed semantics of the information. With proper namespace maintenance, this eliminates any risk of improperly recognizing a construct's label, though of course this does not prevent an application from making an incorrect assumption of the semantics of the information based on a correct label.

Moreover, an application should be prepared to accommodate namespaces it does not recognize, either through defined processing or perhaps by reporting an error.

2.1.2 Document Style Semantics and Specification Language (DSSSL)

There is a large constituency of people who are not fond of electronic displays that are difficult to navigate when a lot of information appears to flow down infinitely long windows of information. We are all familiar with the printed form of presenting information and the roles played by collections of pages, as well as with the tools used to comfortably navigate through a large collection of pages. The Document Style and Semantics Specification Language (DSSSL) gives information providers the technology to paginate information incorporating familiar page-based navigational tools:

- ISO/IEC–10179:1996
  - `http://www.y12.doe.gov/sgml/wg8/dsssl/readme.htm`

Transforming and formatting structured information. The Document Style Semantics and Specification Language (DSSSL) is the International Standard (IS) for styling information. This IS includes a transformation language to rearrange structured information, pagination semantics for presenting it in printed form, and an extension mechanism for implementing arbitrary formatting semantics.

A programming language for transforming structured information. DSSSL incorporates both a transformation language and a styling language, implemented using a side-effect-free dialect of the Scheme language. This functional programming language is very powerful, and complex algorithms can be implemented succinctly with its tight LISP-like syntax.

Unfortunately, the abundant parentheses in the specification language scared a lot of people away from DSSSL and it never achieved the recognition or acceptance it should have in the industry. As a result of shying away from the specification language, our markup community never learned the style semantics side of this international standard, and DSSSL was often ignored when it should have been an important contribution to a number of efforts.

A standardized set of formatting semantics for paginated output. DSSSL includes extensive pagination semantics — a set of characteristics and their values that are used both to flow information on folios (e.g. printed pages) and format the appearance of that information. Both simple and complex page geometries can be specified. Users specify the desired intent of the result of the formatting process by using the semantics described in the standard.

The design of DSSSL is different from traditional publishing software applications and employs an arms-length model regarding rendering. DSSSL does not specify the rendering process itself, only the interpretation of the formatting intent into what needs to be rendered. A DSSSL stylesheet specifies the intent of what is desired, and a DSSSL engine interprets that intent on the given rendering medium.

The members of the DSSSL development group represented a wide range of users and formatting software vendors. Between them they isolated essential formatting concepts (i.e. semantics), gave them labels (i.e. names), and specified their possible properties and values.

DSSSL is truly internationalized. The semantics have no bias to any particular writing direction. For example, a stylesheet written for the left-to-right writing direction can simultaneously support top-to-bottom or right-to-left writing systems without changes.

A framework for implementation-defined sets of formatting semantics. DSSSL is extensible so that a stylesheet writer can utilize any set of semantics defined by a given DSSSL processor. Stylesheets can declare the existence of a formatting concept and then use that concept in the intent for the result.

James Clark, the author of the JADE DSSSL formatting engine (`http://www.jclark.com/jade/jade.htm`), specified and implemented a set of formatting semantics that represents markup syntax. Using these semantics, one can effect an instance transformation by "styling" one's input document into output markup. The OpenJade project `openjade.sf.net` continues the development of JADE.

Custody of ISO/IEC JTC 1/SC 34/WG 2. The International Organization for Standardization (ISO) has many committees for standardization work in various aspects of our daily lives. The joint technical committee (JTC) with the International Electrotechnical Commission (IEC) is responsible for information technology. The subcommittee (SC) for document description and processing languages is numbered 34 and the second working group (WG) of this subcommittee is responsible for DSSSL and other formatting issues such as fonts.

The full title of the working group is ISO/IEC JTC 1/SC 34/WG 2. Prior designations for the committee that has worked on DSSSL from its inception include ISO/IEC JTC 1/WG 4, and ISO/IEC JTC 1/SC 18/WG 8. The working group continues to support the evolution of the DSSSL International Standard.

Members of the original DSSSL working group are members of the W3C XSL Working Group.

2.1.3 Cascading Style Sheets (CSS)

When displaying web documents in user agents, we are often not satisfied with the expressiveness of the limited formatting properties assumed for HTML documents. The CSS1 and CSS2 Recommendations describe a set of formatting semantics through a collection of property names and values:

- http://www.w3.org/TR/REC-CSS1
- http://www.w3.org/TR/REC-CSS2

Formatting property assignment for web documents (HTML and XML). Not accepting the presentation semantics inferred by HTML browsers for HTML-marked-up information, the web community developed a robust and coherent formatting model for electronic presentation of information. The CSS model standardizes a set of formatting semantics tied to a vocabulary of attribute values that can be attached to hierarchically structured web documents for rendering in browsers. This addressed the incompatibilities being added to HTML interpretation by browser manufacturers.

Unfortunately, the designers of CSS did not adopt the pre-existing DSSSL terminology for the identical formatting semantics, nor did they use all of the value sets for the CSS properties. This resulted in a different set of properties for the same concepts and purposes.

Initially designed for HTML, a subsequent release of CSS described the application of formatting properties to XML documents. These formatting properties do not involve any manipulation of the abstract document tree created from an input file; they are merely attached to the document tree as ornaments and are interpreted by a CSS-aware user agent that can effect the formatting inferred by the semantics triggered by the properties.

Inherent in the formatting model is the notion that the width and length of the presentation canvas are not fixed. The length of the presentation is essentially infinite, in that the browser agent shows a document in its entirety regardless of the length of the information included in the instance. The technology of the presentation is essentially electronic, in that reader of the information can dynamically change the width of the canvas requiring the user agent to re-flow the content within the new dimensions.

Ornamentation of the document tree. A CSS-aware user agent views our information as the document tree represented by the markup we choose to use. The stylistic information with which we decorate the document tree dictates how we want the user agent to render the content.

The formatting model provides for document content to be prefixed and suffixed with supplemental information found in the stylesheet. White space around information can be controlled, and we can place our content in overlapping and transparent rectangular regions of the canvas.

Inheritance plays an important role in CSS. The "cascade" is the application of inherited formatting properties when a given construct does not explicitly supply an inheritable value. Inheritance first starts "up" the ancestry of the document tree, looking for an applicable property specification. The cascade then continues looking at external stylesheets of lesser priority than internal stylesheets, finally accepting the built-in presentation semantics assumed by HTML user agents.

Multiple media type support. The CSS formatting model incorporates a number of layout constructs available to flow our information into a given desired presentation. For example table-oriented constructs are available for us to present our information in a tabular form, even if the information isn't in HTML table markup.

Important to the accessibility of information to all users of the Web, CSS introduced aural presentation properties we can use to shape our information for the visually impaired. Note that not only people with sight disabilities are visually impaired, but sighted users of the Web may be in situations where they are unable to use their sight (e.g. mobile applications, such as browsing for information while in a car). Information providers will find clever use of aural properties a boon to their users' surfing experience.

Doesn't (shouldn't) interfere with legacy browsers not supporting CSS. CSS properties are expressed in HTML documents through reserved attributes and document metadata. Unfortunately, many legacy HTML browsers were not true SGML applications but rather simple "angle bracket processors" unaware of the rules of formal markup practice. Hence, arcane methods of capturing stylesheet information are sometimes required to be resilient to legacy browsers that do not properly implement markup. Even still, there are some non-CSS-aware browsers that end up exposing property specifications on the user's canvas instead of properly recognizing their role as supplemental information to be kept off the canvas.

The property sheets can be external to the document itself, and must indeed be so in XML documents that are not utilizing namespaces.

A browser could choose to render XML documents that are using namespaces by recognizing CSS properties embedded in style attributes from the HTML vocabulary, though this is not seen in practice.

Working group is producing a common formatting model for web documents. A W3C working group is responsible for the common formatting model for web documents. Many W3C Recommendations need to specify formatting or display properties at times, and where applicable, designers of new Recommendations are asked to use the CSS semantics and the property names for those semantics. Members of the original CSS working group are members of the XSL Working Group.

This promotes a widely understood specification of the common requirements for formatting, including properties related to font, spacing, and a number of other useful presentation areas.

2.1.4   Styling structured information

2.1.4.1   *Styling is* transforming *and* formatting *information*

Styling is the rendering of information into a form suitable for consumption by a target audience. Since the audience can change for a given body of information, we often need to apply different styling for that information, to obtain dissimilar renderings to meet the needs of each audience. Perhaps some information needs to be rearranged to make more sense for the reader. Perhaps some information needs to be highlighted differently to bring focus to key content.

It is important, when we think about styling information, to remember that two distinct processes are involved, not just one. First, we must transform the information from the organization used when it was created into the organization needed for consumption. Second, when rendering, we must express the aspects of the appearance of the reorganized information, whatever the target medium.

Consider the flow of information as a streaming process where information is created upstream and processed or consumed downstream. Upstream, in the early stages, we should be expressing the information abstractly, thus preventing any early binding of concrete or final-form concepts. Midstream, or even downstream, we can exploit the information as long as it remains flexible and abstract. Late binding of the information to a final form can be based on the target use of the final product; by delaying this binding until late in the process, we preserve the original information for exploitation for other purposes along the way.

It is a common but misdirected practice to model information based on how you plan to use it downstream. It does not matter if your target is, for example, a presentation-oriented structure, or a structure that is appropriate for another markup-based system. Modeling practice should focus on both the business reasons and inherent relationships existing in the semantics behind the information being described (so, the vocabularies are content-oriented at this stage). For example, emphasized text is often confused with a particular format in which it is rendered. Where you might want to model information using a b element type for eventual rendering in a bold face, we would be better off using an emph element type. In this way, we capture the reason for marking up the information (the fact that it is emphasized compared to surrounding information), and we do not lock any of the downstream targets into only using a bold face for rendering.

Many times the midstream or downstream processes need only rearrange, re-label or synthesize the information for a target purpose and never apply any semantics of style for rendering purposes. Transformation tasks stand alone in such cases, meeting the processing needs without introducing rendering issues.

One caveat regarding modeling content-oriented information is that there are applications where the content orientation is, indeed, presentation-oriented. Consider book publishing where the abstract content is based on presentational semantics. This is meaningful because there is no abstraction beyond the appearance or presentation of the content.

Consider the customer information in Example 2–1. A web user agent doesn't know how to render an element named customer. The HTML vocabulary used to render the customer information could be as in Example 2–2.

Example 2–2   HTML rendering semantics markup for Example 2–1

```
Line 01   <p>From: <i>(Customer Reference) <b>cust123</b></i>
     02   </p>
```

The rendering result would then be as in Figure 2–1, with the user agent interpreting the markup for italics and boldface presentation semantics.

The figure illustrates these two distinct styling steps: *transforming* the instance of the XML vocabulary into a new instance according to a vocabulary of rendering semantics; and *formatting* the instance of the rendering vocabulary in the user agent.

2.1.4.2   W3C XSL Working Group

This working group was chartered to define a style specification language that covers at least the formatting functionality of both CSS and DSSSL. The end result was not intended to replace CSS, but to provide functionality beyond that defined by CSS, such as element reordering and pagination semantics.

2.1.4.3   Two W3C Recommendations

To meet these two distinct processes in a detached (yet related) fashion, the W3C XSL Working Group split the original drafts of their work into two separate Recommendations: one for transforming information and the other for paginating information.

The XSL Transformations (XSLT) Recommendation describes a vocabulary recognized by an XSLT processor to transform information from an

Figure 2–1   HTML rendering for example

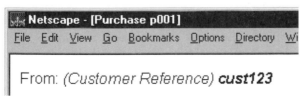

organization in the source file into a different organization suitable for continued downstream processing.

The Extensible Stylesheet Language (XSL) Recommendation describes a vocabulary (often called XSL-FO for "Formatting/Flow Objects," even by the W3C, though the use is unofficial and not formally part of the Recommendation) reflecting the semantics of paginating a stream of information into individual pages. The semantics are defined by a set of formatting objects, properties, and property values, expressible in an XML vocabulary.

The XSL Recommendation normatively includes XSLT by reference in Chapter 2, and historically both Recommendations were expressed in a single document. Indeed, XSLT was designed for use with XSL-FO, incorporating features to make working with the XSL-FO vocabulary easier.

Both XSLT and XSL-FO are endorsed by members of WSSSL, an association of researchers and developers passionate about the application of markup technologies in today's information technology infrastructure.

2.1.5   Extensible Stylesheet Language Transformations (XSLT)

We all have needs to transform our structured information when it is not appropriately ordered for a purpose other than how it is created. The XSLT 1.0 Recommendation describes a transformation instruction vocabulary of constructs that can be expressed in an XML model of elements and attributes:

- `http://www.w3.org/TR/xslt`

2.1.5.1   *Transformation by example*

We can characterize XSLT among other techniques for transmuting information by regarding it simply as "Transformation by Example," whereas many other techniques are better described as "Transformation by Program Logic." This perspective focuses on the fact that we do not need to tell an XSLT processor how to effect the changes we need; rather, we tell an XSLT processor what we want as the end result, and it is the processor's responsibility to do the dirty work.

The XSLT Recommendation gives us, in effect, a templating language. It is a vocabulary for specifying templates that represent "examples of the result." Based on how we instruct the XSLT processor to access the source of the data being transformed, the processor will incrementally build the result by adding the filled-in templates.

We write our stylesheets, or "transformation specifications," primarily with declarative constructs, though we can employ imperative techniques (also known as procedural techniques) if and when needed. We assert the desired behavior of the XSLT processor based on conditions found in our source. We supply examples of how each component of our result is formulated and indicate the conditions of the source that trigger which component is added to the result next. Alternatively, we can selectively add components to the result on demand.

Note: Many programmers unfairly deride XSLT for not being a good programming language, when in fact it is a templating language and not a programming language at all. The idea of declaratively supplying templates of the result and the matching conditions of source tree nodes to the templates is a paradigm that is very different from imperative programming. I find that by far the most disparaging and vociferous attacks against XSLT are from programmers unable or awkwardly trying to follow an algorithm-based imperative approach to the problem instead of the assertion-based declarative approach inherent in the language design.

XSLT is not a panacea, and there are many algorithmic situations (particularly in character-level text manipulation) where XSLT is not the appropriate tool to use. Node tree rearrangement, and in particular mixed content processing, can be handled far more easily declaratively in XSLT than in many imperative approaches. This templating approach is ideal for the rearrangement of information for use with XSL formatting semantics. Critics will continue to claim that XSLT is a "bad" programming language until they stop using it as an incorrect pigeonhole for certain classes of problems.

XSLT is similar to other transmutation approaches in that we deal with our information represented as trees of abstract nodes. We don't deal with the raw markup of our source data. Unlike these other approaches, however, the primary memory management and information manipulation (node traversal and node creation) is handled by the XSLT processor, not by the stylesheet writer. This is a significant difference between XSLT and a transformation programming language or interface, such as the Document Object Model (DOM) where the programmer is responsible for handling the low-level manipulation of information constructs.

Our objective as stylesheet writers is to supply the XSLT processor with enough "templates of the result" so that the processor can build the result we desire when triggered by information in our source. Our data file becomes a hierarchy of nodes in our source tree. Our templates become a hierarchy of nodes in our stylesheet tree. The processor is doing the work building the result node tree from nodes in our stylesheet and source trees. We don't have to be programmers to manipulate the node trees or serialize the result node tree into our result file. It isn't our responsibility to worry about the angle brackets and ampersands that may be needed in the result markup.

Consider once again the customer information in our purchase order in Example 2–1. An example of the HTML vocabulary supplied to the XSLT processor to produce the markup in Example 2–2 could be as in Example 2–3.

Example 2–3 An XSLT template rule for the HTML vocabulary

```
Line 01  <xsl:template match="customer">
     02    <p><xsl:text>From: </xsl:text>
     03      <i><xsl:text>(Customer Reference) </xsl:text>
     04        <b><xsl:value-of select="@db"/></b></i></p>
     05  </xsl:template>
```

An example of XSL vocabulary supplied to the XSLT processor to produce the markup in Example 2–7 is shown in Example 2–4.

Example 2–4 Example XSLT template rule for the XSL vocabulary

```
Line 01  <xsl:template match="customer">
     02    <fo:block space-before.optimum="20pt" font-size="20pt">
     03      <xsl:text>From: </xsl:text>
     04      <fo:inline font-style="italic">
     05        <xsl:text>(Customer Reference) </xsl:text>
     06        <fo:inline font-weight="bold">
     07          <xsl:value-of select="@db"/>
     08        </fo:inline></fo:inline></fo:block>
     09  </xsl:template>
```

Comparing Examples 2–3 and 2–4, we see that our practices as stylesheet writers are not different in any way. The templates are different in that they express different vocabularies for the elements and attributes in the result tree of nodes, but our methodology is not different. Each template is the example of the desired result for the given customer element as expressed in each of two different presentation vocabularies.

Comparing the style shown in both examples above to imperative programming techniques, one can see the XSLT stylesheet writer is not responsible for low-level node manipulation or markup generation. By declaring the nodes to be used in the result tree, one is describing the construction through the use of examples. These templates represent the information we want in the result tree that the processor must effect however it needs to, in order for the information in the example to be correctly included in the result. The processor only takes what is given as an example and is free to use whatever syntactic constructs it wishes; the downstream processor interpreting the result will use these constructs to understand the same information being represented in the template.

XSLT includes constructs that can be used to identify and iterate over structures found in the source information. The information being transformed can be traversed in any order needed and as many times as required to produce the desired result. We can visit source information numerous times if the result of transformation requires that information to be present numerous times.

Users of XSLT also don't have the burden of implementing numerous practical algorithms required to present information. XSLT specifies a number of algorithms that are implemented within the processor itself, and we engage these algorithms declaratively. High-level functions such as sorting and counting are available on demand when we need them. Low-level functions, such as memory-management, node manipulation, and garbage collection, are all integral to the XSLT processor.

This declarative nature of the stylesheet markup makes XSLT much more accessible to non-programmers than the imperative nature of procedurally-oriented transformation languages. Writing a stylesheet is as simple as using markup to declare the behavior of the XSLT processor, much like HTML is used to declare the behavior of the web browser to paint information on the screen.

Not all examples of the result are fixed monolithic sequences of markup, however, as XSLT can conditionally include portions of a template based on testable conditions expressed by the stylesheet writer. Other constructs allow templates to be fragmented and added to the result on demand based on stylesheet logic. Templates can be parameterized to be used in different contexts corresponding to different parameter values.

In this way, XSLT accommodates the programmer as well as non-programmer, in that there is sufficient expressiveness in the declarative constructs so they can be used in an imperative fashion. XSLT is (in programming theory) "Turing complete," thus any arbitrarily complex algorithm could (theoretically) be implemented using the constructs available. While there will always be a trade-off between extending the processor to implement something internally and writing an elaborate stylesheet to implement something portably, there is sufficient expressive power to implement some algorithmic business rules and semantic processing in XSLT constructs.

In short, straightforward and common requirements can be satisfied in a straightforward fashion, while unconventional requirements can be satisfied to an extent with some programming effort.

Note: Theory aside, the necessarily verbose XSLT syntax dictated by its declarative nature and the use of XML markup makes the coding of some complex algorithms a bit awkward. I have implemented some very complex traversals and content generation successfully, but with code that could be difficult to maintain (my own valiant, if not always satisfactory, documentation practices notwithstanding).

Users of XSLT often need to maintain large transformation specifications, and many need to tap prior accomplishments when writing stylesheets. A number of constructs are included supporting the management, maintenance and exploitation of existing stylesheets. Organizations can build libraries of stylesheet components for sharing among their colleagues. Stylesheet writers can tweak the results of a transformation by writing shell specifications that include or import other stylesheets known to solve the problems they are addressing. Stylesheet fragments can be written for particular vocabulary fragments; these fragments can subsequently be used in concert, as part of an organization's strategy for common information description in numerous markup models.

2.1.5.2 Not *intended for general purpose XML transformations*

It is important to remember that XSLT is *primarily for transforming XML vocabularies to the XSL formatting vocabulary*. This doesn't preclude us from using XSLT for other transformation requirements, but it does influence the design of the language and it does constrain some of the functionality from being truly general purpose.

For this reason, the specification *cannot* claim XSLT is a general purpose transformation language. However, it is still powerful enough for *all* downstream processing transformation needs within the assumptions of use of the transformation results. XSLT stylesheets are often called XSLT transformation scripts because they can be used in many areas not at all related to stylesheet rendering. Consider an electronic commerce environment where transformation is not used for presentation purposes. In this case, the XSLT processor may transform a source instance, which is based on a particular vocabulary, and deliver the results to a legacy application that expects a different vocabulary as input. In other words, we can use XSLT in a non-rendering situation when it doesn't matter what markup is utilized to represent the content; when only the parsed result of the markup is material.

An example of using such a legacy vocabulary for the XSLT processor would be as in Example 2–5.

Example 2–5 An XSLT template rule for a legacy vocabulary

```
Line 01   <xsl:template match ="customer">
     02     <buyer><xsl:value-of select="@db"/></buyer>
     03   </xsl:template>
```

The transformation would then produce a result acceptable to the legacy application, as shown in Example 2–6.

Example 2–6 A legacy vocabulary for customer information

```
01   <buyer>cust123</buyer>
```

XSLT assumes that results of transformation will be processed by a rendering agent or some other application employing an XML processor as the means to access the information in the result. The information being delivered represents the serialized result of working with the information in XML instance, and if supplied, the XML document model definition of information set augmentation, expressed as a tree of nodes. The actual markup within either the source XML instance or the XSLT stylesheet is, therefore, not considered material to the application and therefore need not be preserved during transformation. All that counts is that the underlying content of the input is found where required in the structure of the resulting output, regardless of the markup used to represent that result.

Because of this focus on the processed result for downstream applications, there is little or no control in an XSLT stylesheet over the actual XML markup constructs found within the input documents, or over the actual XML markup constructs utilized in the resulting output document. This prevents a stylesheet from being aware of such constructs or controlling how such constructs are used. Any transformation requirement that includes "original markup syntax preservation" would not be suited for XSLT transformations.

Therefore, in comparison to imperative languages and interfaces offering the programmer tight control over the markup of the result of transformation, XSLT cannot be considered a general purpose transformation language because of the lack of control over the markup. For example, when using XSLT one cannot specify the order of attributes in a start tag of the serialized result tree, nor can one specify the technique by which sensitive markup characters present in #PCDATA content are escaped.

When working with the XSL-FO vocabulary, the result of the XSLT transformation is going to be processed by the XML processor inside the XSL-FO processor; therefore, the markup of the result is immaterial as long as it is well formed. The transformation process is, indeed, absolutely general purpose when the result is going to be interpreted for pagination.

2.1.6   Extensible Stylesheet Language (XSL/XSL-FO)

XSL (or XSL-FO) describes formatting and flow semantics for paginated presentation that can be expressed using an XML vocabulary of elements and attributes:

- `http://www.w3.org/TR/xsl`

2.1.6.1   *Paginated flow and formatting semantics vocabulary*

This hierarchical vocabulary captures formatting semantics for rendering textual and graphic information in different media in a paginated form. A rendering agent is responsible for interpreting an instance of the vocabulary for a given medium to reify a final result.

This is no different, in concept and architecture, from using HTML and Cascading Style Sheets (CSS) as a hierarchical vocabulary and formatting properties for rendering a body of information in a web browser. Such user agents are not pagination-oriented and effectively have an infinite page length and variable page width.

Indeed, the printed paged output from a browser of an HTML page is often less than satisfactory. Paginated information includes navigation tools such as page numbers, page number citations, headers, footers, etc. to give the reader methods of finding information or indentifying the current location in a printed document.

In essence, when doing any kind of presentation, we are transforming our XML documents into a final display form by transforming instances of our XML vocabularies into instances of a particular rendering vocabulary that expresses the formatting semantics of our desired result. The vocabulary we choose must be able to express the nature of the formatting we want accomplished. We can choose to transform our information into a combination of HTML and CSS for web browsers and can choose an alternate transformation into XSL-FO for paginated display (be that paginated to a screen, to paper, or perhaps even aurally using sound).

In this way XSL-FO can be considered a pagination markup language.

2.1.6.2 *Target of transformation*

When using the XSL-FO vocabulary as the rendering language, the objective for a stylesheet writer is to convert an XML instance of some arbitrary XML vocabulary into an instance of the formatting semantics vocabulary. This formatting instance is the information rearranged into an expression of the intent of the paginated result as a collection of layout constructs populated with the content to be laid out on the rendered pages.

This result of transformation cannot contain any user-defined vocabulary constructs (such as "address," "customer identifier," or "purchase order number" constructs) because the rendering agent would not know what to do with constructs labeled with these foreign, unknown identifiers.

Consider again the two examples: HTML for rendering on a single page of infinite length in a web browser window, and XSL-FO for rendering on multiple separated pages on a screen, on paper, or audibly. In both cases, the rendering agents only understand the vocabulary expressing their respective formatting semantics and wouldn't know what to do with alien element types defined by the user.

Just as with HTML, a stylesheet writer utilizing XSL-FO for pagination must transform each and every user construct into a rendering construct to direct the rendering agent to produce the desired result. By learning and understanding the semantics behind the constructs of XSL-FO, the stylesheet writer can create an instance of the formatting vocabulary expressing the desired layout of the final result (e.g. area geometry, spacing, font metrics, etc.), with each piece of information in the result coming from either the source data or the stylesheet itself.

Consider once more the customer information in Example 2–1. An XSL-FO rendering agent doesn't know how to render a marked up construct named <customer>. The XSL-FO vocabulary used to render the customer information could be as in Example 2–7.

Example 2–7 XSL-FO rendering semantics markup for Example 2–1

```
Line 01  <fo:block space-before.optimum="20pt" font-size="20pt">From:
     02  <fo:inline font-style="italic">(Customer Reference)
     03  <fo:inline font-weight="bold">cust123</fo:inline>
     04  </fo:inline>
     05  </fo:block>
```

The result rendered in the Portable Document Format (PDF) would then be as in Figure 2–2, with an intermediate PDF generation step interpreting the XSL-FO markup for italics and boldface presentation semantics.

The figure again illustrates the two distinctive styling steps: *transforming* the instance of the XML vocabulary into a new instance according to a vocabulary of rendering semantics; and *formatting* the instance of the rendering vocabulary in the user agent.

The formatting semantics of the XSL-FO vocabulary are described for both visual and aural targets, so we can use one set of constructs regardless of the rendering medium. It is the rendering agent's responsibility to interpret these constructs accordingly. In this way, the XSL-FO semantics can be interpreted for print, display, audio, or other presentations. There are, indeed, some specialized semantics we can use to influence rendering on particular media, though these are just icing on the cake. Dynamic

---

Figure 2–2 XSL-FO rendering for example

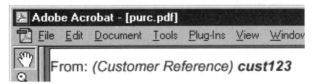

---

behaviors can be specified for interactive media that would not function at all, obviously, in the paper form.

2.1.7 Styling semantics and vocabularies

XSLT and XSL-FO processors implement styling semantics. XSLT and XSL-FO processors are rigorous in implementing styling semantics, or behaviors, for the XSL vocabularies. Well-defined semantics are captured in the two XML vocabularies of elements and their attributes that represent, respectively, instructions and their controls for XSLT and formatting objects and their properties for XSL-FO. Namespaces are important to an XSLT or XSL-FO processor to recognize not only the constructs from their respective vocabularies, but also any extensions to the vocabulary that are specific to a particular brand of processor.

In addition, namespaces allow for rendering vocabularies to be freely used for foreign objects in the XSL-FO stream, and an XSL-FO formatting engine can properly forward rendered content in arbitrary namespaces to the rendering processes incorporated in the tool.

But, as with all XML applications, the assumption is that the names of element types and attributes are just labels referencing the semantics as defined by the specification, and it is up to the user to respect that assumption in order to get the desired formatted result. The use of the XSLT or XSL-FO namespace does not magically confer semantics on the elements; rather, an XSLT or XSL-FO processor assumes that when the names from these vocabularies are used, the application of the semantics defined by the Recommendations is what is desired by the user.

We learn the XSLT and XSL-FO XML vocabularies as representations of the semantics assumed by the processors, and we engage those processors to transform, render, and paginate our information accordingly.

XSLT and XSL-FO document type definitions are described using prose. There are no standardized XML 1.0 DTD representations of the grammar of these vocabularies because DTD semantics and syntax are unable to fully express all of the grammatical constraints of instances representing XSLT and XSL-FO transformations and stylesheets.

The XSLT 1.0 and XSL 1.0 Recommendations describe the document types in English rather than in a formal notation, and it is up to processors to do all aspects of validation and interpretation of the document structure according to the respective document type.

There are, however, snippets of content model-like syntax with Kleene operators ("?" for zero or one, "*" for zero or more, and "+" for one or more) used in the XSL documentation because of the reader's assumed familiarity with DTD syntax.

Otherwise, the normative description of the vocabularies is essentially the detailed prose of the corresponding Recommendations. This prose may override some of the strictness of the abbreviated expression that uses the DTD syntax.

2.1.8 Transforming and rendering XML information using XSLT and XSL-FO

When the result tree in an XSLT process is specified to utilize the XSL-FO pagination vocabulary, the normative behavior of an XSL-FO processor incorporating an XSLT processor is to interpret the result tree. This interpretation reifies the semantics expressed in the constructs of the result tree to some medium, for example pixels on a screen, dots on paper, or sound through a synthesis device (see Figure 2–3).

The stylesheets used in this scenario contain the transformation vocabulary and any custom extensions, as well as the desired result XSL-FO formatting

Figure 2–3   Transformation from XML to XSL Formatting Semantics

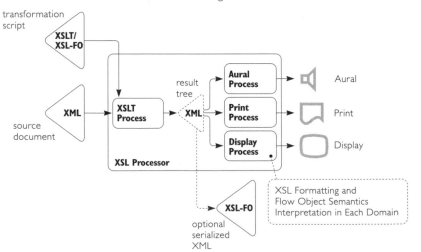

vocabulary and any foreign object vocabularies. There are no element types from other XML vocabularies in the result. If there were, rendering processors would not inherently know what to do with such constructs, for example, with an element of type `custnbr` representing a customer number. It is the stylesheet writer's responsibility to transform the information into information recognized by the rendering agent.

There is no obligation for the formatter to serialize the result tree created during transformation. The feature of serializing the result tree to XML markup is, however, quite useful as a diagnostic tool, revealing to us what we really asked to be rendered, instead of what we thought we were asking to be rendered when we saw incorrect results. There may also be performance considerations of taking the reified result tree in XML markup and rendering it in other media without incurring the overhead of performing the transformation repeatedly.

2.1.9   Interpreting XSL-FO instances directly

The XSL-FO and foreign object vocabularies can also be used in a standalone XML instance, perhaps as the result of an XSLT transformation using an outboard XSLT processor, as shown in Figure 2–4. The XSLT processor serializes a physical entity from the transformation result tree, and that XML file of XSL-FO vocabulary is then interpreted by a standalone XSL-FO processor.

Figure 2–4 delineates three distinct phases of the process. These phases also exist when the XSLT and XSL-FO processors are combined into a single application. The transformation phase creates the XSL-FO expressing our intent for formatting the source XML. The XSL-FO processor first interprets our intent into the information that is to be rendered on the target device, then effects the rendering to reify the result.

2.1.10   Generating XSL-FO instances

XSL-FO need not be generated by XSLT in order to be useful, as shown in Figure 2–5. Consider that when we learned HTML as the rendering vocabulary for a web user agent, we either coded it by hand or wrote applications that generated HTML from our information. This information may have come from some source, such as a database.

Having learned XSLT, we can express our information in XML and then either transform the XML into HTML to send to the user agent, or send the XML directly to an XSLT process in the user agent.

The typical generation of XSL-FO would be from our XML using an XSLT stylesheet, though this need not be the case at all. We may have situations where our applications need to express information in a paginated form, and these applications could generate instances of the XSL-FO vocabulary directly to be interpreted for the output medium.

We need to remember that XSL-FO is just another vocabulary that can be expressed as an XML instance, requiring an application to interpret our

Figure 2–4   Creating standalone XML instances of XSL vocabulary

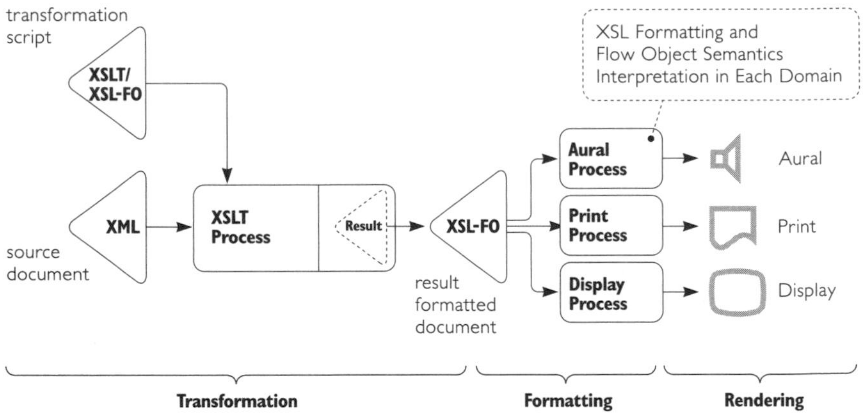

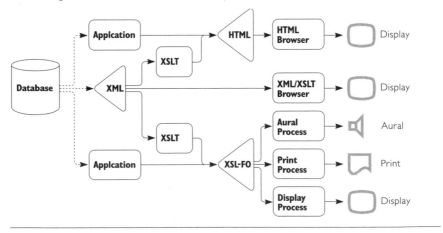

Figure 2–5   Generating XML instances of XSL vocabulary

intent for formatting in order to effect the result. This is no different than the use of the HTML vocabulary for a web browser.

The sole requirement is that the namespace of the vocabulary in the instance be "`http://www.w3.org/1999/XSL/Format`" for the labeled information in the instance to be recognized as expressing the semantics described by the XSL-FO Recommendation.

Note: The default namespace may be used for the XSL-FO vocabulary, just as is true with any vocabulary. Personally, I don't use the popular "`fo:`" prefix in my stylesheets, as it is my habit to use the default namespace and not prefix my XSL-FO names in any way.

This practice reinforces for me that this is just as simple as HTML, where I don't use any namespace at all in my own stylesheets.

There are processors that interpret standalone XSL-FO instances interactively on the screen in a GUI environment. To learn the nuances of XSL-FO, I often hand-author XSL-FO instances experimenting with various objects and properties in elements and attributes, tweaking values repeatedly, and examining the results interactively with the formatting tool. Having hand-authored HTML, using the default namespace for XSL-FO is very natural and saves on the amount of typing as well.

2.1.11 Using XSL-FO on a server

A typical web-based use of XSL-FO is in a three-tiered environment shown in Figure 2–6 where the server is producing "printable versions" of information that people are browsing in HTML using web browsers. In such an architecture, a single XML document is transformed into HTML using

Figure 2–6   Using XSL-FO in a server environment

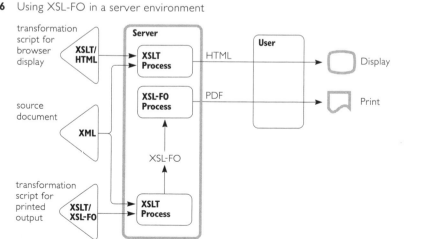

an XSLT stylesheet specifically designed for the best presentation of the information with browser features.

When the user requests a rendition of the information suitable for printing on paper, a separate XSLT stylesheet is applied to the same XML document to produce an XSL-FO structure representing the information on a printed page. An XSL-FO process interprets this structure to produce a representation of the printed output suitable for the user's environment. The Portable Document Format (PDF) is a ubiquitous final-form print format and free readers are available to both view and print paginated documents represented in PDF.

2.2 Examples

2.2.1   Hello world example

Consider a simple, but complete, XSL-FO instance `hellofo.fo` for an A4 page report shown in Example 2–8.

Example 2–8   A simple example

```
Line 01  <?xml version="1.0" encoding="UTF-8"?>
02  <root xmlns="http://www.w3.org/1999/XSL/Format"
03        font-size="16pt">
04    <layout-master-set>
05      <simple-page-master
06            margin-right="15mm" margin-left="15mm"
07            margin-bottom="15mm" margin-top="15mm"
08            page-width="210mm" page-height="297mm"
09            master-name="bookpage">
10        <region-body region-name="bookpage-body"
11              margin-bottom="5mm" margin-top="5mm" />
12      </simple-page-master>
13    </layout-master-set>
14    <page-sequence master-reference="bookpage">
15      <title>Hello world example</title>
16      <flow flow-name="bookpage-body">
17        <block>Hello XSL-FO!</block>
18      </flow>
19    </page-sequence>
20  </root>
```

Note that all examples in this book illustrate instances of the XML-FO vocabulary. How an instance is created is not material to the semantics of the vocabulary. The instance could have been hand-authored in a simple text or XML editor, or created as the result of an XSLT transformation from another XML vocabulary, or generated from any other application.

We can see the declaration on line 2 of the default namespace being the XSL-FO namespace, so all un-prefixed element names refer to element types in the XSL-FO vocabulary. There are no prefixed element-type names used by any of the elements, thus the entire content is written in XSL-FO.

The document model for XSL-FO dictates that the page geometries must be summarized in `layout-master-set` on lines 4 through 13, followed by the content to be paginated in a sequence of pages in `page-sequence` on lines 14 through 19. This instance conforms to these requirements and conveys our formatting intent to the formatter. The formatter needs to know the geometry of the pages being created and the content belonging on those pages.

Think of the parallel where we learned that the document model for HTML requires the metadata in the `head` element and the displayable content in the `body` element. Both elements are required in the document model, the first to contain the mandatory title of the page and the second to contain the rendered information.

Once we learned the vocabulary for HTML, we can create a page knowing where the required components belong in the document. The same is true for XSL-FO, in that we learn what information is required where and we express what we need in the constructs the formatter expects.

In this simple example the dimensions of A4 pages are given in the portrait orientation on line 8. Margins are specified on lines 6 and 7 to constrain the main body of the page within the page boundaries. That body region, described on lines 10 and 11, itself has margins to constrain its content, and is named so that it can be referenced from within a sequence of pages.

The sequence of pages specified on line 14 in this example refers to the only geometry available and specifies on line 16 that the flow of paginated content is targeted to the body region on each page. The sequence is also titled on line 15, which is used by rendering agents choosing to expose the title in some application-dependent fashion (e.g. in a window's title bar).

Consider two conforming XSL-FO processors that processed the simple `hellofo.fo` example as shown in Figure 2–7, one interactively through a GUI window interface, and the other producing a final-form representation of the page:

- Antenna House XSL Formatter (an interactive XSL-FO rendering tool),
- Adobe Acrobat (a Portable Document Format (PDF) display tool),
  - PDF created by RenderX (a batch XSL-FO rendering tool).

Note how the two renderings are not identical. If an XSL-FO instance is insufficient in describing the entire formatting intent, the rendering application may engage certain property values of its own choosing. Page fidelity is not guaranteed if the instance does not express the entire formatting intent. Even within the expressiveness of the XSL-FO semantics, there are some decisions still left up to the formatting tool.

This is not different from two web browsers with different user settings for the display font. A simple web page that does not use CSS stylesheets for font settings relies on the browser's tool options for the displayed font choice. The intent of the web page may be to render "a paragraph," but if two users have different defaults for the font choice, there is no fidelity in the web page between the two renditions if the formatting intent is absent.

Figure 2–7   A simple XSL-FO instance example

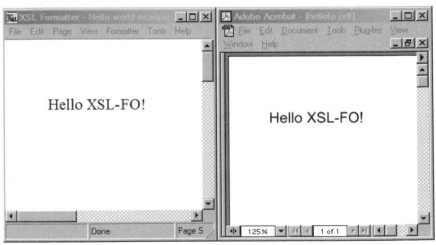

2.2.2 Training material example

Consider a page of content from some instructor-led training material that contains a mixture of a table, a list, a proportionally-spaced paragraph, and monospaced paragraphs shown in Figure 2–8.

Example 2–9 lists the first constructs in the flow that will produce the result shown in Figure 2–8.

The information presented above the horizontal rule is rendered using a borderless table. Lines 1 through 15 describe the three columns of

---

Figure 2–8   A page of handouts rendered in XSL-FO

Practical Formatting Using XSL-FO

Training material example
Module 1 - The context of XSL-FO
Lesson 2 - Examples

This page's material as an instructor-led handout:

   - excerpts of formatting objects created through the use of an XSLT stylesheet

```
01 <flow flow-name="pages-body"><table>
02 <table-column column-width="( 210mm - 2 * 15mm ) - 2in"/>
03 <table-column column-width="1in"/>
04 <table-column column-width="1in"/>
05 <table-body><table-row><table-cell><block text-align="start">
06    <block font-size="19pt">Training material example</block>
07    <block font-size="10pt" space-before.optimum="10pt">Module
08 1 - The context of XSL-FO</block>
09    <block font-size="10pt">Lesson 2 - Examples</block></block>
10 </table-cell>
11 <table-cell><block text-align="end"><external-graphic
12    src="url(&quot;..\whitesml.bmp&quot;)"/></block></table-cell>
13 <table-cell><block text-align="start"><external-graphic
14    src="url(&quot;..\cranesml.bmp&quot;)"/></block></table-cell>
15 </table-row></table-body></table>
16 <block line-height="3px"><leader leader-pattern="rule"
17    leader-length.optimum="100%" rule-thickness="1px"/></block>
18 <block space-before.optimum="6pt" font-size="14pt">
19 This page's material as an instructor-led handout:</block>
20 <list-block provisional-distance-between-starts=".43in"
21    provisional-label-separation=".1in" space-before.optimum="6pt">
22    <list-item relative-align="baseline">
23    <list-item-label text-align="end" end-indent="label-end()">
24      <block>-</block></list-item-label>
25    <list-item-body start-indent="body-start()">
26      <block font-size="14pt">excerpts of formatting objects
27 created through the use of an XSLT stylesheet</block>
28    </list-item-body></list-item></list-block>
29 <block space-before.optimum="12pt div 2" font-family="Courier"
30    linefeed-treatment="preserve" white-space-collapse="false"
31    white-space-treatment="preserve" font-size="12pt"><inline
32 font-size="inherited-property-value(font-size) div 2">01 </inline
33 >&lt;flow flow-name="pages-body"&gt;&lt;table&gt;
34 <inline font-size="inherited-property-value(font-size) div 2"
35 >02 </inline> &lt;table-column column-width...
```

Example 2–9   Formatting objects (excerpt) for a page of handout material

```
Line 01  <flow flow-name="pages-body"><table>
     02  <table-column column-width="( 210mm - 2 * 15mm ) - 2in"/>
     03  <table-column column-width="1in"/>
     04  <table-column column-width="1in"/>
     05  <table-body><table-row><table-cell><block text-align="start">
     06      <block font-size="19pt">Training material example</block>
     07      <block font-size="10pt" space-before.optimum="10pt">Module
     08  1 - The context of XSL-FO</block>
     09      <block font-size="10pt">Lesson 2 - Examples</block></block>
     10    </table-cell>
     11    <table-cell><block text-align="end"><external-graphic
     12      src="url(&quot;..\whitesml.bmp&quot;)"/></block></table-cell>
     13    <table-cell><block text-align="start"><external-graphic
     14      src="url(&quot;..\cranesml.bmp&quot;)"/></block></table-cell>
     15  </table-row></table-body></table>
     16  <block line-height="3px"><leader leader-pattern="rule"
     17      leader-length.optimum="100%" rule-thickness="1px"/></block>
     18  <block space-before.optimum="6pt" font-size="14pt">
     19  This page's material as an instructor-led handout:</block>
     20  <list-block provisional-distance-between-starts=".43in"
     21    provisional-label-separation=".1in" space-before.optimum="6pt">
     22    <list-item relative-align="baseline">
     23    <list-item-label text-align="end" end-indent="label-end()">
     24      <block>-</block></list-item-label>
     25    <list-item-body start-indent="body-start()">
     26      <block font-size="14pt">excerpts of formatting objects
     27  created through the use of an XSLT stylesheet</block>
     28    </list-item-body></list-item></list-block>
     29  <block space-before.optimum="12pt div 2" font-family="Courier"
     30      linefeed-treatment="preserve" white-space-collapse="false"
     31      white-space-treatment="preserve" font-size="12pt"><inline
     32  font-size="inherited-property-value(font-size) div 2">01 </inline
     33  >&lt;flow flow-name="pages-body"&gt;&lt;table&gt;
     34  <inline font-size="inherited-property-value(font-size) div 2"
     35  >02 </inline> &lt;table-column column-width...
```

information: the page title and context, a placebo white box in place of the branding logo for the licensee of the training material, and the Crane registered trademark. The table cell with the page information contains text in different point sizes on lines 6 through 9.

Note how the attribute value specified on line 2 is an expression, not a hard value. There is an expression language in XSL-FO that is a superset of the expression language of XSLT. This can make an XSLT stylesheet easier to write by having it convey property values in a piecemeal fashion in an expression to be evaluated, rather than trying to calculate the resulting value in XSLT. The example shows a calculation involving the page width and twice the margins, less the width of the other two columns. A simpler alternative would be "100% – 2in" since the percentages at this point are calculated relative to the width of the region and not the width of the page.

The horizontal rule below the title information needs to be block-oriented in that it needs to break the flow of information and be separate from the surrounding information. To achieve this effect with the inline-oriented leader construct, note how, on lines 16 and 17, the leader is placed inside of a block. Note also how the line height of the block is adjusted in order to get the desired spacing around the leader.

The block on lines 18 and 19 lays out a simple paragraph.

Lines 20 through 28 lay out a list construct, where the labels and bodies of list items are synchronized and laid out adjacent to each other in the flow of information. This side-by-side effect cannot be achieved with simple paragraphs; it could be achieved to some extent with borderless tables, but the use of list objects gives fine control over the layout nuances of a list construct.

The list block itself has properties on lines 20 and 21 governing all members of the list, including the provisional distance between the start edges of the list item label and the list item body, and the provisional label separation. These provisional values are useful constructs in XSL-FO in that they allow us to specify contingent behavior for the XSL-FO processor to accommodate the start indent of the list label while maintaining the distance between the end of the label and the start of the body.

Note: Remember one of the design goals of XML declared that "terseness is of minimal importance" (they probably could not have found a terser way of saying that)? Note that the attribute name specifying the first of these provisional property values is 35 characters long. It is not uncommon to need to use lengthy element and attribute names, and XSL-FO instances always seem to me to be so very verbose to read, though I admit they certainly are not ambiguous.

Note how, on lines 23 and 25, functions can be used in attribute values. XSL-FO defines a library of functions that can be invoked in the expression language. The `label-end()` and `body-start()` functions engage the appropriate use of one of the two provisional list construct properties based on the start indent of the item's label.

Line 29 begins the block containing the listing of markup. To ensure a verbatim rendering of edited text, line 30 specifies that all linefeeds in the block of content must be preserved, and white-space characters are not to be collapsed. This disengages the default behavior of treating linefeeds as white space and collapsing white space to a single space character, as would be typical for proportional-font paragraphs of prose.

Lines 31 and 32 show an inline sequence of text being formatted differently than the remainder of the text of the block. The desired effect of the line number being half the current font size is achieved through the use of the function "`inherited-property-value(font-size)`", though there are two alternate ways of specifying the same relative value: "50%" and ".5em". Using any of these expressions would produce the same result.

The escaped markup on lines 33 and 35 may look incorrect, but this is an XML serialization of the XSL-FO instance, hence, sensitive markup

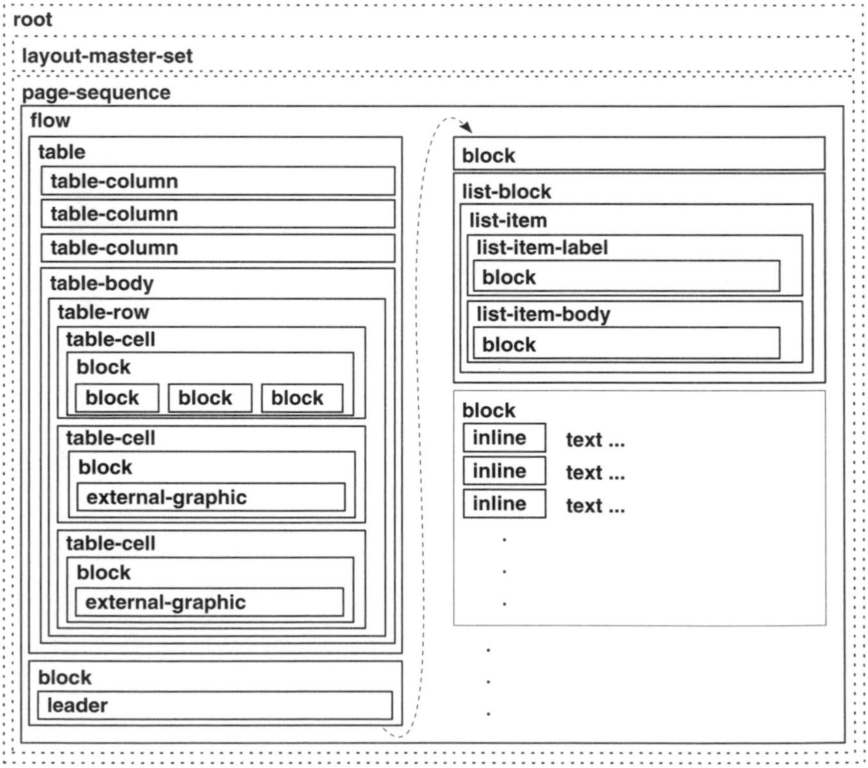

Figure 2–9   The nesting of XSL-FO constructs in the example

characters must be escaped in order to be recognized as text and not as markup. Since this is a page describing markup, the markup being described needs to be distinguished from the markup of the document itself.

The nesting of the hierarchy of the formatting objects is shown in Figure 2–9.

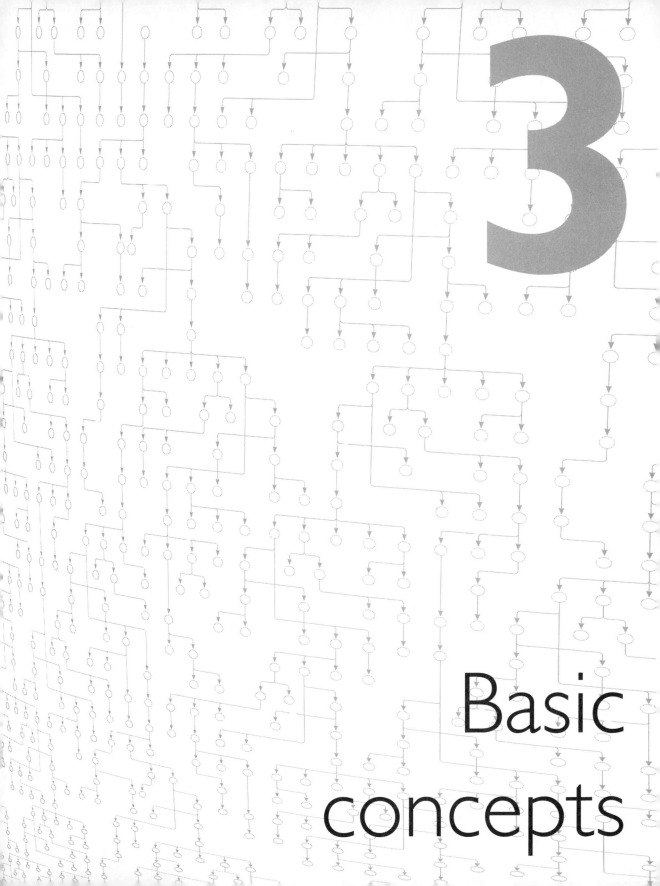

3

Basic concepts

3 Basic concepts

Here we review basic aspects of the XSL-FO semantics and vocabulary, to gain a better understanding of how the technology works and how to use the specification itself.

Layout-based vs. content-based formatting. Two very different approaches to the formatting of information are contrasted. Layout-based formatting respects the constraints of the target medium, where limitations or capacities of the target may constrain the content or appearance of the information on a page. Content-based formatting respects the quantity and identity of the information, while the target medium is made to accommodate the information being formatted according to rules in a stylesheet.

Formatting is different from rendering. The distinction between formatting and rendering is the one between expressing what you want formatted vs. expressing how it is to be accomplished on the target device. This contrast is similar to the difference between declarative and imperative style programming methods, or the difference between XSLT's "transformation by example" paradigm vs. other algorithmic transformation approaches using programming languages.

Differing processing model concepts are expressed using unambiguous terminology. The XSL-FO specification, and this book as well, attempts to be very careful in using precise terminology when what is being referred to has similar concepts in other constructs that it could be confused with. For example, an XSL-FO instance contains elements and their attributes. This is similar to the corresponding formatting object tree with objects and their properties. This is, in turn, similar to the corresponding refined formatting object tree with objects and their area traits. This is, finally, similar to the corresponding area tree with areas and their traits.

The XSL-FO semantics and vocabulary properties address the requirements of arbitrary page boundaries imposed on the presentation of information, which is different from the needs of infinite-length web user agent windows. These new semantics are inspired by the Document Style Semantics and Specification Language (DSSSL) International Standard ISO/IEC 10179, but in practice diverge from DSSSL towards Cascading Style Sheets 2 (CSS2) for compatibility with web-based processing.

Formatting model and vocabulary properties extend what is currently available for web presentation. The semantics are classified based on their relationship to similar CSS properties:

- CSS properties by copy (unchanged CSS2 semantics),
- CSS properties with extended values,
- CSS properties "broken apart" to a finer granularity,
- XSL-FO-specific properties.

The XSL-FO support of multiple writing directions and a reference orientation are important concepts inherited from DSSSL that are not present in CSS2.

What's included in this chapter. This chapter includes discussion of the following XSL-FO objects:

- root (*6.4.2*):
  - is the document element of a XSL-FO instance,
- layout-master-set (*6.4.6*):
  - is the collection of definitions of page geometries and page sequencing and selection patterns,
- page-sequence (*6.4.5*):
  - is the specification of how information is to be paginated over a sequence of pages with common static information,

- flow (*6.4.18*):
  - is the content that is flowed to as many pages as required and formatted according to the appearance properties.

3.1 Formatting and rendering

3.1.1 Layout-based vs. content-based formatting

Layout-based formatting accommodates the medium being used to present information. The constraints of the medium, or the layout design created by the graphic artist, often demands absolute positioning, column location specification, or page number specification. For example, a magazine may need a particular columnist's article to appear on the right-hand edge of page 7, while the three lead stories must be headlined within the first four pages.

This focus on layout places more emphasis on the appearance and location of information than on the information itself, dictating the quantity and presentation of the content. Such layout is typically unstructured in both the authoring and the formatting processes, as typified by desktop publishing, journalism, etc.

Content-based formatting accommodates the information being presented with the available medium. The constraints of layout are expressed as rules associated with the information dictating how given information is to be positioned or presented. For example, a single aircraft maintenance manual cannot have each of its 40,000 to 60,000 pages individually formatted.

This focus on information places more emphasis on the content and rules of layout than on the medium, dictating the automatic layout and presentation of constructs found in the information stream. Such layout is usually highly structured in both the authoring and the formatting processes, as typified by technical publications found in pharmaceutical, aerospace, automotive, or other industries where either vast amounts of information are presented, or the information must be interchanged in a neutral form with other players.

XSL-FO 1.0 is oriented more to content-based formatting than to layout-based formatting, though there do exist certain controls for the positioning, cropping, and flowing of information to particular areas of pages in page sequences. XSL-FO can express the repetition of page geometries, mechanically accommodating the content as flowed by a transformation of the information into the formatting vocabulary. There is only limited support for specifying the order of page sequences, and high-caliber copy-fitting requirements often cannot be met with mechanical unattended transformations.

Note that while XSL-FO is not oriented to loose-leaf publishing, perhaps that will not prevent it from being used by a vendor to express the content of pages being maintained in a loose-leaf-based environment. A loose-leaf environment supports "change pages" (a.k.a. "A pages") through a database of effective pages and page contents.

XSL-FO has no inherent maintenance facilities for past versions of individual pages, and no inherent support for lists of effective pages. Such facilities could be provided outside the scope of individual page presentations. XSL-FO is more oriented to the unrestricted flowing of information to as much of the target medium as required to accommodate the content.

3.1.2   Formatting vs. rendering

When creating XML we should be designing the structures around our business processes responsible for maintaining the information, instead of the structures used for presentation. An XSL-FO instance describes the intent of how that stream of information is to be formatted in the target medium in a paginated fashion. This instance is typically generated by a stylesheet acting on an instance of XML information, rearranging and restructuring it into the order and presentation desired.

This reordering takes the element, attribute, and data content of the instance and repackages it according to our intent based on our understanding of the semantics of the XSL-FO vocabulary. We can reify this hierarchical reordering as an intermediate file of XML syntax which we can use for diagnostic purposes. We could also take the opportunity to store this reordering as an XML instance for "store and forward" strategies where the formatting takes place later or remotely from where the transformation takes place.

Unlike interactive formatting tools, such as desktop publishing products, there is no feedback loop from the XSL-FO formatter to the stylesheet creating the XSL-FO vocabulary. Therefore, the XSL-FO information must be complete with respect to all desired behaviors of the formatter.

Any special formatting cases or conditions can be accommodated through contingencies expressed in the XSL-FO semantics.

The information arranged in the elements, attributes, and data of our source vocabularies is repackaged into the elements and attributes of the XSL-FO formatting vocabulary and the data of the XSL-FO instance that express the formatting objects and their properties of the XSL-FO semantics. Each formatting object specifies an aspect of either layout, appearance and impartation, or pagination and flow.

The layout semantics express the intent of locating information positioned on the target medium. Areas of content are specified as located and nested within other areas, in a hierarchical tree of rectangles on each page.

The appearance and impartation semantics express the intent of how the information is to be conveyed to the reader. For visual media, this conveyance includes font, size, color, weight, etc. For aural synthesis, this conveyance includes voice, volume, azimuth, pitch, etc.

The pagination and flow semantics express the intent of how the stream of information being presented is to be parceled within the layout areas. The final pagination is the result of accommodating the amount of flow being presented within the areas that have been defined.

Each of the formatting objects is expressed in an XSL-FO instance as an element. It is not necessary to know all formatting objects to get effective formatted results.

An XSL-FO formatter is responsible for interpreting the rendering intent, as expressed in the XSL-FO semantics corresponding to the elements and attributes in the instance. Following the Recommendation, the formatter determines what is to be rendered where by interpreting the interaction between formatting objects. How the formatter does this interpretation is defined in excruciating detail in the W3C Recommendation, as this document is written more for implementers than for stylesheet writers or XSL-FO instance creators.

The properties expressed for each of the objects influence or are included in the structure of the resulting areas. Some of these properties are specifically targeted for certain media and are otherwise ignored by media for which they do not apply.

The Recommendation does not describe in detail the semantics of rendering. Any device-specific rendition is effected from the final interpretation of the semantics of the formatting objects that create the trees of areas and the traits found in those areas that are derived from the properties. How the rendering agent actually accomplishes the task of effecting the result of formatting to the target medium is entirely up to the agent, as long as it produces the same result as the intent described by the Recommendation.

The rendering itself may be a multiple-step process, producing the final form through a staged expression of rendering through interpretation on a given medium. For example, the rendering may require production of another intermediate formatting language such as TeX. Rendering may directly produce a final-form page description language such as the Portable Document Format (PDF), or the Standard Page Description Language (International Standard ISO/IEC 10180). The physical final form would then be produced from the intermediate form or final page representation. Indeed, there could be many steps to obtain a final result, e.g. XML to XSL-FO to TeX to PDF to paper.

3.2 Processing model

The Recommendation describes the processing model for XSL-FO as a series of formal steps in the derivation of the areas of content to be rendered from the instance expressing the intent of formatting, as depicted in Figure 3–1. The Recommendation does not cover the creation of the XSL-FO instance, nor the detailed semantics of rendering, but focuses entirely on how to get from the former to the latter (note the thicker arrows in the diagram at the beginning and end of the formatting process).

Note: Although the processing model is described in the Recommendation using constructs and procedural steps following a well-defined sequence, there is no obligation on a vendor that a particular implementation perform the steps as documented. The only obligation on a formatter is that it produce the rendered result *as if it were implemented according to the steps described* in the text.

This nuance is important to vendors in that it allows them to implement any algorithm producing equivalent results, without constraining the innovation or flexibility to accomplish the results using any algorithm they wish.

One ramification of this flexibility is that none of the intermediate results described in the processing model can be standardized or be required of a particular implementation. Conformance testing would be far simpler if there were a serialization of the abstract result of the interpretation of the formatting intent, without needing to interpret a rendered result as having successfully met the criteria.

First, the instance of elements, attributes, and data becomes a node tree of abstract nodes representing these constructs for processing. It is possible that this node tree is passed directly from the result of transforming some source XML into resulting XSL-FO without instantiating the result as markup characters. However, if the information is presented to the formatter as an instance of markup characters, this must be interpreted into a node tree suitable for the formatter to work with.

This node tree of elements, attributes, and text represents the expression of the intent of what the designer desires in the rendered result. This is called the Instance Tree and includes all of the content, including references to external foreign objects not expressible in XML, that is to appear in the target medium. The instance is the mechanism used by the designer to express the information to be presented using the desired semantics as described in the XSL-FO Recommendation.

The Instance Tree is interpreted into the Formatting Object Tree that is comprised entirely of formatting objects and their properties. This requires

Figure 3–1   XSL processing model flow summary

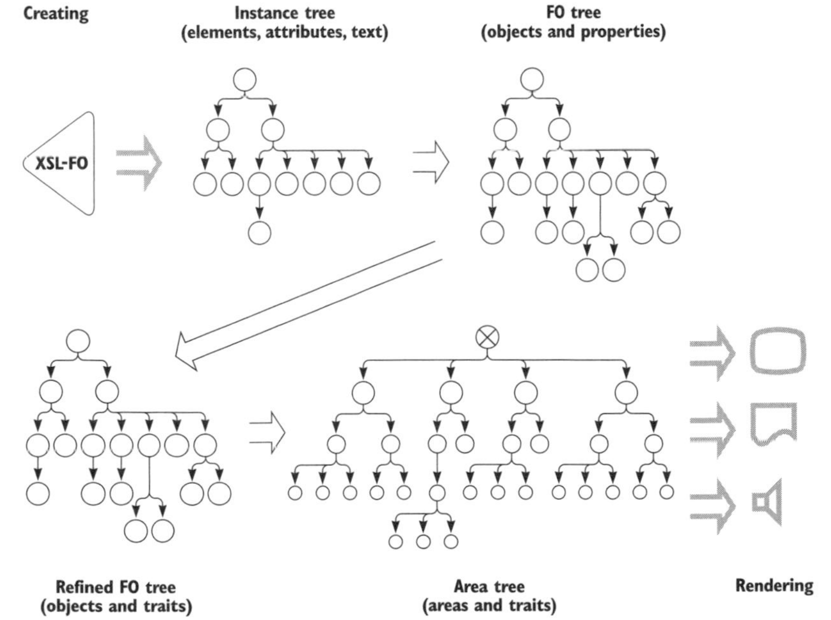

the (abstract) breaking of text nodes into sequences of character formatting objects, and the creation of properties from attributes.

Note that certain white-space-only text nodes of the Instance Tree are irrelevant to the formatting process and do not create text nodes in the Formatting Object Tree. Also removed for later access by the formatter or rendering agent are in-stream foreign objects (expressed in XML but not in the XSL-FO vocabulary, e.g. Scalable Vector Graphics (SVG) fragments), and any objects not from the XSL-FO namespace that are used in the declarations formatting object.

The Formatting Object Tree is interpreted into the Refined Formatting Object Tree that is comprised of objects and traits. Properties can specify two kinds of traits: formatting traits (e.g. size and position) or rendering traits (e.g. style and appearance). Some property specifications are shorthand expressions that encompass a number of separate trait specifications and their values.

Computed property expression values are evaluated and the resulting values assigned to the traits. For example, a property value of 2em when the current font size is 20pt produces a trait value of 40pt.

Inheritance plays an important role in trait derivation. Some traits are derived from the closest ancestral specification of the corresponding property. Some traits that are not inherited by default can have their value inherited by using the explicit inherit property value.

Once all traits that are applicable to all formatting objects are determined, traits not applicable to each object are removed. At this point the information is comprised of all the objects that are used to create areas, and each object has all the traits and only the traits that are applicable to it.

The Refined Formatting Object Tree is interpreted into the Area Tree that is comprised of areas and traits, according to the semantics of the objects. A given object may create areas at different branches of the Area Tree. Most objects produce exactly one area, and some objects do not produce any areas.

Each area has a geometric position, z-layer position, content, background, padding, and borders. Areas are nested in a tree within ancestral areas up to the highest (and largest) area which is the page area.

Page areas are the children of the root node in the Area Tree. Page areas are ordered by their position in the Area Tree, but they are not geometrically related to each other in any way.

The rendering agent effects the impartation of the areas in the Area Tree according to the medium. The Recommendation gives guidelines on the rendering of areas in either visual or aural media. Some missing trait values, such as font or volume, can be arbitrarily inferred by the rendering agent. This allowance leads to differing renderings by different tools in cases when an XSL-FO instance does not express the missing trait values.

The Recommendation document is written to direct a formatter implementer in carrying out the requirements of interpreting the formatting intent. Certain traits are boolean values targeted solely to the implementer and reflecting an area's role or relative order to other areas. These traits are not specifiable in the XSL-FO instance but are indicated in the Recommendation to make implementation easier.

The rigor of the Recommendation language is necessary in order to ensure proper interpretation of finely-tuned typographical nuances. This makes the Recommendation difficult to read for many people who just want to write stylesheets. Fortunately, simple things can be done simply, once you get around the necessary verbosity of the Recommendation document.

3.3 Formatting object XML vocabulary

3.3.1 Vocabulary structure

The semantics of a formatting object are defined in terms of the areas it generates and their traits. The Recommendation describes which areas each object generates (if any), where the areas are placed in the branches of the area tree hierarchy, and how the areas interact with areas generated by other objects.

To trigger the semantics desired, formatting objects and their properties are specified using elements, attributes, and text. This information may be reified in a standalone XML instance being interpreted by a formatter, or it may be represented in a node tree resulting from a transformation process such as XSLT.

All XSL-FO elements input to the processor must be in the namespace with the URI "`http://www.w3.org/1999/XSL/Format`", and may use the default namespace for this URI.

The "X" in XSL-FO does represent "Extensible," so an XSL-FO instance may include extension elements and attributes that are recognized by the formatting processor. Any other processor is not obliged to support an extension recognized by a given processor. Extension elements must be in a namespace other than the XSL-FO namespace. Extension attributes must have a non-null prefix. Extension constructs must be ignored if not recognized by an XSL-FO processor.

The element-type and attribute names are all specified with letters in lowercase (remember that XML is case sensitive). Hyphens separate multiple words in a single name and dots separate names from their compound components. Some abbreviations are used in XSL-FO if the name is already used in XML or HTML.

Any property is allowed to be specified on any object in the elements and attributes of the input. This flexibility provides for inheritance in the formatting object tree. Only those traits meaningful to a formatting object are in the refined formatting object tree and are utilized by the areas created by the object. Some properties not defined to be inheritable by default can be inherited if their values explicitly specify this.

Every object may have a unique identifier specified using the `id` property. This is used as the target of references from other objects. This value is never inherited from other objects and is assigned to the first child area generated by the object. For the reference to work properly, the identifier must be found somewhere in the area tree, so if the object doesn't generate any areas, the identifier is lost and the reference is broken.

Extension objects and/or properties are allowed in any namespace other than the XSL-FO namespace. For example, `xmlns:rx=` "`http://www.renderx.com/XSL/Extensions`" is recognized by the RenderX formatter tool for unique objects and properties implemented by it, while `xmlns:axf="http://www.antennahouse.com/names/XSL/Extensions"` is recognized by the Antenna House, Inc. formatter tool for yet other different objects and properties implemented by that tool. Vendors can implement any semantics they wish and have any vocabulary they wish to represent a user's intent to engage those extended semantics. There is no obligation on any tool to support any vendor's extension semantics.

Note: This is an important portability issue. A user who engages extension semantics cannot assume these semantics will be available on any other tool than that which implements the semantics. Taking advantage of an extension will most likely lock a user into a particular brand of formatting engine. This may have repercussions on the user's ability to distribute stylesheets to other users who may not be in a position to take advantage of the custom extension.

Non-XSL-FO namespaces are allowed in an XSL-FO instance when used to embed the representation of a graphic image in the flow. For example, `xmlns:svg="http://www.w3.org/2000/svg"` is W3C's two-dimensional graphics XML vocabulary that can be embedded in allowed places in an XSL-FO instance. It is up to the rendering process in the formatter to recognize the non-XSL-FO namespace and realize the image in the result.

3.3.2 Direct vs. constraint property specification

Properties influence the behavior of an object in the creation of areas for the formatted result. Properties are specified in an XSL-FO XML instance or node tree as attributes and become traits in the area tree.

Properties can be strategically placed in the hierarchy (or specified algorithmically by the stylesheet writer) in order to promote maintainability or consistency in the formatted result.

Some properties directly specify a formatting result, such as the `color` property. The interpretation of a direct property is not influenced by the context of the areas surrounding the area with the property. In this example, the foreground color trait of the area is the given value regardless of where it is used.

Some properties constrain the formatting result based on an interpretation of context in the area tree, such as the `space-before` property. The interpretation of a constraint property specified identically for two areas may be different based on the context of the generated areas (not on the context of the objects that generated the areas). In this example, the amount of space left before an area is constrained, but should that area be at the top of a reference area (say, a page), and the area's conditionality allows to discard the space before, then the actual value used is zero because the space before is discarded.

Compound properties have components for fine-grained specification. These often originate from the CSS2 specification but they specify too many aspects of formatting in a single specification. XSL-FO allows for the components to be individually specified. An example is the `space-before.optimum`, `space-before.minimum`, `space-before.maximum`, `space-before.conditionality`, and `space-before.precedence` components of the `space-before` property.

It is not necessary to know all properties to get effective formatted results. A complete alphabetical list of formatting properties is in Section D.4 on page 344.

3.3.3   Property value expressions

A property's value can be the evaluation of an expression of either fixed values, such as `space-before="20pt div 2"`, or contextually-sensitive values, such as `space-before="from-parent(font-size) div 2"`.

The expression language is similar to that of XPath 1.0 in that it includes the same operators and the same operands, but it also includes length values as operands that are not allowed in XPath 1.0.

Expressions that are influenced by the font size evaluate the font size before evaluating any other components of the expression.

XSL-FO defines a core function library useful for property expressions.

Some functions give access to property values of the current node, such as `inherited-property-value(property-name)`. This obtains a value that may be specified on the current node or may be inherited from the closest ancestral node that specifies the value.

Some functions give access to property values of other nodes, such as `from-parent(property-name)` or `merge-property-values(property-name)`. The former obtains the property value directly from the parent object specification, and the latter looks for the property value in the particular sibling object specification corresponding to a given state of the user interface.

There are numerous property data types including both simple-valued and compound-valued types that are summarized in Section D.2.1 on page 334.

3.3.4 Inherited properties

Inheritable properties need not be specified for a formatting object because during refinement, the formatting object tree is examined for the closest specifications of such properties to obtain values for a given object. All inheritance is completed before the area tree is created. See Section D.3.1 on page 341 for a list of all inherited properties.

Inheritance goes "through" block-level or out-of-line constructs because of the location of such constructs in the formatting object tree. This is often the source of unexpected results in a stylesheet's result. For example, the same `start-indent` property used to indent a table is inherited by the table's cell's content because the table is an ancestor of the cell. In another common example, a footnote's body inherits properties from the block in which the footnote is specified, again because of the ancestral relationship in the formatting object tree. Without explicitly setting the indentation on a footnote's body, any indentation of the block in which the footnote is cited will be inherited by the footnote body's blocks. One's intuition might be that the blocks at the bottom of the page have no relationship to the blocks in the middle of the page, but that is true only for the result of area tree creation from the hierarchically related constructs.

Some functions can obtain property values from outside the ancestry, looking at siblings of ancestral constructs for the traits for the areas the object is generating. Two examples of such functions are `merge-property-values()` and `from-table-column()`.

Some properties look like they are inherited, but do not go "through" block-level or out-of-line constructs. For example, `text-decoration` is used to underscore text in a block and all inline descendants of the block, but not any descendants of any footnotes or tables found in the block.

3.3.5 Shorthand properties

Shorthand properties specify a number of standalone properties using a single specification. This is different from a compound property in that a shorthand property represents a set of standalone properties whereas a compound property is comprised of a set of components. For example, one specification `font="italic small-caps bold 40pt/50pt Courier"` sets each of `font-style`, `font-variant`, `font-weight`, `font-size`, `line-height`, and `font-family` in order with a single specification.

Individual properties of a shorthand property are supported severally in that a shorthand property can be used in conjunction with individual properties: those that are specified are more precise than those that are inferred.

Shorthand properties are processed in the order of increasing precision. The precedence order is independent of attribute specification order (remember that in XML, attributes are unordered). A more-specific attribute name has higher precedence than less-specific attribute name. For example, `border-color` is more precise than `border`, and `border-bottom-color` is more precise than `border-color`.

Named-edge border specifications have higher precedence than generic border specifications, even though they have the same specificity, so that `border-bottom` is more precise than `border-style`.

A processor is not obliged to support shorthand properties. See Section D.3.2 on page 343 for a list of all shorthand properties. It is common problem when writing stylesheets to get no effect from a given formatter because it doesn't support a shorthand you were using with other formatters.

3.3.6 Conformance

There are three levels of conformance defined in the Recommendation: complete, extended, and basic.

- Claiming complete conformance requires the implementation to support the entire Recommendation.
- Claiming extended conformance does not require an implementation to support shorthand properties or a very few esoteric positioning- and font-related properties. The remainder of the Recommendation must be fully supported.
- Claiming basic conformance requires a minimum level of visual pagination or aural rendering support. Fallback behaviors are defined for the unsupported extended facilities.

In a given medium, a processor must support all formatting objects and properties specified for the conformance level claimed. The conformance levels are described for two rendering class distinctions: visual media and aural media. A processor can implement fallback processing in media not supported, but conformance qualification does not include fallback processing.

3.3.7   Top-level formatting objects

All XSL-FO instances must have the `root` and `layout-master-set` formatting objects. The `root` is the document element of an XSL-FO instance. It is a handy location for document-wide inherited attributes to be placed. The `layout-master-set` collects definitions of page geometries available to use for pagination as well as definitions of patterns of geometry sequencing for nuances in changes of page layout.

All XSL-FO instances must have at least one page sequence with flowed content to be paginated. Each `page-sequence` object begins a new page with some content to be paginated using a sequence of page geometries. It defines properties and content common to all pages in the sequence, such as the formatting of page numbers in the sequence and the definitions of any static content (i.e. headers, footers, etc.) for the page geometries selected for the page sequence.

As many pages will be created as is needed to accommodate the flow given for the sequence. An exception is when the number of pages of the sequence or the starting page number of the following sequence is constrained to be an even or odd number, in which case the formatter may need to generate a blank page to accommodate the criterion. This blank page can be defined with static content to inform the reader that the page is intentionally left blank. Also, the use of `break-before` and `break-after` in a sequence can cause information to start at the top of a page in the middle of the sequence.

The formatter will use either the page geometry or the pattern of geometry sequencing to select the pages, in order to accommodate the content and any blank pages.

The `flow` object contains the content to be paginated in a sequence of pages of a given geometry or geometry sequence. This object can only contain block-level formatting objects as its top-level child objects.

3.3.8 The root object

Purpose

- This is the document element of an XSL-FO instance;
- it returns areas generated by children as a sequence of page viewport areas;
  - such areas are ordered but there is no geometric relationship between areas.

Content

- (*6.4.2*) (layout-master-set, declarations?, page-sequence+),
- child objects (listed alphabetically):
  - declarations (*6.4.3*; 297),
  - layout-master-set (*6.4.6*; 65),
  - page-sequence (*6.4.5*; 65).

Optional property

- media-usage (*7.25.11*; 395).

A property of interest

- media-usage is used when establishing either pagination with bounded page length or no pagination with infinite page length.

An XSL-FO instance's document element is shown in Example 3–1.

Example 3–1 The document element

```
Line 01  <?xml version="1.0" encoding="utf-8"?>
02  <root xmlns="http://www.w3.org/1999/XSL/Format" font-size="16pt">
03    <layout-master-set>
04      <simple-page-master master-name="bookpage"
05                          page-height="297mm" page-width="210mm"
06                          margin-top="15mm" margin-bottom="15mm"
07                          margin-left="15mm" margin-right="15mm">
08        <region-body region-name="bookpage-body"
09                     margin-top="5mm" margin-bottom="5mm"/>
10      </simple-page-master>
11    </layout-master-set>
12    <page-sequence master-reference="bookpage">
13      <title>Hello world example</title>
14      <flow flow-name="bookpage-body">
15        <block>Hello XSL-FO!</block>
16      </flow>
17    </page-sequence>
18  </root>
```

3.3.9 The layout-master-set object

Purpose

- This is the collection of definitions of page geometries, available regions, and page selection patterns.

Content

- (*6.4.6*) (simple-page-master | page-sequence-master)+,
- child objects (listed alphabetically):
  - page-sequence-master (*6.4.7*; 220),
  - simple-page-master (*6.4.12*; 114),
- referring object:
  - root (*6.4.2*; 64).

No properties are defined for this formatting object.

A set of layout masters is shown in Example 3–2.

Example 3–2   The collection of all possible page layouts and their respective regions

```
Line 01   <?xml version="1.0" encoding="utf-8"?>
02   <root xmlns="http://www.w3.org/1999/XSL/Format" font-size="16pt">
03     <layout-master-set>
04       <simple-page-master master-name="bookpage"
05                           page-height="297mm" page-width="210mm"
06                           margin-top="15mm" margin-bottom="15mm"
07                           margin-left="15mm" margin-right="15mm">
08         <region-body region-name="bookpage-body"
09                     margin-top="5mm" margin-bottom="5mm"/>
10       </simple-page-master>
11     </layout-master-set>
12     <page-sequence master-reference="bookpage">
13       <title>Hello world example</title>
14       <flow flow-name="bookpage-body">
15         <block>Hello XSL-FO!</block>
16       </flow>
17     </page-sequence>
18   </root>
```

3.3.10 The page-sequence object

Purpose

- This is the definition of information for a sequence of pages with common static information.

- It implies generating as many pages as necessary to accommodate the flowed content that is supplied.
- Each new page sequence begins the flow at the top of a new page;
  - examples include starts of chapters, front matter, back matter, etc.

Content

- (*6.4.5*) `(title?, static-content*, flow)`,
- child objects (listed alphabetically):
  - `flow` (*6.4.18*; 67),
  - `static-content` (*6.4.19*; 202),
  - `title` (*6.4.20*; 117),
- referring object:
  - `root` (*6.4.2*; 64).

Required property

- `master-reference` (*7.25.9*; 394).

Optional properties

- `country` (*7.9.1*; 371),
- `force-page-count` (*7.25.6*; 380),
- `format` (*7.24.1*; 380),
- `grouping-separator` (*7.24.2*; 381),
- `grouping-size` (*7.24.3*; 382),
- `id` (*7.28.2*; 384),
- `initial-page-number` (*7.25.7*; 385),
- `language` (*7.9.2*; 387),
- `letter-value` (*7.24.4*; 390).

Shorthand influencing the object's properties

- `xml:lang` (*7.29.24*; 429).

Properties of interest

- `master-reference` selects the page geometry or sequencing of page geometry and the available regions within those page definitions;
  - it cannot change the page geometry based on content found in the flow.
- `format` governs how the page number is represented as a sequence of glyphs;
  - it applies to page numbers used —

- on the page itself,
- in citations to the page;
- it can specify numbers, roman numerals, etc. —
  - by utilizing `grouping-size`, `grouping-separator`, `country`, and `language` if appropriate;
- it is formally defined by reference to XSLT (see page Section D.2.3 on page 340).

A sequence of pages is shown in Example 3–3.

Example 3–3   A sequence of pages

```
Line 01  <?xml version="1.0" encoding="utf-8"?>
02  <root xmlns="http://www.w3.org/1999/XSL/Format" font-size="16pt">
03    <layout-master-set>
04      <simple-page-master master-name="bookpage"
05                          page-height="297mm" page-width="210mm"
06                          margin-top="15mm" margin-bottom="15mm"
07                          margin-left="15mm" margin-right="15mm">
08        <region-body region-name="bookpage-body"
09                     margin-top="5mm" margin-bottom="5mm"/>
10      </simple-page-master>
11    </layout-master-set>
12    <page-sequence master-reference="bookpage">
13      <title>Hello world example</title>
14      <flow flow-name="bookpage-body">
15        <block>Hello XSL-FO!</block>
16      </flow>
17    </page-sequence>
18  </root>
```

3.3.11   The flow object

Purpose

- This is the content that is flowed to as many pages as required to fit;
  - flowed content is not repeated by the formatter;
- the length of the flow governs the length of the page sequence.

Content

- (*6.4.18*) `(%block;)+`,
- child object:
  - `%block;` (*6.2*; 69),
- referring object:
  - `page-sequence` (*6.4.5*; 65),

- any number of marker children at the beginning.

Required property

- flow-name (*7.25.5*; *376*).

Property use

- flow-name indicates into which area on the page the child information is to be flowed.
  - The area does not have to exist in the particular page geometry being rendered;
    - this is the method to ignore a flow on particular pages.

A flow of information for an area is shown in Example 3–4.

Example 3–4   The flow of information for an area

```
Line 01  <?xml version="1.0" encoding="utf-8"?>
     02  <root xmlns="http://www.w3.org/1999/XSL/Format" font-size="16pt">
     03    <layout-master-set>
     04      <simple-page-master master-name="bookpage"
     05                          page-height="297mm" page-width="210mm"
     06                          margin-top="15mm" margin-bottom="15mm"
     07                          margin-left="15mm" margin-right="15mm">
     08        <region-body region-name="bookpage-body"
     09                     margin-top="5mm" margin-bottom="5mm"/>
     10      </simple-page-master>
     11    </layout-master-set>
     12    <page-sequence master-reference="bookpage">
     13      <title>Hello world example</title>
     14      <flow flow-name="bookpage-body">
     15        <block>Hello XSL-FO!</block>
     16      </flow>
     17    </page-sequence>
     18  </root>
```

3.3.12   Grouping of formatting objects for the flow

There are five groups of formatting objects that can be used in the flow of information being paginated: block-level, inline-level, neutral, out-of-line, and out-of-line inline-level.

Objects of each kind dictate how the areas created by these objects stack next to each other. Areas are added to branches of the area tree and interact with adjacent areas in the area tree. This interaction on the rendered page is the stacking of areas, and stacking can be either in the block-progression direction (e.g. top-to-bottom of the page in a Western European writing direction) or in the inline-progression direction (e.g. left-to-right of the page in a Western European writing direction).

Block-level objects stack next to siblings in the block-progression direction. This has the effect of restarting the flow of information in the block-progression direction, preventing siblings from being "beside" each other in the inline-progression direction. The `block` object is a very frequently used construct, used for typographical constructs such as paragraphs, headings, captions, table cell contents, etc.

Inline-level objects stack next to siblings in the inline-progression direction. These objects do not restart the flow of information in the block-progression direction. Inline objects specify portions of content to be flowed into the lines of the parent block, where such portions are distinct from their sibling portions, such as bold or italic text fragments.

Neutral objects are allowed anywhere and do not impact the stacking of sibling objects, nor interrupt the progression direction of the parent object.

Out-of-line objects generate areas on branches of the area tree different from those of their sibling objects. As such, the areas of these objects stack out of line relative to the areas of sibling objects. These objects do not break the flow of information in any progression direction.

Out-of-line inline-level objects are similar to out-of-line objects in that they generate areas on branches of the area tree different from those of their sibling objects, but they are restricted to be used solely as inline-level constructs and never as block-level constructs.

3.3.13 Block-level objects

These objects, represented by the `%block;` parameter entity in content models, include —

- `block` (*6.5.2*; 100):
  - is the formatting specification for a block of lines, distinct from any preceding block of lines,
- `block-container` (*6.5.3*; 109):
  - is the specification of a block-level reference area for contained descendant blocks,
- `list-block` (*6.8.2*; 131):

- is the parent object of a related set of child list members,
- `table-and-caption` (*6.7.2*; 170):
  - is the parent object of a captioned collection of tabular content,
- `table` (*6.7.3*; 173):
  - is the parent object of an uncaptioned collection of tabular content.

These objects are allowed as children of the `flow` object;

- they may also be nested inside other constructs.

Block-level objects are stacked in the block-progression direction of flow;

- they restart the block-progression flow of information;
- two block-level objects cannot be positioned next to each other in the inline-progression direction within the same containing object;
- note that `block-container` can, selectively, be absolutely positioned outside of the flow and its areas will then not stack with its sibling areas.

3.3.14   Inline-level objects

These objects, represented by the `%inline;` parameter entity in content models, include —

- `basic-link` (*6.9.2*; 145):
  - is the inline content of the start of a unidirectional link to a single end point,
- `bidi-override` (*6.6.2*; 293):
  - overrides the inherent Unicode text direction for a sequence of characters,
- `character` (*6.6.3*; 294):
  - is both the abstract formatting object implied by a simple character in an XSL-FO instance and the concrete formatting object available to be used in place of a simple character,
- `external-graphic` (*6.6.5*; 139):
  - is the inline display of graphical or other externally-supplied information,
- `inline` (*6.6.7*; 103):
  - is the formatting specification for inline content that is distinct from its preceding content within a line generated in a block,
- `inline-container` (*6.6.8*; 108):
  - is an inline reference area for contained blocks,
- `instream-foreign-object` (*6.6.6*; 141):
  - is the inline display of graphical or other instance-supplied information,
- `leader` (*6.6.9*; 152):

- is the inline display of a rule or a sequence of glyphs,
- `multi-toggle` (*6.9.5*; 276):
  - is the definition of interaction-sensitive objects within a candidate rendered sequence of formatting objects,
- `page-number` (*6.6.10*; 204):
  - is an inline-level placeholder replaced with the page number of the current page,
- `page-number-citation` (*6.6.11*; 105):
  - is an inline-level placeholder replaced with the page number of the first normal area of the cited formatting object.

These blocks are not allowed as children of the `flow` object;

- they may be nested inside constructs (including other inline constructs).

Inline-level objects are stacked in the inline-progression direction of flow;

- they do not restart the block-progression flow of information;
- they reside in the line areas generated by the formatter.

3.3.15 Neutral objects

These objects, typically allowed anywhere where `#PCDATA`, `%inline;`, or `%block;` constructs are allowed, include —

- `multi-properties` (*6.9.6*; 268):
  - is the collection of candidate property sets from which exactly one set influences the properties of a formatting object based on its status or the status of user interaction,
- `multi-switch` (*6.9.3*; 271):
  - is the collection of candidate formatting object sequences from which exactly one is rendered at any given time based on an interactive condition influenced by the user while being tracked by the formatter,
- `retrieve-marker` (*6.11.4*; 209):
  - is a placeholder replaced with the formatting objects of the indicated marker and allowed only within static content,
- `wrapper` (*6.11.2*; 100):
  - is a generic container construct for specifying inherited properties for descendent constructs.

Note that individual flow objects above may have constraints preventing their use in particular objects.

Areas returned by the interpretation of these objects are stacked in the progression direction of the siblings of these objects.

- Except for `retrieve-marker`, the others may be children of the `flow` object.

3.3.16   Out-of-line objects

These objects, typically allowed anywhere where `#PCDATA`, `%inline;`, or `%block;` constructs are allowed, include —

- `float` (*6.10.2*; 233):
    - is the content to be rendered towards either the before, start, or end edges of a region regardless of where in the region the content is defined.

These objects are not stacked in the progression direction of the sibling objects;

- areas returned are contained within and governed by ancestral `page-sequence` object.

Out-of-line objects are allowed as children of the `flow` object;

- they may also be nested inside other constructs.

3.3.17   Out-of-line inline-level objects

Out-of-line objects allowed only inline, i.e. anywhere where `#PCDATA` or `%inline;` constructs are allowed, include —

- `footnote` (*6.10.3*; 237):
    - is the content to be rendered towards the after edge of a region regardless of where in the region the content is defined.

One of the two generated areas is stacked in the progression direction of the sibling inline objects;

- the other area returned is contained within and governed by ancestral `page-sequence` object.

Out-of-line inline objects are not allowed as children of the `flow` object;

- they must be placed in a block to behave at the block level.

4

Areas
and
pages

4 Areas and pages

Here we review the area model and how areas interact with each other and within defined regions of the page. Understanding areas and pages is critical to writing successful XSL-FO instances.

Area model. The rendering process renders the area tree created by formatting objects. Thus, to get the desired rendered result, one must know how to position and nest areas of content and set their traits. Formatting objects are chosen to give the desired layout result, but note that the names of formatting objects may be totally irrelevant to the reason they are used in an XSL-FO instance to get the particular areas desired.

The area model describes the nature of the areas of content that are created for rendering from the formatting specification. XSL-FO 1.0 only defines rectangular areas (some of which of course may be square) in the area model, and these areas are arranged in hierarchical order in the area tree. Child areas that stack normally are arranged within their parent's area. A given formatting object may add areas to multiple branches of the hierarchy, thus placing areas outside of their parent's area. Objects in a given branch of the area tree typically stack next to each other.

There are many different types of areas that define the formatter's behavior for the content of the areas, as depicted in the four rectangles shown in Figure 4–1. An area is spaced between its siblings and within the content rectangle of its parent using a transparent spacing specification in the outermost rectangle. An opaque border may be specified around content where the thickness of the border is defined by the distances between respective edges of two rectangles: the border rectangle (outside edge) and the padding rectangle (inside edge). The border may also be patterned, and if so, any background to the border is transparent and shows through the parent's area. The border is distanced from the area's content rectangle by transparent padding. Note in the left example how these rectangles are coincident when there is no border or padding.

The number of rectangles in play and their nuances can be overwhelming to the novice stylesheet writer. Thankfully, it is not necessary to know all the rectangles to get simple, good quality results. It is, however, important to be aware of the different rectangles to better understand the interplay of areas and the controls available in XSL-FO properties, especially when your requirements evolve beyond simple arrangements of your information.

The two concepts of writing direction and reference orientation govern the visual placement of areas on a page. These values define the block-progression and inline-progression directions for the stacking of descendants of an area. Their combinations support natural directions for common writing systems of the world, and the orientation can be overridden to produce special effects in the rendered result. These values also define the before and after sides in the block-progression direction and the start and end sides in the inline-progression direction.

Figure 4–1   The rectangles describing an area

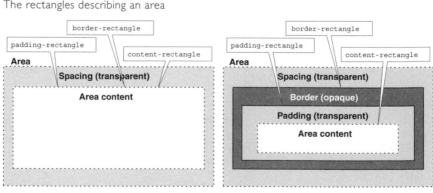

Most child areas inherit unspecified behaviors from the parent areas. Block and inline content stack in the layout areas as specified by the stacking properties, and it is often not necessary to specify most behaviors as these are already implied from the ancestral areas.

Child "container" objects are used to create areas that override orientation behavior specified by an ancestral area. Areas created by container objects can alter their behavior to meet specific requirements that differ from those of the parent area. As examples, consider specifying an absolute position outside of the parent for a block container; or specifying an overflow behavior; or specifying a writing direction or reference orientation that is different from that of the parent. Both block-level and inline-level container objects can be used within their respective types of parent objects.

Areas on the page are not mutually exclusive. Areas can be formatted to overlap other areas in whole or in part, and when they overlap and the backgrounds are transparent, the areas behind show through. Common formatting problems occur when areas from different branches of the tree occupy the same real estate on the page, so you must plan ahead so the stacking of areas in one branch doesn't interfere with the stacking of areas in other branches.

Page geometry.   A page in XSL-FO is described by the geometry of its size and the various regions and sub-regions on the page where information is placed by the formatting objects, as shown in Figure 4–2. Note in this diagram that the page on the left has page margins but no body region margins, therefore the body region perimeter matches locations of the page margins. In the two pages on the right, the body region has margins pulling in the perimeter away from the page margins. In each case all four perimeter regions are defined, the default is shown in the center where the before and after regions are bounded within the extents of the start and end regions whose perimeters extend to the page margins. On the right hand page, the precedence of the before and after regions has been changed to override the start and end regions, thus extending their respective perimeters to the page margins.

Every page has a `region-body` region whose default name is "`xsl-region-body`". This is typically (but not necessarily) the region receiving the flow that triggers the pagination and generation of pages.

Four available perimeter regions defined by `region-before`, `region-after`, `region-start`, and `region-end` can incur into the body region along its four edges. The writing direction and reference orientation of the page reference area defined by the page geometry determine the before, after, start, and end edges of the body for the perimeter regions. The `precedence` property on `region-before` and `region-after` dictates whether the before/after regions or start/end regions occupy the corners of the perimeter. These four regions have the initial names, respectively, of "`xsl-region-before`", "`xsl-region-after`", "`xsl-region-start`", and "`xsl-region-end`".

Regions are referenced in XSL-FO by their names, which can be changed from their initial values by the user.

The five available page regions in the simple geometry of XSL-FO 1.0 are targets for either paginated flow or static content.

The paginated flow triggers as many pages as needed by the amount of the flowed content. When a page's region accepting flow overflows, a new page in the page sequence is triggered to accommodate the continuing flow of content. The flow indicates the name of the target region for the content.

Each page that is triggered by the amount of flow instantiates all regions for the page. The user can define static content for regions, indicating to

Figure 4–2   Regions and sub-regions of a page

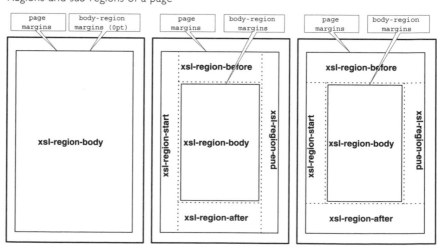

which named region the static content is targeted. Whenever the named region is created by its presence on a new page, the static content is placed into the region. The static content can have dynamic components such as the page number or the content of user-defined markers appearing on the page being formatted.

Page regions are parents and ancestors of the formatting objects flowed (for paginated content) or copied (for static content) in the region. Therefore, the formatting objects in each region are descendant areas of that region's branch in the area tree, so the sibling areas in each branch stack separately from the sibling areas in other branches. Without proper body region margins, the perimeter region areas and the body region areas will overlap.

Included in this chapter. This chapter includes discussion of the following XSL-FO objects.

Content-oriented formatting objects:

- `wrapper` (*6.11.2*):
  - is a neutral construct for specifying inherited properties for descendent constructs,
- `block` (*6.5.2*):
  - is the description of canvas content that is distinct from its preceding area content,
- `initial-property-set` (*6.6.4*):
  - is an auxiliary construct for specifying properties applied to the first line of the parent,
- `inline` (*6.6.7*):
  - is the specification of inherited and non-inherited properties for content within a line generated in a block,
- `page-number-citation` (*6.6.11*):
  - is an inline-level placeholder replaced with the page number of the first normal area of the cited formatting object.

Container formatting objects:

- `block-container` (*6.5.3*):
  - is the specification of a block-level reference area for contained descendant blocks,
- `inline-container` (*6.6.8*):
  - is the specification of an inline-level reference area for contained descendant blocks.

Page-oriented formatting objects:

- `simple-page-master` (*6.4.12*):
  - is the specification of a given page's physical geometry,
- `region-body` (*6.4.13*):
  - is the definition of the middle area inside any perimeter defined for the page,
- `title` (*6.4.20*):
  - is a page sequence's ancillary description not rendered on the page canvas.

4.1 Area model details

4.1.1 Geometric rendered areas

The result of formatting is the generation of geometric areas for rendering based upon an area model which:

- is a superset of CSS2 box formatting model,
- includes references to areas by other areas,
- defines relationships and space adjustment between areas generated for letters, words, lines, and blocks.

Areas are arranged hierarchically as a result of interpreting formatting objects.

- Each branch of the tree collects areas that are related.
  - A single XSL-FO object can generate areas for multiple area tree branches.
- Each area has a relative or absolute position described by a spacing constraint.
- Each area may have content to display.
- Each area may have visual or aural presentations different from those of other areas.
- Areas define placement of every glyph, shape, and image with spacing constraints.

Not all kinds of areas can be directly specified by the XSL-FO instance.

- For example, lines in a block are areas synthesized only by the formatter during the flowing of information.
- Objects and properties in the XSL-FO instance can influence the presentation of the synthesized areas;
  - e.g., `initial-property-set` object influences the first generated line of a block;

- it is an empty formatting object that does not generate any areas;
- e.g., `line-height` property governs how much of a block is taken up by each of the lines.

A paginated area and static areas can be defined for each page.

- Paginated areas accept content to be flowed and trigger the generation of as many pages as needed to fit the flow of information to be rendered;
  - they are defined as descendants of `flow` objects.
- Static areas are rendered on every page that is generated by pagination;
  - they are defined as descendants of `static-content` objects.
- A page's geometry need not contain any region that is accepting flow;
  - such a page is rendered with only the static content, and the formatter moves to the next page geometry in the sequence of pages.

A single object can create many areas.

- Not all generated areas of a given sequence need be adjacent, nor hierarchically related to each other.
  - One object can add areas to separate area tree branches.
- The name of the formatting object that produces the desired areas is not important.
  - The objective is to position information on the page; the choice of which formatting object to use to create the needed areas is based on the semantics of the formatting object, not its name.
    - E.g., a `list-block` can be used to lay out synchronized pairs of paragraphs of different languages, even though the essence of the information being formatted is not a list.

The hierarchical area tree has familial relationships between nodes of the tree;

- a node can be child, sibling, parent, descendant, ancestor, or root;
- a set of nodes are ordered within the parent;
  - there is only one order of sibling nodes;
  - this ordering defines initial, preceding, following, and final relationships;
- there are two traversals of the tree when dealing with child nodes of the parent;
  - pre-order traversal orders the parent before the children, e.g.:
    - determining the "next" area for `keep-with-next`,
    - determining preference in markers for `retrieve-marker`;
  - post-order traversal orders the parent after the children, e.g.:
    - determining the "previous" area for `keep-with-previous`;

- neither traversal order changes the order of the children themselves.

The root node is not an area.

- All other nodes are rectangular areas on the result canvas.
- Areas in the tree may be of zero size;
  - this may be useful for placing identification information in the tree without occupying real estate on the page;
  - a page with only a zero-sized area is not an empty page and is considered to have an area present on the page for the purposes of resolving the first and last areas in a reference area.

The area tree can have very many areas described.

- Even every glyph (character shape) has its own area.
- Every area has its own placement direction and spacing constraint.
- There is no obligation on the formatter to serialize or externalize the area tree.

Most nodes generate a singular area.

- There is an exception for ligatures that have leaf nodes combined to produce a single area, e.g.:
  - combinations of English letters into a single glyph such as "a" and "e" becoming "æ",
  - combinations of Arabic characters based on location and sibling characters.

The formatter has sufficient information in the finalized areas to effect the rendering.

- Missing or conflicting constraints are resolved by the formatter in an implementation-dependent fashion;
  - these may be constrained by the rendering technology used by the formatter.
- Page fidelity is an important portability issue.
  - Two conforming XSL-FO formatters need not produce identical renderings.
  - Formatters can create different area trees based on different interpretation of unspecified traits, e.g.:
    - hyphenation and justification rules,
    - default value for inter-line leading.
  - The rendering process can create different results depending on unspecified traits, e.g.:
    - font.

4.1.2   Directions and writing modes

Orientations and directions are defined for a reference area.

- Every reference area has an orientation with respect the definition of the "top" of the area and its writing direction.
- Descendent reference areas can have orientations modified relative to the containing reference area.
- Descendent areas that are not reference areas cannot have their orientations changed.

Reference areas are found in many places in the area tree, including —

- region reference area (perimeter regions),
- main reference area (page bodies),
- before-float reference area (before floats),
- footnote reference area (footnotes),
- span reference area (spanned columns),
- normal-flow reference area (columns),
- lines in a block,
- `title`,
- `block-container` and `inline-container`,
- `table`, `table-caption`, and `table-cell`.

Stacking rules govern how adjacent areas created by objects in flow are related along directions.

- All objects are defined as stacking in a particular direction relative to their adjacent objects or other objects.
- Some objects are "out of line" in the stacking order;
    - their position is related to objects other than those that are adjacent.
- General rules of thumb with powerful nuances are available for specific requirements.

Various directions govern the placement of objects relative to their siblings.

- Block-progression direction:
    - is the stacking of lines and blocks relative to other lines and blocks in an area,
    - is the stacking of rows in a table.
- Inline-progression direction:

- is the stacking of glyph areas and other inline areas within a line,
- is the stacking of cells in a table row,
- defines the shift direction which:
    - is used for subscripts and superscripts rendered in inline areas,
    - is perpendicular to inline-progression direction,
    - is inverse of the initial block-progression direction,
- defines glyph direction which:
    - is oriented to the top of the glyph,
    - initially is the same as the direction of the top of the reference area,
    - can be rotated or inverted clockwise relative to top of reference area.

Writing-mode-related properties reflect cultural practices of flowing information on a page, as shown in Figure 4–3.

- For example, an indent at the start of a line in a left-to-right writing mode is on the opposite side of the page compared to the indent at the start of a line in a right-to-left writing mode.
- Before, after, start, and end edges of each writing mode are relative to the reference orientation that defines the top edge of the area.
    - Using top, bottom, left, and right ignores the writing mode and is less portable.

Two properties govern progression direction of adjacent areas on the page.

- `reference-orientation`:
    - defines the direction of the top edge of a reference area relative to containing reference area,

Figure 4–3   Possible writing modes

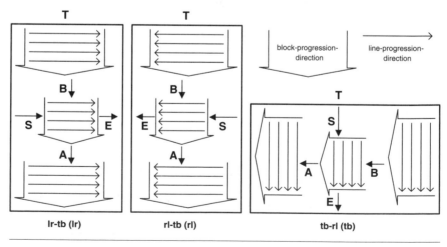

| lr-tb (lr) | rl-tb (rl) | tb-rl (tb) |

- can be positive (counter-clockwise) or negative, in multiples of 90 degrees.
- `writing-mode`:
  - specifies the inline-progression direction and the block-progression direction, in the form of two-letter codes separated by a hyphen, relative to the top of the reference area,
  - can be `lr-tb` or `lr` meaning left-to-right for inline, top-to-bottom for block, e.g.:
    - Western European writing systems,
  - can be `rl-tb` or `rl` meaning right-to-left for inline, top-to-bottom for block, e.g.:
    - Hebrew and Arabic writing systems,
  - can be `tb-lr` or `tb` meaning left-to-right for inline, top-to-bottom for block, e.g.:
    - traditional Japanese and Chinese writing systems.
- A combination of these properties can be used on other objects to define other direction-related traits, e.g.:
  - placement and orientation of perimeter regions within pages,
  - placement of columns within body region,
  - placement and orientation of rows and columns within tables,
  - changes within paginated content and static content in a region, e.g.:
    - by using `block-container` objects at the block level,
    - by using `inline-container` objects at the inline level.
- These properties can only be specified for reference areas.

Bidirectional writing is inherently supported by XSL-FO processors.

- One of the most powerful features of XSL-FO is that the stylesheet writer need not be aware of the writing direction of the characters used in the XML documents being formatted;
  - e.g., right-to-left characters can be intermixed with left-to-right characters.
- The formatter automatically accommodates bidirectional writing based upon the inherent properties of the Unicode characters in the content.
  - It makes the job easier for the stylesheet writer in that the directions of the individual characters do not need to be detected and accommodated.
- `bidi-override` object is only used when direction inferred by the Unicode character is not as desired.
  - A common misconception is that this must be used to support bidirectionality when, in fact, it is used only when the bidirectionality needs to be embedded or overridden.

4.1.3   Margins, spaces, and positioning

Areas are positioned by specifying the spaces around them.

- Areas that are flowed adjacent to each other are separated by their spacing specifications.
- Floats and footnotes are positioned out-of-line as defined by the Recommendation.
- Only a `block-container` can be positioned arbitrarily on the page.
  - This is indicated by using `absolute-position` which implies —
    - either a relative distance from its siblings,
      - as if it were a simple block ("`auto`"),
    - or an absolute distance from an ancestor, in particular:
      - from the parent area boundaries ("`absolute`"),
      - from the page area boundaries ("`fixed`").
  - Distances from ancestral area edges are specified using `top`, `bottom`, `left`, or `right`.

Spaces and non-page margins define the same values, but from different perspectives.

- `space-*` specifications are relative to the writing direction:
  - `space-before`, `space-after`, `space-start`, `space-end`.
- `margin-*` specifications are relative to the reference orientation:
  - `margin-top`, `margin-bottom`, `margin-left`, `margin-right`.

Page margins

- Margins of page regions are fixed to the page boundaries and physical orientation:
  - `margin-top`, `margin-bottom`, `margin-left`, `margin-right`.

Discarding space

- A space specification can have a property of being discarded when the area it is associated with is the first or last in a reference area.

4.1.4   Lengths and spacing

Lengths can be specified in both absolute and relative terms.

- `cm` is centimeter;
- `mm` is millimeter;
- `in` is inch = 2.54 cm;

- pt is point = 1/72 in;
- pc is pica = 12 pt = 1/6 in;
- px is pixel = 1 device dot (nominally 1/90" or .28 mm);
- em is the current font size (the only relative unit of measure);
  - use em-based values for spacing to protect relative appearance from changes in font size (e.g., "2em" is twice the current font size).
- Note that there is no "ex" measurement.
  - Sometimes it is used in formatting specifications as the height of a lowercase letter in the current font size.
  - This is not a concept that is easily interpreted in all international character repertoires.
  - It is used in XSL-FO in the definition of one of the baselines for those scripts that have an ex value.

Spaces are used to position areas within other areas and can be influenced by —

- specifying minimum, maximum, and optimum;
  - the preferred value is the optimum, but it cannot be less than minimum or more than maximum,
- specifying conditionality;
  - the retain or discard values control whether the space specification is preserved at the start or end of a reference area,
- specifying precedence;
  - the value of force or an integer value controls which of the space specifications is in play after constraint calculation resolution,
- interaction of adjacent siblings' space specifications;
  - sizes and precedence determine rendered amount of space;
  - this is detailed on page 256.

Some properties can be specified using a percentage.

- When inherited, percentages are relative to their inherited value, e.g.:
  - font-size="150%".
- When not inherited, percentages are relative to a reference rectangle;
  - for XSL-defined properties, this is the content rectangle;
  - for CSS-defined properties, this is closest non-line-area content rectangle;
  - exceptions exist for out-of-line constructs and the regions in which they are used (detailed in Recommendation, Section 7.3).

4.1.5 Area types

Different areas are characterized by their different purposes and uses.

- Reference area is an area that can have reference-related properties different from those of its parent area;
  - it can change the reference orientation and/or writing mode;
  - it also has special behaviors for first and last space specifications.
- Viewport area is the clipping/scrolling visible portion of a reference area.
- Allocation area is the basis of positioning and alignment of content within parent;
  - it defines the mechanics of how the stacking works.
- Block area is a collection of lines in the block-progression direction;
  - it creates a new set of lines, even if the block has a zero dimension.
- Line area is a collection of inline constructs in a block.
- Inline area is an atomic construct or collection of glyph constructs in the inline-progression direction.
- Glyph area is a single text character.

4.1.6 Stacking area and rectangle relationships

Areas stack in either the block-progression direction or the inline-progression direction using rectangles.

- The parent area's content rectangle constrains the position of the child areas therein.
- The child areas can only stack in one direction relative to the parent reference orientation.
  - One set of opposing edges of a child coincides with the parent content rectangle;
  - the other set of opposing edges of child coincides with the adjacent content rectangle,
    - or with the parent content rectangle if first or last in the stack.

Areas that are stacked adjacent to their siblings are considered "normal."

- Other areas are considered "non-normal" and stack elsewhere in the area tree, e.g.:
  - floats to the before, start, or end sides of the body region,
  - footnote bodies to the after edge of the body region,

- absolutely positioned block containers to arbitrary locations.

A block area without borders is positioned between siblings;

- `space-before` and `space-after` determine its position between siblings;
- `start-indent` and `end-indent` determine its position within parent.

Initial property values are for "common sense" formatting.

- A lot of work can be done without changing initial values.
- A lot of finesse can be accomplished by specifying available alternatives.

A child area with a border contains nested rectangles.

- This allows for a rigorous specification of formatting intent, spaced relative to the directions of the parent area.
- Border rectangle is positioned relative to the parent or adjacent area using `margin-*` or `space-*` spacing properties.
  - Edges of border rectangle are identified by parent reference orientation.
- Padding rectangle is positioned relative to border rectangle using `border-*` width properties.
  - Edges of padding rectangle are identified by parent reference orientation.
- Content rectangle is positioned relative to padding rectangle using `padding-*` spacing properties.
  - Edges of content rectangle are identified by child reference orientation.

Border and padding widths are sometimes ignored.

- For example, they are not applicable to regions, floats, or footnote bodies.
- `border-style` value of "`none`" or "`hidden`" will set the border width to `0pt`.
- `border-before-width` and `border-after-width` have `.conditionality` component with the initial value of "`discard`";
  - it sets the `.length` component to `0pt` if it is, respectively, the first or last area in a reference area;
  - they may be set to "`retain`" to preserve the `.length` component value.

An area is stacked within its parent's content rectangle using spacing extents, as shown in Figure 4–4.

- Names of extents are suffixed using the names of the edges from which they extend.
  - Each edge of the spaces, border, or padding may thus have individual values.

- Shorthand properties are available to set all extents in one specification.
- Reference areas can have a location of "top" different from that of their parent area.

The border rectangle is different from the spacing and padding rectangles.

- Spacing and padding rectangles and dimensions define invisible non-rendered areas.
- The border rectangle and border width properties define the thickness of a visible rendered border.
- Not shown are the `*-top`, `*-bottom`, `*-left`, and `*-right` properties for `padding-*` and `border-*` which directly correspond to the writing direction dependent properties.

An area's content rectangle in turn contains the area's children.

- The area's type governs what is allowed for the child areas.
    - Only a reference area's children can discard conditional spaces.

Figure 4–4 Nested rectangles in stacked block areas

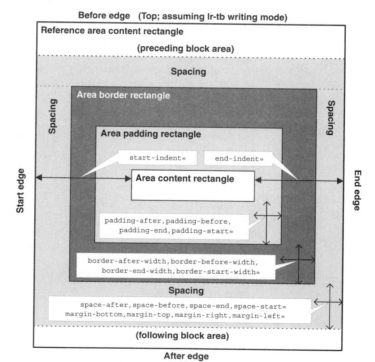

- Only when the area is a reference area can the content rectangle have orientation properties different from itself.
  - Orientation properties and traits are relative to the "top" of the area.
  - Examples include `reference-orientation`, block-progression direction, etc.
  - An area's content rectangle orientation properties are relative to the content's own reference orientation, not the area's reference orientation.
- Proportional `*-indent` and `margin-*` specifications are calculated differently.
  - A proportional `*-indent` specification is based on the ancestral reference area.
  - A proportional `margin-*` specification is based on the containing block.
- Specifying conflicting values will over-constrain requirements.
  - `margin-*` properties take precedence over `*-indent` properties.
    - A specified `start-indent` or `end-indent` value is ignored if the corresponding `margin-*` property within the indent value is specified.
  - `*-indent` properties take precedence over `space-*` properties.
    - A specified `space-*` value is ignored if the corresponding `start-indent` or `end-indent` property within the indent value is in effect.
  - `start-indent` and the content's specified inline-progression dimension take precedence over `end-indent`.
    - Examples are `inline-progression-dimension` on the object or specified for the objects children's sizes.
    - If the inline-progression dimension is not explicitly set for the object or its children, the `end-indent` is respected.

4.1.7 Allocation rectangles and alignment

A child area's allocation rectangle describes constraints of position within parent.

- It defines the mechanics of the stacking of adjacent areas.
- Dimension is based on either the parent, border, or content edges.
  - Block and inline areas use different edges.
  - Inline areas of two different types (normal and large) use different edges.
- Orientation is based on parent area.
  - It may be different from content area.
- The start edge of an inline area's allocation rectangle defines the alignment point of the area.
  - This is used in glyph and other inline rendering.
- The space outside of the allocation rectangle can be discarded.
  - This happens only when the space is the first or last in a reference area.

- The `space-*.conditionality` default of "discard" can be overridden to be "retain".

Block area stacking and allocation rectangle definition is shown in Figure 4–5.

- All block areas are defined with the same relationship between sibling block areas.

Inline areas defined with a normal allocation rectangle are shown in Figure 4–6.

- Most inline areas are defined with the normal relationship between areas.

Figure 4–5   Block-area allocation rectangle

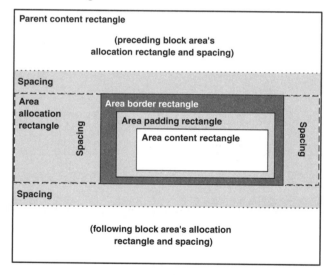

Figure 4–6   Normal inline area allocation rectangle

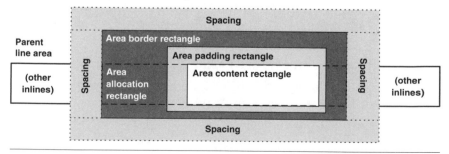

- An example is text.
- Note how the bordering of such an area will not influence the line stacking and may cause undesirable overwriting of content on the previous and following lines.

Inline areas defined with a large allocation rectangle are shown in Figure 4–7.

- Some inline areas are defined with an alternative relationship between areas.
  - Examples are inline containers and graphic images.
- Note how the bordering of such an area will influence the line stacking and will not cause undesirable overwriting of content on the previous and following lines when the line-stacking strategy is based on the height of the content.

4.1.8 Line areas

Line areas are special areas only created by creating a block area.

- Line area traits are specified in the block properties.
- They stack in the block-progression direction.
- They have no borders or padding.

Line stacking strategy determines which rectangle describes the line.

- "`nominal-requested-line-rectangle`" is based on font height and:
  - is selected using the `line-stacking-strategy` value of "`font-height`",
  - reaches above the text baseline by the text altitude,
  - reaches below the text baseline by the text depth,
  - provides constant baseline-to-baseline spacing.

Figure 4–7   Large inline-area allocation rectangle

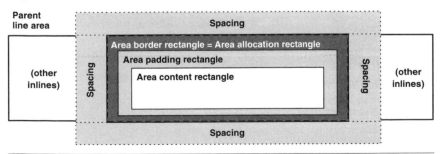

- "maximum-line-rectangle" (the initial value for this property) is based on inline objects within line and:
  - is selected using the line-stacking-strategy value of "max-height",
  - is equal to the maximum of the allocation-rectangle heights of all contained inline objects as well as that of the nominal-requested-line-rectangle,
  - provides constant space between line areas.
- "per-inline-height-rectangle" is based on leading and:
  - is selected using the line-stacking-strategy value of "line-height",
  - provides CSS-style line box stacking when using zero space before and space after.

Leading is calculated as difference between line height and font size.

- Leading is the space found between the lines of a block.
- The half-leading trait is used by the formatter before and after lines.
  - The use of half-leading accommodates adjacent lines with vastly different font sizes without having to decide which line's leading should apply.
  - Both lines' half-leading traits apply to the gap between lines.
- The initial value of line-height is "normal".
  - Processor can implement any "reasonable" (sic) value based on font size.
  - A value between 1.0 and 1.2 is recommended.
  - When not specified, different initial values in different processors will yield different area trees and resulting formatting.
    - This is an important portability issue.
- You can override "normal" by specifying a number (e.g. "1" or "1.1") or percentage factor of the current font size.
- You can also specify absolute length value.

Geometric font characteristics are based on the em box.

- This refers to the relative measure of the height of the glyphs in the font.
- A box that is 1 em wide by 1 em high is called the design space.
  - Note that creating an inline-container with a square dimension of 1 em, aligned on the after edge of the line and with a visible border, will render a checkbox without having to use a graphic image.
- Design space origin (dominant baseline) is different for ideographic, Indic, and other scripts (e.g. alphabetic and syllabic).

Inline constructs align along one of many baselines defined at the same time, as detailed in Area Alignment Properties (7.13). When not specified, the automatic dominant baseline is based on the current font. Different baselines are —

- `alphabetic`:
  - is used for most alphabetic and syllabic scripts, e.g.:
    - Western, Southern Indic, non-ideographic Southeast Asian, etc.,
- `ideographic`:
  - is used by ideographic scripts for the bottom of the ideographic em box,
- `hanging`:
  - is used for certain Indic scripts,
- `mathematical`:
  - is used for mathematical symbols,
- `after-edge`:
  - is at the after edge of the reference area after accommodating line contents,
- `before-edge`:
  - is at the before edge of the reference area after accommodating line contents,
- `central`:
  - is at the computed center of the em box,
- `middle`:
  - is at the center of the ex box sitting on the alphabetic baseline,
  - is approximated by central when the script doesn't have x-height,
- `text-after-edge`:
  - is equal to the ideographic baseline for ideographic scripts,
  - is equal to the bottom of the space for descending characters for non-ideographic scripts,
    - often is slightly after than the ideographic baseline,
- `text-before-edge`:
  - is 1 em before the text-after edge.

Different values for `alignment-adjust` are shown in Figure 4–8.

1: This shows a bordered block with simple text along the dominant baseline with descending letters.

2: A graphic image sits on the dominant baseline (default).
  - Without manipulating `alignment-adjust`, the graphic sits "high" on the line.

3: A square inline container of size 1 em sits on the dominant baseline (default; alphabetic in this example).
  - Without manipulating `alignment-adjust`, the container sits "high" on the line.

4: A graphic image is aligned to the after-edge baseline.

- This often looks more appealing by having a common edge with the text.

5: A container is aligned to the after-edge baseline.

- This effect aligns everything with the "bottom" of the text box.
- This often looks more appealing by not going above the top of the text characters.

6: A graphic image is aligned to the middle baseline.

- The after edge of the graphic sits on the "middle" of the text box.

7: A container is aligned to the middle baseline.

- The center line of the inline container is centered to the "middle" of the text box.

8: The leading is turned off by using `line-height="1"`.

- This shows the before/after edges of the inline container touching the inside edges of the parent line area.
- The half-leading seen in the previous example above and below the inline container has been removed by adjusting the line height.

4.1.9 References in the area tree

The first normally-flowed area created by an object with a specified `id` property will have the value as a trait.

- The application generating the XSL-FO instance is responsible for the uniqueness of `id` values.

Figure 4–8   Alignment of inline constructs

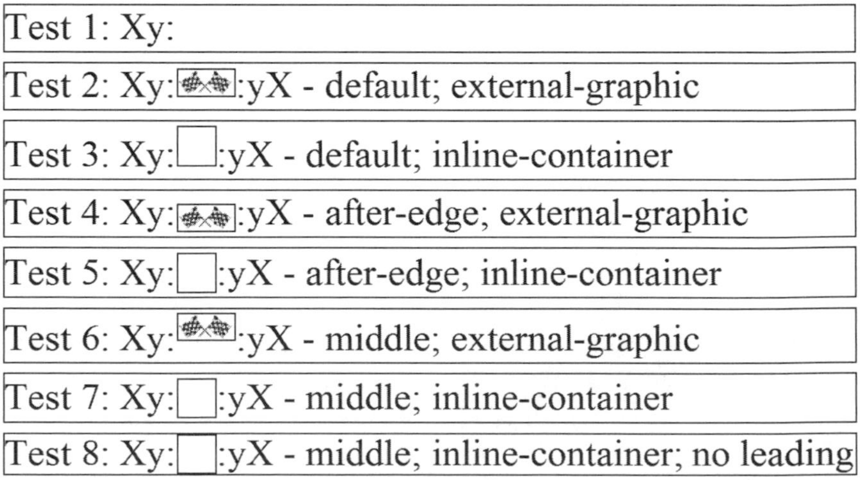

Objects can refer to other objects in the tree creating a reference to the area produced.

- Page number citations use `ref-id`.
- Hyperlink targets use `internal-destination`.
- When more than one object has the same identifier, references are resolved to the first area in the area tree created by the first object with the identifier.
- When no object has the required identifier, the formatter signals an error of being unable to meet the requirements.

Note it is unsafe to use XML ID and IDREF constructs directly in an XSL-FO instance when combining XML source documents.

- Each document has an independent value space for unique ID values.
- Using the ID values from multiple documents in a single XSL-FO document can introduce value conflicts.
  - The same ID may have been used in two documents and will end up being doubly used in the XSL-FO document.

It is safest when using XSLT to convert every ID and corresponding IDREF to the `generate-id()` value for the node corresponding to the element with the ID.

- The value space for `generate-id()` is guaranteed to be unique for every node of all node trees used in a single transformation process.
- For an element with an ID identifier, use the generated identifier of the element, e.g.:
  - `id="{generate-id(.)}"`.
- For a reference with an IDREF identifier, use the generated identifier of the referenced element, e.g.:
  - `ref-id="{generate-id(id(@idref))}"`,
  - `internal-destination="{generate-id(id(@idref))}"`.

This is also the safest approach when synthesizing relationships where ID/IDREF is not used, e.g.:

- `generate-id()` can be used for automatically generated tables of contents.

4.2 **Block and inline basics**

4.2.1 Simple block and inline objects

The `wrapper` object is a semantic-free container used by other objects or for inherited properties.

- It does not generate any areas by itself.
    - It returns the areas generated by its descendants.
- It is used by `multi-properties` as a wrapper for the objects to which the multiple properties apply.
- It can be a generic branch in the formatting object tree from which descendent objects obtain inherited property settings.

Empty wrappers are not useful constructs.

- Area tree will not have any child areas to which an `id` property is attached.

Line properties for a given block can be set by different objects.

- `block:`
    - has one property for the first line in the block;
        - `text-indent:`
            - with a positive value, incurs into the block (indent),
            - with a negative value, hangs outside the block (outdent);
    - has two properties for the last line in the block;
        - `last-line-end-indent:`
            - with a positive value, incurs into the block (indent),
            - with a negative value, hangs outside the block (outdent);
        - `text-align-last:`
            - governs the alignment of only the last line in the block;
    - has a number of properties for all lines in the block (including first and last).
        - Note that for `text-align`, the value "`justify`" doesn't apply to the last line of the block.
- `initial-property-set:`
    - is solely a container of properties applicable to the first line;
        - only the formatter can determine how much of the flowed information in the block will end up on the first line of the block;
        - neither XSLT nor any other XSL-FO generation process can know ahead of time how much will be formatted on the first line of a block;
    - must be a child of the block defining the lines to be influenced.

- The line of a single-line block is considered to be both the first line and the last line of the block.

Constructs designed to be used only inline can be rendered on their own line.

- Inline constructs cannot live between two blocks, e.g.:
  - graphics rendered between paragraphs,
  - a rule-styled leader rendered between paragraphs.
- To render an inline construct between two blocks, it must be placed within its own block.

Inline areas can have non-inheritable properties set for the area contents.

- `inline`:
  - is distinct from `wrapper` in that it creates an area in the area tree,
  - is necessary for properties such as `baseline-shift` for doing superscript and subscript of the contained text.

The formatter can supply glyphs to be rendered in a line.

- Consider `page-number-citation`;
  - the format of the glyphs is dictated by the page sequence for the cited area;
  - e.g., consider a book with the front matter pages numbered in lower-case roman numerals and the book body pages, in digits;
    - citing a page of the body when in the front matter returns the digits as used in the body;
    - citing a page of the front matter when in the body returns the roman numerals as used in the front matter.

`page-number-citation` can also be used to generate a total page count.

- Citing the page number of the last page of the document gives the total page count.
- An empty block with an area with zero dimensions can be flowed on the last page.
  - It's provably not robust for all possible documents, but this works for most documents and is the only way possible in XSL-FO 1.0.
  - Nuances of interaction with floats, float separator sub-regions, and discarded space specifications prevent guaranteed page numbering.
- When using XSLT, here's a tip to guarantee uniqueness of the last block identifier.
  - Use `id="{generate-id(/)}"` to identify the last block of the document.
    - The root node of the source node tree cannot be referenced by IDREF.

- It is guaranteed to be unique among all source documents' uses of IDREF if all identifiers are translated using the `generate-id()` function.

4.2.2 The wrapper object

Purpose

- This is a neutral container construct for specifying inherited properties for descendent constructs.

Content

- (*6.11.2*) (#PCDATA | %inline; | %block;)*,
- child objects (listed alphabetically):
  - %block; (*6.2*; 69),
  - %inline; (*6.2*; 70),
- referring object:
  - multi-properties (*6.9.6*; 268),
- any number of marker children at the beginning.

Optional property

- id (*7.28.2*; 384).

4.2.3 The block object

Purpose

- This is the description of canvas content that is distinct from its preceding area content.

Content

- (*6.5.2*) (#PCDATA | %inline; | %block;)*,
- child objects (listed alphabetically):
  - %block; (*6.2*; 69),
  - %inline; (*6.2*; 70),
- these objects at the beginning (in the following order):
  - zero or more marker objects,
  - at most one initial-property-set object.

Property sets

- Common accessibility properties (*7.4*; 326),
- common aural properties (*7.6*; 327),

- common border, padding, and background properties (*7.7*; 328),
- common font properties (*7.8*; 331),
- common hyphenation properties (*7.9*; 332),
- common margin properties — block (*7.10*; 332),
- common relative position properties (*7.12*; 333).

Other optional properties

- break-after (*7.19.1*; 366),
- break-before (*7.19.2*; 367),
- color (*7.17.1*; 369),
- hyphenation-keep (*7.15.1*; 383),
- hyphenation-ladder-count (*7.15.2*; 383),
- id (*7.28.2*; 384),
- intrusion-displace (*7.18.3*; 385),
- keep-together (*7.19.3*; 386),
- keep-with-next (*7.19.4*; 386),
- keep-with-previous (*7.19.5*; 387),
- last-line-end-indent (*7.15.3*; 387),
- linefeed-treatment (*7.15.7*; 391),
- line-height (*7.15.4*; 390),
- line-height-shift-adjustment (*7.15.5*; 390),
- line-stacking-strategy (*7.15.6*; 391),
- orphans (*7.19.6*; 396),
- span (*7.20.4*; 415),
- text-align (*7.15.9*; 421),
- text-align-last (*7.15.10*; 421),
- text-altitude (*7.27.4*; 421),
- text-depth (*7.27.5*; 422),
- text-indent (*7.15.11*; 422),
- visibility (*7.28.8*; 425),
- white-space-collapse (*7.15.12*; 427),
- white-space-treatment (*7.15.8*; 427),
- widows (*7.19.7*; 427),
- wrap-option (*7.15.13*; 428).

Shorthands influencing the above properties

- font (*7.29.13*; 377),
- page-break-after (*7.29.16*; 401),
- page-break-before (*7.29.17*; 401),
- page-break-inside (*7.29.18*; 402).

Property of interest

- clear:
  - applies but is not included in the list of properties in the Recommendation,
  - specifies whether a block clears a side-float.

4.2.4   Preserving white space

It is often necessary to preserve the exact text content of an element, e.g.:

- see example on Section 2.2.2 on page 41,
- in program listings,
- in markup listings,
- in text drawings.

A combination of properties is required to ensure all text is preserved.

- linefeed-treatment="preserve":
  - preserves linefeed characters during refined formatting object tree generation;
- white-space-treatment="preserve":
  - preserves white space around linefeed characters during refined formatting object tree generation;
- white-space-collapse="false":
  - preserves consecutive white space during area tree generation.

Optionally, one could also specify the behavior of content which is too long for a line.

- wrap-option="no-wrap":
  - clips the line and triggers an overflow error for lines that are too long.

Note that all four properties can be manipulated using the white-space shorthand.

- Remember that shorthand properties are not required to be supported by a processor.

4.2.5 The initial-property-set object

Purpose

- This is an auxiliary construct for specifying properties applied to the first line of the parent block.

  - The information to which the properties applies is determined by the formatter and not by the generation of the block.

Content

- (*6.6.4*) EMPTY.

Property sets

- Common accessibility properties (*7.4*; 326),
- common aural properties (*7.6*; 327),
- common border, padding, and background properties (*7.7*; 328),
- common font properties (*7.8*; 331),
- common relative position properties (*7.12*; 333).

Other optional properties

- color (*7.17.1*; 369),
- id (*7.28.2*; 384),
- letter-spacing (*7.16.2*; 389),
- line-height (*7.15.4*; 390),
- score-spaces (*7.28.6*; 412),
- text-decoration (*7.16.4*; 422),
- text-shadow (*7.16.5*; 423),
- text-transform (*7.16.6*; 423),
- word-spacing (*7.16.8*; 428).

Shorthand influencing the above properties

- font (*7.29.13*; 377).

4.2.6 The inline object

Purpose

- This is the specification of inherited and non-inherited properties for content within a line generated in a block.

Content

- (*6.6.7*) (#PCDATA | %inline; | %block;)*,
- child objects (listed alphabetically):
  - %block; (*6.2*; 69),
  - %inline; (*6.2*; 70),
- referring object:
  - footnote (*6.10.3*; 237),
- any number of marker children at the beginning.

Property sets

- Common accessibility properties (*7.4*; 326),
- common aural properties (*7.6*; 327),
- common border, padding, and background properties (*7.7*; 328),
- common font properties (*7.8*; 331),
- common margin properties — inline (*7.11*; 333),
- common relative position properties (*7.12*; 333).

Other optional properties

- alignment-adjust (*7.13.1*; 346),
- alignment-baseline (*7.13.2*; 346),
- baseline-shift (*7.13.3*; 351),
- block-progression-dimension (*7.14.1*; 352),
- color (*7.17.1*; 369),
- dominant-baseline (*7.13.5*; 374),
- height (*7.14.4*; 382),
- id (*7.28.2*; 384),
- inline-progression-dimension (*7.14.5*; 385),
- keep-together (*7.19.3*; 386),
- keep-with-next (*7.19.4*; 386),
- keep-with-previous (*7.19.5*; 387),
- line-height (*7.15.4*; 390),
- text-decoration (*7.16.4*; 422),
- visibility (*7.28.8*; 425),
- width (*7.14.12*; 428),
- wrap-option (*7.15.13*; 428).

Shorthands influencing the above properties

- font (*7.29.13*; 377),
- page-break-after (*7.29.16*; 401),
- page-break-before (*7.29.17*; 401),
- page-break-inside (*7.29.18*; 402),
- vertical-align (*7.29.22*; 424).

Properties of interest

- baseline-shift is used for subscripting and superscripting;
- text-decoration is used for underscored text;
- font-style is used for italicized text;
- font-weight is used for boldfaced text.

4.2.7   The page-number-citation object

Purpose

- This is an inline-level placeholder replaced with the page number of the first normal area of cited formatting object using the format of the page numbers for the page sequence in which the cited area is found.

Content

- (*6.6.11*) EMPTY.
- This object is used as an inline-level object;
  - the number value is converted to a string according to page-sequence format property using XSLT format strings.

Property sets

- Common accessibility properties (*7.4*; 326),
- common aural properties (*7.6*; 327),
- common border, padding, and background properties (*7.7*; 328),
- common font properties (*7.8*; 331),
- common margin properties — inline (*7.11*; 333),
- common relative position properties (*7.12*; 333).

Other required property

- ref-id (*7.28.5*; 407).

Other optional properties

- `alignment-adjust` (*7.13.1*; 346),
- `alignment-baseline` (*7.13.2*; 346),
- `baseline-shift` (*7.13.3*; 351),
- `dominant-baseline` (*7.13.5*; 374),
- `id` (*7.28.2*; 384),
- `keep-with-next` (*7.19.4*; 386),
- `keep-with-previous` (*7.19.5*; 387),
- `letter-spacing` (*7.16.2*; 389),
- `line-height` (*7.15.4*; 390),
- `score-spaces` (*7.28.6*; 412),
- `text-altitude` (*7.27.4*; 421),
- `text-decoration` (*7.16.4*; 422),
- `text-depth` (*7.27.5*; 422),
- `text-shadow` (*7.16.5*; 423),
- `text-transform` (*7.16.6*; 423),
- `visibility` (*7.28.8*; 425),
- `word-spacing` (*7.16.8*; 428),
- `wrap-option` (*7.15.13*; 428).

Shorthands influencing the above properties

- `font` (*7.29.13*; 377),
- `page-break-after` (*7.29.16*; 401),
- `page-break-before` (*7.29.17*; 401),
- `vertical-align` (*7.29.22*; 424).

Property of interest

- `ref-id` must point to an area with an identifier on the desired page.

4.3　Container basics

4.3.1　Containers

Containers are used to introduce new reference areas in their context.

- Reference properties can only be changed for reference areas.
  - Examples are `reference-orientation` and `writing-mode`.

- This is useful for temporarily changing the direction of text in the rendered result.

Consider the example shown in Figure 4–9. The nesting of the constructs used to create the example is depicted in Figure 4–10.

The following considerations are worthy of note.

- To prevent a break in the line, an `inline-container` is used in the text.
- The container's reference orientation is changed by 90 degrees counter-clockwise.
- The container only contains block-level constructs, so a block is used to contain the text.
- The text is in an inline construct (though in this particular example this is redundant).

Container objects are named by where they are used.

- `inline-container` can only be used inside of a block.
  - Note that by default, an inline container sits on top of the dominant baseline.
  - Use `alignment adjust="after-edge"` for the container to sit on the same after edge as the text.
- `block-container` is typically used between blocks.
  - Using it inside a block would break the block-progression direction.

Figure 4–9   Changing the reference orientation inline

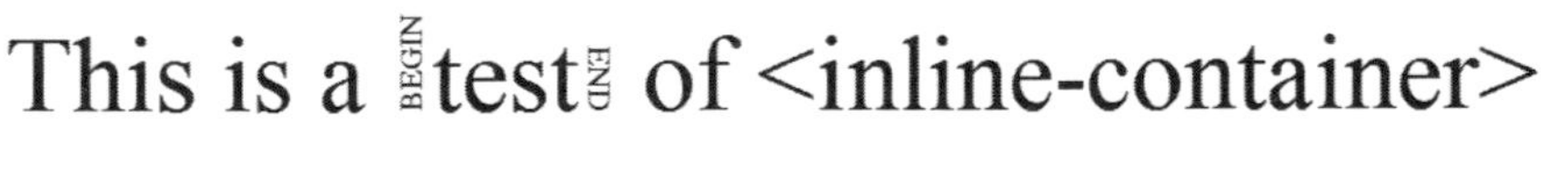

This is a ᴮᴱᴳᴵᴺtestᴱᴺᴰ of <inline-container>

Figure 4–10   The nesting of an `inline-container`

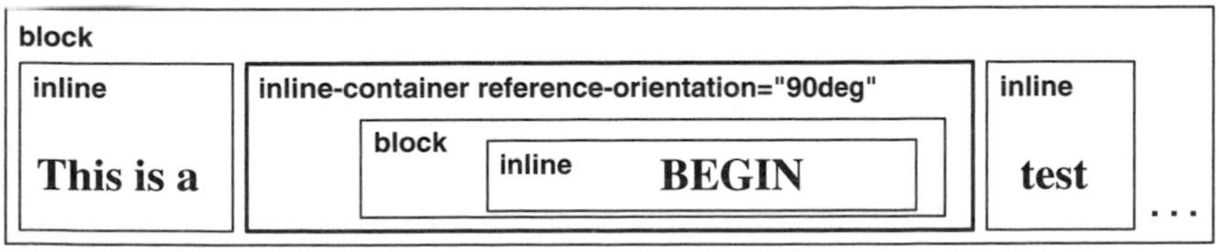

4.3.2 The inline-container object

Purpose

- This is the specification of an inline-level reference area for contained descendant blocks.
  - It is used to place block-oriented constructs inline.

Content

- *(6.6.8)* `(%block;)+`,
- child object:
  - `%block;` *(6.2*; 69),
- any number of `marker` children at the beginning.

Property sets

- Common border, padding, and background properties *(7.7*; 328),
- common margin properties — inline *(7.11*; 333),
- common relative position properties *(7.12*; 333).

Other optional properties

- `alignment-adjust` *(7.13.1*; 346),
- `alignment-baseline` *(7.13.2*; 346),
- `baseline-shift` *(7.13.3*; 351),
- `block-progression-dimension` *(7.14.1*; 352),
- `clip` *(7.20.1*; 368),
- `display-align` *(7.13.4*; 373),
- `dominant-baseline` *(7.13.5*; 374),
- `height` *(7.14.4*; 382),
- `id` *(7.28.2*; 384),
- `inline-progression-dimension` *(7.14.5*; 385),
- `keep-together` *(7.19.3*; 386),
- `keep-with-next` *(7.19.4*; 386),
- `keep-with-previous` *(7.19.5*; 387),
- `line-height` *(7.15.4*; 390),
- `overflow` *(7.20.2*; 397),
- `reference-orientation` *(7.20.3*; 407),
- `width` *(7.14.12*; 428),

- writing-mode (*7.27.7*; 429).

Shorthands influencing the above properties

- font (*7.29.13*; 377),
- page-break-after (*7.29.16*; 401),
- page-break-before (*7.29.17*; 401),
- page-break-inside (*7.29.18*; 402),
- vertical-align (*7.29.22*; 424).

An excerpt from the Figure 4–9 is shown in Example 4–1.

Example 4–1   Containers in Figure 4–9

```
Line 01   <block font-size="40pt">This is a
02          <inline-container reference-orientation="90deg">
03            <block font-size="12pt">BEGIN</block>
04          </inline-container>test<inline-container
05                             reference-orientation="270deg">
06            <block font-size="12pt">END</block>
07          </inline-container>
08          of &lt;inline-container>
09        </block>
```

4.3.3 The block-container object

Purpose

- This is the specification of a block-level reference area for contained descendant blocks.

Content

- (*6.5.3*) (%block;)+,
- child object:
  - %block; (*6.2*; 69),
- any number of marker children at the beginning (unless absolutely positioned).

Property sets

- Common absolute position properties (*7.5*; 325),
- common border, padding, and background properties (*7.7*; 328),
- common margin properties — block (*7.10*; 332).

Other optional properties

- `block-progression-dimension` (*7.14.1*; 352),
- `break-after` (*7.19.1*; 366),
- `break-before` (*7.19.2*; 367),
- `clip` (*7.20.1*; 368),
- `display-align` (*7.13.4*; 373),
- `height` (*7.14.4*; 382),
- `id` (*7.28.2*; 384),
- `inline-progression-dimension` (*7.14.5*; 385),
- `intrusion-displace` (*7.18.3*; 385),
- `keep-together` (*7.19.3*; 386),
- `keep-with-next` (*7.19.4*; 386),
- `keep-with-previous` (*7.19.5*; 387),
- `overflow` (*7.20.2*; 397),
- `reference-orientation` (*7.20.3*; 407),
- `span` (*7.20.4*; 415),
- `width` (*7.14.12*; 428),
- `writing-mode` (*7.27.7*; 429),
- `z-index` (*7.28.9*; 429).

Shorthands influencing the above properties

- `page-break-after` (*7.29.16*; 401),
- `page-break-before` (*7.29.17*; 401),
- `page-break-inside` (*7.29.18*; 402).

4.4 Page definition and sequencing

4.4.1 Simple page layout definition

Every different page layout to be rendered must be described separately.

- `simple-page-master`:
  - must be named using the `master-name` property.
- It can be used to specify differences in reference orientations of regions.
- It can be used to specify differences in column progression directions.
  - Changes from defaults are specified by explicitly setting the `writing-mode` property.

- It can be used to specify differences in geometry, including —
    - page dimensions,
    - region dimensions.

A page's page viewport area's content rectangle defines the page dimensions.

- The page's page reference area's content rectangle is within page margin boundaries.
- The body region's region viewport area is the page reference area's content rectangle.

Every page layout has at least a "middle" body region (see Figure 4–2).

- `region-body`:
    - may be named differently than the default "`xsl-region-body`" name;
        - typically, it is explicitly named to distinguish regions in sequenced pages;
        - where the same name is used on more than one page master, all uses of the name must be for the same kind of region,
    - is distinct from optional perimeter regions in definition but not in page area.

Perimeter regions cut into the body region.

- They may be named differently from the default names using `region-name`.
    - Renaming regions promotes good maintenance practice.
    - `region-before` is named "`xsl-region-before`" by default.
    - `region-after`is named "`xsl-region-after`" by default.
    - `region-start`is named "`xsl-region-start`" by default.
    - `region-end` is named "`xsl-region-end`" by default.
- If the body region doesn't have margins, then the perimeter region content will overlap the body content.
    - Perimeter regions do not automatically shrink the size of the content rectangle of the body region.
- Before and after regions can indicate they have precedence over the start and end regions.

Regions may have different reference orientations and writing modes.

- A common need to have a landscape body region orientation inside of a portrait page geometry with portrait before and after regions.

There are important region name constraints on multiple page masters.

- Once a given custom name is used, it must be used for the same region position wherever else it is used on other page masters.

- The reserved names cannot be used by regions other than those that already use them per the Recommendation.
- For example, the region name "myheader", when used for a region-before, can only be used for a region-before in other page masters.

4.4.2   Spans and columns in simple page geometry

Hierarchy of reference areas within page includes spans and columns.

- Body region contains main reference area;
  - this area occupies the entire region width;
  - it sits between before-float reference area and footnote reference area.
- main reference area contains span reference areas;
  - these are groups of columns with the same number of columns spanned;
  - groups are stacked in the block-progression direction.
- span reference area contains normal-flow reference areas (columns);
  - the normally-flowed blocks of information in the flow are flowed into the columns;
  - columns are stacked in the inline-progression direction.

Only evenly-spaced columns are allowed.

- Only the column count and column gap can be specified;
- the fixed column specification applies to entire page;
  - you cannot change column count within a page, other than by spanning all columns.

Only main reference area wide spans are allowed.

- A block can span all columns or only one column.

Columns are balanced within each span reference area.

- A given span reference area accepts blocks in its normal-flow reference areas, until the number of columns spanned by a block changes;
  - a new span reference area is then introduced on the page;
  - all blocks flowed in the interrupted span reference area are re-flowed across all columns;
  - the balancing depends not on the count of blocks, but on the content of each block and the contained lines.
- All blocks flowed into the last span reference area of the main reference area are balanced across all columns.

Consider a before/after situation of a formatter flowing a mixture of spanned and un-spanned blocks shown in the two sides of Figure 4–11.

- Six un-spanned blocks flow into a normal-flow reference area as normal blocks;
- a seventh block spans all columns and triggers the generation of a new span reference area;
- the content of the first six blocks is flowed across all normal-flow reference areas of the first span reference area based on the length of the content in the sum total of the six blocks.
  - The count of blocks is irrelevant;
  - the total length of all blocks is balanced across the columns while accommodating keeps, widows, and orphans.

Figure 4–11   Hierarchy of span areas

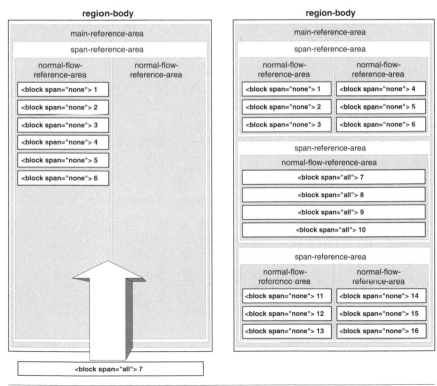

4.4.3   The simple-page-master object

Purpose

- This is the specification of a given page's physical geometry.

Content

- (*6.4.12*) (region-body, region-before?, region-after?, region-start?, region-end?),
- child objects (listed alphabetically):
    - region-after (*6.4.15*; 197),
    - region-before (*6.4.14*; 195),
    - region-body (*6.4.13*; 114),
    - region-end (*6.4.17*; 199),
    - region-start (*6.4.16*; 198),
- referring object:
    - layout-master-set (*6.4.6*; 65).

Property sets

- Common margin properties — block (*7.10*; 332).

Other required property

- master-name (*7.25.8*; 393).

Other optional properties

- page-height (*7.25.13*; 402),
- page-width (*7.25.15*; 403),
- reference-orientation (*7.20.3*; 407),
- writing-mode (*7.27.7*; 429).

Shorthand influencing the above properties

- size (*7.29.21*; 413).

The use of the XSL-FO page description element is shown in Example 4–2.

4.4.4   The region-body object

Purpose

- This is the definition of the middle area inside all perimeter regions defined for the page.

Example 4–2	The use of the XSL-FO page description element

```
Line 01  <?xml version="1.0" encoding="utf-8"?>
    02  <root xmlns="http://www.w3.org/1999/XSL/Format" font-size="16pt">
    03    <layout-master-set>
    04      <simple-page-master master-name="bookpage"
    05                          page-height="297mm" page-width="210mm"
    06                          margin-top="15mm" margin-bottom="15mm"
    07                          margin-left="15mm" margin-right="15mm">
    08        <region-body region-name="bookpage-body"
    09                     margin-top="5mm" margin-bottom="5mm"/>
    10      </simple-page-master>
    11    </layout-master-set>
    12    <page-sequence master-reference="bookpage">
    13      <title>Hello world example</title>
    14      <flow flow-name="bookpage-body">
    15        <block>Hello XSL-FO!</block>
    16      </flow>
    17    </page-sequence>
    18  </root>
```

Content

- $(6.4.13)$ EMPTY,
- referring object:
    - simple-page-master $(6.4.12; 114)$.

Property sets

- Common border, padding, and background properties $(7.7; 328)$,
- common margin properties — block $(7.10; 332)$.

Other required property

- region-name $(7.25.17; 407)$.

Other optional properties

- clip $(7.20.1; 368)$,
- column-count $(7.25.2; 369)$,
- column-gap $(7.25.3; 369)$,
- display-align $(7.13.4; 373)$,
- overflow $(7.20.2; 397)$,
- reference-orientation $(7.20.3; 407)$,
- writing-mode $(7.27.7; 429)$.

Properties of note

- The `region-name` property is required, but the default name of "`xsl-region-body`" is used as this required property if a name is not supplied in the XSL-FO instance.

- Even though `padding` and `border-width` properties are indicated as available indirectly through the common property set, these values are fixed at "`0pt`" in XSL-FO 1.0.

- `display-align` is used to keep the information in the region snug against the before edge, snug against the after edge, or centered in the middle of the two in the block-progression direction.

The page body description element is shown in Example 4–3.

Example 4–3   The page body description element

```
Line 01  <?xml version="1.0" encoding="utf-8"?>
02  <root xmlns="http://www.w3.org/1999/XSL/Format" font-size="16pt">
03    <layout-master-set>
04      <simple-page-master master-name="bookpage"
05                          page-height="297mm" page-width="210mm"
06                          margin-top="15mm" margin-bottom="15mm"
07                          margin-left="15mm" margin-right="15mm">
08        <region-body region-name="bookpage-body"
09                    margin-top="5mm" margin-bottom="5mm"/>
10      </simple-page-master>
11    </layout-master-set>
12    <page-sequence master-reference="bookpage">
13      <title>Hello world example</title>
14      <flow flow-name="bookpage-body">
15        <block>Hello XSL-FO!</block>
16      </flow>
17    </page-sequence>
18  </root>
```

4.4.5   Page sequence titling

A sequence of pages can be assigned a title —

- presented to the user by the formatter in an implementation dependent fashion;
  - the formatter may choose to render the title on the result canvas, e.g.:
    - once per page sequence,
    - once per page;

- an interactive user agent could display the title in the title bar of a screen window;
- the title may be suppressed altogether by the formatter.

This is a portability issue with respect to development.

- A stylesheet writer may be using a formatter that presents the title information outside of the page canvas.
- The user of a stylesheet may be using a formatter that presents the title information on the page canvas.
  - The result may not be as desired by the stylesheet writer.

4.4.6   The title object

Purpose

- This is a page sequence's ancillary description not rendered on the page canvas.

Content

- (*6.4.20*) (`#PCDATA` | `%inline;`)*,
- child object:
  - `%inline;` (*6.2*; 70),
- referring object:
  - `page-sequence` (*6.4.5*; 65).
- This object must not have a marker or out-of-line descendant, i.e.:
  - `marker`,
  - `float`,
  - `footnote`,
  - `block-container` with an absolute position specification.

Property sets

- Common accessibility properties (*7.4*; 326),
- common aural properties (*7.6*; 327),
- common border, padding, and background properties (*7.7*; 328),
- common font properties (*7.8*; 331),
- common margin properties — inline (*7.11*; 333).

Other optional properties

- `color` (*7.17.1*; 369),

- line-height (*7.15.4*; 390),
- visibility (*7.28.8*; 425).

Shorthand influencing the above properties

- font (*7.29.13*; 377).

The XSL-FO page body description element is shown in Example 4–4.

Example 4–4   The XSL-FO page body description element

```
Line 01  <?xml version="1.0" encoding="utf-8"?>
02  <root xmlns="http://www.w3.org/1999/XSL/Format" font-size="16pt">
03    <layout-master-set>
04      <simple-page-master master-name="bookpage"
05                          page-height="297mm" page-width="210mm"
06                          margin-top="15mm" margin-bottom="15mm"
07                          margin-left="15mm" margin-right="15mm">
08        <region-body region-name="bookpage-body"
09                     margin-top="5mm" margin-bottom="5mm"/>
10      </simple-page-master>
11    </layout-master-set>
12    <page-sequence master-reference="bookpage">
13      <title>Hello world example</title>
14      <flow flow-name="bookpage-body">
15        <block>Hello XSL-FO!</block>
16      </flow>
17    </page-sequence>
18  </root>
```

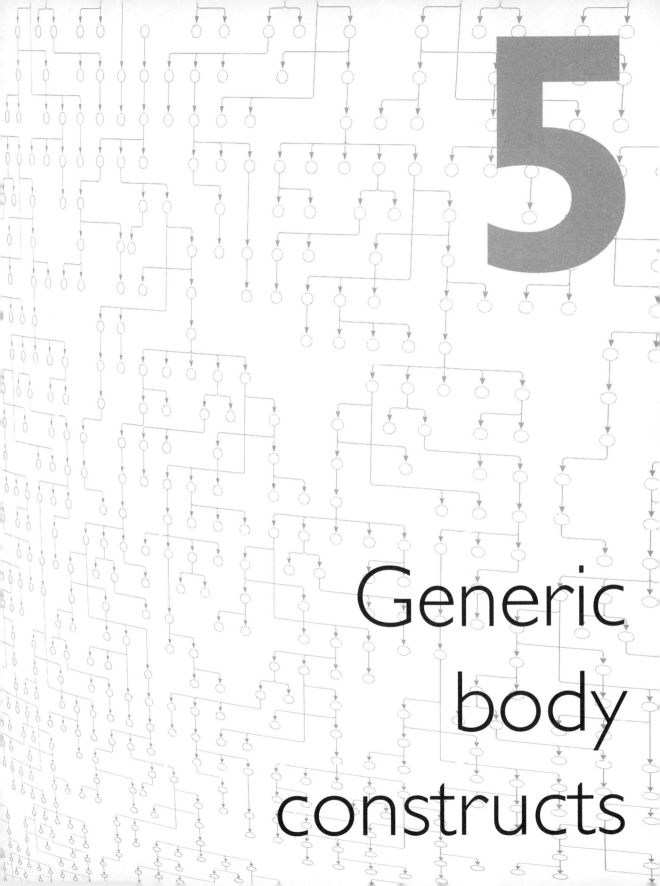

5

Generic
body
constructs

5 Generic body constructs

Many publishing requirements involve commonly-used constructs for pairs of layout areas, for non-textual information, for unidirectional associations, and for visual navigation and barrier lines. These are termed "generic" constructs in this book because of their wide use in many formatted results.

It is often necessary to format pairs of aligned block-level areas in the inline-progression direction, perhaps to present side-by-side language translation text, or an unordered list, or an ordered list. Block-level areas do not normally stack next to each other in the inline-progression direction because they are lined in the block-progression direction, flowing the following area after the preceding area. To align the layout of two block-level areas, XSL-FO provides a number of objects for the layout of the components of the pairs, without any bias to what goes into each member of the pair of areas and on the rendered result. These two areas are aligned on their respective before edges. A list is only a layout construct in XSL-FO, and the name is not to prejudice the use of the construct to only lists; rather, it can be used any time this association of pairs of aligned areas is required. This leaves the user in complete control over what is rendered in the list, by the XSL-FO objects only specifying the layout of the nested components of the list.

Non-textual information is typically a static graphic or photograph of some kind, though an electronic implementation of the presentation of structured information using XSL-FO can provide for dynamic components such as windows into live applications. When the non-textual information is not expressed in XML syntax, it must be external to the XSL-FO instance and is pointed to through properties. When the non-textual information is expressed in XML syntax (e.g. in the Scalable Vector Graphics (SVG) vocabulary), it may be either external to the XSL-FO instance or embedded within the XSL-FO instance.

Unidirectional associations can be defined in the XSL-FO instance for interactive user agents to render in an electronic format. The user can specify links from "hot" areas of the area tree to a target external resource, or to a target area in the same area tree. Interactivity engaged by the operator viewing the rendered result can cause navigating to the target location when the user interface triggers a traversal of the link. Once you have traversed a link, unidirectional links provide no inherent knowledge or "back link" information on where you started. Such behavior in web browsers and page turner applications is implemented by the application itself by remembering where the user had been before traversal, and is not found in the inherent properties of the link.

Both elastic and inelastic rules and patterns can be useful in formatting. Flowing two inline areas to the opposite ends of a line is a common need. Visual guidance or assistance is often necessary when the eye travels from one side of a page to the opposite side, as used in entries in tables of contents. Such areas can be filled with patterned sequences of characters joining information on a single line (e.g. a dot-leader), or with straight-ruled marks, in the inline-progression direction. The length of such areas cannot always be predetermined, so the elasticity of these areas gives the power that is needed because the construct grows to meet the requirements. It is also useful at times to break up the flow of information with visual barriers, with fixed length rules and patterns.

Examples of generic body constructs. Two example uses of aligned pairs of block-level layout areas are side-by-side presentation of simultaneously translated paragraphs in different languages (illustrated in Figure 6–1 in the discussion on tables), and traditional list structures including numbered lists, bulleted lists, terminology definitions, etc., as shown in Figure 5–1. The same XSL-FO semantic is used for both these kinds of layout because of the need to align two block-level areas in the inline-progression direction.

The example depicted in Figure 5–2 illustrates leaders, links and graphics in a mock-up of a table of contents page. The fact that the titles and page numbers of each of the entries in the table of contents is a hyperlink for jumping to the start of the corresponding chapter cannot be shown in the diagram.

The text of each line of the table of contents is "hot" in that the operator can interact with a hot area on the page in order to traverse the link, e.g. with a mouse click. The operator will thus move the focus to the target of the association, e.g. another page in the same XSL-FO formatted result, a page in the another XSL-FO formatted result, or perhaps a web browser with a web page address.

The graphic image shown below the subtitle in this example is an external static bit image, but it could as well be a window into a live application if that is supported by the user agent.

Figure 5–1   Aligned layout areas

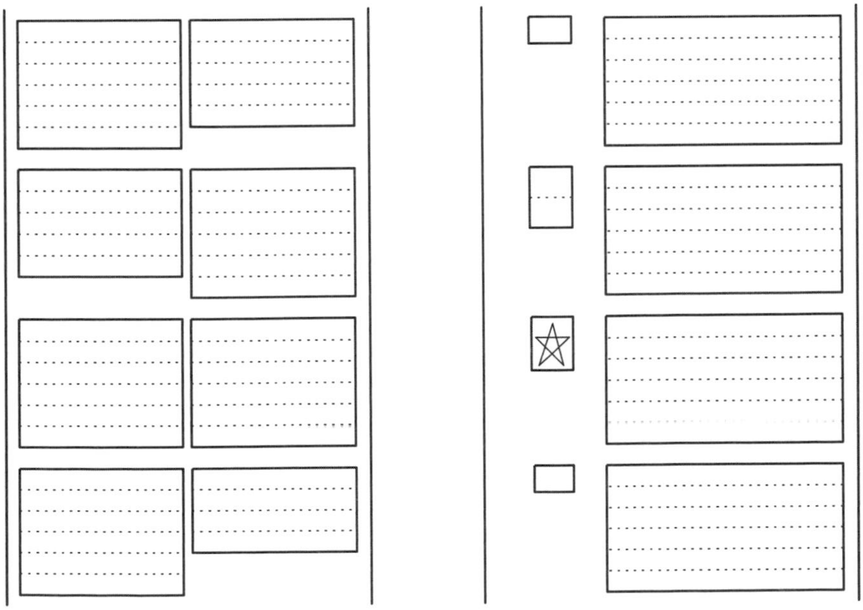

Various leaders are used on the page, including near the top where there are inelastic rule leaders 100% of the width of the page, above the page count where there is an inelastic rule leader 60% the width of the page, and in each entry where there is an elastic dot leader that stretches between the start-aligned titles and the end-aligned page numbers.

Included in this chapter. This chapter includes discussion of the following XSL-FO objects.

List objects:

- `list-block` (*6.8.2*):
    - is the collection object of a related set of child member pairs of aligned block-level areas,
- `list-item` (*6.8.3*):
    - is a member pair of aligned block-level areas in a collection,
- `list-item-label` (*6.8.5*):
    - is the start-side member of a pair of aligned block-level areas,
- `list-item-body` (*6.8.4*):
    - is the end-side member of a pair of aligned block-level areas.

Graphic objects:

- `external-graphic` (*6.6.5*):
    - is the inline display of graphical or other externally-supplied information,

---

Figure 5–2   Example for leaders, links, and graphics

The Leader/Link/Graphic Example

$$\overline{\overline{}}$$

Table of Contents

- `instream-foreign-object` (*6.6.6*):
  - is the inline display of graphical or other instance-supplied information.

Link object:

- `basic-link` (*6.9.2*):
  - is the inline display of the start resource of a unidirectional link to a single end point.

Leader/rule object:

- `leader` (*6.6.9*):
  - is the inline elastic or rigid display of a rule or a repeated sequence of glyphs.

5.1 Lists

5.1.1 Aligned pairs of block-level constructs

Standalone blocks cannot be adjacent to each other in the inline-progression direction.

- A block-level construct typically continues the block-progression direction.

Pairs of adjacent blocks are useful to associate the information in one of the blocks to the information in the other block. This includes —

- side-by-side language text, e.g.:
  - aligned translation paragraphs,
- terms and their definitions,
- generic list item formatting, i.e.:
  - the item enumerator and the item content.

The name of the construct shouldn't prejudice how the construct is used.

- Don't think that only lists in your XML information can use this construct for layout.
- Regard the construct as a layout facility for pairs of block-level constructs in the inline-progression direction of the parent block.
- A two-column table construct may suffice or offer other layout features you need.

Specialized properties are available for the behaviors characteristic of list processing.

- Provisional property values can be used to make the calculated property values of the two blocks relative to each other instead of independent of each other.
- There is no obligation to use the specialized properties.

The content of the blocks does not impact the start/end edges of the blocks.

- The start and end edges of each block are set absolutely or relative to each other, but not relative to the length of the content.
- The edges are fixed to the same values for all members of the entire list.
  - Planning ahead is necessary to ensure any undesired wrapping within edges is avoided.

5.1.2 List constructs

A list is a block-level object shown in two different ways in Figure 5–3.

- It contains only list items (pairs).
  - It requires a nested list to itself be a list item unless it is already in a list item.
- When using provisional values and functions, the edges are fixed to the same values for all members of the entire list.
  - Planning ahead is necessary to ensure any undesired wrapping within edges is avoided.

Figure 5–3   The blocks of information that comprise a list

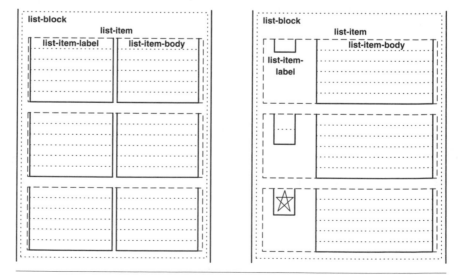

- When specifying margins on a per list item basis, the edges can be explicitly specified differently from other list items.
  - One cannot measure the content of a label or body in order to set the margins relative to the content.

Block alignment can involve more than two blocks, as shown in Figure 5–4.

- The body of a list item can itself contain a list with two aligned blocks.
- The initial value of relative alignment is the before edge for all blocks.

Consider using a table for more than two blocks.

- Table properties allow the block widths to be proportional.
- Table cells do not overlap.

Horizontal indentation of the list item components is the responsibility of the stylesheet writer.

- The item label's `start-indent` is specified explicitly (or inherited).
- The item body's `end-indent` is specified explicitly (or inherited).
- The item label's `end-indent` and item body's `start-indent` can be set independently.

Figure 5–4   Aligning more than two blocks

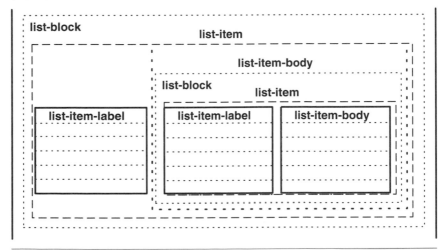

- Without proper planning, this can inadvertently result in display problems, e.g.:
  - overlapping label content on top of body content,
  - undesired wrapping of label content.
- The item label's `end-indent` and item body's `start-indent` can be set relative to the `start-indent` of the item label.
  - The stylesheet can ask the processor to dynamically set these values on a per list item basis.
  - This protects the content of the two areas from sharing the same place on the rendered output.

Vertical alignment of list item label defaults to a common before edge.

- This ensures that the before edge of the first block on each side is aligned on the page.
- `relative-align` can be set to common text baseline of first lines;
  - when different font sizes are used without aligning to the text baseline, the smaller of the two font sizes will appear to be superscripted.

You are not obliged to use `body-start()` or `label-end()`.

- You can specify the distances from the parent edges explicitly for each of the labels and bodies, as shown in Figure 5–5.

Risk of overlap is borne by the stylesheet writer.

Figure 5–5   Simple adjacent blocks in a list

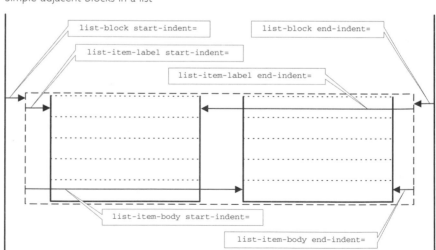

- A common error when starting a stylesheet is to forget to set any margins and to witness both blocks of content superimposed within the parent area.
- Another common error is to change, after writing a stylesheet, the page width and not think to change the list item member indents;
  - e.g., when narrowing the page from US letter to A4 format, the blocks could overlap in the middle when the distances from the edges are used.

Using body-start() or label-end() will prevent edges from overlapping, as shown in Figure 5–6.

Indentation of the list item components can be relative.

- Processor notes provisional-distance-between-starts and provisional-label-separation values for built-in functions.
  - The term "provisional" indicates the value is used as part of an arithmetic calculation.
  - These values are properties of the list as a whole and cannot be set on an individual item.
  - Specifying a separation prevents overlapping of the label and body.
- Two built-in functions reflect the above two values in the context of the item label's start-indent and can (should) be used to protect the adjacent area boundaries from running into each other.

Figure 5–6   Basic edges on relative calculations

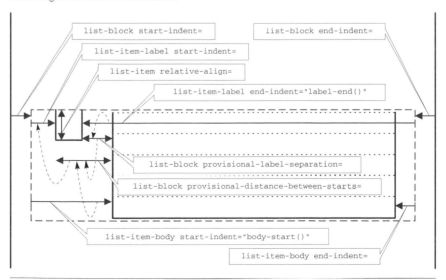

- `label-end()`:
  - is the distance from the end of the label to the end of the line accommodating the indent of the label,
  - is used as the value for the `end-indent` property of the item label;
- `body-start()`:
  - is the distance from the start of the line to the start of the body accommodating the indent of the item label,
  - is used as the `start-indent` property of the item body.

5.1.3 Nested list constructs

The nesting of lists may require the use of hidden list item members.

- A nested list in the user's XML vocabulary is usually one of either:
  - a block within an existing list item;
    - an example is `list/listitem/list`;
    - the block-level `list-block` formatting object can flow with other blocks inside a `list-item-body`,
  - its own list item;
    - an example is `list/list`;
    - this requires a hidden `list-item` within which the list block is placed in the body;
    - a `list-block` can only contain `list-item` children;
    - the hidden `list-item` children must have blocks for labels;
      - the label blocks can be empty to hide the fact they are list items.

The choice of one of these depends on:

- the need for dependence of the indentation of the nested list;
  - is its indentation fixed?
    - use the body of a hidden list item with a fixed indentation for the body;
  - is its indentation relative to the indentation of the label of the list item in which it is flowed?
    - use the calculated body start indentation of the preceding list item,
- the nature of the source list;
  - is the nested list inside one of the list items (typical; e.g. HTML, DocBook)?
    ```
    <list>
      <item>
        <p>...</p>
        <list>nested list</list>
      </item>
      <item>...
    ```

- is the nested list a sibling of other list items (atypical)?

```
<list>
  <item>
    <p>...</p>
  </item>
  <list>nested list</list>
  <item>...
```

The use of a ghost list item, shown in Figure 5–7, prevents violating the content model rules for the containing list.

You cannot use just a `block` or `list-block` in this situation.

- A `list-block` can only contain `list-item` children.
- The ghost list item contains the nested list in the body of the item.
  - It requires an empty block in the label to not be visible on the page.

5.1.4 The list-block object

Purpose

- This is the parent object of a related set of pairs of aligned block-level areas laid out in the inline-progression direction.

Figure 5–7   Two methods of nesting a list

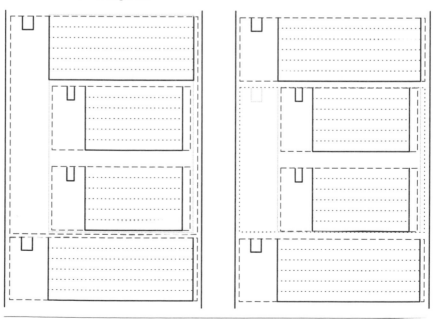

Content

- (*6.8.2*) (list-item+),
- child object:
  - list-item (*6.8.3*; 133),
- any number of marker children at the beginning.

Property sets

- Common accessibility properties (*7.4*; 326),
- common aural properties (*7.6*; 327),
- common border, padding, and background properties (*7.7*; 328),
- common margin properties — block (*7.10*; 332),
- common relative position properties (*7.12*; 333).

Other optional properties

- break-after (*7.19.1*; 366),
- break-before (*7.19.2*; 367),
- id (*7.28.2*; 384),
- intrusion-displace (*7.18.3*; 385),
- keep-together (*7.19.3*; 386),
- keep-with-next (*7.19.4*; 386),
- keep-with-previous (*7.19.5*; 387),
- provisional-distance-between-starts (*7.28.4*; 406),
- provisional-label-separation (*7.28.3*; 407).

Shorthands influencing the above properties

- page-break-after (*7.29.16*; 401),
- page-break-before (*7.29.17*; 401),
- page-break-inside (*7.29.18*; 402).

Properties of interest

- provisional-distance-between-starts specifies the desired distance between the start of the list item label and the start of the list item body;
- provisional-label-separation specifies the desired distance between the end of the list item label and the start of the list item body.

A list-block construct from the earlier Figure 2–8 is shown in Example 5–1.

Separation between the label and body is specified;

- the label is .33 inches wide and .1 inches away from the body.

Example 5–1   The list block

```
Line 01  <block space-before.optimum="6pt" font-size="14pt">
    02    This page's material as an instructor-led handout:</block>
    03  <list-block provisional-distance-between-starts=".43in"
    04              provisional-label-separation=".1in"
    05              space-before.optimum="6pt">
    06    <list-item relative-align="baseline">
    07      <list-item-label text-align="end" end-indent="label-end()">
    08        <block>-</block>
    09      </list-item-label>
    10      <list-item-body start-indent="body-start()">
    11        <block font-size="14pt">excerpts of formatting objects created
    12              through the use of an XSLT stylesheet</block>
    13      </list-item-body>
    14    </list-item>
    15  </list-block>
```

5.1.5   The list-item object

Purpose

- This is the parent of a single pair of aligned block-level areas laid out in the inline-progression direction.
  - Indents are relative to containing `list-block` object.

Content

- (*6.8.3*) (`list-item-label`, `list-item-body`),
- child objects (listed alphabetically):
  - `list-item-body` (*6.8.4*; 136),
  - `list-item-label` (*6.8.5*; 134),
- referring object:
  - `list-block` (*6.8.2*; 131),
- any number of `marker` children at the beginning.

Property sets

- Common accessibility properties (*7.4*; 326),
- common aural properties (*7.6*; 327),
- common border, padding, and background properties (*7.7*; 328),

- common margin properties — block (*7.10*; 332),
- common relative position properties (*7.12*; 333).

Other optional properties

- break-after (*7.19.1*; 366),
- break-before (*7.19.2*; 367),
- id (*7.28.2*; 384),
- intrusion-displace (*7.18.3*; 385),
- keep-together (*7.19.3*; 386),
- keep-with-next (*7.19.4*; 386),
- keep-with-previous (*7.19.5*; 387),
- relative-align (*7.13.6*; 408).

Shorthands influencing the above properties

- page-break-after (*7.29.16*; 401),
- page-break-before (*7.29.17*; 401),
- page-break-inside (*7.29.18*; 402).

Properties of interest

- relative-align determines the alignment of the list item with either the before edge of the list body (default) or the baseline of the first line area generated by the list body;
  - the value "baseline" is typically used when both sides are using text;
  - the value "before" is typically used when one or both sides are graphics.

A list-item construct from the earlier Section 2.2.2 on page 41 is shown in Example 5–2.

5.1.6   The list-item-label object

Purpose

- This is the start-side member of a pair of aligned block-level areas laid out in the inline-progression direction.

Content

- (*6.8.5*) (%block;)+,
- child object:
  - %block; (*6.2*; 69),

Example 5–2   The list item

```
Line 01   <block space-before.optimum="6pt" font-size="14pt">
   02       This page's material as an instructor-led handout:</block>
   03   <list-block provisional-distance-between-starts=".43in"
   04               provisional-label-separation=".1in"
   05               space-before.optimum="6pt">
   06     <list-item relative-align="baseline">
   07       <list-item-label text-align="end" end-indent="label-end()">
   08         <block>-</block>
   09       </list-item-label>
   10       <list-item-body start-indent="body-start()">
   11         <block font-size="14pt">excerpts of formatting objects created
   12               through the use of an XSLT stylesheet</block>
   13       </list-item-body>
   14     </list-item>
   15   </list-block>
```

- referring object:
  - list-item (*6.8.3*; 133),
- any number of marker children at the beginning.

Property sets

- Common accessibility properties (*7.4*; 326).

Other optional properties

- id (*7.28.2*; 384),
- keep-together (*7.19.3*; 386).

Shorthand influencing the above properties

- page-break-inside (*7.29.18*; 402).

Property of interest

- end-indent can utilize the label-end() function.

A list-item-label construct from the earlier Section 2.2.2 on page 41 is shown in Example 5–3.

Of note:

- the end alignment is specified on the label to move the content of the label as close as possible to the body;
- this supports the appearance of variable length labels (i.e. Roman characters) with a common distance between the label and the body.

Example 5–3   The list item's label

```
Line 01  <block space-before.optimum="6pt" font-size="14pt">
02       This page's material as an instructor-led handout:</block>
03     <list-block provisional-distance-between-starts=".43in"
04                 provisional-label-separation=".1in"
05                 space-before.optimum="6pt">
06       <list-item relative-align="baseline">
07        <list-item-label text-align="end" end-indent="label-end()">
08          <block>-</block>
09        </list-item-label>
10         <list-item-body start-indent="body-start()">
11
12           <block font-size="14pt">excerpts of formatting objects created
13                 through the use of an XSLT stylesheet</block>
14         </list-item-body>
15       </list-item>
16     </list-block>
```

5.1.7   The list-item-body object

Purpose

- This is the end-side member of a pair of aligned block-level areas laid out in the inline-progression direction.

Content

- (*6.8.4*) (%block;)+,
- child object:
  - %block; (*6.2*; 69),
- referring object:
  - list-item (*6.8.3*; 133),
- any number of marker children at the beginning.

Property sets

- Common accessibility properties (*7.4*; 326).

Other optional properties

- id (*7.28.2*; 384),
- keep-together (*7.19.3*; 386).

Shorthand influencing the above properties

- page-break-inside (*7.29.18*; 402).

Property of interest

- `start-indent` can utilize the `body-start()` function.

A `list-item-body` construct from the earlier Section 2.2.2 on page 41 is shown in Example 5–4.

Example 5–4   The list item's body

```
Line 01   <block space-before.optimum="6pt" font-size="14pt">
    02      This page's material as an instructor-led handout:</block>
    03   <list-block provisional-distance-between-starts=".43in"
    04              provisional-label-separation=".1in"
    05              space-before.optimum="6pt">
    06     <list-item relative-align="baseline">
    07       <list-item-label text-align="end" end-indent="label-end()">
    08         <block>-</block>
    09       </list-item-label>
    10       <list-item-body start-indent="body-start()">
    11         <block font-size="14pt">excerpts of formatting objects created
    12               through the use of an XSLT stylesheet</block>
    13       </list-item-body>
    14     </list-item>
    15   </list-block>
```

5.1.8 When is a list not a list?

Some formatting requirements for lists cannot be satisfied with the `list-block` construct.

- You are not obliged to use `list-block` to format a list-like source construct.
- `list-block` forces the stylesheet writer to specify the start and end edges of the labels and bodies of the items, which may not be what is desired.

Figure 5–8 shows three alternative approaches to formatting three list items where the item labels have distinctly different lengths, none of which is known by the stylesheet writer.

One approach is basing the indentation of all item bodies on the longest length of all item labels.

- You can use one table for entire list contents (Figure 5–8, left);
  - hidden borders and auto-calculated column widths in all rows reflect a single set of column widths;

- use one row for each list item, with auto width calculation of the first column determining longest label;
  - it may not work well if the label has spaces that will promote cell balancing.

Another approach is basing the indentation of each item body on the length of corresponding item labels.

- You can use a one-row table for each list item (Figure 5–8, center);
  - use hidden borders and auto-calculated column widths for each individual row in separate table;
  - use as many tables as there are list items.
- You can use a side float aligned with the block (Figure 5–8, right);
  - each body block is prefaced with a side float block with the label whose size squeezes the body block width.

5.2 Graphics and foreign objects

5.2.1 Non-textual information

Graphic and other non-textual constructs can come from two possible sources.

- External files:
  - are referenced by `external-graphic`,
  - use URIs to specify how to obtain the external resource.
- Embedded non-XSL-FO-namespace constructs:
  - are referenced by `instream-foreign-object`,
  - will not be confused with XSL-FO objects because of namespace distinction,
  - may include Scalable Vector Graphics (SVG), Math Markup Language (MathML), etc.,
  - promote the generation of images from the stylesheets that generate the XSL-FO;

Figure 5–8   Three alternatives to using a list construct for a list

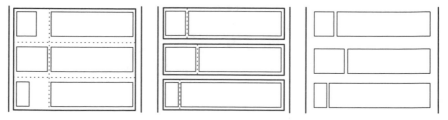

- e.g., numbers can be charted using SVG constructs from the XML instance.

XSL-FO processor need not recognize the formats, only pass on the content from whatever source to rendering agent for imaging.

- The formatter is only responsible for measuring and allocating the required area on the page as indicated by the properties.
- Rendering agent must recognize the file type by either name or content.
  - No notation information is communicated through the stylesheet from the DTD.

Content need not be a static graphic image;

- it could be a window into an application user interface, e.g.:
  - a spreadsheet.

The `src` property has specific syntactic requirements.

- It is safest to use `url("`*`uri-value-here`*`")`.
  - The author of the XML document may be creating the URI being used in the resulting syntax.
  - The URI character set includes the single quote that would bring about an improperly formed attribute value if the single quote is used as the delimiter.
- You could use no quote delimiters, unless the URI contains a single quote.
- You could use single quote delimiters, unless the URI contains a single quote.
- Make sure the XML syntax for attribute quotes is acceptable, e.g.:
  - `src='url("`*`uri-value-here`*`")'`,
  - `src="url(&quot;`*`uri-value-here`*`&quot;)"`.
- This is not a function call, but a syntactic convention.
  - Without it, the URI syntax could be misinterpreted as expression syntax.
  - Without it, any embedded single quotes (which are allowed in URI syntax and could be in the source XML without the stylesheet writer knowing) could confuse the interpretation of the literal string.

5.2.2 The external-graphic object

Purpose

- This is the inline-level display of graphical or other externally-supplied information.
  - Displayed matter is not part of the XSL-FO instance content;

- it is a reference to an addressed external resource.
- It can be placed in a `block` object for block-level display.

Content

- (*6.6.5*) EMPTY.

Property sets

- Common accessibility properties (*7.4*; 326),
- common aural properties (*7.6*; 327),
- common border, padding, and background properties (*7.7*; 328),
- common margin properties — inline (*7.11*; 333),
- common relative position properties (*7.12*; 333).

Other required property

- src (*7.28.7*; 417).

Other optional properties

- alignment-adjust (*7.13.1*; 346),
- alignment-baseline (*7.13.2*; 346),
- baseline-shift (*7.13.3*; 351),
- block-progression-dimension (*7.14.1*; 352),
- clip (*7.20.1*; 368),
- content-height (*7.14.2*; 370),
- content-type (*7.28.1*; 371),
- content-width (*7.14.3*; 371),
- display-align (*7.13.4*; 373),
- dominant-baseline (*7.13.5*; 374),
- height (*7.14.4*; 382),
- id (*7.28.2*; 384),
- inline-progression-dimension (*7.14.5*; 385),
- keep-with-next (*7.19.4*; 386),
- keep-with-previous (*7.19.5*; 387),
- line-height (*7.15.4*; 390),
- overflow (*7.20.2*; 397),
- scaling (*7.14.10*; 411),
- scaling-method (*7.14.11*; 412),

- text-align (*7.15.9*; 421),
- width (*7.14.12*; 428).

Shorthands influencing the above properties

- font (*7.29.13*; 377),
- page-break-after (*7.29.16*; 401),
- page-break-before (*7.29.17*; 401),
- vertical-align (*7.29.22*; 424).

Property of interest

- text-align and display-align are used to align the scaled image's reference area within the viewport area;
  - ancestral specifications will align the viewport area within its parent area.

An excerpt from Figure 5–2 is shown in Example 5–5.

Example 5–5   An example of referencing an external resource

```
Line 01  <block font-size="24pt" space-after="16pt" space-before="1cm"
      02         text-align="center">
      03         Table    of    Contents
      04         <block/>
      05         <external-graphic src='url(&quot;smflags.bmp&quot;)'/>
      06  </block>
```

Note the following regarding the structure of this example.

- By default, white space is collapsed so that the words "Table of Contents" are flowed on the page as if separated by only one space each.
- An empty block is used to introduce a line of zero size thus breaking the title and the graphic onto separate lines.
- The protected quoted syntax is used for the URI of the graphic image.
- All inline constructs on all lines of the outside block are centered using text-align.

5.2.3 The instream-foreign-object object

Purpose

- This is the inline display of graphical or other instance-supplied information.
  - Displayed matter is a part of the XSL-FO instance content.

- Descendent content of the object uses a non-XSL-FO namespace.
- The object can be placed in a `block` object for block-level display.

Content (6.6.6)

- a single child element from a non-XSL-FO namespace.

Property sets

- Common accessibility properties (*7.4*; 326),
- common aural properties (*7.6*; 327),
- common border, padding, and background properties (*7.7*; 328),
- common margin properties — inline (*7.11*; 333),
- common relative position properties (*7.12*; 333).

Other optional properties

- `alignment-adjust` (*7.13.1*; 346),
- `alignment-baseline` (*7.13.2*; 346),
- `baseline-shift` (*7.13.3*; 351),
- `block-progression-dimension` (*7.14.1*; 352),
- `clip` (*7.20.1*; 368),
- `content-height` (*7.14.2*; 370),
- `content-type` (*7.28.1*; 371),
- `content-width` (*7.14.3*; 371),
- `display-align` (*7.13.4*; 373),
- `dominant-baseline` (*7.13.5*; 374),
- `height` (*7.14.4*; 382),
- `id` (*7.28.2*; 384),
- `inline-progression-dimension` (*7.14.5*; 385),
- `keep-with-next` (*7.19.4*; 386),
- `keep-with-previous` (*7.19.5*; 387),
- `line-height` (*7.15.4*; 390),
- `overflow` (*7.20.2*; 397),
- `scaling` (*7.14.10*; 411),
- `scaling-method` (*7.14.11*; 412),
- `text-align` (*7.15.9*; 421),
- `width` (*7.14.12*; 428).

Shorthands influencing the above properties

- font (*7.29.13*; 377),
- page-break-after (*7.29.16*; 401),
- page-break-before (*7.29.17*; 401),
- vertical-align (*7.29.22*; 424).

Property of interest

- text-align and display-align are used to align the scaled image's reference area within the viewport area;
  - ancestral specifications will align the viewport area within its parent area.

Example 5–6 shows embedding alternate namespace content (in this case, Scalable Vector Graphics, SVG) into an XSL-FO instance.

Example 5–6   Embedding of SVG into XSL-FO

```
Line 01  <block text-align="center">
   02      <block>
   03        <instream-foreign-object>
   04          <svg:svg xmlns:svg="http://www.w3.org/2000/svg"
   05                   width="170" height="145">
   06            <svg:g style="stroke:black; fill:black">
   07              <svg:polygon points="  5, 50,  5, 81, 12, 64"/>
   08              <svg:polygon points="  5, 45, 41,116, 41, 73"/>
   09              <svg:polygon points=" 44, 76, 44,119, 61,115"/>
   10              <svg:polygon points=" 46, 73, 75,140,105, 73"/>
   11              <svg:polygon points="107, 76,107,119, 89,115"/>
   12              <svg:polygon points="144, 45,110,116,110, 74"/>
   13              <svg:polygon points="145, 41,167,  4,109, 71"/>
   14              <svg:polygon points=" 66, 70, 75, 63, 84, 70"/>
   15            </svg:g>
   16          </svg:svg>
   17        </instream-foreign-object>
   18      </block>
   19      <block font-size="20pt" font-weight="bold">Crane Logo</block>
   20  </block>
```

The rendering of the embedded image is shown in Figure 5–9.

5.3 **Links**

5.3.1 Link requirements

Unidirectional hyperlinks traverse from clickable content to a target location.

- A `basic-link` object is used for creating a hyperlink.
    - Its content is the clickable content used by the document reader to traverse to the target of the link;
        - it requires support by the user agent;
        - there is no need to be supported for a print-only medium;
        - any content can be wrapped up in a link construct.
    - A strict interpretation of the XSL-FO Recommendation implies that only the construct's inline area is "hot" and not the areas generated by descendants of the formatting object.
- The target location can be another point within the document.
    - For this, use the `internal-destination` property.
    - The user agent software reading the document would navigate the reader to the target page.
- The target location can be a point outside the document.
    - For this, use the `external-destination` property.

Figure 5–9   An embedded SVG image

- The operating system running the user agent software would probably invoke the application associated with the file being pointed to, e.g.:
  - a web browser for an HTML page.

The object is an inline construct.

- It must be placed in a block to be a block-level construct.
- It may contain either block-level or inline-level constructs.

The construct is unidirectional.

- There is no back-link property associated with the link itself.
- The ability for a user agent to "go back" to where the link originated is a function of the user agent based on a history of the user's locations.
  - The user agent is not using a property of the link itself that indicates where the link was made from.

5.3.2 The basic-link object

Purpose

- This is the inline display of the start resource of a unidirectional link to a single end point.

Content

- (*6.9.2*) (`#PCDATA | %inline; | %block;`)*,
- child objects (listed alphabetically):
  - `%block;` (*6.2*; 69),
  - `%inline;` (*6.2*; 70),
- any number of `marker` children at the beginning.

Property sets

- Common accessibility properties (*7.4*; 326),
- common aural properties (*7.6*; 327),
- common border, padding, and background properties (*7.7*; 328),
- common margin properties — inline (*7.11*; 333),
- common relative position properties (*7.12*; 333).

Other optional properties

- `alignment-adjust` (*7.13.1*; 346),
- `alignment-baseline` (*7.13.2*; 346),

- baseline-shift (*7.13.3*; 351),
- destination-placement-offset (*7.22.5*; 373),
- dominant-baseline (*7.13.5*; 374),
- external-destination (*7.22.6*; 376),
- id (*7.28.2*; 384),
- indicate-destination (*7.22.7*; 384),
- internal-destination (*7.22.8*; 385),
- keep-together (*7.19.3*; 386),
- keep-with-next (*7.19.4*; 386),
- keep-with-previous (*7.19.5*; 387),
- line-height (*7.15.4*; 390),
- show-destination (*7.22.9*; 412),
- target-presentation-context (*7.22.12*; 420),
- target-processing-context (*7.22.13*; 420),
- target-stylesheet (*7.22.14*; 420).

Shorthands influencing the above properties

- font (*7.29.13*; 377),
- page-break-after (*7.29.16*; 401),
- page-break-before (*7.29.17*; 401),
- page-break-inside (*7.29.18*; 402),
- vertical-align (*7.29.22*; 424).

An excerpt from Figure 5–2 is shown in Example 5–7.

5.4 Leaders

5.4.1 Elastic and inelastic inline areas

A leader provides the stylesheet writer with a number of basic features —

- fixed-length horizontal rules or patterns, typically used as separators between information,
- elastic leader rules or patterns, used in tables of contents to aid the eye movement across a page,
- elastic inline gaps, used to push away adjacent areas.

Example 5–7   Link constructs in example

```
Line 01  <block text-align-last="justify"
     02        end-indent="1cm" start-indent="1cm">
     03    <basic-link internal-destination="N66">Third Title</basic-link>
     04    <leader leader-pattern="dots"/>
     05    <basic-link internal-destination="N66">
     06      <page-number-citation ref-id="N66"/>
     07    </basic-link>
     08  </block>
     09  ...
     10  <block space-before="10pt" text-align-last="justify"
     11        end-indent="1cm" start-indent="1cm">
     12    <basic-link internal-destination="N1">Page count</basic-link>
     13    <leader leader-pattern="dots"/>
     14    <basic-link internal-destination="N1">
     15      <page-number-citation ref-id="N1"/>
     16    </basic-link>
     17  </block>
     18  ...
     19  <page-sequence master-reference="bookpage">
     20    <title>The Third Chapter Title</title>
     21    <flow flow-name="bookpage-body">
     22      <block id="N66" font-size="16pt * 1.5">Third Title</block>
     23
     24      <block space-before="16pt">Third entry is very short.</block>
     25      <block id="N1"/>
     26    </flow>
     27  </page-sequence>
```

`leader` is an inline construct that stretches a leader along the text baseline of the line.

- It must be put into a standalone block to act as a block construct.
  - Note that the default line height of the block is the font size, not the line height of the highest construct;
  - without specifying a small line height on the block, adjacent blocked lines will not appear close together.
- All leaders on a justified line are expanded before any space character or inter-character space on the line is expanded.
  - Expansion grows evenly across all leaders on the line until the line is full.
  - No justification expansion is done on any space characters or inter-character spacing.

When running a leader from one margin to the other margin, you must use the `text-align-last` property on the containing block.

- Using `text-align` with the value "`justify`" is insufficient because the line of a single-line block is considered the last line of the block.
- The leader grows between the information at the start of the line and the information at the end of the line, e.g.:
  - a dot leader, as used in table of contents entries,
  - an empty leader, used to push two pieces of information to the ends of a line.

Figure 5–2 illustrates leaders;

- block-level leaders are used as separators and decoration;
  - there are special block-level considerations for tightly-spaced leaders;
  - block-level leaders need not be full block width;
- title entries are short;
  - leaders expand between end of title and start of page number.

Figure 5–10 illustrates formatting requirements for a complex table of contents.

Figure 5–10   Example for long leaders

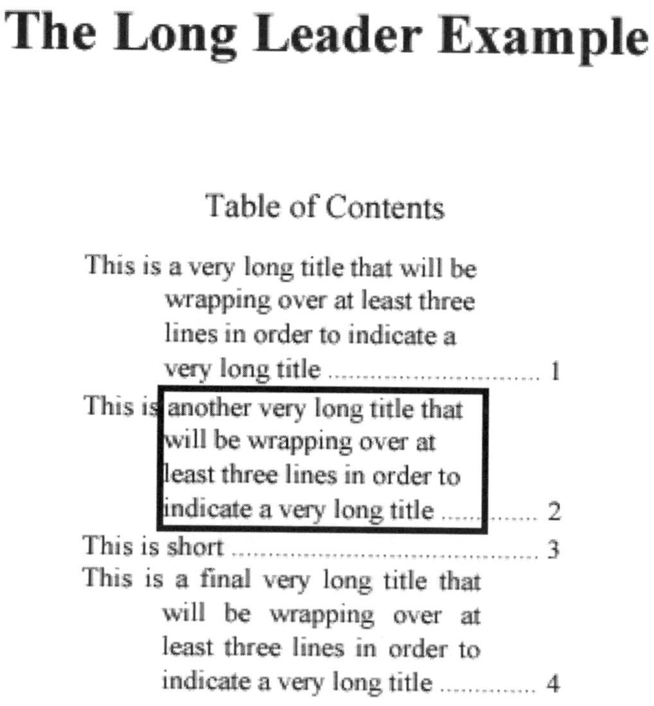

The Long Leader Example

Table of Contents

This is a very long title that will be
wrapping over at least three
lines in order to indicate a
very long title 1
This is another very long title that
will be wrapping over at
least three lines in order to
indicate a very long title 2
This is short 3
This is a final very long title that
will be wrapping over at
least three lines in order to
indicate a very long title 4

- The author of the XML being formatted is responsible for the length of titles.
- The stylesheet is collecting and presenting the titles in a table of contents.
- Short titles are easily accommodated through simple margin specifications.
- If the user could possibly create long titles, the stylesheet writer should be prepared to accommodate wrapping conditions to avoid confusion when reading the table.
  - Wrapping at the start of the line could make it difficult to count the entries in the table of contents;
    - the wrapping point should be indented on the start side.
  - Wrapping at the end of the line could clash with the presentation of page numbers;
    - the wrapping point should be indented on the end side.
- A block's first and last lines can be hanging in respective outdents to give the desired unambiguous presentation at the starts and ends of the lines.

Note that the borders of the block are shown only to illustrate the size of the block construct itself; this was done simply by turning on the `border-style="solid"` property.

- The indents of the first and last lines of the block are clearly shown to be outside the dimensions of the block.

Multiple-line table-of-contents-entry blocks are more complex than single-line blocks, as shown in Figure 5–11.

- There are special considerations for overhanging first and last lines of block;
  - negative values for indents specify outdents and allow the content to go beyond the boundaries of the box.
- You can also specify text alignment for the body of the block.

Of note:

- the last line is justified in order to grow the leader to the complete width of the last line including the outdent;
- the net indents of the first and last line are the differences between the indents of the block and the respective outdents of the first and last line.

5.4.2 Multiple leaders on a single line

When using multiple leaders on a single line, the length of each leader grows evenly in tandem, as shown in Figure 5–12.

- The length of all leaders on a single justified line is the same.
- Lengths grow until the line is filled.

Figure 5–11 Properties of blocks utilizing leaders

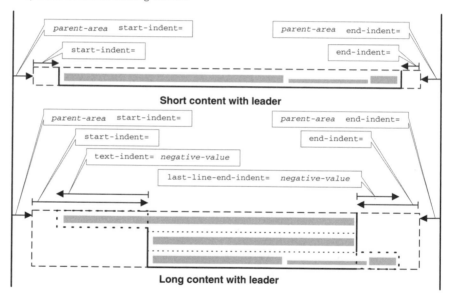

Figure 5–12 Using multiple leaders on a single line

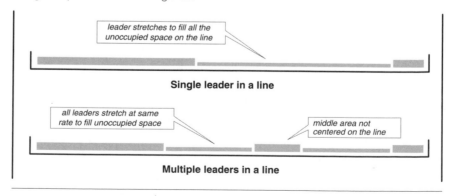

- This cannot be used to reliably position a middle area of content to the center of the line;
  - this only positions a middle area of content to the center of the closest edges of the two surrounding areas;
  - The middle area will then only be centered on the page if the content at the start and end edges happens to be of equal length.

5.4.3 Controlling the distance between leaders

The intuitive approach to controlling the distance between lines does not apply, as shown in Figure 5–13.

- Consider two standalone leaders that necessarily require two standalone blocks, one leader in each block, as in Figure 5–2.
- The line height of the block is governed by block properties and by default is the maximum of the font size and any inline constructs found on the line.
- It is intuitive to adjust the line height of the leader, but if that line height is less than the line height of the block, there will be no change in the result because the line height of the block will govern the placement of the leaders.

It is important to keep font size consistent when positioning adjacent lines.

Figure 5–13   Controlling the distance between leaders

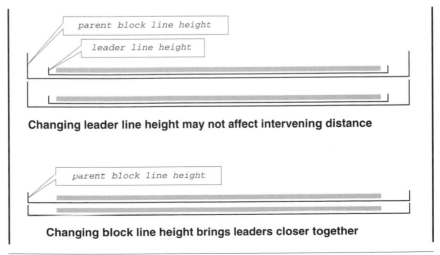

Changing leader line height may not affect intervening distance

Changing block line height brings leaders closer together

- Leaders are drawn along the font baseline.
- Changing the line height does not change the font size.
- Changing the font size will change both the distance between the alignment point and the baseline and the height of the line in the block.
- Changing only the line height will not change the distance between the alignment point and the baseline.
- More consistent distances are rendered when only changing one variable instead of two.

5.4.4   The leader object

Purpose

- This is the inline display of a rule or a sequence of glyphs.
  - This object can be placed in a `block` object for block-level display.

Content

- *(6.6.9)* `(#PCDATA | %inline;)*`,
- child object:
  - `%inline;` *(6.2;* 70),
- no `leader`, `inline-container`, `block-container`, `float`, `footnote`, or `marker` objects as a child or descendant.

Property sets

- Common accessibility properties *(7.4;* 326),
- common aural properties *(7.6;* 327),
- common border, padding, and background properties *(7.7;* 328),
- common font properties *(7.8;* 331),
- common margin properties — inline *(7.11;* 333),
- common relative position properties *(7.12;* 333).

Other optional properties

- `alignment-adjust` *(7.13.1;* 346),
- `alignment-baseline` *(7.13.2;* 346),
- `baseline-shift` *(7.13.3;* 351),
- `color` *(7.17.1;* 369),
- `dominant-baseline` *(7.13.5;* 374),
- `id` *(7.28.2;* 384),

- keep-with-next (*7.19.4*; 386),
- keep-with-previous (*7.19.5*; 387),
- leader-alignment (*7.21.1*; 388),
- leader-length (*7.21.4*; 388),
- leader-pattern (*7.21.2*; 388),
- leader-pattern-width (*7.21.3*; 389),
- letter-spacing (*7.16.2*; 389),
- line-height (*7.15.4*; 390),
- rule-style (*7.21.5*; 411),
- rule-thickness (*7.21.6*; 411),
- text-altitude (*7.27.4*; 421),
- text-depth (*7.27.5*; 422),
- text-shadow (*7.16.5*; 423),
- visibility (*7.28.8*; 425),
- word-spacing (*7.16.8*; 428).

Shorthands influencing the above properties

- font (*7.29.13*; 377),
- page-break-after (*7.29.16*; 401),
- page-break-before (*7.29.17*; 401),
- vertical-align (*7.29.22*; 424).

Property of note

- The line-height property of the leader does not impact the line-height property of the containing block.
  - It may be necessary to adjust the line-height property of the block to achieve the desired result.

An excerpt from Figure 5–2 is shown in Example 5–8.

Example 5–8   Leader constructs in Figure 5–2

```
Line 01  <block font-weight="bold" font-size="16pt * 2"
     02    text-align="center">The Leader/Link/Graphic Example</block>
     03
     04  <block line-height="3px">
     05    <leader leader-pattern="rule" leader-length="100%"/>
     06  </block>
     07  <block line-height="3px">
     08    <leader leader-pattern="rule" leader-length="100%"/>
     09  </block>
     10  <block>
     11    <leader leader-pattern="rule" leader-length="100%"/>
     12  </block>
     13  <block line-height="3px">
     14    <leader leader-pattern="rule" leader-length="100%"/>
     15  </block>
     16  <block line-height="3px">
     17    <leader leader-pattern="rule" leader-length="100%"/>
     18  </block>
     19  ...
     20  <block text-align-last="justify" end-indent="1cm" start-indent="1cm">
     21    <basic-link internal-destination="N9">First Title</basic-link>
     22    <leader leader-pattern="dots"/>
     23    <basic-link internal-destination="N9">
     24      <page-number-citation ref-id="N9"/>
     25    </basic-link>
     26  </block>
     27  ...
     28  <block space-before="10pt" text-align="center">
     29    <leader leader-pattern="rule" leader-length="60%"/>
     30  </block>
```

An excerpt from Figure 5–10 is shown in Example 5–9.

Example 5–9   Complex leader example

```
Line 01   <block text-align-last="justify" border-style="solid"
  02          start-indent="5cm" end-indent="5cm"
  03          text-indent="-2cm" last-line-end-indent="-2cm">
  04     <inline>This is another very long title that will be
  05   wrapping over at least three lines in order to indicate a
  06   very long title</inline>
  07     <leader leader-pattern="dots"/>
  08     <inline>2</inline>
  09   </block>
  10
  11   <block text-align-last="justify"
  12          start-indent="5cm" end-indent="5cm"
  13          text-indent="-2cm" last-line-end-indent="-2cm">
  14     <inline>This is short</inline>
  15     <leader leader-pattern="dots"/>
  16     <inline>3</inline>
  17   </block>
  18
  19   <block text-align-last="justify" text-align="justify"
  20          start-indent="5cm" end-indent="5cm"
  21          text-indent="-2cm" last-line-end-indent="-2cm">
  22     <inline>This is a final very long title that will be
  23   wrapping over at least three lines in order to indicate a
  24   very long title</inline>
  25     <leader leader-pattern="dots"/>
  26     <inline>4</inline>
  27   </block>
```

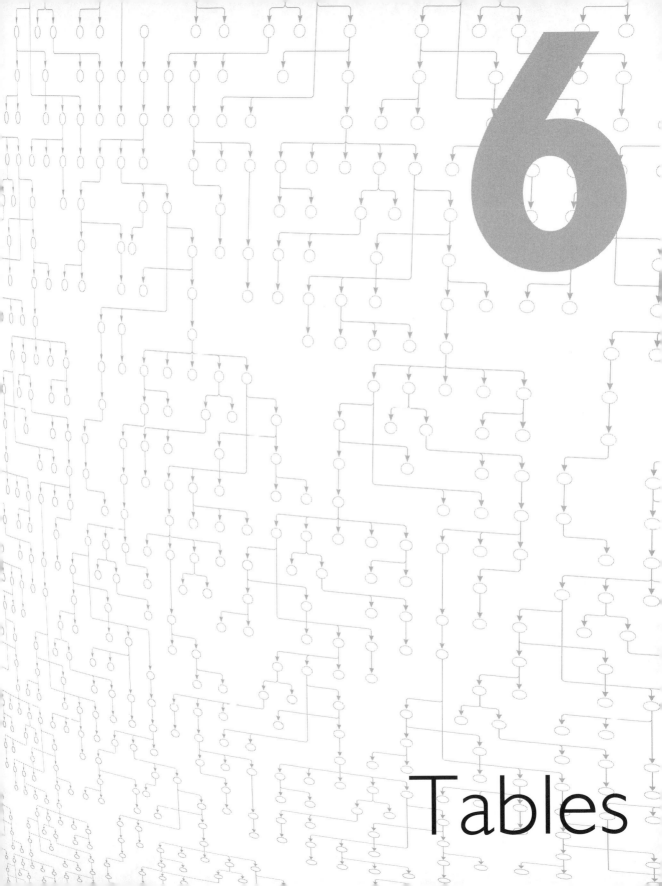

6

Tables

6 Tables

A tabular presentation can help the reader by arranging information in a rigid partitioning of groups.

These groups can be simple tuples of aligned block-level layout areas, where collections (rows) of collections (columns) of information are presented. In this case, the columns and rows are not being used as indices of a Cartesian plane. The grid is only a layout strategy. For example, when laying out columns of aligned formatted paragraphs in multiple languages, each piece of information is a standalone paragraph of a different length, thus requiring that the first lines of all translations of each paragraph be aligned.

An example of a side-by-side bilingual text presentation of an excerpt from the Canadian statute "Employment Equity Act, S.C. 1995, c. 44" is shown in Figure 6–1. Note how the numbered paragraphs are aligned at their before edges even though the lengths of the paragraphs are different.

Alternatively, the groups can be block-level layout areas in a two-dimensional relationship between members of collections. In this case, the information is in a traditional Cartesian arrangement at the intersection of indexed row and column axes.

An example of a Cartesian grid presentation of hockey standings is shown in Figure 6–2. Note how rows are spanned for the "City" and "Points" headings, and columns are spanned for the "Games" heading.

This layout facility supports numerous block-level areas arranged in the inline-progression direction, where the table contains rows (in block-progression direction) of cells (in inline-progression direction) where each cell contains block-level areas (in block-progression direction). Without such a construct, block-level areas would be arranged only in the block-progression direction.

Column widths are fixed for the length of the table. Width values can be specified in the supplied objects and properties, or they can be based on an automatic weighing of the contents of all cells of the table, as when an HTML browser balances column widths based on content.

The two layout objectives using the same layout constructs are illustrated in Figure 6–3. The page on the left shows a collection of tuples of information, where each tuple is in a row and each member of each tuple is in a column. The page on the right shows a coordinate-based layout of cells

---

Figure 6–1   English and French side-by-side tabular presentation

13. Every employer shall, at least once during the period in respect of which the short term numerical goals referred to in paragraph 10(1)(d) are established, review its employment equity plan and revise it by

(a) updating the numerical goals, taking into account the factors referred to in subsection 10 (2); and

(b) making any other changes that are necessary as a result of an assessment made pursuant to paragraph 12(b) or as a result of changing circumstances.

14. Every employer shall provide information to its employees explaining the purpose of employment equity and shall keep its employees informed about measures the employer has undertaken or is planning to undertake to implement employment equity and the progress the employer has made in implementing employment equity.

15. (1) Every employer shall consult with its employees' representatives by inviting the representatives to provide their views concerning

13. Au moins une fois au cours de la période pour laquelle les objectifs quantitatifs à court terme sont fixés, l'employeur procède à la révision de son plan en lui apportant les aménagements rendus nécessaires du fait du suivi ou du changement de sa situation et en adaptant les objectifs quantitatifs, compte tenu des facteurs visés au paragraphe 10(2).

14. L'employeur informe ses salariés sur l'objet de l'équité en matière d'emploi et leur fait part des mesures qu'il a prises ou qu'il entend prendre pour réaliser l'équité en matière d'emploi, ainsi que des progrès qu'il a accomplis dans ce domaine.

15. (1) L'employeur consulte les représentants des salariés et les invite à donner leur avis sur les questions suivantes :

of information, where the ordinate is along the columns and the abscissa is along the rows. In neither case are the heights of the individual cells constrained to be either different or the same; the layout supports any cell to be any height and will align the before edge of all cells of a given row along a common position.

Note that the column widths can differ from each other and are fixed to the same values for all rows in the entire table. As in HTML, the widths may be based on balancing of the content of the columns in all of the rows (which is the default in XSL-FO tables).

The source information needn't be modeled by a table construct, though historical use of structured information tools often forced information designers to model explicit table constructs in their structures. Such models may fail to fully capture the semantics of the information, resulting in a loss of richness and utility in the information source.

Information from any model can be presented in a tabular fashion. XSLT or any other transformation technology can be used to rearrange the source

Figure 6–2   Cartesian grid tabular presentation

Division standings - 2001-03-26
Eastern Conference

Northeast Division

City	Games					Points
	Total	Wins	Losses	Ties	OTL	
Ottawa	76	44	20	9	3	100
Buffalo	75	42	27	5	1	90
Toronto	76	34	26	11	5	84
Boston	75	31	29	8	7	77
Montreal	76	25	39	7	5	62

Atlantic Division

City	Games					Points
	Total	Wins	Losses	Ties	OTL	
New Jersey	75	42	18	12	3	99
Philadelphia	76	40	23	11	2	93
Pittsburgh	75	37	27	9	2	85
NY Rangers	75	28	41	5	1	62
NY Islanders	75	20	45	7	3	50

Southeast Division

City	Games					Points
	Total	Wins	Losses	Ties	OTL	
Washington	75	38	25	10	2	88
Carolina	75	34	30	8	3	79
Florida	76	20	35	12	9	61
Atlanta	76	22	40	12	2	58
Tampa Bay	75	23	42	6	4	56

information into the tabular relationships by expressing the information found in the source XML vocabulary into the table constructs of the XSL-FO XML vocabulary.

It is important to remember that the table is a layout construct in XSL-FO, not an information construct. A table is a block-level construct that itself continues the flow in the block-progression direction.

Tables in XSL-FO have a compound structure with many well-defined behaviors. The caption, header rows, and footer rows are constructs repeated on all pages where the table's body rows are rendered.

Column properties can be specified once for all cells that are in a given column. This is because the linear serialization of a two-dimensional construct necessarily favors one dimension over the other — cells are contained within rows, not columns, so a column-oriented construct is necessary to address the second dimension of property assignment. Column-spanning and row-spanning features provide flexible table cell definition for special needs.

Included in this chapter. This chapter includes discussion of the following XSL-FO objects:

- `table-and-caption` (*6.7.2*):
    - is the parent object of a captioned collection of tabular content,

---

Figure 6–3   Differing uses of the tabular layout construct

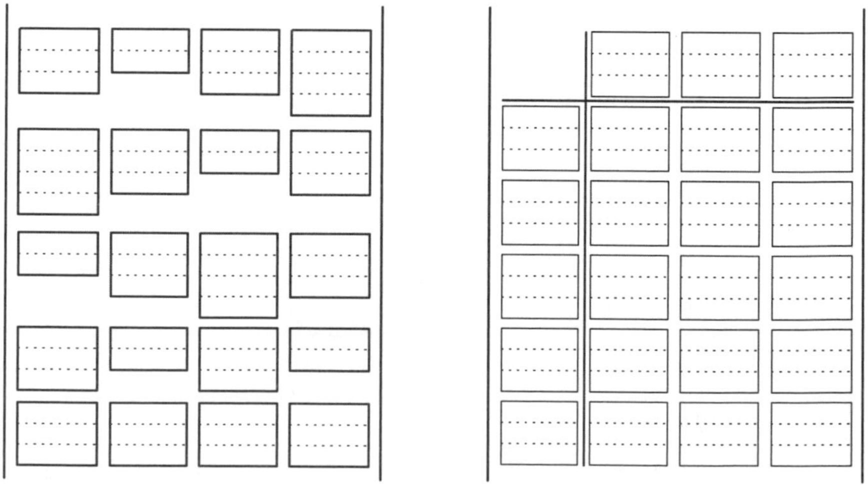

- `table-caption` (*6.7.5*):
  - is the caption of a captioned collection of tabular content,
- `table` (*6.7.3*):
  - is the parent object of an uncaptioned collection of tabular content,
- `table-column` (*6.7.4*):
  - is the specification of common columnar properties,
- `table-header` (*6.7.6*):
  - specifies rows of tabular content repeated at the before edge of every break in body content,
- `table-footer` (*6.7.7*):
  - specifies rows of tabular content repeated at the after edge of every break in body content,
- `table-body` (*6.7.8*):
  - contains rows of tabular content flowed as the body content,
- `table-row` (*6.7.9*):
  - is a row of tabular content,
- `table-cell` (*6.7.10*):
  - is a column of a row of tabular content.

6.1 Tabular structure

6.1.1 Aligned tuples of block-level constructs

Standalone blocks cannot be adjacent to each other in the inline-progression direction.

- A block-level construct typically continues the block-progression direction.

Tuples of adjacent blocks are useful for associating pieces of information, including —

- sets of one-dimensional information;
  - each row of the table is a set of information items;
  - as many rows exist as there are sets of information,
- two-dimensional information;
  - the columns represent one axis of the information;
  - the rows represent another axis of the information;
  - the cells represent the relationship between the members of each axis.

The name of the construct shouldn't prejudice how the construct is used.

- Don't think that only tables in your XML information can use this construct for layout.
- Regard the construct as a layout facility for multiple block-level constructs in the inline-progression direction of the parent block.
- For two-column tables, a list construct may suffice or offer other layout features you need.

The content of the blocks may determine the edges of the blocks.

- An auto-layout table adapts column widths to the widths of the cell contents.
  - The start and end edges of each block in a set are relative to the edges of respective members of all sets.
- The fixed-width table layout ignores the widths of the cell contents.
- Once determined, the widths of the columns are fixed for the entire table.

6.1.2   Table-related formatting objects

A table is a block-level construct.

- There are two ways to begin a table-related hierarchy.
  - `table-and-caption`:
    - lets you specify a caption that is copied to every page in which a portion of the table is presented,
  - `table`:
    - is the collection of header, footer, and body contents of the table.
- Table widths are specified as with other block-level constructs, by providing —
  - possible fixed width,
  - possible width relative to containing block,
  - possible sum of all column widths.
- There are no limitations on the location of `table` or `table-and-caption` objects in an instance.
  - Tables can be nested within table cells.
  - Tables can be positioned inline through the use of the `inline-container` object.
- Tables have the same kinds of attributes as other block-level constructs.

The indeterminate room for rows on a page necessitates special handling of page breaks.

- The transformation creating the XSL-FO instance cannot know how much of the table will fit on each page.
  - The formatter is in charge of determining where the page breaks belong.
- Body content dictates how many pages are used by the rows.
  - `table-body` (mandatory and possibly repeated):
    - contains the rows of the table that are not repeated and make up the body of the table content.

Constructs of a global nature are rendered on each page that gets table content.

- `table-caption` (optional):
  - is positioned according to the `caption-side` property,
  - is optional so that the `table-and-caption` properties can be used to align the nested `table`.
- `table-header` (optional):
  - is rendered before the before edge of the rows of the table body used on each page with table body content,
  - may be unnecessary; if the header need not be repeated, define all rows of the header once in the body before the first row of the body content.
- `table-footer` (optional):
  - is rendered after the after edge of the rows of the table body used on each page with table body content,
  - may be unnecessary; if the footer need not be repeated, define all rows of the footer once in the body after the last row of the body content.

One strategy for building rows in a header, footer, or body row group is to make everything containerized; the other strategy is to have these groups triggered by cell properties.

- The containerized strategy implies the use of `table-row` objects;
  - each one contains `table-cell` objects;
  - it supports transformation of row-related container constructs in source information;
  - this is an opportunity for row-wide inheritance of properties.
- The triggered strategy implies the use of only `table-cell` objects;
  - you'll have to use `starts-row` and `ends-row` properties;
  - this supports algorithmic breaking of cells into rows when source is not containerized;
  - properties represent conditions to be met and not actions to be performed;
    - a cell with `starts-row` following a cell with `ends-row` does not produce an empty row.

- Multiple `table-body` objects are allowed in a single table;
  - each `table-body` object allows a portion of the table to use a different row strategy;
  - each row group may be defined differently than other row groups, but a single row group can only be either containerized or triggered.

Column widths may be calculated from content.

- This requires that the table has the `table-layout` property of "auto".
- This is the initial value for the property and must be changed to get fixed layout behavior.
- Implementation-defined algorithms will not ensure the same presentation between different processors.

Table column properties are specified using `table-column`.

- This is an empty formatting object that does not generate any areas.
- The column number need not be specified if it is equal to the previous sibling specification's column number plus one.
  - The first column specification is assumed to be for column one, if the column number is not specified.
- Formatting properties in this object can be utilized by cells by explicitly using the `from-table-column()` function.

Column widths specified by `column-width` can be relative or explicit.

- It may need to be specified either way for all columns.
  - This is the case when `inline-progression-dimension` is an explicit length and the `table-layout` property is "fixed".
- A relative value can be given with a "unit" specification.
  - Each relatively sized column width is specified as a quantity of abstract units.
  - The sum of units in all unit-specified columns is the basis of a single unit's value.
  - The function `proportional-column-width(`*number-of-units*`)`:
    - returns the length value equal to the length of the number of units requested.
  - The `table-layout` must be "fixed" and the `inline-progression-dimension` cannot be "auto" (but may be "100%" to be as wide as possible).
- A fixed value can be given with a length specification.
- You can mix columns with relative and fixed specifications;
  - the relative values are calculated from the remainder of the table width after subtracting all of the fixed values.

A summary of table structures and row grouping strategies is shown in Figure 6–4.

- Thick lines indicate only those objects that can be the apex of a table structure.
- The choice of row strategy is within each sibling row group (header, footer, or body).
  - A choice for a given row group does not dictate any specific choice for the sibling row groups.

6.2 Tabular appearance

6.2.1 Table and cell borders

Table and cell borders can be visible or invisible.

- Border sides are named by writing directions.
- Visible borders can have a specified thickness, pattern, or color.
  - They can be specified for the table, table row, or table cell perimeters.
  - The formatter can have any default value for thickness if not specified by the property.

Figure 6–4   Possible table formatting object hierarchies

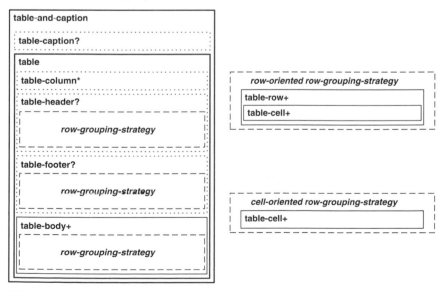

- Some border-related properties are not inherited unless explicitly specified as "inherit".

Co-incident cell and table borders can be arbitrated or separated.

- Use the border-collapse property to specify one of these behaviors.
- "collapse" (initial value) specifies the arbitration of properties based on relative values.
  - The formatter arbitrates border-width, border-style, and border-color.
    - This is summarized later in Section 9.5 on page 256.
- "collapse-with-precedence" limits arbitration to only a numeric precedence value (implied or specified).
- "separate" will separate borders of adjacent cells and cells adjacent to table borders.
  - The amount of separation is specified by the border-separation property.
- Border properties are allowed on table-row only when using collapsed borders.

Precedence guides the arbitration between two conflicting border specifications.

- Each table construct has a different initial value for border precedence;
  - 5 — table,
  - 4 — table-cell,
  - 3 — table-row,
  - 2 — table-body,
  - 1 — table-header,
  - 0 — table-footer.
- A numeric value can be explicitly specified using border-*-precedence.
- A value of "force" overrides all numeric values.

Empty cells can be treated specially.

- By default, an empty cell will have its border properties respected.
- By using empty-cells with the value of "hide" on table-cell, you can hide the border of a cell that has no content, as is typically done for HTML tables in browsers.
  - The initial value is "show" to render separated borders for empty cells.
- If all cells of a row are hidden, the row disappears entirely.

6.2.2 Spanning cells

Cells can occupy more than one column or row.

- It is useful in headers and stubs for "span heads" across multiple columns or rows.
- It is useful in body content to display a single value for multiple rows or columns.
- Spanned cells are specified using an integer count greater than or equal to 1;
  - floating values are rounded;
  - numbers less than 1 are interpreted as 1;
  - a value calculated as 1 does not do any spanning.

Cell spanning progresses towards the end and after edges, starting with the current cell —

- in the column-progression direction for column spanning —
  - using `number-columns-spanned`,
- in the row-progression direction for row spanning —
  - using `number-rows-spanned`.

Spanning rows takes away from subsequent rows' unnumbered columns.

- The cell does not exist that would be in a row except for the cell above whose spanning value affects the row.
- An unnumbered cell will "skip" over spanned cells from preceding rows.
- A numbered cell will override the spanning cells from preceding rows.

6.2.3 Table and cell alignment

Two ways to position a table in the inline-progression direction within its parent area are —

- `start-indent` on given `table`,
- `text-align` on parent `table-and-caption`;
  - the `table-caption` is optional, thus not obliging an aligned table to have a caption.

Inheritable property values will be inherited by the table cells, usually producing undesirable results.

- You could specify resetting values for properties on `table-body`, `table-header`, or other suitable ancestral location to be inheritable by descendant cells.

The content of cells can be aligned through inherited properties.

- Cell vertical alignment is specified by the `display-align` property;
  - its default value is "`auto`".
- Cell row alignment is specified by the `relative-align` property;
  - its default value is "`before`".
  - You may want to use "`baseline`" if fonts of different sizes are used.
  - This only applies if `display-align` is "`auto`".
- Cell column alignment is specified by the individual blocks' `text-align` properties.
  - This is the only significant use of a string argument for `text-align`.
    - For example, you can use the decimal separator character as the string to align a column of cells with financial information vertically.
    - A string argument in the property used in any other context is interpreted as the value "`start`".
  - It need not be specified in the cell object (though it could be specified to be inherited by blocks).

6.2.4   The table-and-caption object

Purpose

- This is the parent object of a captioned collection of tabular content.

Content

- (*6.7.2*) (`table-caption?, table`),
- child objects (listed alphabetically):
  - `table-caption` (*6.7.5*; 172),
  - `table` (*6.7.3*; 173),
- any number of `marker` children at the beginning.

Property sets

- Common accessibility properties (*7.4*; 326),
- common aural properties (*7.6*; 327),
- common border, padding, and background properties (*7.7*; 328),
- common margin properties — block (*7.10*; 332),
- common relative position properties (*7.12*; 333).

Other optional properties

- break-after (*7.19.1*; 366),
- break-before (*7.19.2*; 367),
- caption-side (*7.26.7*; 367),
- id (*7.28.2*; 384),
- intrusion-displace (*7.18.3*; 385),
- keep-together (*7.19.3*; 386),
- keep-with-next (*7.19.4*; 386),
- keep-with-previous (*7.19.5*; 387),
- text-align (*7.15.9*; 421).

Shorthands influencing the above properties

- page-break-after (*7.29.16*; 401),
- page-break-before (*7.29.17*; 401),
- page-break-inside (*7.29.18*; 402).

Property of interest

- text-align is used to align the table.
  - This is the only non-mathematical way of aligning a table within its parent area.

An example is shown in Figure 6–5.

Figure 6–5   Table constructs

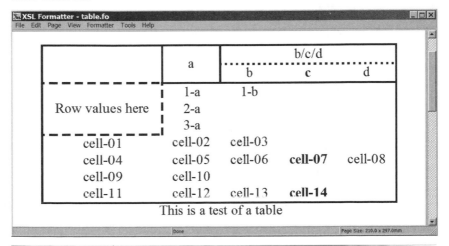

Note in the example:

- the table has adjacent body segments whose boundaries cannot be distinguished;
- all the cells in the column with the "c" heading are bold;
- the caption follows after the table.

An excerpt from Figure 6–5 is shown in Example 6–1.

Example 6–1   The use of `table-and-caption` object in Figure 6–5

```
Line 01  <table-and-caption caption-side="after">
02         <table-caption>
03           <block text-align="center">This is a test of a table</block>
04         </table-caption>
05         <table border="solid" border-collapse="collapse">
06           ...
07           <table-header>
08             ...
09           </table-header>
10           <table-body>
11             ...
12           </table-body>
13           <table-body text-align="center">
14             ...
15           </table-body>
16         </table>
17       </table-and-caption>
```

6.2.5 The table-caption object

Purpose

- This is the caption of a captioned collection of tabular content.

Content

- (*6.7.5*) (`%block;`)+,
- child object:
  - `%block;` (*6.2*; 69),
- referring object:
  - `table-and-caption` (*6.7.2*; 170),
- any number of `marker` children at the beginning.

Property sets

- Common accessibility properties (*7.4*; 326),
- common aural properties (*7.6*; 327),
- common border, padding, and background properties (*7.7*; 328),
- common relative position properties (*7.12*; 333).

Other optional properties

- `block-progression-dimension` (*7.14.1*; 352),
- `height` (*7.14.4*; 382),
- `id` (*7.28.2*; 384),
- `inline-progression-dimension` (*7.14.5*; 385),
- `intrusion-displace` (*7.18.3*; 385),
- `keep-together` (*7.19.3*; 386),
- `width` (*7.14.12*; 428).

Shorthand influencing the above properties

- `page-break-inside` (*7.29.18*; 402).

Properties of interest

- `caption-side` indicates where the caption is relative to the table.

Properties of descendent blocks within the caption block

- `text-align` is used to align the caption content.
- The typical CSS use of `vertical-align` does not apply.

An excerpt from Figure 6–5 is shown in Example 6–2.

6.2.6 The table object

Purpose

- This is the parent object of an uncaptioned collection of tabular content.

Content

- (*6.7.3*) (`table-column*`, `table-header?`, `table-footer?`, `table-body+`),
- child objects (listed alphabetically):
  - `table-body` (*6.7.8*; 180),
  - `table-column` (*6.7.4*; 176),

Example 6–2   The use of `table-caption` object in Figure 6–5

```
Line 01  <table-and-caption caption-side="after">
     02    <table-caption>
     03      <block text-align="center">This is a test of a table</block>
     04    </table-caption>
     05    <table border="solid" border-collapse="collapse">
     06      ...
     07      <table-header>
     08        ...
     09      </table-header>
     10      <table-body>
     11        ...
     12      </table-body>
     13      <table-body text-align="center">
     14        ...
     15      </table-body>
     16    </table>
     17  </table-and-caption>
```

- table-footer (*6.7.7*; 178),
- table-header (*6.7.6*; 177),
- referring object:
  - table-and-caption (*6.7.2*; 170),
- any number of marker children at the beginning.

Property sets

- Common accessibility properties (*7.4*; 326),
- common aural properties (*7.6*; 327),
- common border, padding, and background properties (*7.7*; 328),
- common margin properties — block (*7.10*; 332),
- common relative position properties (*7.12*; 333).

Other optional properties

- block-progression-dimension (*7.14.1*; 352),
- border-after-precedence (*7.26.1*; 353),
- border-before-precedence (*7.26.2*; 354),
- border-collapse (*7.26.3*; 357),
- border-end-precedence (*7.26.4*; 358),
- border-separation (*7.26.5*; 362),
- border-start-precedence (*7.26.6*; 363),

- break-after (*7.19.1*; 366),
- break-before (*7.19.2*; 367),
- height (*7.14.4*; 382),
- id (*7.28.2*; 384),
- inline-progression-dimension (*7.14.5*; 385),
- intrusion-displace (*7.18.3*; 385),
- keep-together (*7.19.3*; 386),
- keep-with-next (*7.19.4*; 386),
- keep-with-previous (*7.19.5*; 387),
- table-layout (*7.26.16*; 419),
- table-omit-footer-at-break (*7.26.17*; 419),
- table-omit-header-at-break (*7.26.18*; 419),
- width (*7.14.12*; 428),
- writing-mode (*7.27.7*; 429).

Shorthands influencing the above properties

- border-spacing (*7.29.9*; 362),
- page-break-after (*7.29.16*; 401),
- page-break-before (*7.29.17*; 401),
- page-break-inside (*7.29.18*; 402).

An excerpt from Figure 6–5 is shown in Example 6–3.

Example 6–3   The use of table object in Figure 6–5

```
Line 01  <table-and-caption caption-side="after">
     02    <table-caption>
     03      <block text-align="center">This is a test of a table</block>
     04    </table-caption>
     05    <table border="solid" border-collapse="collapse">
     06      ...
     07      <table-header>
     08        ...
     09      </table-header>
     10      <table-body>
     11        ...
     12      </table-body>
     13      <table-body text-align="center">
     14        ...
     15      </table-body>
     16    </table>
     17  </table-and-caption>
```

6.2.7 The table-column object

Purpose

- This is the specification of common columnar properties.

Content

- (*6.7.4*) EMPTY,
- referring object:
  - table (*6.7.3*; 173).

Property sets

- Common border, padding, and background properties (*7.7*; 328).

Other optional properties

- border-after-precedence (*7.26.1*; 353),
- border-before-precedence (*7.26.2*; 354),
- border-end-precedence (*7.26.4*; 358),
- border-start-precedence (*7.26.6*; 363),
- column-number (*7.26.8*; 370),
- column-width (*7.26.9*; 370),
- number-columns-repeated (*7.26.12*; 396),
- number-columns-spanned (*7.26.13*; 396),
- visibility (*7.28.8*; 425).

Property of interest

- column-width="proportional-column-width(*number-of-units*)":
  - is calculated as a unit proportion of calculated table width less all specified column widths.
- Inheritable properties specified here are not automatically inherited by cells of the column.
  - The cells are not descendants of this object in the formatting object tree during refinement.
  - Cells must use the from-table-column() function to find out the table column properties.

An excerpt from Figure 6–5 is shown in Example 6–4.

Example 6–4   The use of `table-column` object in Figure 6–5

```
Line 01  <table-and-caption caption-side="after">
   02      <table-caption>
   03        <block text-align="center">This is a test of a table</block>
   04      </table-caption>
   05
   06      <table border="solid" border-collapse="collapse">
   07        <table-column column-width="proportional-column-width(2)"/>
   08        <table-column column-width="proportional-column-width(1)"/>
   09        <table-column column-width="proportional-column-width(1)"/>
   10        <table-column column-width="proportional-column-width(1)"
   11                      font-weight="bold"/>
   12        <table-column column-width="proportional-column-width(1)"/>
   13
   14      <table-header>
   15         ...
   16      </table-header>
   17      <table-body>
   18         ...
   19      </table-body>
   20      <table-body text-align="center">
   21         ...
   22        <table-cell font-weight="from-table-column(font-weight)">
   23          <block>cell-06</block></table-cell>
   24
   25        <table-cell font-weight="from-table-column(font-weight)">
   26          <block>cell-07</block></table-cell>
   27        <table-cell font-weight="from-table-column(font-weight)"
   28                    ends-row="true">
   29          <block>cell-08</block></table-cell>
   30         ...
   31      </table-body>
   32     </table>
   33  </table-and-caption>
```

6.2.8   The table-header object

Purpose

- This object contains rows of tabular content that are repeated at the before edge of every break in body content.
- You must choose one row grouping strategy for the entire header.

Content

- (*6.7.6*) `(table-row+ | table-cell+),`

- child objects (listed alphabetically):
    - `table-cell` (*6.7.10*; 184),
    - `table-row` (*6.7.9*; 182),
- referring object:
    - `table` (*6.7.3*; 173),
- any number of `marker` children at the beginning.

Property sets

- Common accessibility properties (*7.4*; 326),
- common aural properties (*7.6*; 327),
- common border, padding, and background properties (*7.7*; 328),
- common relative position properties (*7.12*; 333).

Other optional properties

- `border-after-precedence` (*7.26.1*; 353),
- `border-before-precedence` (*7.26.2*; 354),
- `border-end-precedence` (*7.26.4*; 358),
- `border-start-precedence` (*7.26.6*; 363),
- `id` (*7.28.2*; 384),
- `visibility` (*7.28.8*; 425).

An excerpt from Figure 6–5 is shown in Example 6–5.

6.2.9   The table-footer object

Purpose

- This object contains rows of tabular content that are repeated at the after edge of every break in body content.
- You must choose one row grouping strategy for the entire footer.

Content

- (*6.7.7*) (`table-row+` | `table-cell+`),
- child objects (listed alphabetically):
    - `table-cell` (*6.7.10*; 184),
    - `table-row` (*6.7.9*; 182),
- referring object:
    - `table` (*6.7.3*; 173),
- any number of `marker` children at the beginning.

Example 6–5   The use of `table-header` object in Figure 6–5

```
Line 01  <table-and-caption caption-side="after">
  02       <table-caption>
  03         <block text-align="center">This is a test of a table</block>
  04       </table-caption>
  05       <table border="solid" border-collapse="collapse">
  06         ...
  07         <table-header>
  08           <table-row>
  09             ...
  10           </table-row>
  11           <table-row>
  12             ...
  13           </table-row>
  14         </table-header>
  15         <table-body>
  16           <table-row text-align="center">
  17           ...
  18           <table-row text-align="center">
  19           ...
  20         </table-body>
  21         <table-body text-align="center">
  22           <table-cell font-weight="from-table-column(font-weight)">
  23             <block>cell-01</block></table-cell>
  24           ...
  25           <table-cell font-weight="from-table-column(font-weight)">
  26             <block>cell-14</block></table-cell>
  27         </table-body>
  28       </table>
  29  </table and caption>
```

Property sets

- Common accessibility properties (*7.4*; 326),
- common aural properties (*7.6*; 327),
- common border, padding, and background properties (*7.7*; 328),
- common relative position properties (*7.12*; 333).

Other optional properties

- `border-after-precedence` (*7.26.1*; 353),
- `border-before-precedence` (*7.26.2*; 354),
- `border-end-precedence` (*7.26.4*; 358),
- `border-start-precedence` (*7.26.6*; 363),

- id (*7.28.2*; 384),
- visibility (*7.28.8*; 425).

6.2.10 The table-body object

Purpose

- This object contains the rows of tabular content that are flowed as the body content.
- You must choose one row grouping strategy for each set of body rows.
    - Different sets of body rows may use different strategies.
    - The boundaries between sets of body rows are seamless.

Content

- (*6.7.8*) (table-row+ | table-cell+),
- child objects (listed alphabetically):
    - table-cell (*6.7.10*; 184),
    - table-row (*6.7.9*; 182),
- referring object:
    - table (*6.7.3*; 173),
- any number of marker children at the beginning.

Property sets

- Common accessibility properties (*7.4*; 326),
- common aural properties (*7.6*; 327),
- common border, padding, and background properties (*7.7*; 328),
- common relative position properties (*7.12*; 333).

Other optional properties

- border-after-precedence (*7.26.1*; 353),
- border-before-precedence (*7.26.2*; 354),
- border-end-precedence (*7.26.4*; 358),
- border-start-precedence (*7.26.6*; 363),
- id (*7.28.2*; 384),
- visibility (*7.28.8*; 425).

An excerpt from Figure 6–5 is shown in Example 6–6.

Example 6–6   The use of `table-body` object in Figure 6–5

```
Line 01  <table border="solid" border-collapse="collapse">
  02       ...
  03       <table-header>
  04         ...
  05       </table-header>
  06       <table-body>
  07         <table-row text-align="center">
  08           ...
  09         </table-row>
  10         <table-row text-align="center">
  11           <table-cell font-weight="from-table-column(font-weight)">
  12             <block>2-a</block></table-cell>
  13         </table-row>
  14         <table-row text-align="center">
  15           <table-cell font-weight="from-table-column(font-weight)">
  16             <block>3-a</block></table-cell>
  17         </table-row>
  18       </table-body>
  19       <table-body text-align="center">
  20         <table-cell font-weight="from-table-column(font-weight)">
  21           <block>cell-01</block></table-cell>
  22         ...
  23         <table-cell font-weight="from-table-column(font-weight)"
  24                     starts-row="true">
  25           <block>cell-04</block></table-cell>
  26         ...
  27         <table-cell font-weight="from-table-column(font-weight)"
  28                     ends-row="true">
  29           <block>cell-08</block></table-cell>
  30         ...
  31         <table-cell font-weight="from-table-column(font-weight)"
  32                     starts-row="true">
  33           <block>cell-11</block></table-cell>
  34         <table-cell font-weight="from-table-column(font-weight)">
  35           <block>cell-12</block></table-cell>
  36       </table-body>
  37     </table>
```

Note in the example:

- the first set of body rows is using the row-based row grouping strategy;
- the second set of body rows is using the cell-based row grouping strategy.

6.2.11   The table-row object

Purpose

- This is a row of tabular content.

Content

- (*6.7.9*) (table-cell+),
- child object:
    - table-cell (*6.7.10*; 184),
- referring objects:
    - table-header (*6.7.6*; 177),
    - table-footer (*6.7.7*; 178),
    - table-body (*6.7.8*; 180).

Property sets

- Common accessibility properties (*7.4*; 326),
- common aural properties (*7.6*; 327),
- common border, padding, and background properties (*7.7*; 328),
- common relative position properties (*7.12*; 333).

Other optional properties

- block-progression-dimension (*7.14.1*; 352),
- border-after-precedence (*7.26.1*; 353),
- border-before-precedence (*7.26.2*; 354),
- border-end-precedence (*7.26.4*; 358),
- border-start-precedence (*7.26.6*; 363),
- break-after (*7.19.1*; 366),
- break-before (*7.19.2*; 367),
- height (*7.14.4*; 382),
- id (*7.28.2*; 384),
- keep-together (*7.19.3*; 386),
- keep-with-next (*7.19.4*; 386),
- keep-with-previous (*7.19.5*; 387),
- visibility (*7.28.8*; 425).

Shorthands influencing the above properties

- page-break-after (*7.29.16*; 401),

- page-break-before (*7.29.17*; 401),
- page-break-inside (*7.29.18*; 402).

An excerpt from Figure 6–5 is shown in Example 6–7.

Example 6–7   The use of table-row object in Figure 6–5

```
Line 01  <table-and-caption caption-side="after">
     02    <table-caption>
     03      <block text-align="center">This is a test of a table</block>
     04    </table-caption>
     05    <table border="solid" border-collapse="collapse">
     06      ...
     07    <table-header>
     08      <table-row>
     09        <table-cell number-rows-spanned="2">
     10          ...
     11      </table-row>
     12      <table-row>
     13        <table-cell border-before-style="dotted"
     14                    border-after-style="solid">
     15          ...
     16      </table-row>
     17    </table-header>
     18    <table-body>
     19      <table-row text-align="center">
     20          ...
     21      </table-row>
     22
     23      <table-row text-align="center">
     24        <table cell font-weight="from-table-column(font-weight)">
     25          <block>2-a</block></table-cell>
     26      </table-row>
     27      <table-row text-align="center">
     28        <table-cell font-weight="from-table-column(font-weight)">
     29          <block>3-a</block></table-cell>
     30      </table-row>
     31    </table-body>
     32    <table-body text-align="center">
     33      <table-cell font-weight="from-table-column(font-weight)">
     34        <block>cell-01</block></table-cell>
     35        ...
     36      <table-cell font-weight="from-table-column(font-weight)">
     37        <block>cell-14</block></table-cell>
     38    </table-body>
     39    </table>
     40  </table-and-caption>
```

6.2.12 The table-cell object

Purpose

- This is a column of a row of tabular content.

Content

- (*6.7.10*) (%block;)+,
- child object:
    - %block; (*6.2*; 69),
- referring objects:
    - table-header (*6.7.6*; 177),
    - table-footer (*6.7.7*; 178),
    - table-body (*6.7.8*; 180),
    - table-row (*6.7.9*; 182),
- any number of marker children at the beginning.

Property sets

- Common accessibility properties (*7.4*; 326),
- common aural properties (*7.6*; 327),
- common border, padding, and background properties (*7.7*; 328),
- common relative position properties (*7.12*; 333).

Other optional properties

- block-progression-dimension (*7.14.1*; 352),
- border-after-precedence (*7.26.1*; 353),
- border-before-precedence (*7.26.2*; 354),
- border-end-precedence (*7.26.4*; 358),
- border-start-precedence (*7.26.6*; 363),
- column-number (*7.26.8*; 370),
- display-align (*7.13.4*; 373),
- empty-cells (*7.26.10*; 374),
- ends-row (*7.26.11*; 375),
- height (*7.14.4*; 382),
- id (*7.28.2*; 384),
- inline-progression-dimension (*7.14.5*; 385),
- number-columns-spanned (*7.26.13*; 396),
- number-rows-spanned (*7.26.14*; 396),

- relative-align (*7.13.6*; 408),
- starts-row (*7.26.15*; 418),
- width (*7.14.12*; 428).

Example 6–8   The use of table-cell object in Figure 6–5

```
Line 01  <table-and-caption caption-side="after">
02       ...
03         <table-header>
04           <table-row>
05             <table-cell font-weight="from-table-column(font-weight)"
06                         number-rows-spanned="2">
07               <block/>
08             </table-cell>
09             <table-cell font-weight="from-table-column(font-weight)"
10                         number-rows-spanned="2" border="solid"
11                         display-align="center">
12               <block text-align="center">a</block>
13             </table-cell>
14             <table-cell font-weight="from-table-column(font-weight)"
15                         number-columns-spanned="3">
16               <block text-align="center">b/c/d</block>
17             </table-cell>
18           </table-row>
19           ...
20         </table-header>
21         <table-body>
22           <table-row text-align="center">
23             <table-cell font-weight="from-table-column(font-weight)"
24                         number-rows-spanned="3" border="dashed"
25                         display-align="center">
26               <block>Row values here</block>
27             </table-cell>
28             <table-cell font-weight="from-table-column(font-weight)">
29               <block>1-a</block></table-cell>
30             <table-cell font-weight="from-table-column(font-weight)">
31               <block>1-b</block></table-cell>
32           </table-row>
33           <table-row text-align="center">
34             <table-cell font-weight="from-table-column(font-weight)">
35               <block>2-a</block></table-cell>
36           </table-row>
37           <table-row text-align="center">
38             <table-cell font-weight="from-table-column(font-weight)">
39               <block>3-a</block></table-cell>
40           </table-row>
41         </table-body>
```

Excerpts from Figure 6–5 in Examples 6–8 and 6–9 show, respectively, the use of the row-based and cell-based row grouping strategies.

Example 6–9	The use of `table-cell` object in Figure 6–5

```
Line 01   <table-and-caption caption-side="after">
02     ...
03       <table-body text-align="center">
04       <table-cell font-weight="from-table-column(font-weight)">
05         <block>cell-01</block></table-cell>
06       <table-cell font-weight="from-table-column(font-weight)">
07         <block>cell-02</block></table-cell>
08       <table-cell font-weight="from-table-column(font-weight)">
09         <block>cell-03</block></table-cell>
10       <table-cell font-weight="from-table-column(font-weight)"
11                 starts-row="true">
12         <block>cell-04</block></table-cell>
13       <table-cell font-weight="from-table-column(font-weight)">
14         <block>cell-05</block></table-cell>
15       <table-cell font-weight="from-table-column(font-weight)">
16         <block>cell-06</block></table-cell>
17       <table-cell font-weight="from-table-column(font-weight)">
18         <block>cell-07</block></table-cell>
19       <table-cell font-weight="from-table-column(font-weight)"
20                 ends-row="true">
21         <block>cell-08</block></table-cell>
22       <table-cell font-weight="from-table-column(font-weight)">
23         <block>cell-09</block></table-cell>
24       <table-cell font-weight="from-table-column(font-weight)">
25         <block>cell-10</block></table-cell>
26       <table-cell font-weight="from-table-column(font-weight)"
27                 starts-row="true">
28         <block>cell-11</block></table-cell>
29       <table-cell font-weight="from-table-column(font-weight)">
30         <block>cell-12</block></table-cell>
31       <table-cell font-weight="from-table-column(font-weight)">
32         <block>cell-13</block></table-cell>
33       <table-cell font-weight="from-table-column(font-weight)">
34         <block>cell-14</block></table-cell>
35       </table-body>
36     </table>
37   </table-and-caption>
```

7

Static content
and
page geometry
sequencing

7 Static content and page geometry sequencing

A screen-based web browser user agent can accommodate a non-predetermined amount of information on a web page by flowing the content in an elastic window of practically infinite length. A paginated presentation is very different, in that bounded areas (the pages) repeat to accommodate a non-predetermined amount of information (the flow). This pagination concept differentiates XSL-FO semantics from traditional web browser display semantics, including the inherent HTML display semantics and those of CSS. The complete collection of pages, split into separate sequences of pages, is used as an entity for reading the information, just as a complete web browser window is used as an entity.

Static content. Static content is distinguished from flowed content in that while the flowed content triggers new pages, the static content is what is copied on each new page triggered by the flow. The flow never repeats automatically, but the static content is designed to be repeated on pages in a page sequence.

The pages in the collection need navigational aids repeated on each page that are necessarily different from the navigational aids on a browser screen. These aids are used by the reader to understand a page's role when not in the context of neighboring pages. Such aids include, among other constructs, the page number, page number citations, headers and footers, and directly cited information found in the content formatted on the page.

The page number gives a focus to the specific bounded area of a portion of the information being flowed. It is used on a given page for navigation purposes and used on other pages for citations to the given page. These citations might be cross references or index information.

Headers and footers provide contextual information about a collection of pages in which the given page is found. For example, the chapter title could be repeated in each header of the page. The footer could include a total page count reflecting information about the entire production and not just the page sequence.

Cited information found from the page being formatted can be contextual information useful for navigation. This information would not be known about a page by the stylesheet at the time of transformation. It is the act of pagination that dictates the page boundaries, not the act of processing the source information, thus the stylesheet writer doesn't know a priori what information belongs in a given page's header and footer. Two examples of information drawn from the flow itself into the static content are dictionary headers (where one needs to find one of many items on a page) and subsection citations (where one needs to find breaks in the information that are not triggering new page sequences).

Every page sequence has its own definitions for static content, and it is the stylesheet writer's responsibility to supply all candidate uses that might be required in each sequence. It is usually the case that the generation of information (e.g. using an XSLT stylesheet) cannot accurately predict the pages where pagination of that information will position different areas. If the same behavior is desired in some or all of the page sequences, it is the stylesheet writer's responsibility to repeat the content in each sequence where it might be needed. Citing the dynamic content in the static content allows one to modify headers and footers without forcing the new page that is triggered at the beginning.

Static content is associated with the name of a page region, not with a particular region's position. This is sometimes confusing to the stylesheet writer, as the writer must organize the region names in each page geometry and then bind, in each page sequence, the static content to the named regions. It is not an error to supply static content for a named region that isn't being used on a given page geometry or even that isn't being used on any page geometry referenced by a sequence of pages. Static content can also be defined for named sub-regions that are triggered by the formatter.

Page sequencing.   Differences in page geometry are allowed from page to page when more than one page is being rendered in a sequence of pages. The tests for differences are performed within each page sequence construct's flow. These differences can be changes in the dimensions of the page, the choices of the regions and their names and margins, the presence or selection of headers and/or footers, the column count, etc.

One can describe a sequence with odd and even page number differences to implement features such as alternating headers and footers. Two different static contents are defined with the page number to be rendered on the outside edge of each side of a bound publication. Differences in headers and footers of the geometries alternate the names of the flows for the static content between odd and even numbered pages. The page geometry for each of the two kinds of page can have different region names, then the static content for each presentation of the page number can be assigned to each of the two region names.

One can describe a sequence of pages with first, last, and middle page differences, for example to have no heading on the first page of a chapter sequence.

One can describe a sequence to replace absent content for forced un-flowed pages. When forcing a particular number of pages, there may be insufficient flow to fit on the last page of the sequence. Such pages are commonly seen with a "this page is intentionally left blank" banner.

Consider the choreography in each of two possible page plans for a set of chapters, as shown in Figure 7–1. Here, the plan on the left does not accommodate the parity of pages, but the plan on the right has differences for even and odd pages, typically formatted in Western European publications as, respectively, the left-hand and right-hand sides of an open book.

A single-sided presentation is shown on the left with all page sequences consecutive, so that no pages are found between the TOC and the chapters. The document title is centered at the top of document content pages (but not the TOC), and the page number and total page count centered at the bottom of all pages.

A double-sided presentation is shown on the right with contents of the TOC and the first chapter each starting on a right-hand page. This requires the page sequence for the table of contents to have an even number of pages, regardless of the amount of flow occupying the sequence, thus perhaps needing a forced page. The document title is at the bottom left of odd pages and the bottom right of even pages. The chapter title is at the top right of odd pages and the top left of even pages. The page number and total page count are centered at the bottom of all pages.

Figure 7–1   Page sequence and static content planning

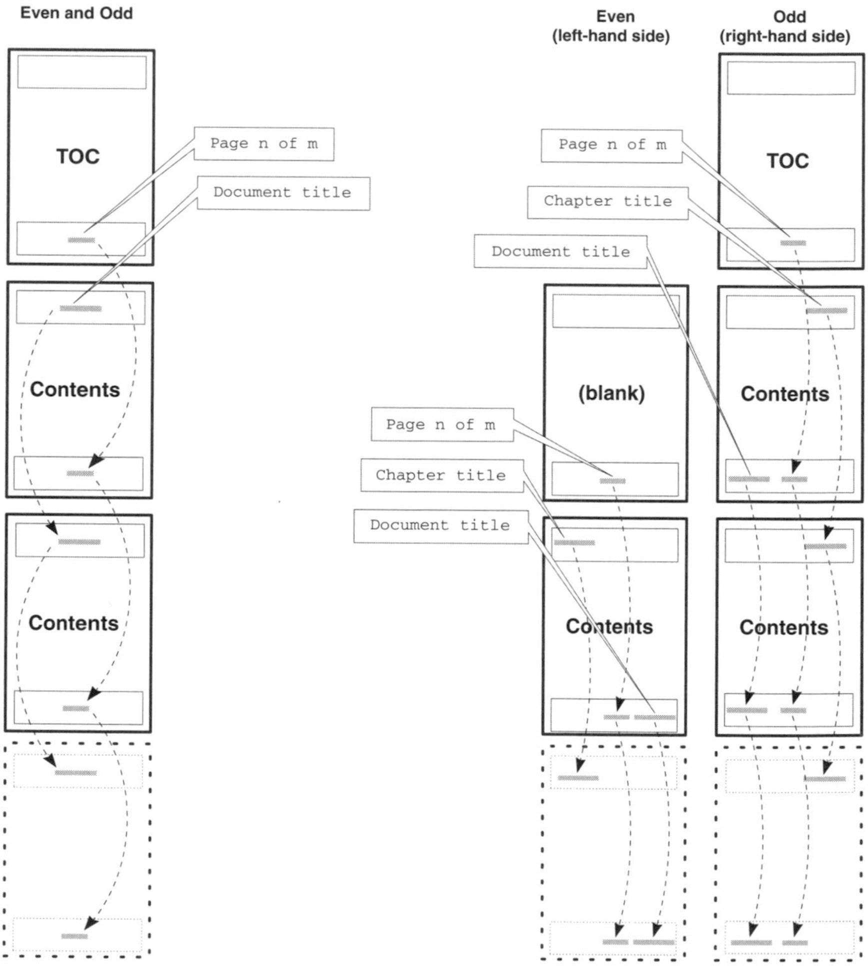

Successful choreography requires a lot of planning ahead by the stylesheet writer in order to ensure that all possible formatting situations have contingencies in the stylesheet to accommodate the desired result.

Included in this chapter. This chapter includes discussion of the following XSL-FO objects.

Formatting objects related to static content:

- `region-before` (*6.4.14*):
    - is the definition of the body region perimeter area whose before edge is co-incident with the before edge of the page's content rectangle;
        - in the `lr-tb` mode, this is the header at the top of the page,
- `region-after` (*6.4.15*):
    - is the definition of the body region perimeter area whose after edge is co-incident with the after edge of the page's content rectangle;
        - in the `lr-tb` mode, this is the footer at the bottom of the page,
- `region-start` (*6.4.16*):
    - is the definition of the body region perimeter area whose start edge is co-incident with the start edge of the page's content rectangle;
        - in the `lr-tb` mode, this is the sidebar at the left of the page,
- `region-end` (*6.4.17*):
    - is the definition of the body region perimeter area whose end edge is co-incident with the end edge of the page's content rectangle;
        - in the `lr-tb` mode, this is the sidebar at the right of the page,
- `static-content` (*6.4.19*):
    - is the definition of content that is primarily unchanged from page to page in a page sequence;
        - entire sequence is repeated on each page except for page numbers and user-defined markers,
- `page-number` (*6.6.10*):
    - is an inline-level placeholder replaced with the page number of the current page,
- `retrieve-marker` (*6.11.4*):
    - is an inline-level placeholder replaced with the formatting objects of the indicated marker,
- `marker` (*6.11.3*):
    - is the replacement formatting object content for a marker retrieved in static content.

Formatting objects related to page geometry sequencing:

- `page-sequence-master` (*6.4.7*):
  - is the definition and name of a particular sequence of using page masters,
- `single-page-master-reference` (*6.4.8*):
  - is the specification of the single use of a page master within a sequence of page masters,
- `repeatable-page-master-reference` (*6.4.9*):
  - is the specification of the repeated use of a page master within a sequence of page masters,
- `repeatable-page-master-alternatives` (*6.4.10*):
  - is the collection of possible page-master references from which one is to be used based on status conditions detected by the formatter,
- `conditional-page-master-reference` (*6.4.11*):
  - is a page-master choice available to the formatter when selecting from a collection of candidate page masters.

7.1   Page regions, headers, and footers

7.1.1   Region dimensions

Page definition is slightly different from region definitions.

- The page reference edges are top, bottom, left, and right relative to the physical medium.
  - Region reference edges are relative to the reference orientation.
- The page's viewport area is larger than the page's reference area.
  - A region's viewport area is equal to the region's reference area.

The perimeter region incursions must be accommodated explicitly by the body region, as shown in Figure 7–2.

- The incursion is illustrated in Figure 4–2.
  - Precedence determines which perimeter region occupies the before or after pairs of corners of a page.
  - The default is to keep before/after region boundaries between start/end regions.
- You must move the border of body region within extents of perimeter regions for the border not to interfere.
  - This is not automatic and may result in overwritten content if not accommodated.
- Neither the page nor regions have border or padding rectangles.
  - In future versions of XSL-FO, they may have border and padding.

7.1.2 The region-before object

Purpose

- This is the definition of the perimeter area whose before edge is co-incident with the before edge of the page's content rectangle.

Content

- (*6.4.14*) EMPTY,
- referring object:
    - simple-page-master (*6.4.12*; 114).

Property sets

- Common border, padding, and background properties (*7.7*; 328).

Other required property

- region-name (*7.25.17*; 407).

Other optional properties

- clip (*7.20.1*; 368),
- display-align (*7.13.4*; 373),
- extent (*7.25.4*; 375),
- overflow (*7.20.2*; 397),
- precedence (*7.25.16*; 406),
- reference-orientation (*7.20.3*; 407),
- writing-mode (*7.27.7*; 429).

Figure 7–2   Incursion of perimeter regions into the body region

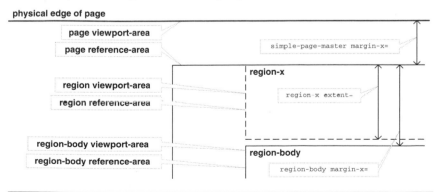

Properties of note

- The `region-name` property is required, but the default name of "xsl-region-before" is used for this property if a name is not supplied in the XSL-FO instance.

- `precedence` defaults to "false" indicating that the before region does not override the start and end regions, but can be changed to "true" to stretch the region to the content rectangle of the page reference area.

- Even though `padding` and `border-width` properties are indicated as available indirectly through the common property set, these values are fixed at "0pt" in XSL-FO 1.0.

- `display-align` is used to keep the information in the region snug against the before edge, snug against the after edge, or centered in the middle of the two in the block-progression direction.

Excerpts from a draft of a training rendition of this material are shown in Example 7–1.

Example 7–1   Regions on a page

```
Line 01  <layout-master-set>
02    <simple-page-master master-name="frame-left"
03      page-height="11in" page-width="8.5in"
04      margin-top=".45in - .3in" margin-bottom=".45in - .3in"
05      margin-left=".6in" margin-right=".6in">
06      <region-body region-name="pages-body"
07        margin-top=".3in" margin-bottom=".3in"/>
08      <region-before extent=".3in" region-name="pages-before"/>
09      <region-after extent=".3in" region-name="pages-after-left"/>
10    </simple-page-master>
11    <simple-page-master master-name="frame-right"
12      page-height="11in" page-width="8.5in"
13      margin-top=".45in - .3in" margin-bottom=".45in - .3in"
14      margin-left=".6in" margin-right=".6in">
15      <region-body region-name="pages-body"
16        margin-top=".3in" margin-bottom=".3in"/>
17      <region-before extent=".3in" region-name="pages-before"/>
18      <region-after extent=".3in" region-name="pages-after-right"/>
19    </simple-page-master>
20    ...
```

7.1.3 The region-after object

Purpose

- This is the definition of the perimeter area whose after edge is co-incident with the after edge of the page's content rectangle.

Content

- (*6.4.15*) `EMPTY`,
- referring object:
  - `simple-page-master` (*6.4.12*; 114).

Property sets

- Common border, padding, and background properties (*7.7*; 328).

Other required property

- `region-name` (*7.25.17*; 407).

Other optional properties

- `clip` (*7.20.1*; 368),
- `display-align` (*7.13.4*; 373),
- `extent` (*7.25.4*; 375),
- `overflow` (*7.20.2*; 397),
- `precedence` (*7.25.16*; 406),
- `reference-orientation` (*7.20.3*; 407),
- `writing-mode` (*7.27.7*; 429).

Properties of note

- The `region-name` property is required, but the default name of "`xsl-region-after`" is used for this property if a name is not supplied in the XSL-FO instance.
- `precedence` defaults to "`false`" indicating the after region does not override the start and end regions, but can be changed to "`true`" to stretch the region to the content rectangle of the page reference area.
- Even though `padding` and `border-width` properties are indicated as available indirectly through the common property set, these values are fixed at "`0pt`" in XSL-FO 1.0.

- display-align is used to keep the information in the region snug against the before edge, snug against the after edge, or centered in the middle of the two in the block-progression direction.

7.1.4 The region-start object

Purpose

- This is the definition of the perimeter area whose start edge is co-incident with the start edge of the page's content rectangle.

Content

- (*6.4.16*) EMPTY,
- referring object:
  - simple-page-master (*6.4.12*; 114).

Property sets

- Common border, padding, and background properties (*7.7*; 328).

Other required property

- region-name (*7.25.17*; 407).

Other optional properties

- clip (*7.20.1*; 368),
- display-align (*7.13.4*; 373),
- extent (*7.25.4*; 375),
- overflow (*7.20.2*; 397),
- reference-orientation (*7.20.3*; 407),
- writing-mode (*7.27.7*; 429).

Properties of note

- The region-name property is required, but the default name of "xsl-region-start" is used for this property if a name is not supplied in the XSL-FO instance.
- Even though padding and border-width properties are indicated as available indirectly through the common property set, these values are fixed at "0pt" in XSL-FO 1.0.

7.1.5 The region-end object

Purpose

- This is the definition of the perimeter area whose end edge is co-incident with the end edge of the page's content rectangle.

Content

- (*6.4.17*) EMPTY,
- referring object:
  - simple-page-master (*6.4.12*; 114).

Property sets

- Common border, padding, and background properties (*7.7*; 328).

Other required property

- region-name (*7.25.17*; 407).

Other optional properties

- clip (*7.20.1*; 368),
- display-align (*7.13.4*; 373),
- extent (*7.25.4*; 375),
- overflow (*7.20.2*; 397),
- reference-orientation (*7.20.3*; 407),
- writing-mode (*7.27.7*; 429).

Properties of note

- The region-name property is required, but the default name of "xsl-region-end" is used for this property if a name is not supplied in the XSL-FO instance.
- Even though padding and border-width properties are indicated as available indirectly through the common property set, these values are fixed at "Opt" in XSL-FO 1.0.

7.2 Content definition

7.2.1 Flowed content vs. static content

The flow, the headers, and the footers are defined by assigning content to the region name, not to the region position.

- The page's geometry defines at which position (if any) a named region is on the page.
- Regions are just well-defined areas of the page into which content can be placed.
- Regions have default names but can be renamed.
  - The same names can be used for the same regions in different page definitions.
- The content of flows, headers, and footers is placed into regions by the region name.

Flowed content triggers the pages to be produced from a `page-sequence`.

- Each `page-sequence` construct must have exactly one flow specified.
  - A flow must indicate the region (by name) to which the content is targeted.
- Flowed content fills a region (any region) until the region overflows.
  - The `overflow` property dictates whether another page is generated to create a new region.
  - You can choose to signal an error on overflow.
- A page geometry in the page sequence need not have the named region accepting the flow.
  - Such a page is produced using only static content for the regions named on the page definition.
  - The next page is obtained from the page sequence and examined for the named region accepting the flow.

The formatter generates a page using the next page geometry in the page sequence.

- The amount of the flowed content dictates how many pages get generated for the sequence.
- The page geometry or pattern of page geometries dictate which regions are there on each generated page to accommodate the flow.

Static content is repeated in the named regions that appear on each generated page.

- `static-content` is used to define static content.
- Each `page-sequence` construct may have any number of static content specifications.
  - You must indicate the region (by name) to which the content is targeted.
- It is common to include a `page-number` object in the static content.
  - It generates a sequence of glyph areas reflecting the page number.

- The choice in glyphs used in the generated areas is governed by properties of the `page-sequence` object.
  - Formal definition of these properties comes from XSLT.
- The generated areas inherit properties ancestral to the referencing object, not the referred object.

Flowed and static content are defined on a page sequence basis.

- Every page sequence must have its own definitions of flowed content and static content.
  - It cannot point to another page sequence's content.
- `flow` and `static-content` constructs are children of the `page-sequence` construct.

It is not an error when content is defined for a named region and that region is not present on the page being generated.

- Nothing is rendered from the definition of the flowed content.
- If there is no region for the flowed content, the static content (if any) is rendered and a new page is generated.
- Consider the example where one interleaves pages of normally flowed content with pages entirely made of static content displaying a set of ruled lines; the resulting publication is in a workbook-like format where the pages opposite to the material are used for keeping notes.

It is a common requirement for different pages to have different static content.

- Consider the need for rendering page numbers on alternate sides of the footer —
  - on the right side of odd pages,
  - on the left side of even pages.
- Use different region names for the same regions on different pages.
  - The odd page `region-after` constructs could be named "`footer-odd`".
  - The even page `region-after` constructs could be named "`footer-even`".
  - The page sequence would then define two different `static-content` constructs.
    - The construct flowed to the region named "`footer-odd`" would place the page number on the right.
    - The construct flowed to the region named "`footer-even`" would place the page number on the left.

It is a common requirement for different pages to have the same content in different places.

- Consider the need for rendering information in the outside edge of all pages.
  - Here, the content is the same but it must use the right side on odd pages and the left side on even pages.
- You cannot use the same region name for different regions on different pages.
  - Each time you use a given custom name in the set of page geometries, it must always be for the same body or perimeter region wherever else that name is used in other page geometries.
- You must duplicate the content if there are two differently named regions in two page geometries in order to obtain identical results.
  - The odd pages' `region-end` construct could be named "`outside-odd`".
  - The even pages' `region-start` construct could be named "`outside-even`".
  - The page sequence would define two identical `static-content` constructs to get the same appearance in both regions.
  - The same results would be better obtained by using the same region names in the two geometries.

It is the author's responsibility to supply in each page sequence the definitions of all content desired for the possible regions triggered by the sequence of pages.

- Stylesheets are often repetitive in order to satisfy this requirement.

7.2.2 The static-content object

Purpose

- This is the definition of content that is primarily unchanged from page to page in a page sequence.

Content

- (*6.4.19*) (`%block;+`),
- child object:
  - `%block;` (*6.2*; 69),
- referring object:
  - `page-sequence` (*6.4.5*; 65).

Required property

- flow-name (*7.25.5*; 376).

Excerpts from a draft of a training rendition of this material are shown in Example 7–2.

Example 7–2	Static content definition of regions

```
Line 01  <page-sequence id="fo_region-before" master-reference="frames">
     02    <static-content flow-name="pages-before" font-style="italic">
     03      <block text-align="center">Practical Formatting
     04  Using XSL-FO</block></static-content>
     05    <static-content flow-name="pages-after-right"
     06               font-style="italic" font-size="9pt">
     07      <table>...<block text-align="start">Slide 173 of
     08  287 <inline font-size="8pt">&lt;frame_static-content&gt;</inline
     09  ></block>...<block text-align="center">
     10            <inline font-size="8pt" font-style="normal"
     11  >Information subject to restrictive legend on title page.</inline>
     12            </block>...
     13            <block text-align="end">Page <page-number/> of
     14  <page-number-citation ref-id="N0"/></block>...
     15      </table></static-content>
     16    <static-content flow-name="pages-after-left"
     17               font-style="italic" font-size="9pt">
     18      <table>...<block text-align="start">Page <page-number/> of
     19  <page-number-citation ref-id="N0"/></block>...
     20            <block text-align="center">
     21               <inline font-size="8pt" font-style="normal"
     22  >Information subject to restrictive legend on title page.</inline>
     23            </block>...
     24            <block text-align="end"><inline
     25  font-size="8pt">&lt;frame_static-content&gt;</inline> Slide 173 of
     26  287</block>...</table></static-content>
     27    <flow>...
```

Of note:

- the header is a single centered title;
- two footers are defined, one for the right-hand pages and the other for the left-hand pages;
  - the right-hand footer has the page number on the right-hand side of the page;
  - the left-hand footer has the page number on the left-hand side of the page;
- each footer is a table of three columns;

- the start-side column is aligned to the start edge;
- the center column is aligned at the center;
- the end-side column is aligned to the end edge.

7.2.3 The page-number object

Purpose

- This is an inline-level placeholder replaced with the page number of the current page.
- The formatter supplies the glyphs to be inserted into the flow as `character` objects.
  - The glyphs used by the formatter are specified by the `format` property of the `page-sequence` for the page.

Content

- (*6.6.10*) EMPTY.

Property sets

- Common accessibility properties (*7.4*; 326),
- common aural properties (*7.6*; 327),
- common border, padding, and background properties (*7.7*; 328),
- common font properties (*7.8*; 331),
- common margin properties — inline (*7.11*; 333),
- common relative position properties (*7.12*; 333).

Other optional properties

- alignment-adjust (*7.13.1*; 346),
- alignment-baseline (*7.13.2*; 346),
- baseline-shift (*7.13.3*; 351),
- dominant-baseline (*7.13.5*; 374),
- id (*7.28.2*; 384),
- keep-with-next (*7.19.4*; 386),
- keep-with-previous (*7.19.5*; 387),
- letter-spacing (*7.16.2*; 389),
- line-height (*7.15.4*; 390),
- score-spaces (*7.28.6*; 412),
- text-altitude (*7.27.4*; 421),

- text-decoration (*7.16.4*; 422),
- text-depth (*7.27.5*; 422),
- text-shadow (*7.16.5*; 423),
- text-transform (*7.16.6*; 423),
- visibility (*7.28.8*; 425),
- word-spacing (*7.16.8*; 428),
- wrap-option (*7.15.13*; 428).

Shorthands influencing the above properties

- font (*7.29.13*; 377),
- page-break-after (*7.29.16*; 401),
- page-break-before (*7.29.17*; 401),
- vertical-align (*7.29.22*; 424).

7.2.4 Dynamic content in static content

It is often necessary to redefine header information more often than once per page sequence.

- Starting a new page sequence starts a new page.
- A page sequence of chapter content may require section headings to change when section breaks do not start a new page.
- "Dictionary heads" are used in a dictionary presentation with many entries per page.
  - The top left of the left-page header indicates the first word found on the page.
  - The top right of the right-page header indicates the last word found on the page.
  - The formatter must be told which of the possibilities is desired for choosing the first or last entry on the page.
    - Is it the first or last entry that begins on the page?
    - Is it the first or last entry where any part of the definition is on the page?

Dynamic content that is a candidate for inclusion in static content is captured in the flow using the marker object.

- The marker's parent's total area is called a "qualifying area" for the marker.
  - The marker is associated with all of the non-normal areas in the qualifying area.

- The "containing page" is the page containing the first of the areas that would have been rendered for the marker if the marker were rendered in place.
  - Marker descendants do not inherit inheritable properties of the marker or its ancestors.
  - Marker descendants do inherit inheritable properties of where the marker is retrieved.
- Two markers with the same parent object must not have the same `marker-class-name` property.
  - A marker must either be the first child of its parent object, or only have other sibling markers before it.

It is necessary to have canvas information duplicated to be retrieved.

- The marker definition is not rendered on the canvas, only the retrieval.
- If the static content needs to be the same as the canvas content, the content must be duplicated in the flow.

Preference is afforded to the parents of nested markers based on their position in the area tree hierarchy.

- Areas higher in the tree (pre-order traversal) are preferred to the areas lower in the tree.
- Higher preference is given to a page than to the page that precedes it.

Areas in the area tree have associated markers for each marker class.

- The retrieval algorithm notes the first, last, or any areas of a marker on a page.
- A page may validly not contain any first or last area for a given marker class.

Consider Figure 7–3 that shows four pages generated in the area tree.

- The first page has only one first or last area associated with any marker.
  - "A" is the first and last marker whose first area is on the page.
- The second page doesn't have the first or last area associated with any marker.
  - "A" is the only marker with any area on the page.
- The third page has a number of such areas.
  - "A" is the first marker where any of its areas is on the page.
  - "B" is the first marker whose first area is on the page.
  - "B" is the last marker whose last area is on the page.

- • "C" is the last marker whose first area is on the page.
- • The fourth page has only one first or last area associated with any marker.
  - • "C" is the first and last marker whose last area or any area is on the page.

Only static content may contain `retrieve-marker` constructs.

- • They reference the marker named by the `retrieve-class-name` property.
  - • The marker's content is added to the static content in place of the retrieval construct.

Dynamic content inherits properties ancestral to the referencing `retrieve-marker` construct.

- • Properties are inherited as if the formatting objects of the marker content existed at the retrieval point.

You can scope the search for a marker to be retrieved by using `retrieve-boundary` property —

- • looking only on the page,

Figure 7–3   Adding to the area tree the first, last, and other areas for a marker

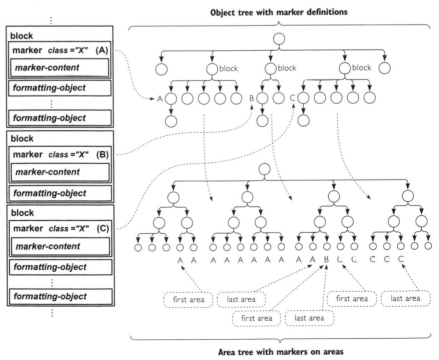

- looking either on the page or on an earlier page in the same page sequence (default),
- looking either on the page or on any earlier page in the document.

You can ask for the areas of a particular marker based on the marker's position by using `retrieve-position` property —

- first marker where any area within its parent is in the scope,
- first marker whose first area within its parent is in the scope (default),
- last marker whose last area within its parent is in the scope,
- last marker whose first area within its parent is in the scope.

Consider the production of "dictionary heads" where every entry in the dictionary includes a `marker` child and the header reflects the first and last entry on the page for navigation purposes, as shown in Figure 7–4.

7.2.5   The marker object

Purpose

- This is the replacement formatting object content for a marker retrieved in static content.

Figure 7–4   Options for retrieving markers

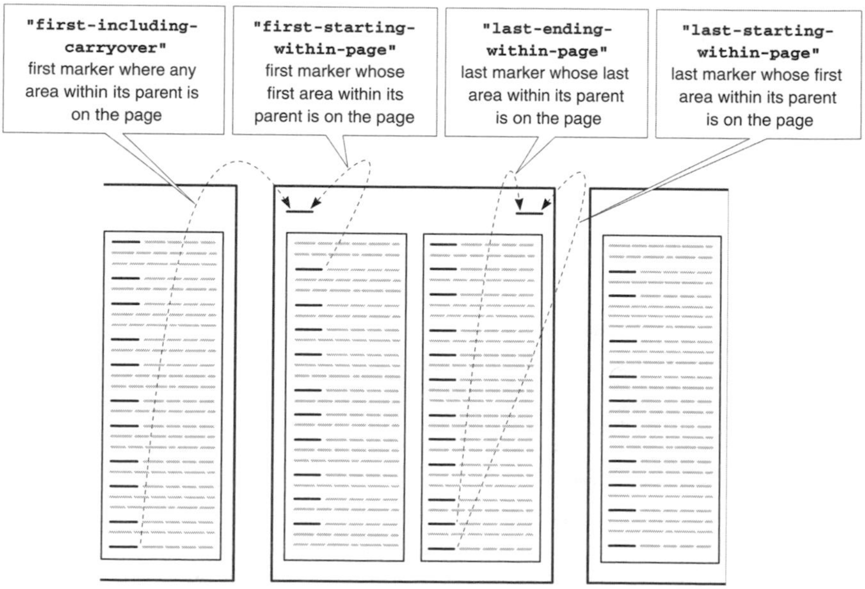

- It is associated with all of the areas generated by its parent formatting object.

Content

- (*6.11.3*) (#PCDATA | %inline; | %block;)*,
- child objects (listed alphabetically):
  - %block; (*6.2*; 69),
  - %inline; (*6.2*; 70).
- Content validity is dependent on the context of the corresponding retrieve-marker object that the marker object replaces.

Required property

- marker-class-name (*7.23.1*; 393).

Consider in Example 7–3 a single-sided presentation where the header retrieves a section's title. Each section is surrounded by a block that includes a marker (highlighted in the example) that is thereby associated with the contents of the surrounding block. Note how the arrangement of the section title in the marker is different than that used in the body of the page.

7.2.6   The retrieve-marker object

Purpose

- This is an inline-level placeholder replaced with the formatting objects of the indicated marker.

Content

- (*6.11.4*) EMPTY.

Required property

- retrieve-class-name (*7.23.2*; 409).

Optional properties

- retrieve-boundary (*7.23.4*; 409),
- retrieve-position (*7.23.3*; 409).

Example 7–3   Defining markers

```
Line 01  <page-sequence master-reference="frame">
     02    <static-content flow-name="frame-before">
     03      <block text-align="end" font-weight="bold"
     04            color="silver" font-size="12pt">
     05        <retrieve-marker retrieve-class-name="section"/>
     06      </block>
     07    </static-content>
     08    ...
     09    <flow flow-name="frame-body">
     10      ...
     11      <block>
     12       <marker marker-class-name="section">Section One - 1.</marker>
     13       <block>1. Section One</block>
     14       <block space-before="1em">This is a test</block>
     15       <block space-before="1em">This is a test</block>
     16       ...
     17       <block space-before="1em">This is a test</block>
     18       <block space-before="1em">This is a test</block>
     19      </block>
     20
     21      <block space-before="2em">
     22       <marker marker-class-name="section">Section Two - 2.</marker>
     23       <block>2. Section Two</block>
     24       <block space-before="1em">This is a test</block>
     25       <block space-before="1em">This is a test</block>
     26       ...
     27       <block space-before="1em">This is a test</block>
     28       <block space-before="1em">This is a test</block>
     29      </block>
```

Properties of note

- retrieve-boundary can be used to limit the search for a marker within the page, to the beginning of the page sequence (default), or to the beginning of the document.

- retrieve-position is illustrated in Figure 7–3.

This is highlighted in Example 7–4 using the earlier example of section title citations in a header.

7.2.7 Planning a simple page sequence specification

Figure 7–5 shows how planning ahead can make page sequence specifying easier.

Example 7–4   Retrieving markers

```
Line 01  <page-sequence master-reference="frame">
     02    <static-content flow-name="frame-before">
     03      <block text-align="end" font-weight="bold"
     04            color="silver" font-size="12pt">
     05        <retrieve-marker retrieve-class-name="section"/>
     06      </block>
     07    </static-content>
     08    ...
     09    <flow flow-name="frame-body">
     10      ...
     11      <block>
     12        <marker marker-class-name="section">Section One - 1.</marker>
     13        <block>1. Section One</block>
     14        <block space-before="1em">This is a test</block>
     15        <block space-before="1em">This is a test</block>
     16        ...
     17        <block space-before="1em">This is a test</block>
     18        <block space-before="1em">This is a test</block>
     19      </block>
     20
     21      <block space-before="2em">
     22        <marker marker-class-name="section">Section Two - 2.</marker>
     23        <block>2. Section Two</block>
     24        <block space-before="1em">This is a test</block>
     25        <block space-before="1em">This is a test</block>
     26        ...
     27        <block space-before="1em">This is a test</block>
     28        <block space-before="1em">This is a test</block>
     29      </block>
```

- Consider planning a book with a table of contents followed by content in separate page sequences each using the same page geometry for before and after regions.
- A single-sided presentation with the page number is at the bottom of all pages.
  - Static content indicates the current and last page numbers.
- Headers are formatted differently for the table of contents and for chapter contents.
  - The document title is shown in the content page sequences but not in the TOC page sequence.
    - The TOC page sequence has a different definition of static content than the content page sequences.

7.3 **Page Sequence Master Interleave (PSMI)**

Sometimes it is necessary to change page geometry based on content.

- Consider the need to change the geometry for a lengthy landscaped table.
  - You cannot use a rotated table because the table length is limited by the container.
  - You must switch to a landscape body region so the lengthy table can flow to subsequent pages.
- Consider the need to flow certain figures into double-sized pages.

Figure 7–5   Page sequence planning simple example

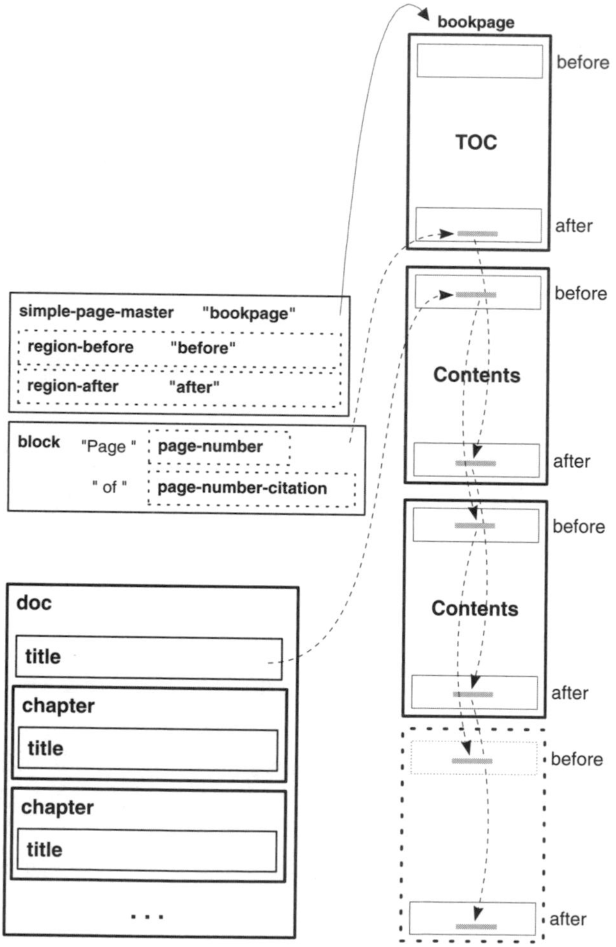

- You must selectively choose a geometry with different dimensions.
- The construct may be deep within the structure of the document being processed.

To use XSL-FO, you must package all content for each page geometry into the flow of a page sequence.

- This can involve a difficult and wasteful recursive process —
  - finding all information up to the change in geometry,
  - packaging the information into a page sequence,
  - packaging the special constructs into a different page sequence,
  - recursively finding all information up to the next change in geometry.
- This breaks the XSLT model of hierarchical processing.
  - This approach is susceptible to development and maintenance problems.

A two-step process can make this very easy to implement.

- The first step creates the flow with supplemental indications of the need to change geometries.
  - You can come from any depth of processing of the source document.
  - Block-level constructs of a page are the immediate children of the flow.
- The second step repackages flow children in as many sequences as necessary.
  - It recursively checks all flow child constructs for any changes in geometry.
  - It is not necessary to check any depth deeper than the children.
- The resulting document is then processed by a standard XSL-FO engine.

The Page Sequence Master Interleave (PSMI) semantic implements this algorithm.

- The public resource is freely available from Crane Softwrights Ltd. —
  - `http://www.CraneSoftwrights.com/links/res-dxslfo.htm`
- A one-element vocabulary is designed to express the semantic of this two-step intermediate process.
- An XSLT stylesheet implements the semantic for any XSL-FO+PSMI sequence.

Consider the need to flow a landscape table in a portrait page geometry, as shown in Figure 7–6. Here's how this is addressed using the PSMI.

- You could rotate a short table in a block container to present it in landscape orientation.
  - A long table would overflow and not trigger a new page in pagination.

- Using PSMI, you could flow the landscape table into an interleaved page geometry where the body region of that geometry is landscape.
- The PSMI stylesheet reads the XSL-FO+PSMI instance and produces a pure XSL-FO instance where three page sequences are created instead of one.
- A long table in the landscape body region will correctly trigger new pages in pagination.

Figure 7–6   Page Sequence Master Interleave (PSMI)

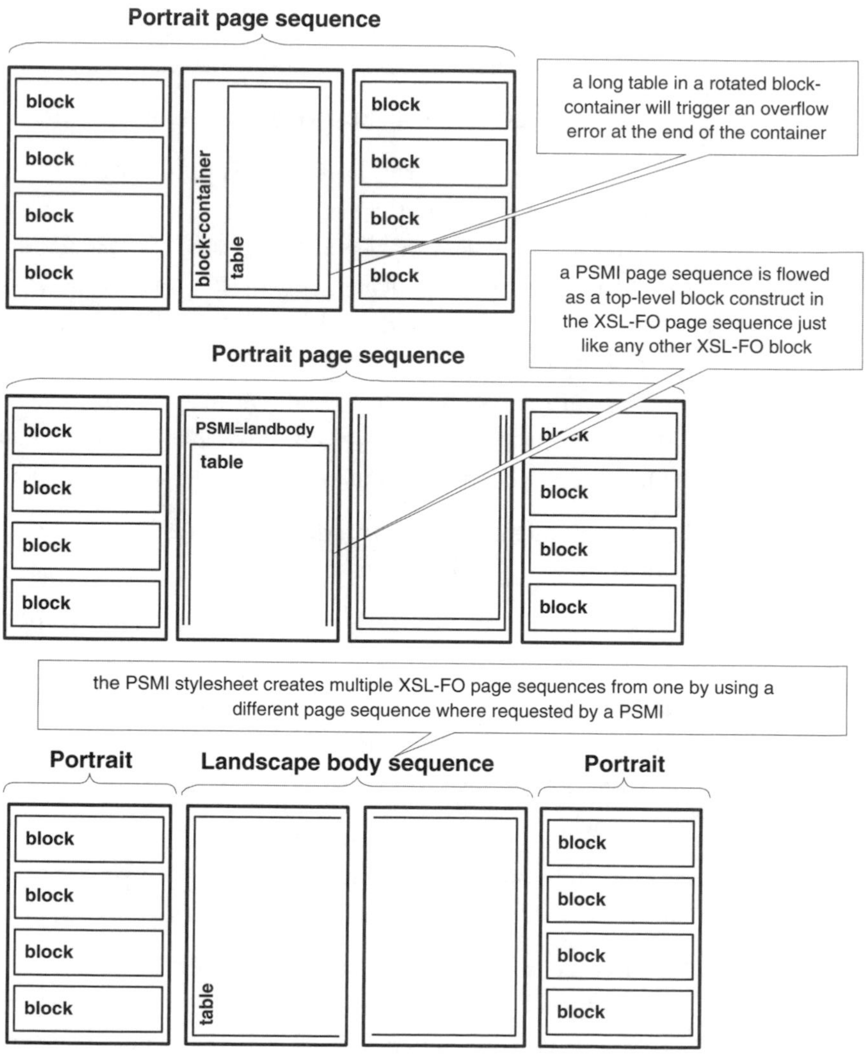

Portrait page sequence

block block block block

block-container table

block block block block

a long table in a rotated block-container will trigger an overflow error at the end of the container

a PSMI page sequence is flowed as a top-level block construct in the XSL-FO page sequence just like any other XSL-FO block

Portrait page sequence

block block block block

PSMI=landbody table

block block block block

the PSMI stylesheet creates multiple XSL-FO page sequences from one by using a different page sequence where requested by a PSMI

Portrait   **Landscape body sequence**   **Portrait**

block block block block

table

block block block block

An example of flow implementing the change in page geometry is shown in Example 7–5.

Example 7–5   PSMI constructs in example

```
Line 01   <simple-page-master master-name="frame-portraitbody" ...>
      02     <region-body region-name="frame-body" .../>
      03     <region-before region-name="frame-before" .../>
      04     <region-after region-name="frame-after" .../>
      05   </simple-page-master>
      06   <simple-page-master master-name="frame-landbody" ...>
      07     <region-body region-name="frame-body"
      08                   reference-orientation="90deg" .../>
      09     <region-before region-name="frame-before" .../>
      10     <region-after region-name="frame-after" .../>
      11   </simple-page-master>
      12   ...
      13   <page-sequence master-reference="frame-portraitbody">
      14     <flow flow-name="frame-body">
      15       <block>Portrait information</block>
      16       ...
      17       <block>Next is landscaped</block>
      18       <psmi:page-sequence master-reference="frame-landbody"
      19         xmlns:psmi="http://www.CraneSoftwrights.com/resources/psmi">
      20         <flow flow-name="frame-body">
      21           <table>
      22             <table-body>
      23               <table-row>
      24                 <table-cell border="solid">
      25                   <block>This is a test</block>
      26                   <block>This is a test</block>
      27                   ...
      28                   <block>This is a test</block>
      29                   <block>This is a test</block>
      30                 </table-cell>
      31               </table-row>
      32             </table-body>
      33           </table>
      34         </flow>
      35       </psmi:page-sequence>
      36       <block>Back to portrait</block>
      37       ...
      38     </flow>
```

7.4 **Page geometry sequencing**

7.4.1 Patterning the page geometry in a sequence of pages

Every different page geometry must be in a separate `simple-page-master` construct.

- Each master is uniquely named.
- Not all regions utilized in the page sequence need be defined on every page geometry.

A `page-sequence` defines the flow for a sequence of pages.

- You can create a new page sequence for a change in static content.
- You can create a new page sequence to start the flow on a new page.
- The page sequence utilizes page geometries referenced by the `master-reference` property.
- You can force a sequence to create a blank page at end if necessary —
  - so the page sequence automatically accommodates the first page number of the following page sequence (default);
    - the following page sequence may be forced to start on an odd or even page number thereby requiring a filler page after the end of the given page sequence,
  - so the total number of pages in the page sequence is an even or odd count,
  - so the last of the page sequence is an even or odd page number.

The simplest case is not to sequence the pages.

- A `page-sequence` that points to a `simple-page-master` repeats that one page for the entire sequence.

A `page-sequence-master` defines an ordering of sub-sequences of page geometries.

- A `page-sequence` that points to a `page-sequence-master` obtains each page geometry from the specified ordering.
- The need for new pages in the flow takes the next page geometry from the next ordered sub-sequence in the master.
  - Each `page-sequence-master` must specify at least one sub-sequence of geometries.
- The formatter may signal an error if it exhausts available sub-sequences.
  - Otherwise it could just repeat the last sub-sequence.

- To prevent possible error, a robust stylesheet should provide an infinitely repeatable sub-sequence as the last sub-sequence.
- Each master is named uniquely and also differently from the page geometry names.

A single required `layout-master-set` specifies all masters.

- Both single-page masters and page-sequence masters are specified.
- There is no semantic order to the set of layout masters.

7.4.2 Page geometry sub-sequences

A sub-sequence defines some or all of the page geometries used in a page sequence.

- The first page of the flow comes from the first qualifying geometry of the first sub-sequence of the page sequence.
- When one sub-sequence is exhausted, the next page uses the first qualifying geometry from the next sub-sequence.

A sub-sequence can specify the use of only one geometry.

- Use `single-page-master-reference` to use one geometry once.
- Use `repeatable-page-master-reference` to use one geometry more than once.
  - It can be unbounded (default) or bounded by a maximum number of repetitions.

A sub-sequence can specify the choice of one of a set of geometries.

- Use `repeatable-page-master-alternatives` to collect the set of geometries from which to choose.
- Use `conditional-page-master-reference` to specify the choice criteria.
- Each choice criterion is tested in the document order of choices specified in the set.
  - The first choice where all criteria test true specifies the geometry used for the page of the flow.
- The set of choices is repeated indefinitely by default.
  - It can be bounded by a maximum number of repetitions.

The choice criteria are made up of three sub-conditions.

- All three criteria must be true for the choice to be used.

- An unspecified criterion is considered to be "any" which is true for each test.
  - You only need to specify the criteria desired for uniqueness.
- All criteria values are unambiguous.
  - It doesn't matter in what order the criteria are specified.
  - Each page tests true for exactly one value for each criterion.

A criterion can be based on the parity of the page number.

- Use odd-or-even to test the criterion;
- "any" (initial value) tests true for all pages;
- "odd" tests true if the page number is odd;
- "even" tests true if the page number is even.

A criterion can be based on the position of the page within the page sequence.

- Use page-position to test the criterion;
- "any" (initial value) tests true for all pages;
- "first" tests true if the page is the first in the page sequence;
- "last" tests true if the page is the last in the page sequence;
- "rest" tests true if the page is neither the first nor the last in the page sequence.
- Note that a one-page page sequence will test true for both "first" and "last".
  - This requires the stylesheet writer to decide which of the two possible geometries is desired for a one-page sequence.
  - The tests in the alternatives must be ordered so that the desired geometry is selected for the one-page sequence situation before the undesired geometry would be selected.

A criterion can be based on the page being generated by the flow or not.

- Use blank-or-not-blank to test the criterion;
- "any" (initial value) tests true for all pages;
- "not-blank" tests true if the page contains flow;
- "blank" tests true if the page does not contain flow because of the page being generated to meet sequence conditions (a "forced" page) —
  - e.g. ensuring that the last page of a chapter is on an even page number.

7.4.3 Forced blank pages

A forced blank page is a page not containing any paginated flow, but created by the formatter in response to page sequencing requirements.

- It is referred to as a "blank page" in a page sequence.
  - This is tested in `conditional-page-master-reference` using `blank-or-not-blank`.
- If no page master is supplied for a blank page, a page with no content is rendered.
- It is always rendered as the last page in a page sequence.

There are two ways a blank page can be triggered.

- It may be triggered by the page numbering of the last page in the given page sequence.
  - This is determined by `force-page-count`;
  - the values of `even`, `odd`, `end-on-even`, and `end-on-odd` may require a blank page to be created.
- It may be triggered by the page numbering of the first page of the following page sequence.
  - A value of `auto` on the given page sequence will cause a final blank page to be created if the page number of the first page of the following page sequence is explicitly specified and requires a blank page for continuous page numbering;
  - the value of `initial-page-number` for the following page sequence is taken into account;
  - it is tested for odd or even (including a specified value of "1") forcing the given page sequence to end on even or odd page respectively;
  - sometimes a blank page appears "unexpectedly" whereas the influence of the following page sequence is the actual trigger.

There are four ways a blank page can be triggered by breaking to a new page.

- You can use `break-before="odd-page"` or `break-after="odd-page"` when in the middle of an odd page.
- You can use `break-before="even-page"` or `break-after="even-page"` when in the middle of an even page.
- It is important to remember the intuitive use of two `break-before="page"` or `break-after="page"` blocks in a row does not constitute a blank page for the purposes of geometry testing.

- It is a "not-blank" page since there is an empty area on the page from the first of the two blocks.

7.4.4   The page-sequence-master object

Purpose

- This is the definition and name of a particular sequence of using page masters.

Content

- (*6.4.7*) (single-page-master-reference | repeatable-page-master-reference | repeatable-page-master-alternatives+),
- child objects (listed alphabetically):
  - repeatable-page-master-alternatives (*6.4.10*; 222),
  - repeatable-page-master-reference (*6.4.9*; 222),
  - single-page-master-reference (*6.4.8*; 221),
- referring object:
  - layout-master-set (*6.4.6*; 65).

Required property

- master-name (*7.25.8*; 393).

Excerpts from a draft XSLT stylesheet for producing a training material are shown in Example 7–6.

The page sequence used in this example prepares to alternately use differently named page masters.

- Each page master has the same name for the before region and a different name for the after region.
- The page sequence defines the static content to be rendered for every possible named region in all simple page masters triggered by the page sequence master.
- Only the static content for the regions that are used on a given page is rendered.
  - Any defined static content for regions that are not on the page is ignored.

The production environment for this example responds to a parameterized request for single-sided copies.

- For single-sided output, master-reference="frame-right" will be used for both odd and even pages.

- `master-reference="frame-left"` is never used, but maintenance of the stylesheets is easy by not having two separate page sequences.

- For double-sided output, each page geometry will be used accordingly.

Example 7–6   A master of a sequence of pages

```
Line 01  <xsl:param name="single-sided"/><!--assume double sided-->
02  <xsl:variable name="use-left"><!--determine left side geometry-->
03    <xsl:choose>
04      <xsl:when test="$single-sided">frame-right</xsl:when>
05      <xsl:otherwise>frame-left</xsl:otherwise>
06    </xsl:choose>
07  </xsl:variable>
08  ...
09  <layout-master-set>
10    <simple-page-master master-name="frame-left" ...>
11      <region-body region-name="pages-body" .../>
12      <region-before extent=".3in" region-name="pages-before"/>
13      <region-after extent=".3in" region-name="pages-after-left"/>
14    </simple-page-master>
15    <simple-page-master master-name="frame-right" ...>
16      <region-body region-name="pages-body" .../>
17      <region-before extent=".3in" region-name="pages-before"/>
18      <region-after extent=".3in" region-name="pages-after-right"/>
19    </simple-page-master>
20
21    <page-sequence-master master-name="frames">
22      <repeatable-page-master-alternatives maximum-repeats="no-limit">
23        <conditional-page-master-reference
24          master-reference="frame-right" odd-or-even="odd"/>
25        <conditional-page-master-reference
26          master-reference="{$use-left}" odd-or-even="even"/>
27      </repeatable-page-master-alternatives>
28    </page-sequence-master>
29  </layout-master-set>
```

7.4.5 The single-page-master-reference object

Purpose

- This is the specification of the single use of a page master within a sequence of page masters.

Content

- *(6.4.8)* EMPTY,

- referring object:
  - `page-sequence-master` (*6.4.7*; 220).

Required property

- `master-reference` (*7.25.9*; 394).

7.4.6   The repeatable-page-master-reference object

Purpose

- This is the specification of the repeated use of a page master within a sequence of page masters.

Content

- (*6.4.9*) `EMPTY`,
- referring object:
  - `page-sequence-master` (*6.4.7*; 220).

Required property

- `master-reference` (*7.25.9*; 394).

Optional property

- `maximum-repeats` (*7.25.10*; 394).

7.4.7   The repeatable-page-master-alternatives object

Purpose

- This is the collection of candidate page master references from which one is to be used based on status conditions detected by the formatter.

Content

- (*6.4.10*) (`conditional-page-master-reference+`),
- child object:
  - `conditional-page-master-reference` (*6.4.11*; 223),
- referring object:
  - `page-sequence-master` (*6.4.7*; 220).

Optional property

- `maximum-repeats` (*7.25.10*; 394).

Excerpts from a draft XSLT stylesheet for the training material document are shown in Example 7–7.

Example 7–7   A master of a sequence of pages

```
Line 01  <xsl:param name="single-sided"/><!--assume double sided-->
     02  <xsl:variable name="use left"><!  determine left side geometry  >
     03    <xsl:choose>
     04      <xsl:when test="$single-sided">frame-right</xsl:when>
     05      <xsl:otherwise>frame-left</xsl:otherwise>
     06    </xsl:choose>
     07  </xsl:variable>
     08  ...
     09  <layout-master-set>
     10    <simple-page-master master-name="frame-left" ...>
     11      <region-body region-name="pages-body" .../>
     12      <region-before extent=".3in" region-name="pages-before"/>
     13      <region-after extent=".3in" region-name="pages-after-left"/>
     14    </simple-page-master>
     15    <simple-page-master master-name="frame-right" ...>
     16      <region-body region-name="pages-body" .../>
     17      <region-before extent=".3in" region-name="pages-before"/>
     18      <region-after extent=".3in" region-name="pages-after-right"/>
     19    </simple-page-master>
     20
     21    <page-sequence-master master-name="frames">
     22      <repeatable-page-master-alternatives maximum-repeats="no-limit">
     23        <conditional-page-master-reference
     24          master-reference="frame-right" odd-or-even="odd"/>
     25        <conditional-page-master-reference
     26          master-reference="{$use-left}" odd-or-even="even"/>
     27      </repeatable-page-master-alternatives>
     28    </page-sequence-master>
     29  </layout-master-set>
```

7.4.8   The conditional-page-master-reference object

Purpose

- This is a page master choice available to the formatter when selecting from a collection of candidate page masters.

Content

- (*6.4.11*) EMPTY,
- referring object:
  - repeatable-page-master-alternatives (*6.4.10*; 222).

Required property

● master-reference (*7.25.9*; 394).

Optional properties

● blank-or-not-blank (*7.25.1*; 351),

● odd-or-even (*7.25.12*; 396),

● page-position (*7.25.14*; 402).

Excerpts from a draft XSLT stylesheet for the training material are shown in Example 7–8.

Example 7–8   A master of a sequence of pages

```
Line 01  <xsl:param name="single-sided"/><!--assume double sided-->
      02  <xsl:variable name="use-left"><!--determine left side geometry-->
      03    <xsl:choose>
      04      <xsl:when test="$single-sided">frame-right</xsl:when>
      05      <xsl:otherwise>frame-left</xsl:otherwise>
      06    </xsl:choose>
      07  </xsl:variable>
      08  ...
      09  <layout-master-set>
      10    <simple-page-master master-name="frame-left" ...>
      11      <region-body region-name="pages-body" .../>
      12      <region-before extent=".3in" region-name="pages-before"/>
      13      <region-after extent=".3in" region-name="pages-after-left"/>
      14    </simple-page-master>
      15    <simple-page-master master-name="frame-right" ...>
      16      <region-body region-name="pages-body" .../>
      17      <region-before extent=".3in" region-name="pages-before"/>
      18      <region-after extent=".3in" region-name="pages-after-right"/>
      19    </simple-page-master>
      20
      21    <page-sequence-master master-name="frames">
      22      <repeatable-page-master-alternatives maximum-repeats="no-limit">
      23        <conditional-page-master-reference
      24          master-reference="frame-right" odd-or-even="odd"/>
      25        <conditional-page-master-reference
      26          master-reference="{$use-left}" odd-or-even="even"/>
      27      </repeatable-page-master-alternatives>
      28    </page-sequence-master>
      29  </layout-master-set>
```

7.4.9   Overview of a page sequence specification

A complicated (and contrived) page sequence is shown in Figure 7–7.

Note there are only two specifications of actual page geometry, while many various sequencing patterns of using these geometries are defined and utilized by the five page sequence specifications.

- All sub-sequences are composed only of references to page geometries.

7.4.10   Planning a more complex page sequence specification

Figure 7–8 shows how planning ahead helps when considering more complex requirements.

- Consider planning a book with a table of contents and the contents each starting on the right-hand page.
- You need different formatting of headers and footers for the TOC and for contents;
  - the TOC only has the page number centered in the footer and an even number of pages in total count (to ensure the content starts on an odd page);

Figure 7–7   Page sequence specification options

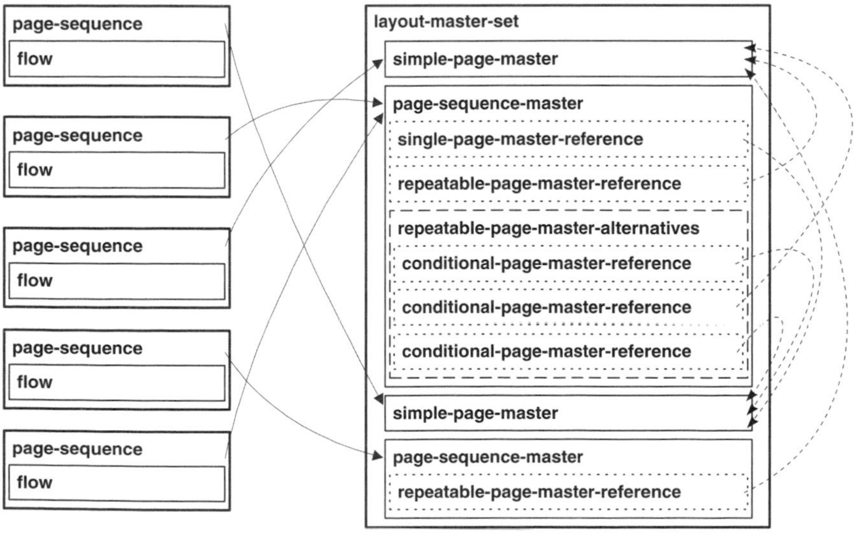

- other pages have the document title at bottom left of odd pages and bottom right of even pages, and chapter title at top right of odd pages and top left of even pages.

Figure 7–8   Page sequence planning: complex example

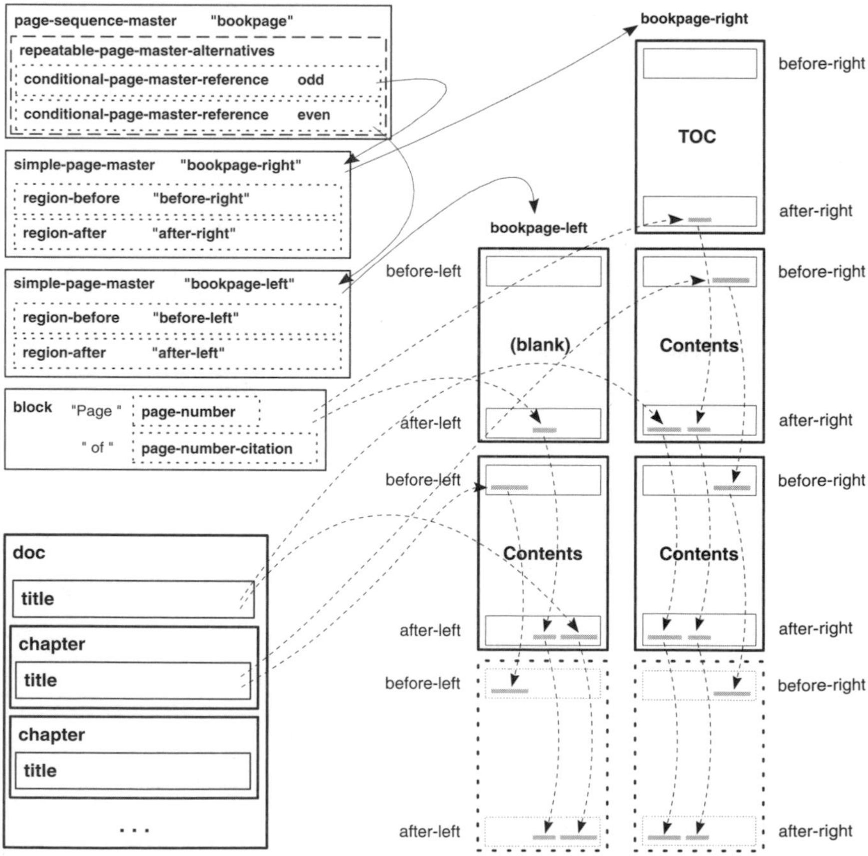

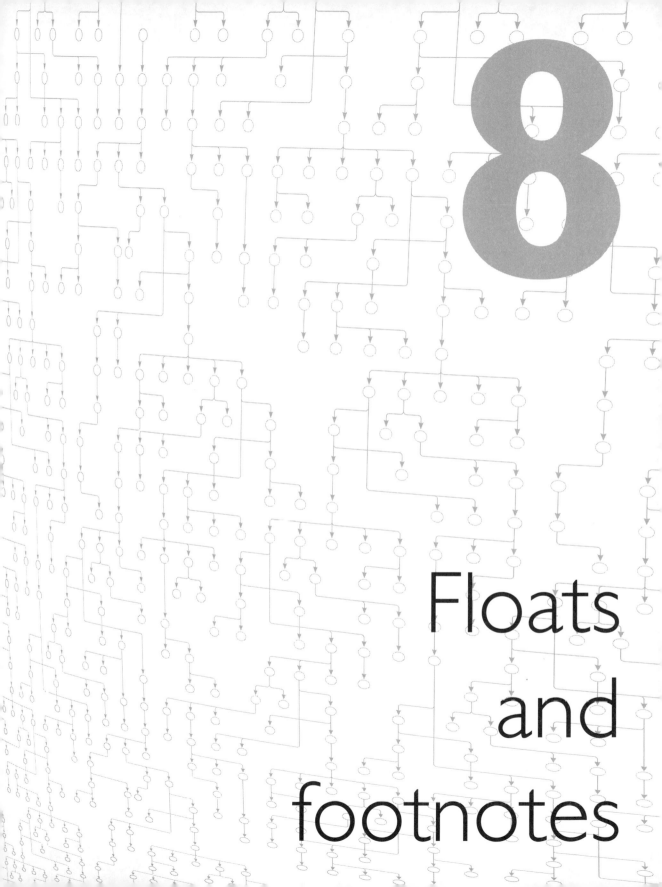

8

Floats
and
footnotes

8 Floats and footnotes

Floats and footnotes are used to render distinctive information that is supplemental to the information found in the flow, making it easy for the reader to find it because of its predetermined location on the page. These constructs are defined "in line" of the flow of information being paginated, but are rendered "out of line" of the flow of information being paginated. Such information is considered auxiliary enough not to disturb the flow itself for the reader, so that the reader can choose to examine a float or footnote at leisure without interrupting the reading of the flow in which it is referenced.

These constructs are dynamically rendered on the page where detected by the formatter in the flow, or perhaps on the immediately following page should it not fit where referenced. They can only be defined in the flow filling the body region of a page, though not in an absolutely positioned area, and are stacked in a different reference area than the main reference area. Floats are moved to either the before, start, or end edges within the body region (not in the perimeter regions). Footnotes are two-part constructs: the footnote citation that is rendered inline in the flow and the footnote body is rendered at the after edge within the body region. An after float is accomplished using a footnote without a footnote citation, but can only be used when not using footnotes since this kind of after float cannot be distinguished from other footnotes on the same page.

Note that the labeling of footnotes is up to the transformation process producing the XSL-FO instance and cannot be generated by the formatter. A feature that is commonly requested but unavailable in XSL-FO 1.0 is numbering the footnotes on a per-page basis. Since the transformation process is unaware of where the page breaks are, yet is responsible for the labeling of the footnote references, this feature cannot yet be realized.

There are no endnote layout constructs in XSL-FO. An endnote is a two-part footnote-like construct with a citation and a definition, but all endnote definitions are collected at the end of a page sequence (e.g. chapter) rather than at the bottom of pages. To render endnotes, it would be the respon-sibility of transformation to cite the endnotes inline in the flow of the scope and then collect and render endnotes at the end of the scope. You could then choose to render the citations as part of the flow on the body, or use empty citations to take advantage of the XSL-FO footnote construct to sink the collection of endnotes to the bottom of the last page.

Judicious use of floats can keep the main flow of information continuous without unseemly breaks at the bottom of pages. The formatter moves the floating object to the perimeter and flows subsequent information in the main flow without interruption, as if the flow had not been present. If the construct is too large to fit on the page, it can be rendered on the next page and the subsequent information continues on the previous page in a seamless fashion.

There are many candidate uses of floating constructs. You can use `float` to float images to the side of a page, e.g. to present sidebar portions of content, or to format lists where the item bodies are indented relative to the corresponding item label's formatted length. It can also be used to implement a multi-line drop initial cap in a paragraph. You can use `footnote` to sink content to the bottom of a page, e.g. for traditional footnotes, acronym expansions, glossary definitions, or images floating to the bottom of a page (using an empty inline construct).

The name of the construct shouldn't prejudice how the construct is used. Consider the need to format a disclaimer at the bottom of the last page of a document. You can flow the disclaimer in the body of a footnote with an empty citation in an empty block at the end of the document. The disclaimer isn't a footnote, yet you'll get the desired effect of the out-of-line placement.

Every page's body region has two sub-regions that are rendered only if necessary. Before floats and footnotes are stacked in the body region with other block level constructs, but the reader needs some separation rendered to distinguish content belonging in a float or footnote from the content belonging in the body. The body region is separated into the before-float reference area, main reference area, and footnote reference area portions, as shown in Figure 8–1.

The act of defining these visual separators does not affect their rendering, as they are only rendered on a page if the floated information is being rendered on the page. Static content defines the rendering of a separator. When needed, the static content associated with `xsl-before-float-separator` is rendered inside and at the end of the before-float reference area. When needed, the static content associated with `xsl-footnote-separator` is rendered inside and at the start of the footnote reference area.

Figure 8–1   Conditional areas and sub-regions

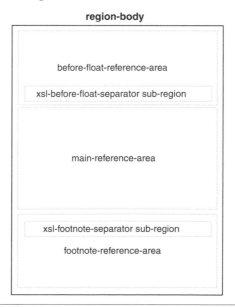

Static content for these sub-regions should always be defined as a contingency if floats and footnotes are being used, for the chance that a given page may have such a construct.

Remember from Figure 4–2 the incursion of the perimeter regions into the body: all reference areas shown above are within the body region's margins and not part of the perimeters.

Included in this chapter. This chapter includes discussion of the following XSL-FO objects:

- `float` (*6.10.2*):
  - is the content to be rendered towards either the before, start, or end edges of the body region regardless of where in the region the content is defined,
- `footnote` (*6.10.3*):
  - is the content to be rendered partly in the flow and partly towards the after edge of the body region regardless of where in the region the content is defined,
- `footnote-body` (*6.10.4*):
  - is the portion of footnote content rendered towards the after edge of the body region.

8.1 Floats

8.1.1 Float definition

Using the `float` object, you can position out-of-line information at the before, start, or end sides of a page.

- The before floats are flowed in the before-float reference area (see Figure 8–1).
- A float creates a dimensionless anchor area in the area tree.
- The anchor is tied to the information that precedes the float in the flow.
- Out-if-line information is placed relative to the anchor —
  - typically at the top or sides of the page in which the anchor is flowed.
- The content of the float is always a set of block-level constructs.

Information can be defined at the block level or at the inline level of the flow.

- The anchor is treated as a block if defined at the block level.

- The anchor is typically treated as an inline construct if defined at the inline level.
  - It is treated as a block object if the line area created by the inline constructs consists only of anchors.
- It must be defined in the body region of the page.
- It must be defined as a descendant of a relatively positioned block.
  - Absolutely positioned areas cannot have float descendants.
- It cannot have any `float`, `footnote`, or `marker` descendants.

The blocks of the float definition are positioned in the area tree accordingly.

- The before floats are stacked in the before-float reference area.
- The side floats are stacked in a side-float reference area.
  - This is a child of the specifying block's ancestral span reference area.
- Float content that does not float is flowed as normal content.
  - This may be the result of a faulty definition or placement.
  - A float is an area that is not normally flowed and cannot be defined within any other area that is not normally flowed (e.g. another float, a footnote, a perimeter region, an absolutely positioned block container, etc.).
- Float lengths cannot be preset and are always derived from the content of the float.

The block areas that float have no border or padding.

- Padding, border, and content rectangles are coincident.

Side floats do not overlap and are typically placed beside each other.

- They make a further incursion into the inline-progression dimension of the block.
- They can be forced to not be placed beside each other by using the `clear` property.
  - Different values control which floats are clear of other floats.

8.1.2   The float object

Purpose

- This is the content to be rendered towards either the before, start, or end edges of the body region regardless of where in the region the content is defined.

Content

- (*6.10.2*) (%block;)+,
- child object:
    - %block; (*6.2*; 69).

Optional properties

- clear (*7.18.1*; 368),
- float (*7.18.2*; 376).

8.1.3 The interaction of blocks and floats

The clear property is used to prevent two side floats from being beside each other or a block-level object from being beside a float.

- It is not documented as a property within the individual block-level object descriptions.
    - It applies to all such constructs as documented in the property definition.
- The default is for side floats to continue intruding into the main reference area.
    - Use clear to start a side float back at the edge, clear of any previous float.
- The default is for the lines of a block to contour around the accumulation of side floats.
    - Use clear to start a block back at the edge, clear of any previous float.
- Those constructs with the clear value clear the float they would otherwise be beside.

Consider three situations in Figure 8–2 that illustrate the use of clear on each of floats and blocks;

- the numbers reflect the order in which the constructs are flowed;

Figure 8–2   The clearing of slide floats by new constructs

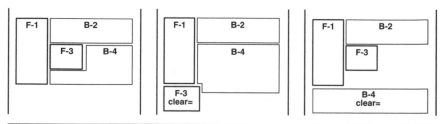

- the thick-lined blocks with "F-" prefixes are floats;
- the thin-lined blocks with "B-" prefixes are blocks.

Of note in the diagram:

- the left-most page fragment shows the default situation where side floats intrude and blocks flow around floats;
    - the second float ("F–3") is to the right of the first float ("F–1");
    - the second block ("B–4") wraps around both floats;
- the center page fragment shows the second float being clear of the first float;
    - the second block ("B–4") starts abutted to the first block ("B–2");
- the right-most page fragment shows the second block being clear of all floats;
    - the second float ("F–3") is to the right of the first float ("F–1");
    - the second block ("B–4") is clear of both floats.

The `intrusion-displace` property indicates the strategy of locating the start (or end) edges and indents of the lines of the block being intruded upon.

- Note that displacing the edge of a block necessarily displaces all lines in that block.

Consider three situations in Figure 8–3 that illustrate the use of `intrusion-displace` on a block with both `text-indent` and `start-indent`.

- "`indent`" respects `text-indent` and `start-indent`;
- "`block`" respects `text-indent` but limits all lines by the width of the float;
- "`line`" ignores `text-indent` if occupied by the float, and respects `start-indent`.

Figure 8–3   The behavior of lines in a block next to a float

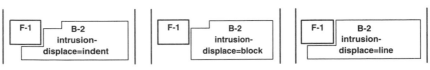

8.2 **Footnotes**

8.2.1 Footnote definition

Using the `footnote` object, you can position out-of-line information at the bottom of a page.

- The anchor area is the last area defined by the `inline` child.
- Out-of-line information is placed relative to the anchor —
  - typically at the bottom of the page in which the anchor is flowed.
- Out-of-line content is the content of the `footnote-body` child.
  - It is always a set of block-level constructs.

Information must be defined at the inline level of the flow.

- The object supplies the content of the inline anchor.

The blocks of the footnote body are positioned in the area tree accordingly.

- The footnote body is flowed to the footnote reference area (see Figure 8–1).
- Footnote body length cannot be preset and is always derived from the content of the float.

The same restrictions as for `float` apply.

- A footnote's body is an area that is not normally flowed and cannot be defined within any other area that is not normally flowed (e.g. another footnote, a float, a perimeter region, an absolutely positioned block container, etc.).
- It must be defined in the body region of the page as a descendant of a relatively positioned block.
- It cannot have any `float`, `footnote`, or `marker` descendants.

There exist no built-in semantics of footnote numbering or citations.

- Numbering and presentation is the responsibility of the stylesheet or application generating the flow objects, including —
  - what is displayed inline and how it is displayed,
    - e.g. superscripting, italics, font size, etc.,
  - how the inline reference is reflected in the out-of-line information for correlation by the reader.
- Numbering cannot be restarted on a per-page basis.

- The page boundaries are determined by the formatter and are not known to the transformation process.
- The XSLT process producing the XSL-FO instance can probably use the same criteria for determining the page sequence boundaries to do footnote numbering either across the page sequence or across the entire publication.

There is no automatic copying of the inline content to the start of the footnote body.

- It is the stylesheet writer's responsibility to define both the footnote citation and the footnote body separately.
- You may wish to use different formatting properties for each use of the footnote citation.

8.2.2 The footnote object

Purpose

- This is the content to be rendered partly in the flow and partly towards the after edge of the body region regardless of where in the region the content is defined.
    - It includes the inline content to render in the flow where the footnote body content is defined.

Content

- (*6.10.3*) `(inline, footnote-body)`,
- child objects (listed alphabetically):
    - `footnote-body` (*6.10.4*; 238),
    - `inline` (*6.6.7*; 103).

Property sets

- Common accessibility properties (*7.4*; 326).

No other properties are defined for this formatting object.

The example shown in Figure 8–4 illustrates the use of footnotes.

An excerpt from Figure 8–4 is shown in Example 8–1.

Of note:

- the footnote definitions are embedded in the blocks at the point where the footnote citation is rendered;

- the footnote citation in the block is formatted differently from the footnote citation echoed in the footnote reference area.

8.2.3 The footnote-body object

Purpose

- This is the portion of footnote content rendered towards the after edge of the body region.

Content

- (*6.10.4*) (%block;)+,
- child object:
  - %block; (*6.2*; 69),
- referring object:
  - footnote (*6.10.3*; 237).

Property sets

- Common accessibility properties (*7.4*; 326).

Figure 8–4   Example for footnotes

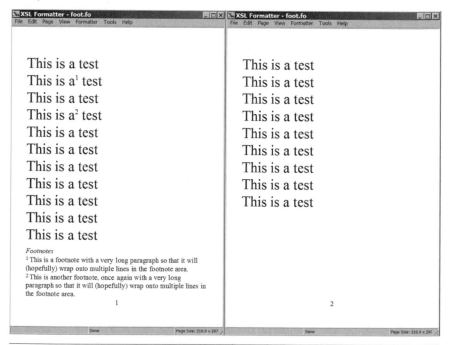

Example 8–1   Footnote constructs in Figure 8–4

```
Line 01  <page-sequence master-reference="frame">
     02    <static-content flow-name="xsl-footnote-separator">
     03      <block font-style="italic">Footnotes</block>
     04    </static-content>
     05
     06    <flow flow-name="frame-body" font-size="40pt">
     07      <block>This is a test</block>
     08      <block>This is a<footnote>
     09      <inline baseline-shift="15pt" font-size="20pt">1</inline>
     10      <footnote-body>
     11        <block font-size="20pt">
     12          <inline baseline-shift="5pt" font-size="15pt"
     13          >1 </inline>This is a footnote with a very
     14  long paragraph so that it will (hopefully) wrap onto
     15  multiple lines in the footnote area.
     16        </block>
     17      </footnote-body>
     18      </footnote> test</block>
     19      <block>This is a test</block>
     20      <block>This is a<footnote>
     21      <inline baseline-shift="15pt" font-size="20pt">2</inline>
     22      <footnote-body>
     23        <block font-size="20pt">
     24          <inline baseline-shift="5pt" font-size="15pt"
     25          >2 </inline>This is another footnote, once
     26  again with a very long paragraph so that it will
     27  (hopefully) wrap onto multiple lines in the footnote area.
     28        </block>
     29      </footnote-body>
     30      </footnote> test</block>
     31      <block>This is a test</block>
     32      <block>This is a test</block>
     33    ...
```

No other properties are defined for this formatting object.

An excerpt from Figure 8–4 highlighting the footnote-body object is shown in Example 8–2.

Example 8–2   Footnote constructs in Figure 8–4

```
Line 01   <page-sequence master-reference="frame">
     02     <static-content flow-name="xsl-footnote-separator">
     03       <block font-style="italic">Footnotes</block>
     04     </static-content>
     05
     06     <flow flow-name="frame-body" font-size="40pt">
     07       <block>This is a test</block>
     08       <block>This is a<footnote>
     09       <inline baseline-shift="15pt" font-size="20pt">1</inline>
     10     <footnote-body>
     11       <block font-size="20pt">
     12         <inline baseline-shift="5pt" font-size="15pt"
     13           >1 </inline>This is a footnote with a very
     14   long paragraph so that it will (hopefully) wrap onto
     15   multiple lines in the footnote area.
     16       </block>
     17     </footnote-body>
     18     </footnote> test</block>
     19       <block>This is a test</block>
     20       <block>This is a<footnote>
     21       <inline baseline-shift="15pt" font-size="20pt">2 </inline>
     22     <footnote-body>
     23       <block font-size="20pt">
     24         <inline baseline-shift="5pt" font-size="15pt"
     25           >2 </inline>This is another footnote, once
     26   again with a very long paragraph so that it will
     27   (hopefully) wrap onto multiple lines in the footnote area.
     28       </block>
     29     </footnote-body>
     30     </footnote> test</block>
     31       <block>This is a test</block>
     32       <block>This is a test</block>
     33     ...
```

9

Breaks, borders, and backgrounds

9 Breaks, borders, and backgrounds

An area's placement is governed by the XSL-FO stacking rules and the area's traits refined from the properties of the objects. This placement happens at the block level in each of the before-float reference areas, normal-flow reference areas (page columns), and footnote reference areas on a page, at the line level inside a block where the lines are generated by the formatter (not the stylesheet), and at the inline level within a line containing characters, rules, graphics, and other inline constructs.

Areas stacked normally are stacked in the pertinent progression direction. Page-level reference areas stack in the block-progression direction. Lines and table rows also stack in the block-progression direction. Page column, table column, and inline areas stack in the inline-progression direction.

Recall from Figure 4–3 that these directions are based on the combination of writing mode and reference orientation.

The "natural" stacking of areas may produce typographically unpleasant results. While the initial values implement common-sense formatting control for consistent presentation, many traditional conventions break initial values. For example, you often need to keep a heading in the body on the same page as the first paragraph to which the heading applies when the naturally occurring page break could otherwise separate these two items. These settings override the physical arrangement of information implied by the default area properties.

Conditionality and precedence can eliminate certain areas from being rendered, to prevent the unnecessary use of inter-block spacing when pagination renders a block without an adjacent sibling. For example, a block forced to the top of a new page doesn't always need the space defined for between blocks to be rendered.

Formatting special cases can be accommodated easily with simple specifications of intent where the formatter determines the applicability of spaces based on object properties. Not only can the transformation process ascribe such properties more easily than it can determine space behaviors; it would be impossible for the transformation process to know where the result information will end up in the rendered result to make such a decision.

Numerous properties are available to be used in formatting objects to specify these nuances of layout, such as breaking the flow of content to a new column or page, maintaining a minimum number of widow and orphan lines of a block on a page, keeping information together in the same reference area, drawing borders around information, and painting backgrounds behind information.

9.1 Breaks

One often needs to arbitrarily continue flowing information at the start of the next line, column, or page.

- If there is no change to static content, you need not use a new page sequence to begin on a new page.
- You may need to continue at the top of an even page number or odd page number.
  - You may need to introduce a blank page that can be accommodated in the page sequence master.

Breaking at the line level can be done with an empty `block` object.

- Adding a block of zero lines to the flow interrupts the block-progression direction.
- `<block/>` behaves somewhat like the HTML `br` element.
- Multiple breaks in a row do not create multiple lines, unlike HTML;

- the areas created by the blocks do not have any dimensions;
- they can be nested inside of a block of lines without being considered an error.
- This is not appropriate for typical program listings or other monospace presentations.
  - See discussion of preservation of white space in Section 4.2.4 on page 102.

Breaking at the column or page level can be done with the `break-before` and `break-after` properties on a block.

- The block may be empty;
- it can specify a break to the next column;
- it can specify a break to the next page —
  - regardless of page parity,
  - to the next even or odd page.

Specifying a break does *not* mean forcing a break.

- The property specifies a condition to be met, not an action to be performed.
- If the information already satisfies the break requirement, nothing is added to the rendering of the flow.

Forcing a break requires two uses of `break-before`.

- One is with an empty block to put an empty block at the top of the blank page.
  - An empty block on a page is not a blank page even though the block cannot be seen.
- The other is with the first block of the subsequent page to move off the page with the empty block.

9.2 Widows and orphans

The natural breaking of blocks of lines may result in an unpleasant appearance.

- Seeing only one line of a block at the bottom or top of a page may leave the impression there is only one line of information;
  - having two or more lines can better suggest that there is more than just those lines in the block on the other side of the page break.
- The effect is magnified when blocks are justified;

- the last line of a justified block is typically not justified;
- when positioned at the top of a page, the unjustified last line may look more like a heading.

Widows are the lines at the end of a block overflowing to the start of a page.

- You can specify the minimum number of line areas allowed in the first area of the page generated by the last lines of a block.
- The initial value of widows is "2".

Orphans are the lines at the start of a block overflowing at the end of a page.

- You can specify the minimum number of line areas allowed in the last area of the page generated by the first lines of a block.
- The initial value of orphans is "2".

Figure 9–1 illustrates the lines of that are widows and the lines that are orphans created when a block breaks over the edge of a column or page.

Breaking happens to the next logical reference area —

- a column break if there are multiple columns in the page,
- a page break if at the end of the last column.

The entire block is moved to the next reference area if neither condition can be satisfied.

Figure 9–1   Widows and orphans of a block

- Widows and orphans are not tested until there are widow lines to be accommodated.
- The entire block is moved when there are not enough orphan lines remaining after accommodating the minimum number of widow lines.

Figure 9–2 illustrates the setting of different values.

Note the following regarding the three examples of the six-line block wrapping.

- In each test the values of widows and orphans ("W=" and "O=") are different to illustrate the behavior for a six-line long block that wraps at the end of each column.
- In Test 1, the widows specification is 0 which is less than or equal to the actual one widow line in the block.
    - The block is left untouched and shows what would result when widows and orphans are not defined.
    - Remember that when not specified, the values are defined as "2", not "0".
- In Test 2, the widows specification is 4 which is greater than what would be only one widow line in the block as in Test 1.
    - Three orphan lines are moved to the next column to satisfy the widow count.
    - The remaining orphan count of 2 does satisfy the specified orphan count of 0.
- In Test 3, the widows specification is 4 which is greater than what would be only one widow line in the block as in Test 1.
    - Three orphan lines are first moved to the next column to satisfy the widow count, reducing the orphan count to two, as in Test 2.
    - The remaining orphan count of 2 does not, however, satisfy the specified orphan count of 4, so all remaining orphans are then moved to the next column as well.

Figure 9–2   An illustration of widows and orphans

Test 1	W=0,O=0.	**Test 2**	W=4,O=0;	**Test 3**	Block:
Block:		Block:	W=4,O=0;		W=4,O=4;
W=0,O=0;		W=4,O=0;	W=4,O=0;		W=4,O=4;
W=0,O=0;			W=4,O=0.		W=4,O=4;
W=0,O=0;					W=4,O=4;
W=0,O=0;					W=4,O=4.

9.3 **Keeps**

9.3.1 Keep conditions

You can prevent information from separating over line, column, or page contexts, by using —

- line-oriented keeps for inline-level constructs only;
  - use *keep*.within-line= for the line context,
- column- and page-oriented keeps for block-level constructs;
  - use *keep*.within-column= for the column context;
  - use *keep*.within-page= for the page context.

Overriding widows and orphans with the keep-together property:

- keeps descendants together,
- adds a context break to the flow before an area whose entire content will not fit within the keep-together component context.

Injecting context breaks with the keep-with-previous and keep-with-next properties:

- keeps siblings together,
- adds a context break to the flow before an area when —
  - the following area has a keep-with-previous property component and both areas will not fit within the component context,
  - the area has a keep-with-next property component and both areas will not fit within the component context.

Relative strengths of keeps can be specified to ensure "more important" areas are kept together when "less important" areas cannot be kept together.

- Consider a safety publication where a list of steps is attempted to be kept together.
  - There may be warnings found in the list of steps.
  - If the steps cannot be kept together, the more important blocks associated with the warning are to be kept together.

9.3.2 Examples of keeps

Consider the "before and after" comparison of using keeps and not using keeps shown in Figure 9–3.

The markup in Example 9–1 illustrates controlling the keeps for descendants.

Of note:

- the lines reading "Block in block" spread over the column break on page 1;
- these lines are kept together within the column on page 2.

Consider the "before and after" comparison of not using keeps of siblings and then using keeps shown in Figure 9–4.

Note that the space at the head of each reference area is conditional and is therefore discarded.

The markup in Example 9–2 illustrates controlling the keeps for siblings.

Of note:

- on page 1 the heading for the third group of names is not in the same column as the names;

Figure 9–3   Examples of keeps

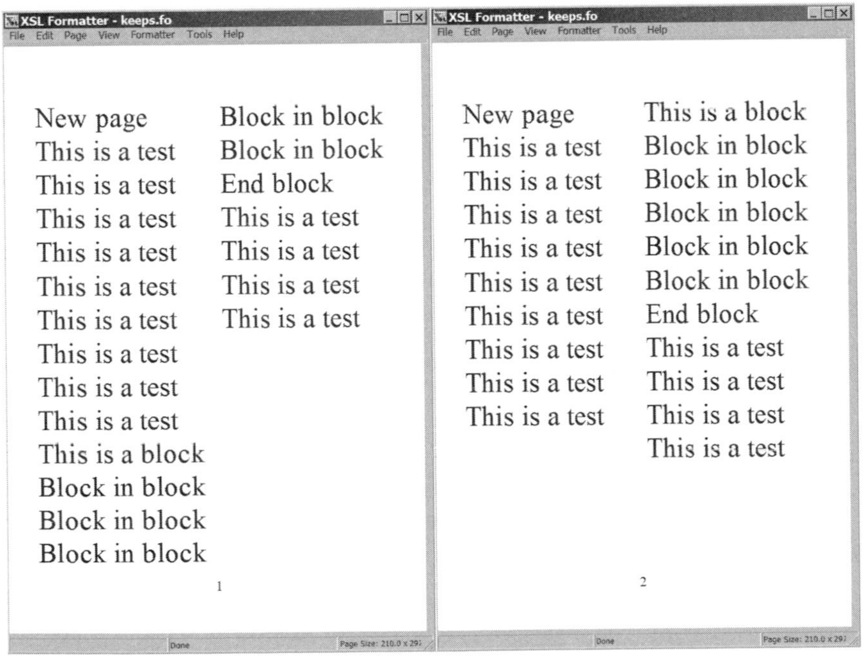

Example 9–1   Keeping a group of areas together in a reference area

```
Line 01  <layout-master-set>
     02    ...
     03      <region-body region-name="frame-body" column-count="2" .../>
     04    ...
     05  </layout-master-set>
     06    ...
     07  <flow flow-name="frame-body" font-size="40pt">
     08   <block break-before="page">New page</block>
     09   <block>This is a test</block>
     10    ...
     11   <block>This is a test</block>
     12   <block>This is a block
     13     <block>Block in block</block>
     14     ...
     15     <block>Block in block</block>
     16     End block</block>
     17   <block>This is a test</block>
     18    ...
     19   <block>This is a test</block>
     20   <block break-before="page">New page</block>
     21   <block>This is a test</block>
     22    ...
     23   <block>This is a test</block>
     24   <block keep-together.within-column="always">This is a block
     25     <block>Block in block</block>
     26     ...
     27     <block>Block in block</block>
     28     End block</block>
     29   <block>This is a test</block>
     30    ...
     31   <block>This is a test</block>
     32  </flow>
```

- on page 2 the heading for the third group of names is kept together with the names.

9.3.3   Keep strength

The strength of a keep is specified in the corresponding property's value.

- "auto" indicates no keep condition imposed.
- "integer-number" indicates a relative keep strength that can be ignored;
  - it is ignored without overflow condition if the keep area doesn't fit.
- "always" indicates a keep that cannot be ignored;

- it implies an overflow condition if the keep area doesn't fit.
- Consider the situation where the pieces of a warning notice have to be kept together within a set of blocks that would be nice to keep together but may not fit on a page;
  - the keep of the warning components would have a higher value than the keep of the set of blocks.

A keep is attempted to be fit first into what remains within the context.

- If a keep doesn't fit what remains, it begins within the next context (e.g. next column or next page).
- A keep is ignored if the amount being kept doesn't fit an entire context.
  - When ignored, the keep's content is flowed as if there was no keep specified.
  - It does not begin at the start of the next context, but after the last flowed area.
- The keeps of next higher strength within the flow of the keep being ignored are attempted to be kept together.
  - Any keeps of lower strength are ignored as that strength has already been addressed.

Figure 9–4   Examples of sibling keeps

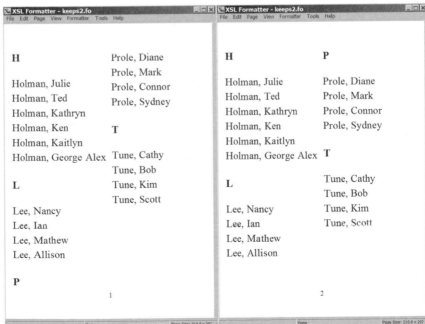

Example 9–2   Keeping a group of areas together in a reference area

```
Line 01  <block space-before="1.5cm" space-after="1.3cm"
     02         font-weight="bold">L</block>
     03  <block space-before=".2em">Lee, Nancy</block>
     04  <block space-before=".2em">Lee, Ian</block>
     05  <block space-before=".2em">Lee, Mathew</block>
     06  <block space-before=".2em">Lee, Allison</block>
     07
     08  <block space-before="1.5cm" space-after="1.3cm"
     09         font-weight="bold">P</block>
     10  <block space-before=".2em">Prole, Diane</block>
     11  <block space-before=".2em">Prole, Mark</block>
     12  <block space-before=".2em">Prole, Connor</block>
     13  <block space-before=".2em">Prole, Sydney</block>
     14  ...
     15  <block space-before="1.5cm" space-after="1.3cm"
     16         keep-with-next.within-column="always"
     17         font-weight="bold">L</block>
     18  <block space-before=".2em">Lee, Nancy</block>
     19  <block space-before=".2em">Lee, Ian</block>
     20  <block space-before=".2em">Lee, Mathew</block>
     21  <block space-before=".2em">Lee, Allison</block>
     22
     23  <block space-before="1.5cm" space-after="1.3cm"
     24         keep-with-next.within-column="always"
     25         font-weight="bold">P</block>
     26  <block space-before=".2em">Prole, Diane</block>
     27  <block space-before=".2em">Prole, Mark</block>
     28  <block space-before=".2em">Prole, Connor</block>
     29  <block space-before=".2em">Prole, Sydney</block>
```

- The keep of the next higher strength is then ignored if the length of that keep's flow cannot fit within the context.
  - That keep's content is flowed as if there was no keep specified.
- A keep of "always" is never ignored; if the areas do not fit in the context, an overflow condition is triggered.

The size of the flow for a keep doesn't affect the choice of page geometry.

- A page-level keep will be tested on the next page geometry chosen by page sequencing.
- A smaller page geometry is not simply ignored if it cannot accommodate the information in the keep and a subsequent page happens to fit the content.

- The choice of page geometry is solely based on page sequencing and never on flow.

Explicit break conditions are stronger than any keep conditions.

- A keep is ignored if a break is specified.

Consider two situations in Figure 9–5 where keeps are allowed to be ignored and not allowed to be ignored.

Of note:

- for each of the two examples, the blocks on the left depict the blocks in the flow, while the pages on the right depict where the blocks end up on the pages;
- the pages are depicted with the odd page numbers on the right and the even page numbers on the left as is typical in left-to-right writing systems.

In this example, each labeled block includes an area with that label plus the areas of the labeled blocks found therein.

Using a numeric value allows the keep to be ignored.

- A has no keep and flows as usual.

Figure 9–5 Keep strength

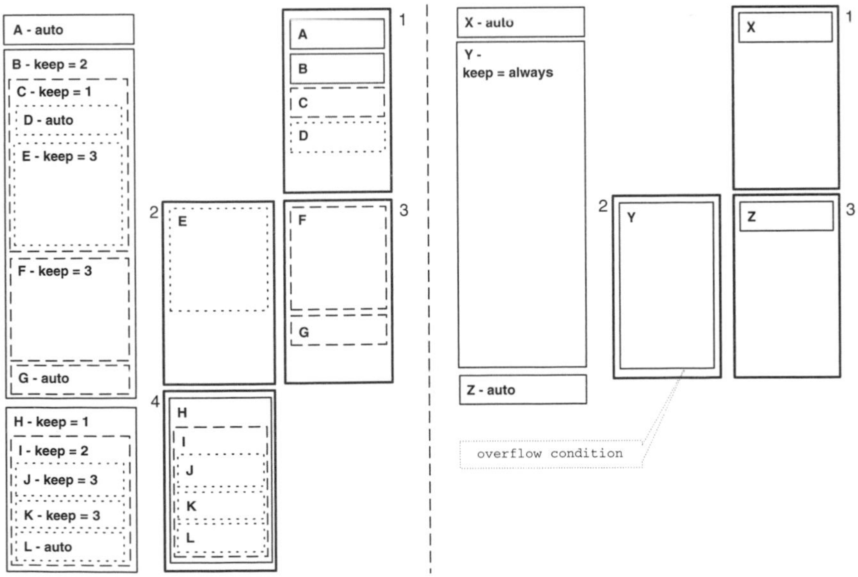

- B has `keep="2"` and contains C, F, and G.
  - All of B is longer than what remains on the first page, so the second page is attempted.
  - Because it doesn't fit on the second page, the B keep is ignored and its content is flowed as if no keep was specified for B.
- C has `keep="1"` and contains D and E.
  - Though all of C would fit on the next page, the keep strength specified is less than what has already been rejected, so the keep has no force and is ignored as if no keep was specified for C.
- D has no keep and flows as usual.
- E has `keep="3"` and doesn't fit on the rest of the first page.
  - The keep strength is higher than what has been rejected, so it is respected.
  - Content is placed on the second page.
- F has `keep="3"` and doesn't fit on the second page.
  - The keep strength is higher than what has been rejected, so it is respected.
  - Content is placed on the third page.
- G has no keep and flows as usual.
- H has `keep="1"` and doesn't fit on the rest of the third page.
  - It hasn't been part of any keep that has been rejected, and it fits in its entirety on a page, so it is moved to the next page.
- I through L do not break over a page so their keep values are not considered.

Using "`always`" does not allow the keep to be ignored.

- X has no keep and flows as usual.
- Y doesn't fit on the remainder of the first page;
  - because of the "`always`" it begins on the second page;
  - because it is longer than the second page, an overflow condition exists;
    - whatever doesn't fit is lost.
- Z has no keep and flows as usual.
  - It ends up at the start of the third page because the second page is full.

9.4 Spacing, conditionality, and precedence

Many components of compound properties specify the space before or after formatting objects.

- `space-before` and `space-after` are used for block-level constructs.
- `space-start` and `space-end` are used for inline-level constructs.

- Components offer fine-tuned control over behaviors.
  - *space*.optimum is used for the preferable amount of space;
    - the shorthand property without a sub-field sets the optimum to the shorthand value.
  - *space*.minimum and *space*.maximum are used for the limits to the actual amount of space;
    - not specifying the limits implies the limits do not vary from the optimum.
  - *space*.conditionality is used for the discarding of unwanted space —
    - at the start or end of reference areas.
  - *space*.precedence is used for the arbitration of conflicting space —
    - where abutted space specifications are not desired.
- Spacing specifications are conditions to be met, not actions to be performed.
  - This makes stylesheet writing easier by allowing redundant specifications for adjacent areas.

You can prevent border, padding, and spacing from being used under certain conditions.

- The pagination of flow may result in space specifications leading or trailing in reference areas;
  - e.g., the space specified before a paragraph is to be discarded when it is at the top of a page.
    - The stylesheet generating the blocks for paragraphs cannot know where the page breaks will occur in order to turn off the space specification.
    - The default is to discard spacing used at the start or end of a reference area.
- It is often easy to write the stylesheet to always specify spacing and arbitrate between two coincident space specifications —
  - e.g. between a space specified before paragraphs in a section and a space specified after the title of a section.
    - It may not be desirable to have the two spaces combine to too large a space before the first paragraph.

Conditionality dictates whether space specifications are discarded.

- The value "retain" can be specified to change the initial value of "discard".
- All contiguous space specifications that can be discarded, if flowed to the start or end of a reference area, are suppressed.
  - Each such area's size in the tree is set to zero.

- All space specifications after the first non-discarded area (either space, padding, border, or content) and before the last non-discarded area are not suppressed as a result of conditionality.
  - They may be suppressed as a result of precedence or optimum size.

Precedence dictates arbitration between adjacent space specifications.

- For example, the `space-after` of a block may be adjacent to the `space-before` of the following block.
- An integer value (default is zero) is used for arbitration of precedence between adjacent space specifications.
  - All unsuppressed areas whose precedence is less than the highest integer value of precedence are then suppressed.
- The value "`force`" will protect an unsuppressed area from being suppressed due to precedence.

Optimum values are used for arbitration between the areas with equal precedence.

- All unsuppressed areas whose optimum values are less than the greatest optimum value are then suppressed.

Resolved minimum and maximum are derived from all remaining unsuppressed areas.

- By arbitration described above, all have the same (greatest) optimum value.
- Resolved minimum is the greatest of all minimums.
- Resolved maximum is the least of all maximums.

Figure 9–6 illustrates the interaction of the space specifications between adjacent blocks.

9.5 Borders

Both block and inline areas can have their borders visible using a non-zero border width.

- There are properties specified separately on each of the before, after, start, and end sides.
- The `*-width` properties are used to specify border width (precedence is given to wider widths in coincident table borders).

- In table borders, wider widths take precedence over narrower widths.
- A compound value can be specified through individual component settings —
    - `*-width.length="length"`,
    - `*-width.conditionality="conditionality"`;
        - the values of "`discard`" or "`retain`" apply to the border of split areas, i.e. —
            - column and page reference areas for block areas (including table cells),
            - line reference areas for inline areas;
    - a simple `*-width="length"` length value:
        - implies `*-width.conditionality="discard"`,
        - allows user-agent dependent values of "`thin`", "`medium`", and "`thick`".
- The `*-style` properties are used to specify border style (listed in the order of precedence when width is equal for coincident table borders) —
    - "`hidden`":
        - forces `*-width="0pt"`,
        - is a special case for table borders, in that "`hidden`" has higher precedence than any other coincident border specification, so the border is never seen,
    - "`double`" (with both lines and intervening space equal to the width),
    - "`solid`",
    - "`dashed`",
    - "`dotted`",
    - "`ridge`",

Figure 9–6   Optimum size and precedence arbitration

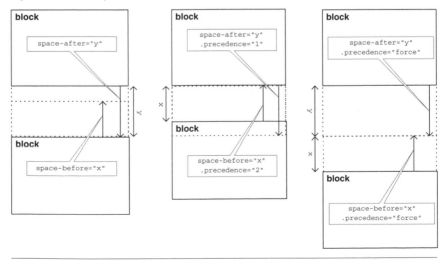

- "outset",
- "groove",
- "inset",
- "none":
  - forces *-width="0pt",
  - is a special case for table borders, in that "none" has lower precedence than any other coincident border specification, so the border may still be seen.
- The *-color properties are used to specify border color (the precedence is to construct nesting in coincident table borders of equal width and style).
  - Any valid color specification can be used.
  - The order of precedence (highest to lowest) is cell, row, row group, column, column group, then table.
- The region areas are fixed at a border width of 0pt and a padding of 0pt.

Borders with a conditionality of "discard" (the default) will have borders along split reference area edges discarded, as shown in Figure 9–7.

- A retained border will be drawn along the reference area's edge.

Figure 9–7   An illustration of border conditionality

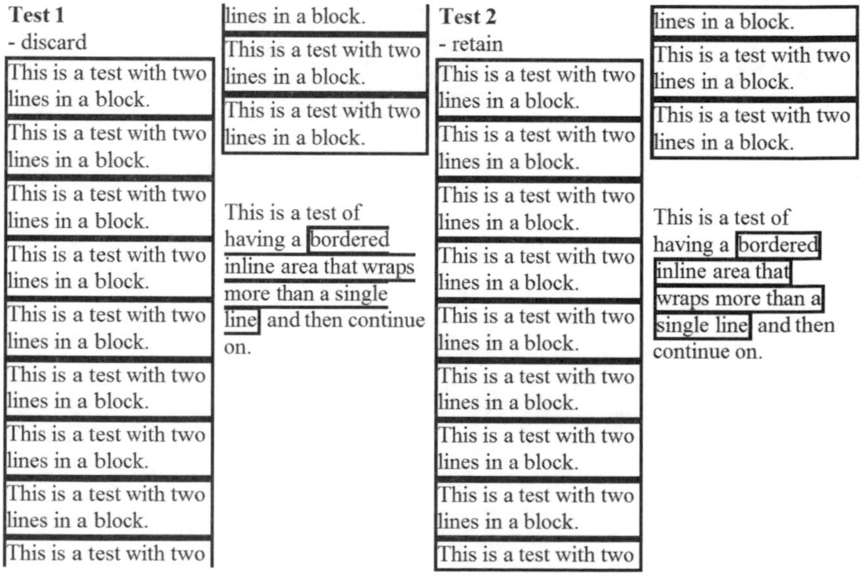

Note the following about the example:

- each test includes a test of both block and inline level bordered areas;
- the split areas have, respectively, open and closed edges along the splits in the first and second tests, implementing each of the "discard" and "retain" property values;
- the presence of the retained border in the inline test changes the amount of text that fits on the third line.

9.6 Backgrounds

9.6.1 Displaying backgrounds

Properties control the background colors and images of areas.

- background-color:
  - is either transparent, to show through the parent area background (default), or a specified color;
- background-image:
  - is a URI of the image to render as the background;
- background-repeat:
  - either repeatedly renders the background image in both directions — in the "x" direction (horizontal left to right according to the reference orientation) and in the "y" direction (vertical top to bottom according to the reference orientation) — or renders it only once;
- background-position-horizontal:
  - is the position of the background image in the horizontal direction (left to right according to the reference orientation);
- background-position-vertical:
  - is the position of the background image in the vertical direction (top to bottom according to the reference orientation);
- background-attachment:
  - specifies whether a background image scrolls in synchronization with the scrolling of an object or, if the presentation is electronic, the background image is fixed in place and the object's content scrolls over the fixed background.

An area's background is always within its padding rectangle, as shown in Figure 9–8.

- Any gaps in a border that is not solid (e.g. a dotted border) are transparent and will show through the parent area background.

Precedence is given to the contained areas.

- A child area's background shows on top of an area's background.
- An area's background shows on top of its parent's background.

9.6.2 Decorating page columns using a background

Consider the need to decorate columns of a page.

- There are no properties to decorate the normal-flow reference area of a column.
- You can create an image of the decoration for the background of the entire page.
  - For a single column, you could center a narrow image of just the decoration —
    - such as a simple vertical line.
  - For multiple columns, you could create a page-wide graphic with strategically placed decorations.
- The graphic of the decoration can be repeated for the entire page.
- This scheme does not work for a portion of the page, only for the entire page.

Example 9–3 shows excerpts from Figure 9–8.

Figure 9–8   Background visibility

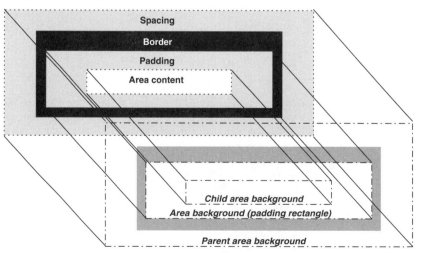

Example 9–3   Keeping a group of areas together in a reference area

```
Line 01   <region-body region-name="frame-body"
   02                 column-count="2" column-gap=".5cm"
   03                 background-position-horizontal="center"
   04                 background-repeat="repeat-y"
   05                 background-image='url("vertical-line.bmp")'/>
   06   ...
   07   <block background-color="silver">This is a test</block>
   08   ...
```

Figure 9–9 shows the rendering of the background image apparently between the two columns.

Of note:

• the silver background is used here only to illustrate the width of the columns on the page.

Figure 9–9   A decoration between page columns

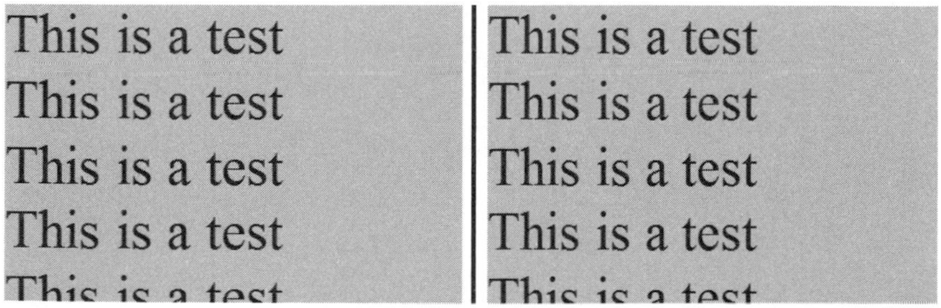

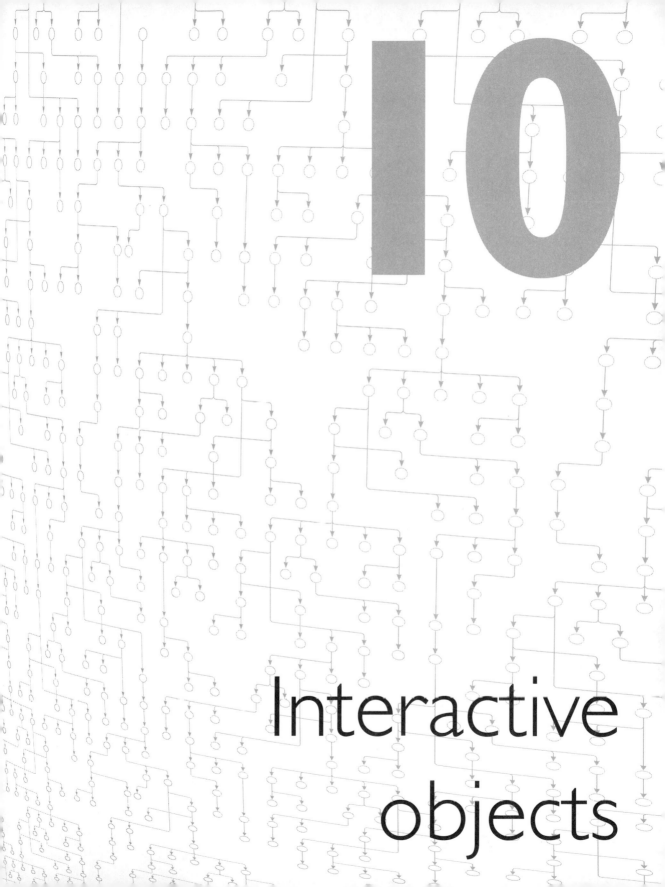

10

Interactive objects

10 Interactive objects

For the active rendering of changing information in an electronic display, XSL-FO supports interactive, operator-influenced presentation of content. The use of interactive formatting objects enables the operator (i.e. the reader of the document) to select from multiple alternatives prepared by the stylesheet writer, where the interactive object itself reflects previous interaction by its state. This results in a dynamically changing presentation of the information, rather than a single static rendering of the information.

XSL-FO 1.0 provides two areas where interactivity can influence presentation: reflecting the active state of a linked object using different property values, and selecting and switching between alternative available presentations using different sub-trees of formatting objects.

Appearance or other impartation differences can distinguish a link that can be but hasn't yet been traversed (future potential for visitation), from a link that would be traversed (active hover), from a link that is about to be traversed (has the focus), from a link that is in the process of being traversed (is activated), from a link that has been traversed (past visitation).

Switching alternative available renderings can be used to implement interactive presentations such as a dynamically expandable and collapsible table of contents. HTML pages accomplish this in an imperative fashion with scripting in a programming language, whereas XSL-FO 1.0 pages accomplish this in a declarative fashion by describing transition paths in a state machine, without having to implement the imperative logic behind the state machine.

Included in this chapter. This chapter includes discussion of the following XSL-FO objects.

Formatting objects related to dynamic properties:

- `multi-properties` (*6.9.6*):
  - is the collection of candidate property sets from which exactly one set influences the properties of a formatting object based on its status or the status of operator interaction,
- `multi-property-set` (*6.9.7*):
  - is the set of properties associated with a single possible state of a formatting object or operator interaction.

Formatting objects related to dynamic presentation:

- `multi-switch` (*6.9.3*):
  - is the collection of candidate formatting object sequences from which exactly one is rendered at any given time based on an interactive condition that is influenced by the operator while being tracked by the formatter,
- `multi-case` (*6.9.4*):
  - is a single formatting object sequence that is a candidate for rendering based on an interactive condition that is influenced by the operator while being tracked by the formatter,
- `multi-toggle` (*6.9.5*):
  - is the definition of the interaction-sensitive objects within a candidate sequence of formatting objects.

10.1 Reflecting formatting object state by appearance

10.1.1 Dynamically changing property values

The formatting object sub-trees sensitive to state reflection are wrapped into a `multi-properties` object.

- It collects the sets of properties and those descendent areas that are to be sensitive to operator interaction.

- You may specify default values for properties to be inherited by descendent areas.
- Each `multi-property-set` object captures the properties for a given state.
  - Use `active-state` to specify the state for the collection of properties.
- Any, some, or all of the following states can have associated properties.
  - "`link`" (unvisited):
    - is `true` when a descendant `basic-link` object hasn't yet been visited;
  - "`hover`":
    - is `true` when a descendant area is under the influence of some pointing device, yet without activation of the interactivity;
  - "`focus`":
    - is `true` when a descendant area is the focus of operator interactivity (e.g., the user has tabbed to the hyperlink instead of using a pointing device);
  - "`active`":
    - is `true` when a descendant area is being activated by operator interactivity (e.g. during the time the pointing device button is being pressed but not released);
  - "`visited`":
    - is `true` when a descendant `basic-link` object has already been visited.

A `multi-properties` object is a neutral construct.

- In general it can be used anywhere the formatting objects it wraps can be used.

The objects that are to be rendered are captured in the `wrapper` object.

- It merges inherited properties with the sibling properties associated with the current state by using the `merge-property-values()` function.
  - Regular ancestor inheritance during formatting object tree refinement would miss the sibling `multi-property-set` constructs.
  - This function cannot be used with any other formatting object, nor with a `wrapper` that has any other parent object.
- You may specify any other inheritable properties for descendant constructs.

The nesting of the constructs is illustrated in Figure 10–1.

10.1.2 The multi-properties object

Purpose

- This is the collection of candidate property sets from which exactly one set influences the properties of a formatting object based on its status or the status of user interaction.
  - It supports reserved states for the `basic-link` object.

Content

- (*6.9.6*) (`multi-property-set+`, `wrapper`),
- child objects (listed alphabetically):
  - `multi-property-set` (*6.9.7*; 269),
  - `wrapper` (*6.11.2*; 100).

Property sets

- Common accessibility properties (*7.4*; 326).

Other optional property

- `id` (*7.28.2*; 384).

Figure 10–1   Structuring multiple sets of properties for a sequence of formatting objects

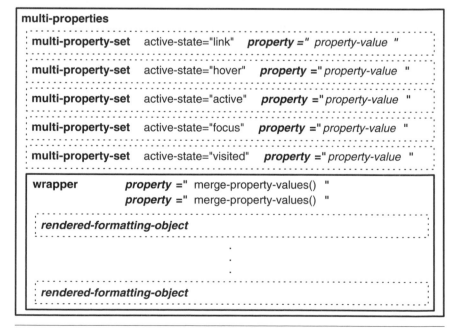

Function of interest

- `merge-property-values()` is used on the `wrapper` object that is ancestral to the formatting objects being rendered.
  - It merges the corresponding values from the properties specified for the active `multi-property-set` according to the current state.

Consider the need to reproduce typical browser colors for unvisited and visited links —

- blue when not yet visited,
- purple when already visited.

Example 10–1 illustrates how this would be accomplished.

Example 10–1   An example of using dynamic formatting properties

```
Line 01  <block>This is a link:
    02   <multi-properties>
    03     <multi-property-set active-state="link" color="blue"/>
    04     <multi-property-set active-state="visited" color="purple"/>
    05     <wrapper color="merge-property-values()">
    06       <basic-link external-destination="http://www.CraneSoftwrights.com"
    07   >http://www.CraneSoftwrights.com</basic-link>
    08     </wrapper>
    09   </multi-properties>
    10   : end of block.
    11   </block>
```

10.1.3 The multi-property-set object

Purpose

- This is the set of properties associated with a single possible state of a formatting object or user interaction.

Content

- (*6.9.7*) EMPTY,
- referring object:
  - `multi-properties` (*6.9.6*; 268).

Required property

- `active-state` (*7.22.1*; 345).

Optional property

- id (*7.28.2*; 384).

Example 10–2 highlights where this formatting object is used in the earlier example of mimicking browser colors.

Example 10–2   An example of using dynamic formatting properties

```
Line 01   <block>This is a link:
    02   <multi-properties>
    03    <multi-property-set active-state="link" color="blue"/>
    04    <multi-property-set active-state="visited" color="purple"/>
    05    <wrapper color="merge-property-values()">
    06       <basic-link external-destination="http://www.CraneSoftwrights.com"
    07   >http://www.CraneSoftwrights.com</basic-link>
    08    </wrapper>
    09   </multi-properties>
    10   : end of block.
    11   </block>
```

10.2 Interactively changing the effective flow

10.2.1 Dynamically changing formatting object sub-trees

The formatting objects participating in two or more renderings with dynamic changes are wrapped into a multi-switch object.

- They are separated into individual mutually exclusive conditions.
- Always exactly one condition is shown at a time.
  - All other conditions are hidden when not shown.
- Operator interactivity can change which condition is shown.
  - The action of doing so will hide all conditions not being shown.

Individual conditions are wrapped by child multi-case objects.

- There is one such child per condition.
- It is named for reference purposes (as the target of a toggle).
- It is titled for display purposes (when selecting from a number of cases).

Changing which condition is shown is enabled by the multi-toggle object.

- It defines a "hot spot" on a page.
- It encloses the flow object sub-trees sensitive to operator interaction.
  - The essence of the operator interaction is defined by the formatter.

- You can have any number of toggles in a given sequence for different behaviors.
  - Each toggle can only change the current shown state of one other case.
    - The formatter may provide a list of case names from which the operator can choose.
      - The list is documented using the respective mandatory case titles.
    - The formatter may cycle through sibling cases in either direction.
  - A toggle can only change states amongst sibling `multi-case` objects.
- Only sensitive areas need to be surrounded, not the entire content.

Descendent `multi-switch` objects within `multi-switch` objects can make for very rich presentation.

- Properties can accommodate an ancestor `multi-switch` object being hidden.
  - They can restore the initial state of the descendent `multi-switch` object.
  - The default is to preserve the active state in the descendant regardless of the behavior of the ancestor.
- They can be nested to any depth.
- The stylesheet writer doesn't need to know programming, but does need to understand basic concepts of changing state as in state machines.

The XSL-FO instance effectively implements a state machine.

- The initial state determines which object sequence is shown;
  - others are hidden.
- Transitions to subsequent states are triggered by operator interaction —
  - showing another one, hiding this one.
- Restoration to the initial state may happen on ancestral change of state;
  - hiding the ancestor may possibly reset the descendant.

Figure 10–2 shows how these constructs are nested and how the toggle constructs refer to the case constructs.

10.2.2 The multi-switch object

Purpose

- This is the collection of candidate formatting object sequences from which exactly one is rendered at any given time based on an interactive condition that is influenced by the operator while being tracked by the formatter.

Content

- (*6.9.3*) (`multi-case+`),
- child object:
    - `multi-case` (*6.9.4*; 274).

Property sets

- Common accessibility properties (*7.4*; 326).

Other optional properties

- `auto-restore` (*7.22.2*; 347),
- `id` (*7.28.2*; 384).

Property of interest

- `auto-restore` is used to indicate whether this `multi-switch` is restored to initial state when an ancestral `multi-switch` causes this `multi-switch` to be hidden.

Figure 10–2   The nesting of dynamically-switched formatting objects

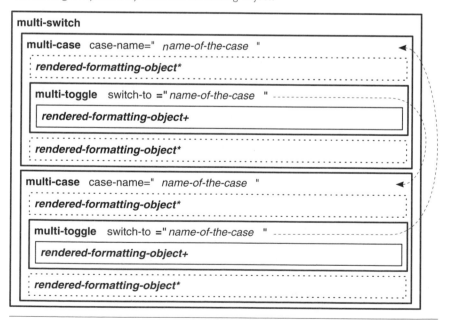

Consider a mockup in Figure 10–3;

- the results are presented without any user input;
- the stylesheet chooses to use underscore to indicate to the reader the hot text to click on to expand the entry.

Continuing from Figure 10–3, the display changes as shown in Figure 10–4;

- the operator has clicked on "Thursday", thus revealing the drop-down timesheet values;
- the stylesheet again chooses to use underscore to indicate to the reader the hot text to click on to expand the entry;
- the stylesheet has used indentation to indicate to the reader that "Thursday" can be clicked on to collapse the entry.

Figure 10–3   Dynamic objects example snapshot 1

Timesheet

Monday: 9 hours
Tuesday: 10 hours
Wednesday: 6 hours
Thursday: 10 hours
Friday: 6 hours

Figure 10–4   Dynamic objects example snapshot 2

Timesheet

Monday: 9 hours
Tuesday: 10 hours
Wednesday: 6 hours
Thursday: (10 hours)
- email: 3 hours
- office: 2 hours
- writing: 2 hours
- profdev: 3 hours
Friday: 6 hours

Continuing from Figure 10–3 again, the display changes as shown in Figure 10–5;

- the operator has clicked on "writing", thus revealing the drop-down timesheet values;
- collapsing the "Thursday" again will restore the original collapsed state of "writing".

An excerpt from Figure 10–5 is shown in Example 10–3.

10.2.3   The multi-case object

Purpose

- This is a single formatting object sequence that is a candidate for rendering based on an interactive condition that is influenced by the operator while being tracked by the formatter.
    - It is comprised of interaction-sensitive (using `multi-toggle`) and interaction-insensitive formatting objects.

Content

- *(6.9.4)* (#PCDATA | %inline; | %block;)*,
- child objects (listed alphabetically):
    - %block; *(6.2;* 69),
    - %inline; *(6.2;* 70),

Figure 10–5   Dynamic objects example snapshot 3

Timesheet

<u>Monday: 9 hours</u>
<u>Tuesday: 10 hours</u>
<u>Wednesday: 6 hours</u>
Thursday: (10 hours)
- email: 3 hours
- office: 2 hours
- writing:
    - pfux: 2 hours
- profdev: 3 hours
<u>Friday: 6 hours</u>

Example 10–3   Mockup of interactive markup

```
Line 01  <list-block>
02       ...
03       <multi-switch auto-restore="true">
04         <multi-case case-title="Roll-up writing"
05                     case-name="roll-up" starting-state="show">
06           <list-item>
07             <list-item-label><block>-</block></list-item-label>
08             <list-item-body start-indent="body-start()">
09               <block text-decoration="underline">
10                 <multi-toggle switch-to="roll-down"
11                                     >writing: 2 hours</multi-toggle>
12               </block>
13             </list-item-body>
14           </list-item>
15         </multi-case>
16         <multi-case case-title="Roll-down writing"
17                     case-name="roll-down" starting-state="hide">
18           <list-item>
19             <list-item-label><block>-</block></list-item-label>
20             <list-item-body start-indent="body-start()">
21               <block>
22                 <multi-toggle switch-to="roll-up"
23                                         >writing: </multi-toggle>
24               </block>
25               <list-block>
26                 <list-item>
27                   <list-item-label><block>-</block></list-item-label>
28                   <list-item-body start-indent="body-start()">
29                     <block>pfux: 2 hours</block>
30                   </list-item-body>
31                 </list-item>
32               </list-block>
33             </list-item-body>
34           </list-item>
35         </multi-case>
36       </multi-switch>
37       ...
38  </list-block>
```

- referring object:
  - multi-switch (*6.9.3*; 271).

Property sets

- Common accessibility properties (*7.4*; 326).

Other required properties

- `case-name` (*7.22.3*; 367),
- `case-title` (*7.22.4*; 368).

Other optional properties

- `id` (*7.28.2*; 384),
- `starting-state` (*7.22.10*; 418).

Example 10–4 is again an excerpt from Figure 10–5.

10.2.4   The multi-toggle object

Purpose

- This is the definition of the interaction-sensitive objects within a candidate sequence of formatting objects.
  - It specifies which candidate sequence is to be the rendered as a result of the interaction.

Content

- (*6.9.5*) `(#PCDATA | %inline; | %block;)*`,
- child objects (listed alphabetically):
  - `%block;` (*6.2*; 69),
  - `%inline;` (*6.2*; 70).
- It must be a descendant of `multi-case`.

Property sets

- Common accessibility properties (*7.4*; 326).

Other optional properties

- `id` (*7.28.2*; 384),
- `switch-to` (*7.22.11*; 419).

Example 10–5 is again an excerpt from Figure 10–5.

Example 10–4   Mockup of interactive markup

```
Line 01  <list-block>
02     ...
03     <multi-switch auto-restore="true">
04       <multi-case case-title="Roll-up writing"
05                   case-name="roll-up" starting-state="show">
06         <list-item>
07           <list-item-label><block>-</block></list-item-label>
08           <list-item-body start-indent="body-start()">
09             <block text-decoration="underline">
10               <multi-toggle switch-to="roll-down"
11                                   >writing: 2 hours</multi-toggle>
12             </block>
13           </list-item-body>
14         </list-item>
15       </multi-case>
16       <multi-case case-title="Roll-down writing"
17                   case-name="roll-down" starting-state="hide">
18         <list-item>
19           <list-item-label><block>-</block></list-item-label>
20           <list-item-body start-indent="body-start()">
21             <block>
22               <multi-toggle switch-to="roll-up"
23                                       >writing: </multi-toggle>
24             </block>
25             <list-block>
26               <list-item>
27                 <list-item-label><block>-</block></list-item-label>
28                 <list-item-body start-indent="body-start()">
29                   <block>pfux: 2 hours</block>
30                 </list-item-body>
31               </list-item>
32             </list-block>
33           </list-item-body>
34         </list-item>
35       </multi-case>
36     </multi-switch>
37     ...
38  </list-block>
```

Example 10–5   Mockup of interactive markup

```
Line 01   <list-block>
  02        ...
  03        <multi-switch auto-restore="true">
  04          <multi-case case-title="Roll-up writing"
  05                      case-name="roll-up" starting-state="show">
  06            <list-item>
  07              <list-item-label><block>-</block></list-item-label>
  08              <list-item-body start-indent="body-start()">
  09                <block text-decoration="underline">
  10                  <multi-toggle switch-to="roll-down"
  11                                       >writing: 2 hours</multi-toggle>
  12                </block>
  13              </list-item-body>
  14            </list-item>
  15          </multi-case>
  16          <multi-case case-title="Roll-down writing"
  17                      case-name="roll-down" starting-state="hide">
  18            <list-item>
  19              <list-item-label><block>-</block></list-item-label>
  20              <list-item-body start-indent="body-start()">
  21                <block>
  22                  <multi-toggle switch-to="roll-up"
  23                                       >writing: </multi-toggle>
  24                </block>
  25                <list-block>
  26                  <list-item>
  27                    <list-item-label><block>-</block></list-item-label>
  28                    <list-item-body start-indent="body-start()">
  29                      <block>pfux: 2 hours</block>
  30                    </list-item-body>
  31                  </list-item>
  32                </list-block>
  33              </list-item-body>
  34            </list-item>
  35          </multi-case>
  36        </multi-switch>
  37        ...
  38   </list-block>
```

Supplemental objects

Supplemental objects

This chapter addresses the final few formatting objects not yet discussed. These objects are not used by many stylesheet writers, but are critically important to those who do need them. The functionality is focused in two particular areas: character-level processing and constructs of a global nature.

- Character-level processing outside of the default behaviors includes —
  - managing the bidirectionality inherent in the Unicode properties of characters,
  - instantiating formatting objects explicitly in the formatting object tree.
- Constructs of a global nature include —
  - specifying a color system recognized by an XSL-FO processor,
  - accommodating a home in the XSL-FO instance for color system specifications.

One of the most powerful features of XSL-FO processors is that they are obliged to respect the inherent direction property of every Unicode character as defined by the Unicode standard. This relieves the stylesheet writer from the responsibility of detecting and acting on the characters in a bidirectional flow where right-to-left characters are intermixed with left-to-right characters. The author of the XML document being transformed into XSL-FO is responsible for the text characters being rendered and will use a mixture of directional character paths as required by their needs. The XSL-FO stylesheet writer can rest assured the inherent properties will be respected by a conformant processor. However, should the stylesheet want to present characters in an alternative character path, overriding the bidi-rectionality inherent in the characters themselves, a formatting object is needed to instruct the processor to act accordingly.

The abstraction of the character formatting object in the formatting object tree, instantiated by text in the XSL-FO instance, is available as a stand-alone object if explicitly specified using the vocabulary. This allows the stylesheet writer to override character-level properties on a per-character basis without relying on inheritance by using wrappers or other inline constructs.

Color is critically important to many compositors. Although XSL-FO supports RGB color values as used in HTML and CSS, many other color systems are available in printing software and hardware. To take advantage of other color systems, one can indicate the system in the stylesheet and then access it from other constructs. This brings up the need for information of a global nature that must reside outside of the information being flowed on the canvas.

Included in this chapter. This chapter includes discussion of the following XSL-FO objects:

- `bidi-override` (*6.6.2*):
  - specifies how to manage and override the inherent Unicode text direction for a sequence of characters,
- `character` (*6.6.3*):
  - represents both the abstract formatting object implied by a single character in an XSL-FO instance and the concrete formatting object available to be used in place of a simple character,
- `color-profile` (*6.4.4*):
  - is the declaration of a profile of candidate color values from which color specifications can be made by formatting objects,
- `declarations` (*6.4.3*):
  - is a global-scope repository of formatting object constructs for an XSL-FO instance, containing —
    - the collection of available color profiles,
    - any collections of extended formatting objects supported by an XSL-FO processor.

- The extended formatting objects must use a processor-recognized namespace URI other than the XSL-FO namespace URI.

11.1 Specialty formatting objects

`bidi-override` overrides the inherent behavior of characters as defined by Unicode.

- Most uses of characters require no special handing.
  - Most Unicode characters have an intrinsic writing direction property utilized by the formatter.
    - Some characters have a weak or neutral writing direction.
  - The processor is supposed to respect the writing direction of all characters so that the stylesheet writer does not have to accommodate any combination of characters used by the author of the source XML document.
- Special formatting may require a behavior different from what is intrinsically defined, e.g.:
  - to protect left-to-right presentation from being influenced by the presence of right-to-left characters,
  - to display right-to-left characters in a left-to-right fashion.

`character` objects:

- govern the presentation of glyphs associated with coded characters,
- are implicitly created by the presence of text nodes (`#PCDATA`) in the XSL-FO instance,
- are explicitly created using an element in the XSL-FO vocabulary, which:
  - prevents the need to represent the character as a coded character,
  - provides for specifying properties on a single character in the flow.

`color-profile` provides alternative color specifications that may be required for rendering.

- Formalized color definitions provide alternatives to the built-in color granularity.
- The stylesheet writer is obliged to always provide an RGB fallback color to accommodate formatters that do not support the requested color profile.

`declarations` provides a home in an XSL-FO instance for constructs out of the pagination.

- A home location is required in the XSL-FO instance for referenced constructs that do not exist in any flow or repeatable construct.
- This object is used for XSL-FO vocabulary purposes, e.g.:
  - `color-profile`;
- it is also used for extension and other vocabulary purposes.

11.2 The importance of bidirectional text

Some international formatting requirements must accommodate mixing text of different writing directions.

- The presentation of right-to-left scripts (e.g. Hebrew, Arabic, Thaana, and Syriac) may be embedded into the presentation of left-to-right scripts.
- The stylesheet may be mixing its boilerplate text with authored content of either possible direction from many different sources to produce the combined result.
- The formatter is responsible for placement and interpretation of glyphs on the page based on the character code points in the XSL-FO instance.
- The stylesheet writer is responsible for protecting text, where possible, from being influenced in the XSL-FO instance being formatted.

Three aspects of writing direction influence the presentation of information in a line.

- A line has an inline-progression direction determined by the writing direction of the closest ancestral reference area.
  - Information is flowed into lines in the inline-progression direction, independent of the visual order of the characters in the information.
- A group of adjacent characters may have semantic affinity and would thus be required to be flowed into the lines in groups.
  - Groups are ordered in the inline-progression direction.
  - E.g., in a right-to-left progression direction there may be groups of left-to-right characters.
    - The groups are rendered right-to-left on the line, but the characters in each group are rendered left-to-right.
    - Without grouping, adjacent strings of the same direction would be rendered as a whole, losing the semantic affinity in the characters.

- E.g., boilerplate information from the stylesheet is often semantically distinct from source file information, needing insulation from undue influence from the content.
- Characters from different scripts have inherent writing directions that may differ from the inline-progression direction.
  - Usually it is necessary to respect the character direction while accommodating the inline-progression direction (this is the responsibility of the formatter).
  - It may be necessary to override the inherent direction for a special effect.
  - Many characters are not associated with any language and are influenced by their proximity to characters from different scripts.
- Stylesheet writers can specify the progression direction of the information, the grouping of characters, and the respect or override of the inherent Unicode direction in characters.

11.3 The mechanics of mixing text of different writing directions

Evolving rendering needs are being documented by Unicode and are influenced by XSL-FO.

- The rendering algorithm is governed primarily by the Unicode Bidirectional Algorithm:
  - http://www.unicode.org/unicode/reports/tr9
- Nuances are described by XSL-FO 1.0 Recommendation (Unicode BIDI Algorithm, Section 5.8) in conjunction with the CSS definition.
  - XSL-FO slightly modifies the CSS definition, e.g. mandating that an unspecified `direction` property is assumed to be that of the `writing-mode` in effect.
- Here, we do not attempt to repeat the detailed algorithms described in the above documents, but only to give a general overview.

There are three categories of direction strength for Unicode characters.

- Strong characters are from language groups with well defined left-to-right or right-to-left character-progression directions.
  - This includes "marks" that are non-spacing invisible characters with strong direction —
    - `&#x200e;` — left-to-right mark (LRM),
    - `&#x200f;` — right-to-left mark (RLM).
  - This includes directional controls that are interpreted by the rendering algorithm —

- ‪ — left-to-right embed begin (LRE),
- ‫ — right-to-left embed begin (RLE),
- ‭ — left-to-right override begin (LRO),
- ‮ — right-to-left override begin (RLO).

- Weak characters are digits, currency symbols, and some punctuation characters.
  - This includes mirroring characters whose presentation on the canvas may be different from their representation in the data.
    - This includes "(", ")", "[", "]", "<", ">", "{", "}", "«", "»", etc.
    - A mirrored character is rendered in the writing direction of adjacent text, which may require it to be flipped by the formatter.
      - The stylesheet writer doesn't have any responsibility for doing the flipping.
  - This includes ‬ — Pop Directional Formatting (PDF) — for embedding levels.
- Neutral characters are white space characters and some separator characters.

The embedding algorithm is based on isolating groups of sequences in "embedding levels."

- An embedded sequence sets a progression direction for the members of the sequence.
  - Members are characters or other embedded sequences.
- The stylesheet writer may need to introduce embedding levels to keep a sequence of characters together.
  - The stylesheet would need to recognize or predict the semantic affinity of the group to know where to embed a new level.
- Using bidi-override will create an embedding level.
  - The progression direction of the level is either the specified direction, or the current writing-mode direction if not specified.
  - Using a unicode-bidi value of "embed" doesn't change the inherent writing direction of the individual characters in the embedding level.
  - Using a unicode-bidi value of "bidi-override" forces the characters to render in the direction of the embedding level, ignoring the inherent properties of the characters.
    - All characters are assigned the overriding direction as if they were strongly directed; their original nature is forgotten.
- Embedding levels are indicated in the resulting stream using LRE, RLE, LRO, RLO, and PDF Unicode characters.

The resulting stream of characters is grouped according to the Unicode directionality controls.

- The grouping of characters crosses boundaries of embedding levels.
- The act of grouping weak characters with strong characters gives direction to the weak characters.
  - Weak characters are influenced by their proximity to strong characters so they become strongly directed themselves.
  - Weak characters between two strong characters of the same direction adopt that direction.
  - Weak characters preceding a strong character without white space interruption adopt the strong character's direction.
  - Weak characters following a strong character and any intervening white space adopt the strong character's direction.
- The characters are rendered after all of the characters have been assigned a direction.

Examples in this book include sequences of right-to-left language text, as defined in Example 11–1.

- &hebrew-test; is "Hebrew test" in Hebrew;
- &arabic-test; is "Arabic test" in Arabic.

Example 11–1   Sample Unicode sequences of right-to-left language text

```
Line 01   <!ENTITY hebrew-test   "&#x05D1;&#x05D3;&#x05D9;&#x05E7;&#x05D4;
    02                            &#x05E2;&#x05D1;&#x05E8;&#x05D9;&#x05EA;">
    03   <!ENTITY arabic-test1  "&#x0625;&#x062e;&#x062a;&#x0628;&#x0627;">
    04   <!ENTITY arabic-test2  "&#x0631; &#x0639;&#x0631;&#x0628;&#x064a;">
    05   <!ENTITY arabic-test   "&arabic-test1;&arabic-test2;">
```

Consider a detailed example of mixing sequences of different directions in Example 11–2.

- Lines in the test are grouped differently to illustrate how groups are ordered in the writing direction for rendering before the characters found in the group are rendered;
  - test "12" is left-to-right with embedded sequences of right-to-left text;
  - test "23" is right-to-left with the content identical to test "12";
  - test "34" is almost identical to test "23" except for a space introduced after "89";
  - test "45" is right-to-left but the language text inside is in groups without overriding direction;
  - test "56" is left-to-right but the language text inside is in groups that override direction;

Example 11–2   Controlling bidirectionality using grouping

```
Line 01  <block-container>
     02    <block>12 - English Test 13 , Test Français 14
     03    + &hebrew-test; 15 = &arabic-test; 16 / 89end</block>
     04  </block-container>
     05  <block-container writing-mode="rl-tb">
     06    <block>23 - English Test 13 , Test Français 14
     07    + &hebrew-test; 15 = &arabic-test; 16 / 89end</block>
     08  </block-container>
     09  <block-container writing-mode="rl-tb">
     10    <block>34 - English Test 13 , Test Français 14
     11    + &hebrew-test; 15 = &arabic-test; 16 / 89 end</block>
     12  </block-container>
     13  <block-container writing-mode="rl-tb">
     14    <block>45 - <bidi-override unicode-bidi="embed"
     15                        >English Test 13</bidi-override>
     16            , <bidi-override unicode-bidi="embed"
     17                        >Test Français 14</bidi-override>
     18            + <bidi-override unicode-bidi="embed"
     19                        >&hebrew-test; 15</bidi-override>
     20            = <bidi-override unicode-bidi="embed"
     21                        >&arabic-test; 16</bidi-override>
     22            / 89 end</block></block-container>
     23  <block-container>
     24    <block>56 - <bidi-override unicode-bidi="bidi-override"
     25                        >English Test 13</bidi-override>
     26            , <bidi-override unicode-bidi="bidi-override"
     27                        >Test Français 14</bidi-override>
     28            + <bidi-override unicode-bidi="bidi-override"
     29                        >&hebrew-test; 15</bidi-override>
     30            = <bidi-override unicode-bidi="bidi-override"
     31                        >&arabic-test; 16</bidi-override>
     32            / 89 end</block></block-container>
     33  <block-container writing-mode="rl-tb">
     34    <block>67 - <bidi-override unicode-bidi="bidi-override"
     35                        >English Test 13</bidi-override>
     36            , <bidi-override unicode-bidi="bidi-override"
     37                        >Test Français 14</bidi-override>
     38            + <bidi-override unicode-bidi="bidi-override"
     39                        >&hebrew-test; 15</bidi-override>
     40            = <bidi-override unicode-bidi="bidi-override"
     41                        >&arabic-test; 16</bidi-override>
     42            / 89 end</block></block-container>
```

- test "67" is right-to-left but the language text inside is in groups that override direction.

- Note that where the direction isn't specified, it is inferred by the writing mode;
  - this is different from CSS that assumes left-to-right when not specified.
- Weak punctuation characters separate the strong script characters.
  - The first three tests illustrate the differences in assignment of direction to weak characters.
  - Note how the introduction of a space at the end of the "34" test changes the direction assignment to the "89" characters, compared to the "89" characters in the "23" test.
- Embedding groups arrange the groups of left-to-right sequences;
  - in test "34", the English text is shown to the left of the French text;
  - in test "45", the French text is shown to the left of the English text.
- Overriding the direction results in an improper presentation of language text;
  - in test "56", the Hebrew and Arabic sequences are inappropriately presented;
  - in test "67", the English and French sequences are inappropriately presented.

Figure 11–1 illustrates the on-screen interpretation of Example 11–2.

- The line annotations are only for illustrative purposes; they visualise the groupings of characters and the character writing directions.
- This test does not incorporate explicit use of Unicode directionality characters;
  - the use of `bidi-override` introduces these characters into the rendering stream.
- Note how the grouping of characters for strength purposes goes over the bounds of embedded levels.

11.4 The bidirectional support challenge

The challenge for the stylesheet writer is to recognize when it is necessary to add marks or add embedding levels in the flow.

- Always using a single stream of character information will only work if all of the text is in the same direction as the inline-progression direction.
  - An internationally used stylesheet would need to respect the possibility of mixing weak and neutral characters with strong characters of both directions.
- E.g., consider mixing boilerplate text with authored text.

- One may assume that the authored text was correctly presented to the author while being worked on, so the content could be formatted as entered without special concerns.
- If English boilerplate text is to be abutted to language text of an arbitrary language, weak characters in the boilerplate text might be inadvertently influenced by the strong characters of the authored text.
  - The influence could rearrange characters or flip the rendering of mirrored characters found in the boilerplate.
- Add LRM (‎) before and after the left-to-right boilerplate text;
- add RLM (‏) before and after the right-to-left boilerplate text.

Be careful when formatting generated content, such as table of contents entries.

- Leaders and page numbers follow the arbitrary title text.
- The content of the title is abutted to the leaders and page numbers.

Figure 11–1   Example of bidirectionality

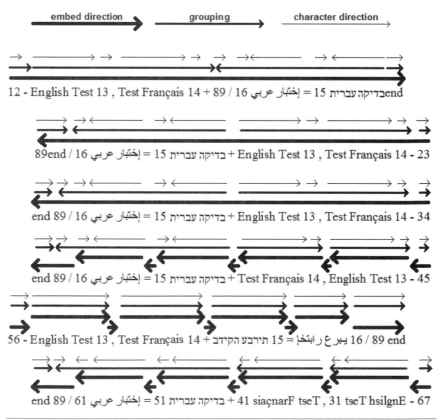

- Wrapping the leaders and page numbers in marks will protect them from being influenced by the characters at the end of the title.

The sample files in Example 11–3 and Example 11–4 illustrate the importance of adding marks.

- The table of contents entries are extracting arbitrary title contents.
- If the characters preceding and following the title are not protected with strong marks, the display is corrupted;
    - the weak characters of the boilerplate are influenced by the strong characters of the title.

Example 11–3 formats two tables of contents, the first without protection and the second protecting the boilerplate of the entries from the arbitrary text directions of the characters in the titles.

Example 11–3   Adding marks

```
Line 01  <!ENTITY LRM "&#x200e;">
     02  <!ENTITY RLM "&#x200f;">
     03  ...
     04  <block space-after=".5cm">
     05    This is a table of contents without using marks:
     06  </block>
     07  <xsl:for-each select="/doc/section">
     08    <block text-align-last="justify">
     09      <xsl:value-of select="position()"/>.
     10      <xsl:value-of select="title"/>
     11      (<xsl:value-of select="count(subsection)"/>)
     12      <leader leader-pattern="dots"/>
     13      <page-number-citation ref-id="{generate-id(.)}"/>
     14    </block>
     15  </xsl:for-each>
     16
     17  <block space-before="1.5cm" space-after=".5cm">
     18    This is a table of contents using marks:
     19  </block>
     20  <xsl:for-each select="/doc/section">
     21    <block text-align-last="justify">
     22      <xsl:value-of select="position()"/>.&LRM;
     23      <xsl:apply-templates select="title"/>
     24      &LRM;(<xsl:value-of select="count(subsection)"/>)
     25      <leader leader-pattern="dots"/>
     26      <page-number-citation ref-id="{generate-id(.)}"/>
     27    </block>
     28  </xsl:for-each>
```

Example 11–4 includes titles utilizing text of different writing directions.

Example 11–4 A test file with mixed character directions

```
Line 01  <!DOCTYPE doc [
     02  <!ENTITY hebrew-test  "&#x05D1;&#x05D3;&#x05D9;&#x05E7;&#x05D4;
     03                        &#x05E2;&#x05D1;&#x05E8;&#x05D9;&#x05EA;">
     04  <!ENTITY arabic-test1 "&#x0625;&#x062e;&#x062a;&#x0628;&#x0627;">
     05  <!ENTITY arabic-test2 "&#x0631; &#x0639;&#x0631;&#x0628;&#x064a;">
     06  <!ENTITY arabic-test  "&arabic-test1;&arabic-test2;">
     07  ]>
     08  <doc>
     09    <section>
     10      <title>English Test</title>
     11      <subsection>Sub 1 in English</subsection>
     12      ...
     13      <subsection>Sub 15 in English</subsection>
     14    </section>
     15    <section>
     16      <title>&hebrew-test;</title>
     17      <subsection>Sub 1 in Hebrew</subsection>
     18      ...
     19      <subsection>Sub 14 in Hebrew</subsection>
     20    </section>
     21    <section>
     22      <title>&arabic-test;</title>
     23      <subsection>Sub 1 in Arabic</subsection>
     24      ...
     25      <subsection>Sub 14 in Arabic</subsection>
     26    </section>
     27    <section>
     28      <title>Test Fran&#xe7;ais</title>
     29      <subsection>Sub 1 in French</subsection>
     30      ...
     31      <subsection>Sub 12 in French</subsection>
     32    </section>
```

The formatted result in Figure 11–2 illustrates the impact of including the marks for protection from the characters of the titles.

Note the behavior when the marks are not present (top rendering).

- The right-to-left text influences the following weak characters " (14" and makes them all part of a right-to-left group.
  - The "(" character is displayed as ")" because it is a mirror character being displayed right-to-left.

- The "14" still renders left-to-right because the grouping isn't powerful enough to override the inherent writing direction of the digits.
- The original ")" and the following space are influenced by the `leader` and the writing direction of the line, which is left to right, so the mirroring character doesn't change.

11.5 The bidi-override object

Purpose

- It specifies how to manage and override the inherent Unicode text direction for a sequence of characters.
- This is not needed for standard processing of a mixture of writing-mode characters, as the processor will recognize the inherent text direction and act accordingly.

Content

- *(6.6.2)* `(#PCDATA | %inline; | %block;)*`,
- child objects (listed alphabetically):
  - `%block;` (*6.2*; 69),
  - `%inline;` (*6.2*; 70),
- any number of `marker` children at the beginning.

Figure 11–2 Example of using marks

This is a table of contents without using marks:

1:-English Test (15) 2
2:-14) בדיקה עברית) 3
3:-14) إختبار عربي) 4
4:-Test Français (12) 5

This is a table of contents using marks:

1:-English Test (15) 2
2:-בדיקה עברית (14) 3
3:-إختبار عربي (14) 4
4:-Test Français (12) 5

Property sets

- Common aural properties (*7.6*; 327),
- common font properties (*7.8*; 331),
- common relative position properties (*7.12*; 333).

Other optional properties

- color (*7.17.1*; 369),
- direction (*7.27.1*; 373),
- id (*7.28.2*; 384),
- letter-spacing (*7.16.2*; 389),
- line-height (*7.15.4*; 390),
- score-spaces (*7.28.6*; 412),
- unicode-bidi (*7.27.6*; 424),
- word-spacing (*7.16.8*; 428).

Shorthand influencing the above properties

- font (*7.29.13*; 377).

Properties of interest

- unicode-bidi
  - Use "embed" to wrap groups of characters that are to progress in the writing direction of the parent construct;
    - this preserves the inherent writing direction of the characters in the group.
  - Use "bidi-override" to force the wrapped characters to progress in the writing direction of the parent construct;
    - this overrides the inherent writing direction of the characters in the group.
- direction
  - Use "ltr" and "rtl" to specify the direction of the embedded characters.
  - The default direction is that of the parent construct.

11.6 **The character object**

Purpose

- This is both an abstract formatting object implied by a single text character in an XSL-FO instance and the concrete formatting object available to be used in place of a simple character.

Content

- (*6.6.3*) EMPTY.

Property sets

- Common aural properties (*7.6*; 327),
- common border, padding, and background properties (*7.7*; 328),
- common font properties (*7.8*; 331),
- common hyphenation properties (*7.9*; 332),
- common margin properties — inline (*7.11*; 333),
- common relative position properties (*7.12*; 333).

Other required property

- character (*7.16.1*; 368).

Other optional properties

- alignment-adjust (*7.13.1*; 346),
- alignment-baseline (*7.13.2*; 346),
- baseline-shift (*7.13.3*; 351),
- color (*7.17.1*; 369),
- dominant-baseline (*7.13.5*; 374),
- glyph-orientation-horizontal (*7.27.2*; 381),
- glyph-orientation-vertical (*7.27.3*; 381),
- id (*7.28.2*; 384),
- keep-with-next (*7.19.4*; 386),
- keep-with-previous (*7.19.5*; 387),
- letter-spacing (*7.16.2*; 389),
- line-height (*7.15.4*; 390),
- score-spaces (*7.28.6*; 412),
- suppress-at-line-break (*7.16.3*; 418),
- text-altitude (*7.27.4*; 421),
- text-decoration (*7.16.4*; 422),
- text-depth (*7.27.5*; 422),
- text-shadow (*7.16.5*; 423),
- text-transform (*7.16.6*; 423),
- treat-as-word-space (*7.16.7*; 424),

- visibility (*7.28.8*; 425),
- word-spacing (*7.16.8*; 428).

Shorthands influencing the above properties

- font (*7.29.13*; 377),
- page-break-after (*7.29.16*; 401),
- page-break-before (*7.29.17*; 401),
- vertical-align (*7.29.22*; 424).

11.7 The color-profile object

Purpose

- This is the declaration of a profile of candidate color values from which color specifications can be made by formatting objects.

Content

- (*6.4.4*) EMPTY,
- referring object:
  - declarations (*6.4.3*; 297).

Required properties

- color-profile-name (*7.17.2*; 369),
- src (*7.28.7*; 417).

Optional property

- rendering-intent (*7.17.3*; 408).

Functions of interest

- The value of src is a URI recognized by the processor to represent the desired color system.
- rgb-icc() is used for a color property value to reference the named color profile according to the numeric arguments specific to the profile definition.
  - Note the function requires fallback RGB specification in the case the formatter does not recognize the desired color system.

11.8 **The declarations object**

Purpose

- This is a repository of global formatting object constructs including the collection of available color profiles and any collections of extended formatting objects supported by an XSL-FO processor.

Content

- (*6.4.3*) `(color-profile)+`,
- child object:
  - `color-profile` (*6.4.4*; 296),
- referring object:
  - `root` (*6.4.2*; 64).

No properties are defined for this formatting object.

A

Using XSLT with XSL-FO

A Using XSLT with XSL-FO

XSLT was designed primarily for use with XSL-FO.

- The result of an XSLT transform is an XML information set that may or may not be serialized as XML syntax.
  - The result information set can be delivered to XSL-FO formatter without serialization.
- A number of features of XSLT assist the writing of XSL-FO stylesheets.
- The design of XSL-FO is made simpler by the use of XSLT functionality.

XSLT is a normative part of XSL-FO.

- Section 2.1 of XSL-FO states the following:
  - The provisions in "XSL Transformations" form an integral part of this recommendation and are considered normative.

Certain aspects of XSL-FO are defined by XSLT.

- References are made in XSL-FO to the definitions in XSLT.
- Design decisions in XSL-FO pattern themselves after XSLT definitions.

There is no technical reason that XSLT must be used exclusively to create XSL-FO.

- The formatter will accept an instance of XSL-FO regardless of how that instance was generated.

A.1 XSLT language features supporting XSL-FO

A.1.1 The xsl:attribute-set instruction

xsl:attribute-set is a very useful instruction for the manipulation of many attributes targeted for a given formatting object.

- It names a set of attribute instructions that can be called on demand.
- It uses a namespace-qualified name promoting easy sharing of stylesheet fragments.
- It provides well-defined integration with other methods of specifying attributes for a result element.
  - Any xsl:attribute-set collections named in an xsl:use-attribute-sets attribute are added first.
  - Any attribute specifications in the literal result element itself are added next.
  - Any executed xsl:attribute instructions in the literal result element's template are added last.
  - Attribute values defined earlier are replaced with those defined later without an error.
  - The last value assigned to an attribute is what remains in the result tree.

A.1.2 List numbering facilities

The numbering facilities in XSLT allow the list structures in XSL-FO to be defined easier.

- The collection of list formatting objects are layout oriented, not content oriented.
  - A list is a list regardless of how it is labeled or what it contains.
- The content of the objects is defined by XSLT, thereby reducing the number of objects.
  - There is no distinction between numbered and unnumbered lists.
  - The type and structure of the list item labels is entirely out of the scope of formatting and rendering.

A.2 XSL-FO language features similar to XSLT and XPath

The expression language is very close, but not identical.

- The operators are the same;
- there is a wider set of operands in XSL-FO than in XPath.

Nuances of differences can make writing in XSLT confusing;

- this may trigger stylesheet errors.

Consider the situation of arithmetic calculations with lengths, as shown in Example A–1.

Example A–1   An illustration of uses of the expression language with lengths

```
Line 01   <xsl:template name="test">
     02   <xsl:variable name="num" select="100"/>
     03   <xsl:variable name="medium-font" select="'10pt'"/>
     04
     05   <block space-before.optimum="10pt div 2">
     06     First test: <xsl:value-of select="$num div 2"/>
     07   </block>
     08
     09   <block space-before.optimum="{$medium-font} div 2">
     10     Second test
     11   </block>
     12
     13   <block space-before.optimum="{$medium-font div 2}">
     14     Third test
     15   </block>
     16
     17   <block>
     18     <xsl:attribute name="space-before.optimum">
     19       <xsl:value-of select="$medium-font div 2"/>
     20     </xsl:attribute>
     21     Fourth test
     22   </block>
     23
     24   <block>
     25     <xsl:attribute name="space-before.optimum">
     26       <xsl:value-of select="$medium-font"/> div 2<xsl:text/>
     27     </xsl:attribute>
     28     Fifth test
     29   </block>
     30   </xsl:template>
```

There will be no spacing in the third and fourth tests.

- The arithmetic calculation yields the result of NaN because a length is not a number in XSLT, as opposed to XSL-FO.
  - XSLT cannot do arithmetic operations with string operands.
- A formatter may not report an error and assume a value of 0 for NaN since it is a valid number in the floating point arithmetic.
  - There is no indication to the stylesheet writer that anything is wrong, yet results are not as expected.

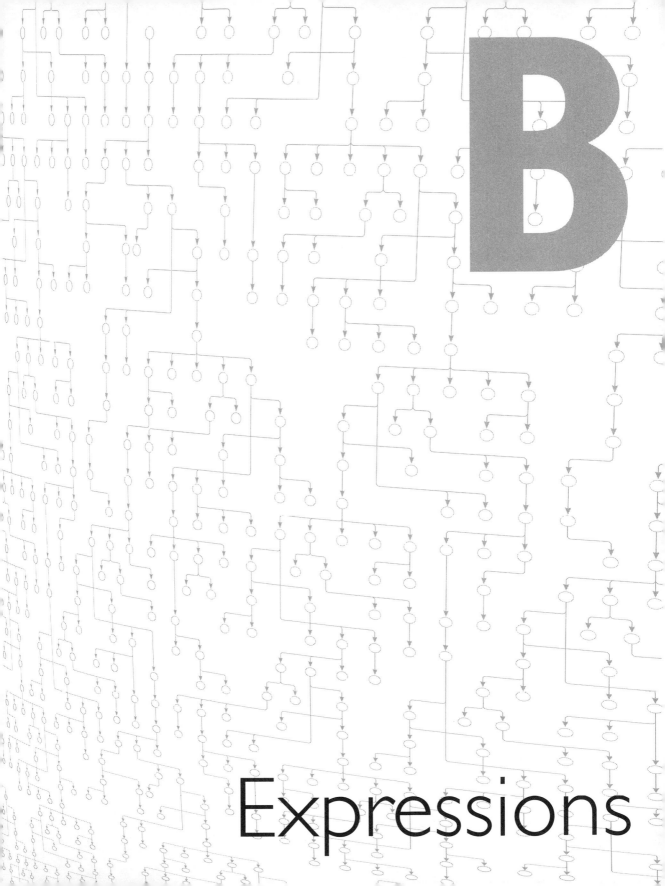

B

Expressions

B Expressions

This annex first summarizes in production order all of the productions in the expression grammar in the Recommendation.

- The left-hand side is the production being defined;
- the right-hand side is the definition of the grammatical construct.

Then, this annex summarizes the built-in functions available in the XSL-FO processor.

B.1 Production summary

```
[1] Expr            ::=  AdditiveExpr[11]

[2] PrimaryExpr     ::=  '(' Expr[1] ')'
                       | Numeric[5]
                       | Literal[20]
                       | Color[18]
                       | Keyword[24]
                       | EnumerationToken[26]
                       | FunctionCall[3]
```

```
[3] FunctionCall          ::=   FunctionName[25] '(' ( Argument[4] ( ','
                                Argument[4])*)? ')'

[4] Argument              ::=   Expr[1]

[5] Numeric               ::=   AbsoluteNumeric[6]
                                | RelativeNumeric[8]

[6] AbsoluteNumeric       ::=   AbsoluteLength[7]

[7] AbsoluteLength        ::=   Number[15] AbsoluteUnitName[27]?

[8] RelativeNumeric       ::=   Percent[9]
                                | RelativeLength[10]

[9] Percent               ::=   Number[15] '%'

[10] RelativeLength       ::=   Number[15] RelativeUnitName[27]

[11] AdditiveExpr         ::=   MultiplicativeExpr[12]
                                | AdditiveExpr[11] '+'
                                MultiplicativeExpr[12]
                                | AdditiveExpr[11] '-'
                                MultiplicativeExpr[12]

[12] MultiplicativeExpr   ::=   UnaryExpr[13]
                                | MultiplicativeExpr[12]
                                MultiplyOperator[23] UnaryExpr[13]
                                | MultiplicativeExpr[12] 'div'
                                UnaryExpr[13]
                                | MultiplicativeExpr[12] 'mod'
                                UnaryExpr[13]

[13] UnaryExpr            ::=   PrimaryExpr[2]
                                | '-' UnaryExpr[13]

[14] ExprToken           ::=   '(' | ')' | '%'
                                | Operator[21]
                                | FunctionName[25]
                                | EnumerationToken[26]
                                | Number[15]

[15] Number              ::=   FloatingPointNumber[16]

[16] FloatingPointNumber ::=   Digits[17] ('.' Digits[17]?)?
                                | '.' Digits[17]

[17] Digits              ::=   [0-9]+

[18] Color               ::=   '#' AlphaOrDigits[19]

[19] AlphaOrDigits       ::=   [a-fA-F0-9]+
```

```
[20] Literal            ::-  '"' [^"]* '"'
                             | "'" [^']* "'"

[21] Operator           ::=  OperatorName[22]
                             | MultiplyOperator[23]
                             | '+' | '-'

[22] OperatorName       ::=  'mod' | 'div'

[23] MultiplyOperator   ::=  '*'

[24] Keyword            ::=  'inherit'

[25] FunctionName       ::=  NCName(XML Namespaces)

[26] EnumerationToken   ::=  NCName(XML Namespaces)

[27] AbsoluteUnitName   ::=  'cm' | 'mm' | 'in' | 'pt' | 'pc' | 'px'

[28] RelativeUnitName   ::=  'em'

[29] ExprWhitespace     ::=  S(XML)
```

B.2 XSL-FO functions

B.2.1 Function summary

Expressions can incorporate numbers and lengths as operands.

- A number does not include a unit of measure;
  - this is termed "a unit power of zero."
- A length does include a unit of measure (inches, mm, etc.);
  - this is termed "a unit power of one."

You can perform numeric operations on lengths.

- Some functions accept either lengths or numbers as operands, e.g.:
  - `font-size="min(10pt,1em)"`,
  - `<table-cell column-number="min(3,5)">`.
  - Sometimes (e.g. for `min()`), both operands must have the same unit power.
- Some functions do not work on lengths, only numbers.
  - E.g. `round()` accepts only numbers, not lengths;
    - to round a length, you need to convert it to a number, round, then convert the result back to a length, e.g.:
      - `round(.75in div 1in)*1in`.

Percentages are counted in 1/100 units.

- They can be utilized in a property as a relation to the property's current value.
  - The following expressions all evaluate to the same value:
    - `font-size="150%"`,
    - `font-size="1.5 * inherited-property-value(font-size)"`,
    - `font-size="1.5em"`.

B.2.2 Function groupings

Color functions (5.10.2)

- `rgb()`,
- `rgb-icc()`,
- `system-color()`.

Font functions (5.10.3)

- `system-font()`.

Number functions (5.10.1)

- `abs()`,
- `ceiling()`,
- `floor()`,
- `max()`,
- `min()`,
- `round()`.

Property value functions (5.10.4)

- `body-start()`,
- `from-nearest-specified-value()`,
- `from-parent()`,
- `from-table-column()`,
- `inherited-property-value()`,
- `label-end()`,
- `merge-property-values()`,
- `proportional-column-width()`.

B.2.3   Functions summarized by name

numeric abs(*numeric*) (*5.10.1*):

- returns the absolute value of number or length argument.

numeric body-start() (*5.10.4*):

- returns the start indent corresponding to the list item body when considering the provisional-valued properties of the list.

numeric ceiling(*numeric*) (*5.10.1*):

- returns the nearest integer closest to positive infinity.

numeric floor(*numeric*) (*5.10.1*):

- returns the nearest integer closest to negative infinity.

object from-nearest-specified-value(*NCName*) (*5.10.4*):

- returns the value of the named property from the nearest ancestor of the formatting object in which the property value is being explicitly specified,
- returns the initial value if there is no parent.

object from-parent(*NCName*) (*5.10.4*):

- returns the value of the named property from the parent of the formatting object of the property being evaluated,
- returns the initial value if there is no parent.

object from-table-column(*NCName*) (*5.10.4*):

- returns the value of the named property from the table-column corresponding to the current column in the table.

object inherited-property-value(*NCName*) (*5.10.4*):

- returns the value of the inherited property named,
- reports an error if the property named is not an inherited property.

numeric label-end() (*5.10.4*):

- returns the end indent corresponding to the list item label when considering the provisional-valued properties of the list.

numeric max(*numeric*, *numeric*) (*5.10.1*):

- returns the maximum of two arguments,
- allows the arguments to be either lengths or numbers, but they must be the same type.

object merge-property-values(*NCName*) (*5.10.4*):

- returns the property calculated from the property set corresponding to the current user-agent state within the parent's child property sets.

numeric min(*numeric*, *numeric*) (*5.10.1*):

- returns the minimum of two arguments,
- allows the arguments to be either lengths or numbers, but they must be the same type.

numeric proportional-column-width(*numeric*) (*5.10.4*):

- returns the length corresponding to the number of units of proportional measure of the current table column's table as indicated in the supplied argument.
- Note: the proportional measure is the length left over after subtracting specified column widths from the table width and dividing the result by the number of columns for which widths are not specified.

color rgb(*numeric*, *numeric*, *numeric*) (*5.10.2*):

- returns a color from the RGB space,
- allows arguments to be numbers, not lengths.

color rgb-icc(*numeric*, *numeric*, *numeric*, *NCName*, *numeric*, *numeric*) (*5.10.2*):

- returns a color from the named ICC color profile,
- interprets the first three arguments as the fallback RGB color if the ICC color is not found,
- interprets the last arguments in a way specific to the color profile.

numeric round(*numeric*) (*5.10.1*):

- returns an integer closest to the given number,
- returns ceiling() on the value .5.

color system-color(*NCName*) (*5.10.2*):

- returns the system-defined color named in the argument.

object system-font(*NCName*, *NCName*) (*5.10.3*):

- returns the font size characteristic named in the second argument of the system font named in the first argument;
- if the second argument is omitted, the characteristic is the one being assigned by the expression.

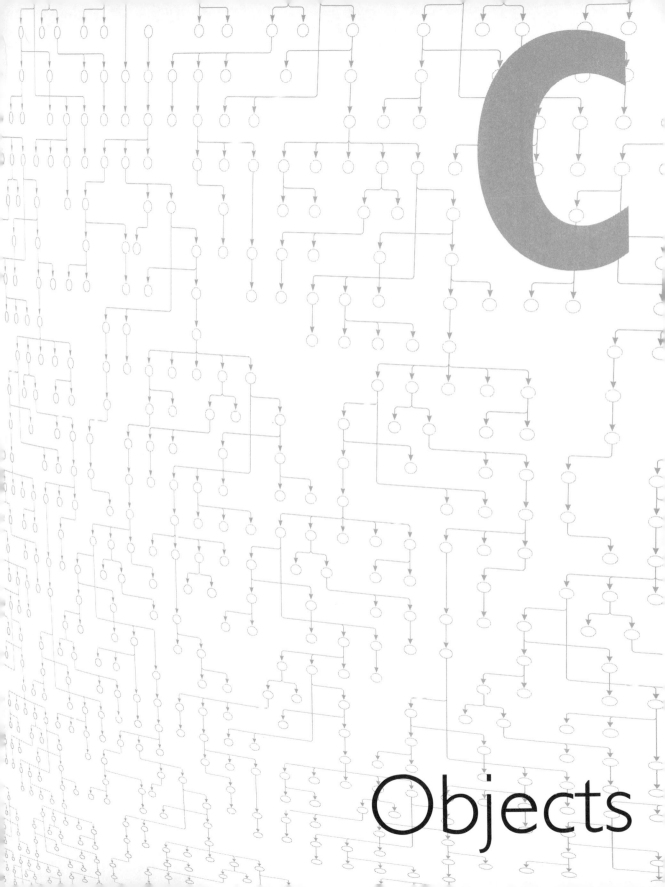

C

Objects

C Objects

In the first of these summaries, a formatting object's conformance level of "basic" or "extended" is indicated for both visual and aural media.

C.1 Objects summarized by name

- basic-link (*6.9.2*; 145) (visual: extended; aural: extended),
- bidi-override (*6.6.2*; 293) (visual: extended; aural: basic),
- block (*6.5.2*; 100) (visual: basic; aural: basic),
- block-container (*6.5.3*; 109) (visual: extended; aural: basic),
- character (*6.6.3*; 294) (visual: basic; aural: basic),
- color-profile (*6.4.4*; 296) (visual: extended; aural: N/A),
- conditional-page-master-reference (*6.4.11*; 223) (visual: extended; aural: extended),
- declarations (*6.4.3*; 297) (visual: basic; aural: basic),
- external-graphic (*6.6.5*; 139) (visual: basic; aural: basic),
- float (*6.10.2*; 233) (visual: extended; aural: extended),
- flow (*6.4.18*; 67) (visual: basic; aural: basic),

- footnote (*6.10.3*; 237) (visual: extended; aural: extended),
- footnote-body (*6.10.4*; 238) (visual: extended; aural: extended),
- initial-property-set (*6.6.4*; 103) (visual: extended; aural: basic),
- inline (*6.6.7*; 103) (visual: basic; aural: basic),
- inline-container (*6.6.8*; 108) (visual: extended; aural: extended),
- instream-foreign-object (*6.6.6*; 141) (visual: extended; aural: extended),
- layout-master-set (*6.4.6*; 65) (visual: basic; aural: basic),
- leader (*6.6.9*; 152) (visual: basic; aural: basic),
- list-block (*6.8.2*; 131) (visual: basic; aural: basic),
- list-item (*6.8.3*; 133) (visual: basic; aural: basic),
- list-item-body (*6.8.4*; 136) (visual: basic; aural: basic),
- list-item-label (*6.8.5*; 134) (visual: extended; aural: basic),
- marker (*6.11.3*; 208) (visual: extended; aural: extended),
- multi-case (*6.9.4*; 274) (visual: basic; aural: basic),
- multi-properties (*6.9.6*; 268) (visual: extended, need not be implemented for extended conformance for non-interactive media; aural: extended),
- multi-property-set (*6.9.7*; 269) (visual: extended, need not be implemented for extended conformance for non-interactive media; aural: extended),
- multi-switch (*6.9.3*; 271) (visual: extended, need not be implemented for extended conformance for non-interactive media; aural: extended),
- multi-toggle (*6.9.5*; 276) (visual: extended, need not be implemented for extended conformance for non-interactive media; aural: extended),
- page-number (*6.6.10*; 204) (visual: basic; aural: extended),
- page-number-citation (*6.6.11*; 105) (visual: extended; aural: extended),
- page-sequence (*6.4.5*; 65) (visual: basic; aural: basic),
- page-sequence-master (*6.4.7*; 220) (visual: basic; aural: basic),
- region-after (*6.4.15*; 197) (visual: extended; aural: extended),
- region-before (*6.4.14*; 195) (visual: extended; aural: extended),
- region-body (*6.4.13*; 114) (visual: basic; aural: basic),
- region-end (*6.4.17*; 199) (visual: extended; aural: extended),
- region-start (*6.4.16*; 198) (visual: extended; aural: extended),

- `repeatable-page-master-alternatives` (*6.4.10*; 222) (visual: extended; aural: extended),
- `repeatable-page-master-reference` (*6.4.9*; 222) (visual: basic; aural: basic),
- `retrieve-marker` (*6.11.4*; 209) (visual: extended; aural: extended),
- `root` (*6.4.2*; 64) (visual: basic; aural: basic),
- `simple-page-master` (*6.4.12*; 114) (visual: basic; aural: basic),
- `single-page-master-reference` (*6.4.8*; 221) (visual: basic; aural: basic),
- `static-content` (*6.4.19*; 202) (visual: extended; aural: extended),
- `table-and-caption` (*6.7.2*; 170) (visual: basic; aural: basic),
- `table` (*6.7.3*; 173) (visual: basic; aural: basic),
- `table-body` (*6.7.8*; 180) (visual: basic; aural: basic),
- `table-caption` (*6.7.5*; 172) (visual: extended; aural: extended),
- `table-cell` (*6.7.10*; 184) (visual: basic; aural: basic),
- `table-column` (*6.7.4*; 176) (visual: basic; aural: basic),
- `table-footer` (*6.7.7*, 178) (visual: extended; aural: extended),
- `table-header` (*6.7.6*; 177) (visual: basic; aural: basic),
- `table-row` (*6.7.9*; 182) (visual: basic; aural: basic),
- `title` (*6.4.20*; 117) (visual: extended; aural: extended),
- `wrapper` (*6.11.2*; 100) (visual: basic; aural: basic).

C.2 Objects summarized by type

Block-level formatting objects (6.5)

- `block` (*6.5.2*; 100),
- `block-container` (*6.5.3*; 109).

Declarations, pagination, and layout formatting objects (6.4)

- `color-profile` (*6.4.4*; 296),
- `conditional-page-master-reference` (*6.4.11*; 223),
- `declarations` (*6.4.3*; 297),
- `flow` (*6.4.18*; 67),
- `layout-master-set` (*6.4.6*; 65),
- `page-sequence` (*6.4.5*; 65),
- `page-sequence-master` (*6.4.7*; 220),

- region-after (*6.4.15*; 197),
- region-before (*6.4.14*; 195),
- region-body (*6.4.13*; 114),
- region-end (*6.4.17*; 199),
- region-start (*6.4.16*; 198),
- repeatable-page-master-alternatives (*6.4.10*; 222),
- repeatable-page-master-reference (*6.4.9*; 222),
- root (*6.4.2*; 64),
- simple-page-master (*6.4.12*; 114),
- single-page-master-reference (*6.4.8*; 221),
- static-content (*6.4.19*; 202),
- title (*6.4.20*; 117).

Dynamic effects: link and multi formatting objects (6.9)

- basic-link (*6.9.2*; 145),
- multi-case (*6.9.4*; 274),
- multi-properties (*6.9.6*; 268),
- multi-property-set (*6.9.7*; 269),
- multi-switch (*6.9.3*; 271),
- multi-toggle (*6.9.5*; 276).

Formatting objects for lists (6.8)

- list-block (*6.8.2*; 131),
- list-item (*6.8.3*; 133),
- list-item-body (*6.8.4*; 136),
- list-item-label (*6.8.5*; 134).

Formatting objects for tables (6.7)

- table-and-caption (*6.7.2*; 170),
- table (*6.7.3*; 173),
- table-body (*6.7.8*; 180),
- table-caption (*6.7.5*; 172),
- table-cell (*6.7.10*; 184),
- table-column (*6.7.4*; 176),
- table-footer (*6.7.7*; 178),

- `table-header` (*6.7.6*; 177),
- `table-row` (*6.7.9*; 182).

Inline-level formatting objects (6.6)

- `bidi-override` (*6.6.2*; 293),
- `character` (*6.6.3*; 294),
- `external-graphic` (*6.6.5*; 139),
- `initial-property-set` (*6.6.4*; 103),
- `inline` (*6.6.7*; 103),
- `inline-container` (*6.6.8*; 108),
- `instream-foreign-object` (*6.6.6*; 141),
- `leader` (*6.6.9*; 152),
- `page-number` (*6.6.10*; 204),
- `page-number-citation` (*6.6.11*; 105).

Other formatting objects (6.11)

- `marker` (*6.11.3*; 208),
- `retrieve-marker` (*6.11.4*; 209),
- `wrapper` (*6.11.2*; 100).

Out-of-line formatting objects (6.10)

- `float` (*6.10.2*; 233),
- `footnote` (*6.10.3*; 237),
- `footnote-body` (*6.10.4*; 238).

D

Properties

D Properties

This annex first summarizes the collections of common properties. Then it lists all the data types of the properties. Finally, it summarizes all shorthand and individual properties in alphabetical order.

- Citations refer to the W3C Recommendation;
- after a citation, there is either "CSS" or "XSL" indicating the heritage of this property.

Note that much of this annex is synthesized by applying an XSLT transformation to the source XML of the W3C Recommendation document itself, demonstrating the power of using these technologies for information processing.

D.1 Common properties

D.1.1 Common absolute position properties

Properties (7.5)

- `absolute-position` (*7.5.1*; 345),
- `bottom` (*7.5.4*; 366),

- left (*7.5.5*; 389),
- right (*7.5.3*; 410),
- top (*7.5.2*; 423).

Referring object

- block-container (*6.5.3*; 109).

Shorthand influencing the above properties

- position (*7.29.20*; 406).

D.1.2   Common accessibility properties

Properties (7.4)

- role (*7.4.2*; 410),
- source-document (*7.4.1*; 413).

Referring objects

- basic-link (*6.9.2*; 145),
- block (*6.5.2*; 100),
- external-graphic (*6.6.5*; 139),
- footnote (*6.10.3*; 237),
- footnote-body (*6.10.4*; 238),
- initial-property-set (*6.6.4*; 103),
- inline (*6.6.7*; 103),
- instream-foreign-object (*6.6.6*; 141),
- leader (*6.6.9*; 152),
- list-block (*6.8.2*; 131),
- list-item (*6.8.3*; 133),
- list-item-body (*6.8.4*; 136),
- list-item-label (*6.8.5*; 134),
- multi-case (*6.9.4*; 274),
- multi-properties (*6.9.6*; 268),
- multi-switch (*6.9.3*; 271),
- multi-toggle (*6.9.5*; 276),
- page-number (*6.6.10*; 204),
- page-number-citation (*6.6.11*; 105),

- table-and-caption (*6.7.2*; 170),
- table (*6.7.3*; 173),
- table-body (*6.7.8*; 180),
- table-caption (*6.7.5*; 172),
- table-cell (*6.7.10*; 184),
- table-footer (*6.7.7*; 178),
- table-header (*6.7.6*; 177),
- table-row (*6.7.9*; 182),
- title (*6.4.20*; 117).

D.1.3 Common aural properties

Properties (7.6)

- azimuth (*7.6.1*; 347),
- cue-after (*7.6.2*; 372),
- cue-before (*7.6.3*; 372),
- elevation (*7.6.4*; 374),
- pause-after (*7.6.5*; 403),
- pause-before (*7.6.6*; 404),
- pitch (*7.6.7*; 404),
- pitch-range (*7.6.8*; 405),
- play-during (*7.6.9*; 405),
- richness (*7.6.10*; 410),
- speak (*7.6.11*; 415),
- speak-header (*7.6.12*; 415),
- speak-numeral (*7.6.13*; 416),
- speak-punctuation (*7.6.14*; 416),
- speech-rate (*7.6.15*; 417),
- stress (*7.6.16*; 418),
- voice-family (*7.6.17*; 425),
- volume (*7.6.18*; 426).

Referring objects

- basic-link (*6.9.2*; 145),
- bidi-override (*6.6.2*; 293),

- block (*6.5.2*; 100),
- character (*6.6.3*; 294),
- external-graphic (*6.6.5*; 139),
- initial-property-set (*6.6.4*; 103),
- inline (*6.6.7*; 103),
- instream-foreign-object (*6.6.6*; 141),
- leader (*6.6.9*; 152),
- list-block (*6.8.2*; 131),
- list-item (*6.8.3*; 133),
- page-number (*6.6.10*; 204),
- page-number-citation (*6.6.11*; 105),
- table-and-caption (*6.7.2*; 170),
- table (*6.7.3*; 173),
- table-body (*6.7.8*; 180),
- table-caption (*6.7.5*; 172),
- table-cell (*6.7.10*; 184),
- table-footer (*6.7.7*; 178),
- table-header (*6.7.6*; 177),
- table-row (*6.7.9*; 182),
- title (*6.4.20*; 117).

Shorthands influencing the above properties

- cue (*7.29.12*; 372),
- pause (*7.29.19*; 403).

D.I.4   Common border, padding, and background properties

Properties (7.7)

- background-attachment (*7.7.1*; 348),
- background-color (*7.7.2*; 348),
- background-image (*7.7.3*; 349),
- background-position-horizontal (*7.7.5*; 350),
- background-position-vertical (*7.7.6*; 350),
- background-repeat (*7.7.4*; 350),
- border-after-color (*7.7.10*; 352),

- border-after-style (*7.7.11*; 353),
- border-after-width (*7.7.12*; 353),
- border-before-color (*7.7.7*; 354),
- border-before-style (*7.7.8*; 354),
- border-before-width (*7.7.9*; 355),
- border-bottom-color (*7.7.22*; 355),
- border-bottom-style (*7.7.23*; 356),
- border-bottom-width (*7.7.24*; 356),
- border-end-color (*7.7.16*; 357),
- border-end-style (*7.7.17*; 358),
- border-end-width (*7.7.18*; 358),
- border-left-color (*7.7.25*; 359),
- border-left-style (*7.7.26*; 359),
- border-left-width (*7.7.27*; 360),
- border-right-color (*7.7.28*; 360),
- border-right-style (*7.7.29*; 361),
- border-right-width (*7.7.30*; 361),
- border-start-color (*7.7.13*; 362),
- border-start-style (*7.7.14*; 363),
- border-start-width (*7.7.15*; 363),
- border-top-color (*7.7.19*; 364),
- border-top-style (*7.7.20*; 365),
- border-top-width (*7.7.21*; 365),
- padding-after (*7.7.32*; 398),
- padding-before (*7.7.31*; 398),
- padding-bottom (*7.7.36*; 398),
- padding-end (*7.7.34*; 399),
- padding-left (*7.7.37*; 399),
- padding-right (*7.7.38*; 400),
- padding-start (*7.7.33*; 400),
- padding-top (*7.7.35*; 401).

Referring objects

- basic-link (*6.9.2*; 145),

- block (*6.5.2*; 100),
- block-container (*6.5.3*; 109),
- character (*6.6.3*; 294),
- external-graphic (*6.6.5*; 139),
- initial-property-set (*6.6.4*; 103),
- inline (*6.6.7*; 103),
- inline-container (*6.6.8*; 108),
- instream-foreign-object (*6.6.6*; 141),
- leader (*6.6.9*; 152),
- list-block (*6.8.2*; 131),
- list-item (*6.8.3*; 133),
- page-number (*6.6.10*; 204),
- page-number-citation (*6.6.11*; 105),
- region-after (*6.4.15*; 197),
- region-before (*6.4.14*; 195),
- region-body (*6.4.13*; 114),
- region-end (*6.4.17*; 199),
- region-start (*6.4.16*; 198),
- table-and-caption (*6.7.2*; 170),
- table (*6.7.3*; 173),
- table-body (*6.7.8*; 180),
- table-caption (*6.7.5*; 172),
- table-cell (*6.7.10*; 184),
- table-column (*6.7.4*; 176),
- table-footer (*6.7.7*; 178),
- table-header (*6.7.6*; 177),
- table-row (*6.7.9*; 182),
- title (*6.4.20*; 117).

Shorthands influencing the above properties

- background (*7.29.1*; 347),
- background-position (*7.29.2*; 349),
- border (*7.29.3*; 352),
- border-bottom (*7.29.4*; 355),

- border-color (*7.29.5*; 357),
- border-left (*7.29.6*; 359),
- border-right (*7.29.7*; 360),
- border-style (*7.29.8*; 364),
- border-top (*7.29.10*; 364),
- border-width (*7.29.11*; 366),
- padding (*7.29.15*; 397).

D.1.5 Common font properties

Properties (*7.8*)

- font-family (*7.8.2*; 377),
- font-selection-strategy (*7.8.3*; 377),
- font-size (*7.8.4*; 378),
- font-size-adjust (*7.8.6*; 378),
- font-stretch (*7.8.5*; 379),
- font-style (*7.8.7*; 379),
- font-variant (*7.8.8*; 379),
- font-weight (*7.8.9*; 380).

Referring objects

- bidi-override (*6.6.2*; 293),
- block (*6.5.2*; 100),
- character (*6.6.3*; 294),
- initial-property-set (*6.6.4*; 103),
- inline (*6.6.7*; 103),
- leader (*6.6.9*; 152),
- page-number (*6.6.10*; 204),
- page-number-citation (*6.6.11*; 105),
- title (*6.4.20*; 117).

Shorthand influencing the above properties

- font (*7.29.13*; 377).

D.1.6 Common hyphenation properties

Properties (7.9)

- country (*7.9.1*; 371),
- hyphenate (*7.9.4*; 382),
- hyphenation-character (*7.9.5*; 383),
- hyphenation-push-character-count (*7.9.6*; 383),
- hyphenation-remain-character-count (*7.9.7*; 384),
- language (*7.9.2*; 387),
- script (*7.9.3*; 412).

Referring objects

- block (*6.5.2*; 100),
- character (*6.6.3*; 294).

Shorthand influencing the above properties

- xml:lang (*7.29.24*; 429).

D.1.7 Common margin properties — block

Properties (7.10)

- end-indent (*7.10.8*; 375),
- margin-bottom (*7.10.2*; 392),
- margin-left (*7.10.3*; 392),
- margin-right (*7.10.4*; 392),
- margin-top (*7.10.1*; 393),
- space-after (*7.10.6*; 413),
- space-before (*7.10.5*; 414),
- start-indent (*7.10.7*; 417).

Referring objects

- block (*6.5.2*; 100),
- block-container (*6.5.3*; 109),
- list-block (*6.8.2*; 131),
- list-item (*6.8.3*; 133),
- region-body (*6.4.13*; 114),

- `simple-page-master` (*6.4.12*; 114),
- `table-and-caption` (*6.7.2*; 170),
- `table` (*6.7.3*; 173).

Shorthand influencing the above properties

- `margin` (*7.29.14*; 391).

D.1.8 Common margin properties — inline

Properties (*7.11*)

- `space-end` (*7.11.1*; 414),
- `space-start` (*7.11.2*; 414).

Referring objects

- `basic-link` (*6.9.2*; 145),
- `character` (*6.6.3*; 294),
- `external graphic` (*6.6.5*; 139),
- `inline` (*6.6.7*; 103),
- `inline-container` (*6.6.8*; 108),
- `instream-foreign-object` (*6.6.6*; 141),
- `leader` (*6.6.9*; 152),
- `page-number` (*6.6.10*; 204),
- `page-number-citation` (*6.6.11*; 105),
- `title` (*6.4.20*; 117).

D.1.9 Common relative position properties

Property (*7.12*)

- `relative-position` (*7.12.1*; 408).

Referring objects

- `basic-link` (*6.9.2*; 145),
- `bidi-override` (*6.6.2*; 293),
- `block` (*6.5.2*; 100),
- `character` (*6.6.3*; 294),
- `external-graphic` (*6.6.5*; 139),

- initial-property-set (*6.6.4*; 103),
- inline (*6.6.7*; 103),
- inline-container (*6.6.8*; 108),
- instream-foreign-object (*6.6.6*; 141),
- leader (*6.6.9*; 152),
- list-block (*6.8.2*; 131),
- list-item (*6.8.3*; 133),
- page-number (*6.6.10*; 204),
- page-number-citation (*6.6.11*; 105),
- table-and-caption (*6.7.2*; 170),
- table (*6.7.3*; 173),
- table-body (*6.7.8*; 180),
- table-caption (*6.7.5*; 172),
- table-cell (*6.7.10*; 184),
- table-footer (*6.7.7*; 178),
- table-header (*6.7.6*; 177),
- table-row (*6.7.9*; 182).

Shorthand influencing the above property

- position (*7.29.20*; 406).

D.2 Data types

D.2.1 Definitions

angle

A representation of an angle consisting of an optional "+" or "-" character immediately followed by a *number* immediately followed by an angle unit identifier. Angle unit identifiers are: "deg" (for degrees), "grad" (for grads), and "rad" (for radians). The specified values are normalized to the range 0deg to 360deg. A property may define additional constraints on the value.

character

A single Unicode character.

color

Either a string of characters representing a keyword or a color function defined in Section B.2.2 on page 310. The list of keyword color names is: aqua, black, blue, fuchsia, gray, green, lime, maroon, navy, olive, purple, red, silver, teal, white, and yellow.

country

A string of characters conforming to an ISO 3166 country code.

family-name

A string of characters identifying a font.

frequency

A *number* immediately followed by a frequency unit identifier. Frequency unit identifiers are: "Hz" (for Hertz) and "kHz" (for Kilohertz).

id

A string of characters conforming to the definition of an NCName in XML Names and unique within the stylesheet.

idref

A string of characters conforming to the definition of an NCName in XML Names and matching an ID property value used within the stylesheet.

integer

A signed integer value which consists of an optional "+" or "-" character followed by a sequence of digits. A property may define additional constraints on the value.

keep

A compound data type with the components of within-line, within-column, and within-page. The value of each component is either "auto", "always", or an *integer*.

language

A string of characters conforming to an ISO 639 3-letter code.

length

A signed length value where the length is a real number plus a unit qualification. A property may define additional constraints on the value.

length-bp-ip-direction

> A compound data type, with the components of `block-progression-direction` and `inline-progression-direction`. Each component is a *length*. A property may define additional constraints on the values.

length-conditional

> A compound data type, with `length` and `conditionality` components. The `length` component is a *length*. The `conditionality` component is either "`discard`" or "`retain`". A property may define additional constraints on the values.

length-range

> A compound data type, with `minimum`, `optimum`, and `maximum` components. Each component is a *length*. If `minimum` is greater than `optimum`, it will be treated as if it had been set to `optimum`. If `maximum` is less than `optimum`, it will be treated as if it had been set to `optimum`. A property may define additional constraints on the values.

name

> A string of characters representing a name. It must conform to the definition of an NCName in XML Names.

number

> A signed real number which consists of an optional "+" or "-" character followed by a sequence of digits followed by an optional "." character and a sequence of digits. A property may define additional constraints on the value.

percentage

> A signed real percentage which consists of an optional "+" or "-" character followed by a sequence of digits followed by an optional "." character and a sequence of digits followed by "%". A property may define additional constraints on the value.

script

> A string of characters conforming to an ISO 15924 script code.

space

> A compound data type, with `minimum`, `optimum`, `maximum`, `precedence`, and `conditionality` components. The `minimum`, `optimum`, and `maximum` components are *lengths*. The `precedence` component is either "`force`"

or an *integer*. The `conditionality` component is either "`discard`" or "`retain`". If `minimum` is greater than `optimum`, it will be treated as if it had been set to `optimum`. If `maximum` is less than `optimum`, it will be treated as if it had been set to `optimum`.

string

A sequence of characters.

time

A *number* immediately followed by a time unit identifier. Time unit identifiers are "`ms`" (for milliseconds) and "`s`" (for seconds).

uri-specification

A sequence of characters starting with "`url(`", followed by optional white space, followed by an optional single quote (`'`) or double quote (`"`) character, followed by a URI reference as defined in RFC 2396, followed by an optional single quote (`'`) or double quote (`"`) character, followed by optional white space, followed by "`)`". The two quote characters must be the same and must both be present or absent. If the URI reference contains a single quote, the two quote characters must be present and be double quotes.

D.2.2 Relevant standards

Many of the data types refer to other standards and recommendations, listed below.

CSS2

World Wide Web Consortium. *Cascading Style Sheets, level 2 (CSS2)*, as amended by Errata document 2001/04/04. W3C Recommendation (`http://www.w3.org/TR/1998/REC-CSS2-19980512/`).

DSSSL

International Organization for Standardization, International Electrotechnical Commission. *ISO/IEC 10179:1996. Document Style Semantics and Specification Language (DSSSL)*. International Standard.

ICC

International Color Consortium. *Specification ICC.1:1998–09, File Format for Color Profiles* (`http://www.color.org/ICC-1_1998-09.PDF`).

IEEE 754

> Institute of Electrical and Electronics Engineers. *IEEE Standard for Binary Floating-Point Arithmetic.* ANSI/IEEE Std 754–1985.

ISO15924

> International Organization for Standardization. *ISO 15924:1998. Code for the representation of names of scripts.* Draft International Standard.

ISO31

> International Organization for Standardization. *ISO 31:1992, Amended 1998. Quantities and units.* International Standard.

JLS

> J. Gosling, B. Joy, and G. Steele. *The Java Language Specification* (`http://java.sun.com/docs/books/jls/index.html`).

OpenType

> Microsoft, Adobe. *OpenType specification v.1.2* (`http://www.micro-soft.com/truetype/tt/tt.htm`).

RDF

> World Wide Web Consortium. *Resource Description Framework (RDF) Model and Syntax Specification.* W3C Recommendation (`http://www.w3.org/TR/REC-rdf-syntax/`).

RFC 2070

> IETF. *RFC 2070. Internationalization of the Hypertext Markup Language* (`http://www.ietf.org/rfc/rfc2070.txt`).

RFC 2119

> IETF. *RFC 2119. Key words for use in RFCs to Indicate Requirement Levels* (`http://www.ietf.org/rfc/rfc2119.txt`).

RFC 2396

> IETF. *RFC 2396. Uniform Resource Identifiers (URI): Generic Syntax* (`http://www.ietf.org/rfc/rfc2396.txt`).

RFC3066

> IETF. *RFC 3066. Tags for the Identification of Languages* (`http://www.ietf.org/rfc/rfc3066.txt`).

sRGB

Anderson, M., Motta, R., Chandrasekar, S., and Stokes, M. *A Standard Default Color Space for the Internet — sRGB* (http://www.w3.org/Graphics/Color/sRGB.html).

UNICODE

Unicode Consortium. *The Unicode Standard, Version 3.0* (http://www.unicode.org/unicode/uni2book/u2.html).

UNICODE Character Database

Unicode Consortium. Unicode Character Database (http://www.unicode.org/Public/UNIDATA/).

UNICODE TR20

Unicode Consortium. Dürst, Martin and Freytag, Asmus. *Unicode Technical Report #20. Unicode in XML and other Markup Languages* Unicode Technical Report (http://www.unicode.org/unicode/reports/tr20/).

UNICODE UAX #9

Unicode Consortium. *The Unicode Standard, Version 3.1.0. Unicode Standard Annex #9: The Bidirectional Algorithm* (http://www.unicode.org/unicode/reports/tr9/).

XML

World Wide Web Consortium. *Extensible Markup Language (XML) 1.0.* W3C Recommendation (http://www.w3.org/TR/2000/REC-xml-20001006).

XML Names

World Wide Web Consortium. *Namespaces in XML.* W3C Recommendation (http://www.w3.org/TR/REC-xml-names/).

XPath

World Wide Web Consortium. *XML Path Language.* W3C Recommendation (http://www.w3.org/TR/xpath).

XSLT

World Wide Web Consortium. *XSL Transformations (XSLT).* W3C Recommendation (http://www.w3.org/TR/xslt).

D.2.3 XSLT format tokens

A token can be used to represent how numbers are to be rendered as a sequence of characters.

- It can be used for `xsl:number` in XSLT.
- It can be used for page numbering in XSL-FO.
- The representation of the numbers, the format of the separator sequences between multiple numbers, and the format of the terminator sequence can all be specified using attributes that accept attribute value templates.
- A token may be omitted to indicate decimal.
  - The default presentation is with a period as the separator (not terminator) sequence.

The `format="token"` attribute specifies the counting scheme to be used when formatting the value.

- `format="1"` gives 1, 2, ..., 9, 10, 11, ..., 99, 100, 101, ...
- `format="01"` gives 01, 02, ..., 09, 10, ..., 99, 100, ...
  - Each `"0"` prefix is a zero-fill indication for number values formatted shorter than the length of the format string.
  - `grouping-separator=","` specifies the character between groups of digits.
  - `grouping-size="3"` specifies the number of digits in each group (e.g. the value of 3 gives "1,000,000").
- `format="a"` gives a, b, ..., z, aa, ab, ac, ...
- `format="A"` gives A, B, ... Z, AA, AB, AC, ...
  - `lang` specifies the alphabet to be used when numbering with an alphabetic sequence.
  - The range of values as the same as for the `xml:lang` attribute in XML 1.0.
- `format="i"` gives i, ii, iii, iv, v, ..., ix, x, xi, ...
- `format="I"` gives I, II, III, IV, V, ..., IX, X, XI, ...
- `format="a-Unicode-character"` specifies a translation.
  - It converts the number into a representation based upon a specific language or character set.
  - The XSLT Recommendation lists a number of examples of Unicode characters representing specific conversions such as Katakana (regular and "iroha" orderings), Thai, Hebrew, Greek, Old Slavic, etc.
  - `letter-value="alphabetic"` and `letter-value="traditional"` are used for ambiguous distinctions.

- These distinguish between numbering schemes in those languages where the first character of the sequence is ambiguous.
- This is unlike English where the different first characters of "a" and "i" distinguish alphabetic and roman numeral formats.

D.3 Inheritance and shorthands

D.3.1 Inherited properties

The following traits are inherited from ancestral property specifications.

- `auto-restore` (*7.22.2*; 347),
- `azimuth` (*7.6.1*; 347),
- `border-collapse` (*7.26.3*; 357),
- `border-separation` (*7.26.5*; 362),
- `border-spacing` (*7.29.9*; 362),
- `caption-side` (*7.26.7*; 367),
- `color` (*7.17.1*; 369),
- `country` (*7.9.1*; 371),
- `direction` (*7.27.1*; 373),
- `display-align` (*7.13.4*; 373),
- `elevation` (*7.6.4*; 374),
- `empty-cells` (*7.26.10*; 374),
- `end-indent` (*7.10.8*; 375),
- `font-family` (*7.8.2*; 377),
- `font-selection-strategy` (*7.8.3*; 377),
- `font-size` (*7.8.4*; 378),
- `font-size-adjust` (*7.8.6*; 378),
- `font-stretch` (*7.8.5*; 379),
- `font-style` (*7.8.7*; 379),
- `font-variant` (*7.8.8*; 379),
- `font-weight` (*7.8.9*; 380),
- `font` (*7.29.13*; 377),
- `glyph-orientation-horizontal` (*7.27.2*; 381),
- `glyph-orientation-vertical` (*7.27.3*; 381),
- `hyphenate` (*7.9.4*; 382),
- `hyphenation-character` (*7.9.5*; 383),

- hyphenation-keep (*7.15.1*; 383),
- hyphenation-ladder-count (*7.15.2*; 383),
- hyphenation-push-character-count (*7.9.6*; 383),
- hyphenation-remain-character-count (*7.9.7*; 384),
- intrusion-displace (*7.18.3*; 385),
- keep-together (*7.19.3*; 386),
- language (*7.9.2*; 387),
- last-line-end-indent (*7.15.3*; 387),
- leader-alignment (*7.21.1*; 388),
- leader-length (*7.21.4*; 388),
- leader-pattern (*7.21.2*; 388),
- leader-pattern-width (*7.21.3*; 389),
- letter-spacing (*7.16.2*; 389),
- linefeed-treatment (*7.15.7*; 391),
- line-height (*7.15.4*; 390),
- line-height-shift-adjustment (*7.15.5*; 390),
- line-stacking-strategy (*7.15.6*; 391),
- orphans (*7.19.6*; 396),
- page-break-inside (*7.29.18*; 402),
- pitch (*7.6.7*; 404),
- pitch-range (*7.6.8*; 405),
- provisional-distance-between-starts (*7.28.4*; 406),
- provisional-label-separation (*7.28.3*; 407),
- reference-orientation (*7.20.3*; 407),
- relative-align (*7.13.6*; 408),
- richness (*7.6.10*; 410),
- rule-style (*7.21.5*; 411),
- rule-thickness (*7.21.6*; 411),
- score-spaces (*7.28.6*; 412),
- script (*7.9.3*; 412),
- speak (*7.6.11*; 415),
- speak-header (*7.6.12*; 415),
- speak-numeral (*7.6.13*; 416),
- speak-punctuation (*7.6.14*; 416),

- speech-rate (*7.6.15*; 417),
- start-indent (*7.10.7*; 417),
- stress (*7.6.16*; 418),
- text-align (*7.15.9*; 421),
- text-align-last (*7.15.10*; 421),
- text-indent (*7.15.11*; 422),
- text-transform (*7.16.6*; 423),
- visibility (*7.28.8*; 425),
- voice-family (*7.6.17*; 425),
- volume (*7.6.18*; 426),
- white-space-collapse (*7.15.12*; 427),
- white-space-treatment (*7.15.8*; 427),
- white-space (*7.29.23*; 426),
- widows (*7.19.7*; 427),
- word-spacing (*7.16.8*; 428),
- wrap-option (*7.15.13*; 428),
- writing-mode (*7.27.7*; 429),
- xml:lang (*7.29.24*; 429).

D.3.2 Shorthand properties

Note the following regarding the shorthand properties.

- They need not be supported by a processor unless it claims complete conformance (the highest XSL-FO conformance level);
  - this is an important portability issue — if one develops a stylesheet using a formatter that does recognize shorthand properties, that stylesheet may not run properly on a formatter that does not recognize shorthand properties.
- If the value "inherit" is being used for a shorthand, it applies to all subproperty values;
  - other subproperty values cannot be specified at the same time.

The following is a summary of shorthand properties.

- background (*7.29.1*; 347),
- background-position (*7.29.2*; 349),
- border (*7.29.3*; 352),
- border-bottom (*7.29.4*; 355),

- border-color (*7.29.5*; 357),
- border-left (*7.29.6*; 359),
- border-right (*7.29.7*; 360),
- border-spacing (*7.29.9*; 362),
- border-style (*7.29.8*; 364),
- border-top (*7.29.10*; 364),
- border-width (*7.29.11*; 366),
- cue (*7.29.12*; 372),
- font (*7.29.13*; 377),
- margin (*7.29.14*; 391),
- padding (*7.29.15*; 397),
- page-break-after (*7.29.16*; 401),
- page-break-before (*7.29.17*; 401),
- page-break-inside (*7.29.18*; 402),
- pause (*7.29.19*; 403),
- position (*7.29.20*; 406),
- size (*7.29.21*; 413),
- vertical-align (*7.29.22*; 424),
- white-space (*7.29.23*; 426),
- xml:lang (*7.29.24*; 429).

D.4 Property summary

This section presents an alphabetical listing of all properties, each indicating —

- the corresponding section number of the Recommendation,
- whether the property is originally from CSS or from XSL,
- the conformance level (basic, extended, complete) required for its support to be expected.

Note the following regarding the property definitions.

- The summary below is extracted from the XSL Recommendation; the references to "prose" refer to the prose found in the Recommendation as noted in the given section numbers, not to the content of this book.

- In certain cases, the XSL Recommendation lists the applicable formatting objects indirectly through the CSS definition and the list is incorrect due to XSL overrides;
  - here, such lists have been replaced with synthesized lists based on explicit references to the property made in the XSL Recommendation definition of the formatting —
    - directly for the object,
    - indirectly through common properties,
    - indirectly through shorthand properties.

Below is the complete alphabetic list of property definitions.

- `absolute-position`   (*7.5.1*; CSS; complete)

  - **Value:** `auto | absolute | fixed | inherit`
  - **Initial:** `auto`
  - **Inherited:** no
  - **Media:** visual
  - This property represents an object's positioning: normally flowed relative to its sibling ("`auto`"), offset from its containing area ("`absolute`"), offset from the medium ("`fixed`"), or the specified value of an ascendant ("`inherit`").
  - **Object to which this property applies:** `block-container`
  - **Shorthand affecting this property:** `position`

- `active-state`   (*7.22.1*; XSL; extended)

  - **Value:** `link | visited | active | hover | focus`
  - **Initial:** no, a value is required
  - **Inherited:** no
  - **Media:** interactive
  - This property represents the state tested for a `basic-link` descendant of the parent `multi-properties`: either not yet visited ("`link`"), ready to be engaged ("`hover`"), in the act of being engaged ("`active`"), given the focus for input ("`focus`"), or having already been visited ("`visited`").
  - **Object to which this property applies:** `multi-property-set`

- alignment-adjust *(7.13.1*; XSL; basic)

  - **Value:** auto | baseline | before-edge | text-before-edge | middle | central | after-edge | text-after-edge | ideographic | alphabetic | hanging | mathematical | *percentage* | *length* | inherit
  - **Initial:** auto
  - **Inherited:** no
  - **Percentages:** see prose
  - **Media:** visual
  - This property sets, relative to the alignment-baseline of the parent, the alignment point with which the formatter aligns areas created by formatting objects (such as graphics) that either do not have a baseline table or don't have a desired baseline in that table.
    - It refers to baseline-shift for suitable (not exclusive) behavior for text.
  - Percentages are relative to either the computed area (for an image), the font size (for a character), or the line height (for other constructs).
  - Positive lengths are opposite to the shift direction.
  - See page 94 for details on the values.
  - **Objects to which this property applies:** basic-link, character, external-graphic, inline, inline-container, instream-foreign-object, leader, page-number, page-number-citation
  - **Shorthand affecting this property:** vertical-align

- alignment-baseline *(7.13.2*; XSL; basic)

  - **Value:** auto | baseline | before-edge | text-before-edge | middle | central | after-edge | text-after-edge | ideographic | alphabetic | hanging | mathematical | inherit
  - **Initial:** auto
  - **Inherited:** no
  - **Media:** visual
  - This property specifies to which of an object's parent's baselines the object's alignment point (as defined by alignment-adjust) is aligned.
  - **Objects to which this property applies:** basic-link, character, external-graphic, inline, inline-container, instream-foreign-object, leader, page-number, page-number-citation

- **Shorthand affecting this property:** vertical-align

- auto-restore   (*7.22.2*; XSL; extended)

  - **Value:** true | false
  - **Initial:** false
  - **Inherited:** yes
  - **Media:** interactive
  - If "true" for an object, that object's multi-case will be restored to its initial value when the object is hidden by the hiding of an ancestral multi-switch construct.
  - **Object to which this property applies:** multi-switch

- azimuth   (*7.6.1*; CSS; basic)

  - **Value:** *angle* | [[left-side | far-left | left | center-left | center | center-right | right | far-right | right-side] || behind] | leftwards | rightwards | inherit
  - **Initial:** center
  - **Inherited:** yes
  - **Media:** aural
  - This property directs from which lateral direction an aural presentation is heard with respect to the listener.
  - **Objects to which this property applies:** basic-link, bidi-override, block, character, external-graphic, initial-property-set, inline, instream-foreign-object, leader, list-block, list-item, page-number, page-number-citation, table-and-caption, table, table-body, table-caption, table-cell, table-footer, table-header, table-row, title

- background   (*7.29.1*; CSS; shorthand)

  - **Value:** [*background-color* || *background-image* || *background-repeat* || *background-attachment* || *background-position*] | inherit
  - **Initial:** not defined for shorthand properties
  - **Inherited:** no
  - **Percentages:** allowed on *background-position*
  - **Media:** visual

- This property provides a shorthand method of specifying the five individual values.
- Any values omitted are given their initial values.

- background-attachment   (*7.7.1*; CSS; extended)
  - **Value:** scroll | fixed | inherit
  - **Initial:** scroll
  - **Inherited:** no
  - **Media:** visual
  - When the background is "fixed", it remains stationary in the viewport while the foreground scrolls in front of it.
  - **Objects to which this property applies:** basic-link, block, block-container, character, external-graphic, initial-property-set, inline, inline-container, instream-foreign-object, leader, list-block, list-item, page-number, page-number-citation, region-after, region-before, region-body, region-end, region-start, table-and-caption, table, table-body, table-caption, table-cell, table-column, table-footer, table-header, table-row, title
  - **Shorthand affecting this property:** background

- background-color   (*7.7.2*; CSS; basic)
  - **Value:** *color* | transparent | inherit
  - **Initial:** transparent
  - **Inherited:** no
  - **Media:** visual
  - This property fills the padding rectangle behind an object's content, thus the color is seen within the inside edge of a visible border.
    - Gaps in a visible border show through the background color of the parent area.
  - **Objects to which this property applies:** basic-link, block, block-container, character, external-graphic, initial-property-set, inline, inline-container, instream-foreign-object, leader, list-block, list-item, page-number, page-number-citation, region-after, region-before, region-body, region-end, region-start, table-and-caption, table, table-body, table-caption, table-cell, table-column, table-footer, table-header, table-row, title

- **Shorthand affecting this property:** background

- background-image   (*7.7.3*; CSS; extended)

  - **Value:** *uri-specification* | none | inherit
  - **Initial:** none
  - **Inherited:** no
  - **Media:** visual
  - The referenced image is positioned (and possibly repeated with background-repeat) within the padding rectangle behind an object's content.
  - The background-color will show through the transparent parts of the background image.
  - **Objects to which this property applies:** basic-link, block, block-container, character, external-graphic, initial-property-set, inline, inline-container, instream-foreign-object, leader, list-block, list-item, page-number, page-number-citation, region-after, region-before, region-body, region-end, region-start, table-and-caption, table, table-body, table-caption, table-cell, table-column, table-footer, table-header, table-row, title
  - **Shorthand affecting this property:** background

- background-position   (*7.29.2*; CSS; shorthand)

  - **Value:** [[*percentage* | *length*]{1,2} | [[top | center | bottom] || [left | center | right]]] | inherit
  - **Initial:** 0% 0%
  - **Inherited:** no
  - **Percentages:** refer to the size of the box itself
  - **Media:** visual
  - A shorthand for specifying one or two positions relative to the upper left corner of the padding rectangle, setting individual values for background-position-horizontal and background-position-vertical.
  - The horizontal value is specified first, followed by the vertical value.
  - An absent value is interpreted as "center" which is placed at 50%.

- background-position-horizontal   (7.7.5; CSS; extended)
  - **Value:** *percentage* | *length* | left | center | right | inherit
  - **Initial:** 0%
  - **Inherited:** no
  - **Percentage:** refers to the size of the padding rectangle
  - **Media:** visual
  - **Objects to which this property applies:** basic-link, block, block-container, character, external-graphic, initial-property-set, inline, inline-container, instream-foreign-object, leader, list-block, list-item, page-number, page-number-citation, region-after, region-before, region-body, region-end, region-start, table-and-caption, table, table-body, table-caption, table-cell, table-column, table-footer, table-header, table-row, title
  - **Shorthand affecting this property:** background-position

- background-position-vertical   (7.7.6; CSS; extended)
  - **Value:** *percentage* | *length* | top | center | bottom | inherit
  - **Initial:** 0%
  - **Inherited:** no
  - **Percentage:** refers to the size of the padding rectangle
  - **Media:** visual
  - **Objects to which this property applies:** basic-link, block, block-container, character, external-graphic, initial-property-set, inline, inline-container, instream-foreign-object, leader, list-block, list-item, page-number, page-number-citation, region-after, region-before, region-body, region-end, region-start, table-and-caption, table, table-body, table-caption, table-cell, table-column, table-footer, table-header, table-row, title
  - **Shorthand affecting this property:** background-position

- background-repeat   (7.7.4; CSS; extended)
  - **Value:** repeat | repeat-x | repeat-y | no-repeat | inherit
  - **Initial:** repeat
  - **Inherited:** no
  - **Media:** visual

- "x" is the horizontal direction, "y" is the vertical direction. Both are relative to the reference orientation but independent of the writing mode.
- **Objects to which this property applies:** basic-link, block, block-container, character, external-graphic, initial-property-set, inline, inline-container, instream-foreign-object, leader, list-block, list-item, page-number, page-number-citation, region-after, region-before, region-body, region-end, region-start, table-and-caption, table, table-body, table-caption, table-cell, table-column, table-footer, table-header, table-row, title
- **Shorthand affecting this property:** background

- baseline-shift   (*7.13.3*; XSL; basic)

  - **Value:** baseline | sub | super | *percentage* | *length* | inherit
  - **Initial:** baseline
  - **Inherited:** no
  - **Percentage:** refers to the line-height of the parent area
  - **Media:** visual
  - Repositions the dominant baseline (and all other entries in the baseline table) of an object relative to the dominant baseline of the parent area.
  - Using the parent area as a reference is more consistent for a set of child objects of different sizes.
  - **Objects to which this property applies:** basic-link, character, external-graphic, inline, inline-container, instream-foreign-object, leader, page-number, page-number-citation
  - **Shorthand affecting this property:** vertical-align

- blank-or-not-blank   (*7.25.1*; XSL; extended)

  - **Value:** blank | not-blank | any | inherit
  - **Initial:** any
  - **Inherited:** no
  - **Media:** visual
  - **Object to which this property applies:** conditional-page-master-reference

- block-progression-dimension (*7.14.1*; CSS; basic)
  - **Value:** auto | *length* | *percentage* | *length-range* | inherit
  - **Initial:** auto
  - **Inherited:** no
  - **Percentage:** see prose
  - **Media:** visual
  - Specifies the block-progression dimension of the content rectangle for each area generated by the formatting object.
  - **Objects to which this property applies:** block-container, external-graphic, inline, inline-container, instream-foreign-object, table, table-caption, table-cell, table-row

- border (*7.29.3*; CSS; shorthand)
  - **Value:** [*border-width* || *border-style* || *color*] | inherit
  - **Initial:** see individual properties
  - **Inherited:** no
  - **Media:** visual
  - Sets any of the border width, style, or color properties for all four borders of a box.

- border-after-color (*7.7.10*; CSS; basic)
  - **Value:** *color* | inherit
  - **Initial:** the value of the color property
  - **Inherited:** no
  - **Media:** visual
  - **Objects to which this property applies:** basic-link, block, block-container, character, external-graphic, initial-property-set, inline, inline-container, instream-foreign-object, leader, list-block, list-item, page-number, page-number-citation, region-after, region-before, region-body, region-end, region-start, table-and-caption, table, table-body, table-caption, table-cell, table-column, table-footer, table-header, table-row, title
  - **Shorthands affecting this property:** border, border-color

- border-after-precedence   (*7.26.1*; XSL; basic)

  - **Value:** force | *integer* | inherit
  - **Initial:** table: 6, table-cell: 5, table-column: 4, table-row: 3, table-body: 2, table-header: 1, table-footer: 0
  - **Inherited:** no
  - **Media:** visual
  - Specifies the precedence of the formatting object's border compared to the precedence of the coincident border of —
    - an adjacent formatting object when borders are collapsed using border-collapse,
    - an overlapping table construct in the formatting object hierarchy.
  - The highest border precedence specification of all of the coincident borders dictates which formatting object's properties that border will exhibit.
  - **Objects to which this property applies:** table, table-body, table-cell, table-column, table-footer, table-header, table-row

- border-after-style   (*7.7.11*; CSS; basic)

  - **Value:** *border-style* | inherit
  - **Initial:** none
  - **Inherited:** no
  - **Media:** visual
  - **Objects to which this property applies:** basic-link, block, block-container, character, external-graphic, initial-property-set, inline, inline-container, instream-foreign-object, leader, list-block, list-item, page-number, page-number-citation, region-after, region-before, region-body, region-end, region-start, table-and-caption, table, table-body, table-caption, table-cell, table-column, table-footer, table-header, table-row, title
  - **Shorthand affecting this property:** border-style

- border-after-width   (*7.7.12*; CSS; basic)

  - **Value:** *border-width* | *length-conditional* | inherit
  - **Initial:** medium
  - **Inherited:** no
  - **Media:** visual

- **Objects to which this property applies:** `basic-link`, `block`, `block-container`, `character`, `external-graphic`, `initial-property-set`, `inline`, `inline-container`, `instream-foreign-object`, `leader`, `list-block`, `list-item`, `page-number`, `page-number-citation`, `region-after`, `region-before`, `region-body`, `region-end`, `region-start`, `table-and-caption`, `table`, `table-body`, `table-caption`, `table-cell`, `table-column`, `table-footer`, `table-header`, `table-row`, `title`
- **Shorthand affecting this property:** `border-width`

- `border-before-color`   (*7.7.7*; CSS; basic)

  - **Value:** *color* | `inherit`
  - **Initial:** the value of the `color` property
  - **Inherited:** no
  - **Media:** visual
  - **Objects to which this property applies:** `basic-link`, `block`, `block-container`, `character`, `external-graphic`, `initial-property-set`, `inline`, `inline-container`, `instream-foreign-object`, `leader`, `list-block`, `list-item`, `page-number`, `page-number-citation`, `region-after`, `region-before`, `region-body`, `region-end`, `region-start`, `table-and-caption`, `table`, `table-body`, `table-caption`, `table-cell`, `table-column`, `table-footer`, `table-header`, `table-row`, `title`
  - **Shorthands affecting this property:** `border`, `border-color`

- `border-before-precedence`   (*7.26.2*; XSL; basic)

  - **Value:** `force` | *integer* | `inherit`
  - **Initial:** `table`: 6, `table-cell`: 5, `table-column`: 4, `table-row`: 3, `table-body`: 2, `table-header`: 1, `table-footer`: 0
  - **Inherited:** no
  - **Media:** visual
  - See `border-after-precedence` for details.
  - **Objects to which this property applies:** `table`, `table-body`, `table-cell`, `table-column`, `table-footer`, `table-header`, `table-row`

- `border-before-style`   (*7.7.8*; CSS; basic)

  - **Value:** *border-style* | `inherit`
  - **Initial:** `none`

- **Inherited:** no
- **Media:** visual
- **Objects to which this property applies:** basic-link, block, block-container, character, external-graphic, initial-property-set, inline, inline-container, instream-foreign-object, leader, list-block, list-item, page-number, page-number-citation, region-after, region-before, region-body, region-end, region-start, table-and-caption, table, table-body, table-caption, table-cell, table-column, table-footer, table-header, table-row, title
- **Shorthand affecting this property:** border-style

- border-before-width   (*7.7.9*; CSS; basic)

  - **Value:** *border-width* | *length-conditional* | inherit
  - **Initial:** medium
  - **Inherited:** no
  - **Media:** visual
  - **Objects to which this property applies:** basic-link, block, block-container, character, external-graphic, initial-property-set, inline, inline-container, instream-foreign-object, leader, list-block, list-item, page-number, page-number-citation, region-after, region-before, region-body, region-end, region-start, table-and-caption, table, table-body, table-caption, table-cell, table-column, table-footer, table-header, table-row, title
  - **Shorthand affecting this property:** border-width

- border-bottom   (*7.29.4*; CSS; shorthand)

  - **Value:** [*border-width* || *border-style* || *color*] | inherit
  - **Initial:** see individual properties
  - **Inherited:** no
  - **Media:** visual
  - This property is a shorthand for specifying a border's width, style, and color.

- border-bottom-color   (*7.7.22*; CSS; basic)

  - **Value:** *color* | inherit
  - **Initial:** the value of the color property

- **Inherited:** no
- **Media:** visual
- **Objects to which this property applies:** basic-link, block, block-container, character, external-graphic, initial-property-set, inline, inline-container, instream-foreign-object, leader, list-block, list-item, page-number, page-number-citation, region-after, region-before, region-body, region-end, region-start, table-and-caption, table, table-body, table-caption, table-cell, table-column, table-footer, table-header, table-row, title
- **Shorthands affecting this property:** border-bottom, border-color

- border-bottom-style (*7.7.23*; CSS; basic)

  - **Value:** *border-style* | inherit
  - **Initial:** none
  - **Inherited:** no
  - **Media:** visual
  - **Objects to which this property applies:** basic-link, block, block-container, character, external-graphic, initial-property-set, inline, inline-container, instream-foreign-object, leader, list-block, list-item, page-number, page-number-citation, region-after, region-before, region-body, region-end, region-start, table-and-caption, table, table-body, table-caption, table-cell, table-column, table-footer, table-header, table-row, title
  - **Shorthands affecting this property:** border-bottom, border-style

- border-bottom-width (*7.7.24*; CSS; basic)

  - **Value:** *border-width* | inherit
  - **Initial:** medium
  - **Inherited:** no
  - **Media:** visual
  - **Objects to which this property applies:** basic-link, block, block-container, character, external-graphic, initial-property-set, inline, inline-container, instream-foreign-object, leader, list-block, list-item, page-number, page-number-citation, region-after, region-before, region-body, region-end, region-start,

table-and-caption, table, table-body, table-caption, table-cell,
table-column, table-footer, table-header, table-row, title

- **Shorthands affecting this property:** border-bottom, border-width

- border-collapse   (*7.26.3*; CSS; extended)

  - **Value:** collapse | collapse-with-precedence | separate | inherit
  - **Initial:** collapse
  - **Inherited:** yes
  - **Media:** visual
  - **Object to which this property applies:** table

- border-color   (*7.29.5*; CSS; shorthand)

  - **Value:** [*color* | transparent]{1,4} | inherit
  - **Initial:** see individual properties
  - **Inherited:** no
  - **Media:** visual
  - Up to four individual values for the border color can be specified in this shorthand.
    - See Section 9.5 on page 256 for a discussion of borders.
  - Four colors specify each of the borders of a table in the following order: before, end, after, start.
  - Three colors specify the borders in the following order: before, end/start, after.
  - Two colors specify the borders in the following order: before/after, end/start.
  - One color specifies the color of all borders.

- border-end-color   (*7.7.16*; CSS; basic)

  - **Value:** *color* | inherit
  - **Initial:** the value of the color property
  - **Inherited:** no
  - **Media:** visual
  - **Objects to which this property applies:** basic-link, block, block-container, character, external-graphic, initial-property-set, inline, inline-container, instream-foreign-object, leader, list-

block, list-item, page-number, page-number-citation, region-after, region-before, region-body, region-end, region-start, table-and-caption, table, table-body, table-caption, table-cell, table-column, table-footer, table-header, table-row, title

- **Shorthands affecting this property:** border, border-color

border-end-precedence   *(7.26.4*; XSL; basic)

- **Value:** force | *integer* | inherit
- **Initial:** table: 6, table-cell: 5, table-column: 4, table-row: 3, table-body: 2, table-header: 1, table-footer: 0
- **Inherited:** no
- **Media:** visual
- See border-after-precedence for details.
- **Objects to which this property applies:** table, table-body, table-cell, table-column, table-footer, table-header, table-row

border-end-style   *(7.7.17*; CSS; basic)

- **Value:** *border-style* | inherit
- **Initial:** none
- **Inherited:** no
- **Media:** visual
- **Objects to which this property applies:** basic-link, block, block-container, character, external-graphic, initial-property-set, inline, inline-container, instream-foreign-object, leader, list-block, list-item, page-number, page-number-citation, region-after, region-before, region-body, region-end, region-start, table-and-caption, table, table-body, table-caption, table-cell, table-column, table-footer, table-header, table-row, title
- **Shorthand affecting this property:** border-style

border-end-width   *(7.7.18*; CSS; basic)

- **Value:** *border-width* | *length-conditional* | inherit
- **Initial:** medium
- **Inherited:** no
- **Media:** visual

- **Objects to which this property applies:** `basic-link`, `block`, `block-container`, `character`, `external-graphic`, `initial-property-set`, `inline`, `inline-container`, `instream-foreign-object`, `leader`, `list-block`, `list-item`, `page-number`, `page-number-citation`, `region-after`, `region-before`, `region-body`, `region-end`, `region-start`, `table-and-caption`, `table`, `table-body`, `table-caption`, `table-cell`, `table-column`, `table-footer`, `table-header`, `table-row`, `title`
- **Shorthand affecting this property:** `border-width`

- `border-left` (*7.29.6*; CSS; shorthand)

  - **Value:** `[ border-width || border-style || color ] | inherit`
  - **Initial:** see individual properties
  - **Inherited:** no
  - **Media:** visual
  - A shorthand for specifying a border's width, style, and color.

- `border-left-color` (*7.7.25*; CSS; basic)

  - **Value:** `color | inherit`
  - **Initial:** the value of the `color` property
  - **Inherited:** no
  - **Media:** visual
  - **Objects to which this property applies:** `basic-link`, `block`, `block-container`, `character`, `external-graphic`, `initial-property-set`, `inline`, `inline-container`, `instream-foreign-object`, `leader`, `list-block`, `list-item`, `page-number`, `page-number-citation`, `region-after`, `region-before`, `region-body`, `region-end`, `region-start`, `table-and-caption`, `table`, `table-body`, `table-caption`, `table-cell`, `table-column`, `table-footer`, `table-header`, `table-row`, `title`
  - **Shorthands affecting this property:** `border-color`, `border-left`

- `border-left-style` (*7.7.26*; CSS; basic)

  - **Value:** `border-style | inherit`
  - **Initial:** `none`
  - **Inherited:** no
  - **Media:** visual

- **Objects to which this property applies:** basic-link, block, block-container, character, external-graphic, initial-property-set, inline, inline-container, instream-foreign-object, leader, list-block, list-item, page-number, page-number-citation, region-after, region-before, region-body, region-end, region-start, table-and-caption, table, table-body, table-caption, table-cell, table-column, table-footer, table-header, table-row, title
- **Shorthands affecting this property:** border-left, border-style

- border-left-width   (*7.7.27*; CSS; basic)

  - **Value:** *border-width* | inherit
  - **Initial:** medium
  - **Inherited:** no
  - **Media:** visual
  - **Objects to which this property applies:** basic-link, block, block-container, character, external-graphic, initial-property-set, inline, inline-container, instream-foreign-object, leader, list-block, list-item, page-number, page-number-citation, region-after, region-before, region-body, region-end, region-start, table-and-caption, table, table-body, table-caption, table-cell, table-column, table-footer, table-header, table-row, title
  - **Shorthands affecting this property:** border-left, border-width

- border-right   (*7.29.7*; CSS; shorthand)

  - **Value:** [*border-width* || *border-style* || *color*] | inherit
  - **Initial:** see individual properties
  - **Inherited:** no
  - **Media:** visual
  - A shorthand for specifying a border's width, style, and color.

- border-right-color   (*7.7.28*; CSS; basic)

  - **Value:** *color* | inherit
  - **Initial:** the value of the color property
  - **Inherited:** no
  - **Media:** visual

- **Objects to which this property applies:** basic-link, block, block-container, character, external-graphic, initial-property-set, inline, inline-container, instream-foreign-object, leader, list-block, list-item, page-number, page-number-citation, region-after, region-before, region-body, region-end, region-start, table-and-caption, table, table-body, table-caption, table-cell, table-column, table-footer, table-header, table-row, title
- **Shorthands affecting this property:** border-color, border-right

- border-right-style   (*7.7.29*; CSS; basic)

  - **Value:** *border-style* | inherit
  - **Initial:** none
  - **Inherited:** no
  - **Media:** visual
  - **Objects to which this property applies:** basic-link, block, block-container, character, external-graphic, initial-property-set, inline, inline-container, instream-foreign-object, leader, list-block, list-item, page-number, page-number-citation, region-after, region-before, region-body, region-end, region-start, table-and-caption, table, table-body, table-caption, table-cell, table-column, table-footer, table-header, table-row, title
  - **Shorthands affecting this property:** border-right, border-style

- border-right-width   (*7.7.30*; CSS; basic)

  - **Value:** *border-width* | inherit
  - **Initial:** medium
  - **Inherited:** no
  - **Media:** visual
  - **Objects to which this property applies:** basic-link, block, block-container, character, external-graphic, initial-property-set, inline, inline-container, instream-foreign-object, leader, list-block, list-item, page-number, page-number-citation, region-after, region-before, region-body, region-end, region-start, table-and-caption, table, table-body, table-caption, table-cell, table-column, table-footer, table-header, table-row, title
  - **Shorthands affecting this property:** border-right, border-width

- border-separation   (*7.26.5*; XSL; extended)
  - **Value:** *length-bp-ip-direction* | inherit
  - **Initial:** .block-progression-direction="0pt" .inline-progression-direction="0pt"
  - **Inherited:** yes
  - **Media:** visual
  - Specifies the distance between the borders of adjacent cells when using borders that are not collapsed using border-collapse.
  - The space between borders is filled with the table background color.
  - **Object to which this property applies:** table
  - **Shorthand affecting this property:** border-spacing

- border-spacing   (*7.29.9*; CSS; shorthand)
  - **Value:** *length length?* | inherit
  - **Initial:** 0pt
  - **Inherited:** yes
  - **Media:** visual
  - This shorthand specifies the two components of the compound border-separation property as separate values in the order of the .inline-progression-direction component from the first value, then in the order of the .block-progression-direction component from the second value.
  - Specifying only one value sets both components simultaneously.

- border-start-color   (*7.7.13*; CSS; basic)
  - **Value:** *color* | inherit
  - **Initial:** the value of the color property
  - **Inherited:** no
  - **Media:** visual
  - **Objects to which this property applies:** basic-link, block, block-container, character, external-graphic, initial-property-set, inline, inline-container, instream-foreign-object, leader, list-block, list-item, page-number, page-number-citation, region-after, region-before, region-body, region-end, region-start,

table-and-caption, table, table-body, table-caption, table-cell, table-column, table-footer, table-header, table-row, title

- **Shorthands affecting this property:** border, border-color

- border-start-precedence (*7.26.6*; XSL; basic)

  - **Value:** force | *integer* | inherit
  - **Initial:** table: 6, table-cell: 5, table-column: 4, table-row: 3, table-body: 2, table-header: 1, table-footer: 0
  - **Inherited:** no
  - **Media:** visual
  - See border-after-precedence for details.
  - **Objects to which this property applies:** table, table-body, table-cell, table-column, table-footer, table-header, table-row

- border-start-style (*7.7.14*; CSS; basic)

  - **Value:** *border-style* | inherit
  - **Initial:** none
  - **Inherited:** no
  - **Media:** visual
  - **Objects to which this property applies:** basic-link, block, block-container, character, external-graphic, initial-property-set, inline, inline-container, instream-foreign-object, leader, list-block, list-item, page-number, page-number-citation, region-after, region-before, region-body, region-end, region-start, table-and-caption, table, table-body, table-caption, table-cell, table-column, table-footer, table-header, table-row, title
  - **Shorthand affecting this property:** border-style

- border-start-width (*7.7.15*; CSS; basic)

  - **Value:** *border-width* | *length-conditional* | inherit
  - **Initial:** medium
  - **Inherited:** no
  - **Media:** visual
  - **Objects to which this property applies:** basic-link, block, block-container, character, external-graphic, initial-property-set,

```
inline, inline-container, instream-foreign-object, leader, list-
block, list-item, page-number, page-number-citation, region-
after, region-before, region-body, region-end, region-start,
table-and-caption, table, table-body, table-caption, table-cell,
table-column, table-footer, table-header, table-row, title
```

- **Shorthand affecting this property:** `border-width`

- `border-style`   (*7.29.8*; CSS; shorthand)

  - **Value:** `border-style{1,4} | inherit`
  - **Initial:** see individual properties
  - **Inherited:** no
  - **Media:** visual
  - Up to four individual values for the border style can be specified in this shorthand.
    - See Section 9.5 on page 256 for a discussion of borders.
  - Four values specify each of the borders of a table in the following order: before, end, after, start.
  - Three values specify the borders in the following order: before, end/start, after.
  - Two values specify the borders in the following order: before/after, end/start.
  - One value specifies the style of all borders.

- `border-top`   (*7.29.10*; CSS; shorthand)

  - **Value:** `[ border-width || border-style || color ] | inherit`
  - **Initial:** see individual properties
  - **Inherited:** no
  - **Media:** visual
  - This property is a shorthand for specifying a border's width, style, and color.

- `border-top-color`   (*7.7.19*; CSS; basic)

  - **Value:** `color | inherit`
  - **Initial:** the value of the `color` property
  - **Inherited:** no

- **Media:** visual
- **Objects to which this property applies:** basic-link, block, block-container, character, external-graphic, initial-property-set, inline, inline-container, instream-foreign-object, leader, list-block, list-item, page-number, page-number-citation, region-after, region-before, region-body, region-end, region-start, table-and-caption, table, table-body, table-caption, table-cell, table-column, table-footer, table-header, table-row, title
- **Shorthands affecting this property:** border-color, border-top

- border-top-style   (*7.7.20*; CSS; basic)

  - **Value:** *border-style* | inherit
  - **Initial:** none
  - **Inherited:** no
  - **Media:** visual
  - **Objects to which this property applies:** basic-link, block, block-container, character, external-graphic, initial-property-set, inline, inline-container, instream-foreign-object, leader, list-block, list-item, page-number, page-number-citation, region-after, region-before, region-body, region-end, region-start, table-and-caption, table, table-body, table-caption, table-cell, table-column, table-footer, table-header, table-row, title
  - **Shorthands affecting this property:** border-style, border-top

- border-top-width   (*7.7.21*; CSS; basic)

  - **Value:** *border-width* | inherit
  - **Initial:** medium
  - **Inherited:** no
  - **Media:** visual
  - **Objects to which this property applies:** basic-link, block, block-container, character, external-graphic, initial-property-set, inline, inline-container, instream-foreign-object, leader, list-block, list-item, page-number, page-number-citation, region-after, region-before, region-body, region-end, region-start, table-and-caption, table, table-body, table-caption, table-cell, table-column, table-footer, table-header, table-row, title

- **Shorthands affecting this property:** border-top, border-width

- border-width   (*7.29.11*; CSS; shorthand)

  - **Value:** *border-width*{1,4} | inherit
  - **Initial:** see individual properties
  - **Inherited:** no
  - **Media:** visual
  - Up to four individual values for the border width can be specified in this shorthand.
    - See Section 9.5 on page 256 for a discussion of borders.
  - Four values specify each of the borders of a table in the following order: before, end, after, start.
  - Three values specify the borders in the following order: before, end/start, after.
  - Two values specify the borders in the following order: before/after, end/start.
  - One value specifies the width of all borders.

- bottom   (*7.5.4*; CSS; extended)

  - **Value:** *length* | *percentage* | auto | inherit
  - **Initial:** auto
  - **Inherited:** no
  - **Percentage:** refers to height of containing block
  - **Media:** visual
  - This property specifies the distance between the margin edge and the containing block.
  - A value other than "auto" overrides a height value of "auto".
  - The percentage is ignored if the containing block height is not specified explicitly.
  - **Object to which this property applies:** block-container

- break-after   (*7.19.1*; XSL; basic)

  - **Value:** auto | column | page | even-page | odd-page | inherit
  - **Initial:** auto
  - **Inherited:** no

- **Media:** visual
- This property has no effect on `table-row` if that row has a row-spanning cell including the following row.
- **Objects to which this property applies:** `block, block-container, list-block, list-item, table-and-caption, table, table-row`
- **Shorthand affecting this property:** `page-break-after`

- `break-before`   (*7.19.2*; XSL; basic)

  - **Value:** `auto | column | page | even-page | odd-page | inherit`
  - **Initial:** `auto`
  - **Inherited:** no
  - **Media:** visual
  - This property has no effect on `table-row` if the previous row has a row-spanning cell including the given row.
  - **Objects to which this property applies:** `block, block-container, list-block, list-item, table-and-caption, table, table-row`
  - **Shorthand affecting this property:** `page-break-before`

- `caption-side`   (*7.26.7*; CSS; complete)

  - **Value:** `before | after | start | end | top | bottom | left | right | inherit`
  - **Initial:** `before`
  - **Inherited:** yes
  - **Media:** visual
  - **Object to which this property applies:** `table-and-caption`

- `case-name`   (*7.22.3*; XSL; extended)

  - **Value:** *name*
  - **Initial:** none, a value is required
  - **Inherited:** no, a value is required
  - **Media:** interactive
  - This name must be unique among the siblings of the `multi-case`.
  - **Object to which this property applies:** `multi-case`

- case-title *(7.22.4*; XSL; extended)

  - **Value:** *string*
  - **Initial:** none, a value is required
  - **Inherited:** no, a value is required
  - **Media:** interactive
  - This string can be displayed in a menu corresponding to the associated multi-case objects of allowed multi-toggle destinations when more than one candidate destination is specified.
  - **Object to which this property applies:** multi-case

- character *(7.16.1*; XSL; basic)

  - **Value:** *character*
  - **Initial:** none, a value is required
  - **Inherited:** no, a value is required
  - **Media:** visual
  - **Object to which this property applies:** character

- clear *(7.18.1*; CSS; extended)

  - **Value:** start | end | left | right | both | none | inherit
  - **Initial:** none
  - **Inherited:** no
  - **Media:** visual
  - This property specifies which side floats whose parent reference area is the nearest ancestor of the reference area of the generated area must be clear of the given block to which this property is specified.
    - The value indicates which side float the given construct is supposed to clear.
  - This property may alter the space-before property to meet the constraints.
  - It also applies to block, even though it is not listed in the Recommendation as a property for that object.
  - **Object to which this property applies:** float

- clip *(7.20.1*; CSS; extended)

  - **Value:** *shape* | auto | inherit
  - **Initial:** auto

- **Inherited:** no
- **Media:** visual
- The only shape supported is rect(top, right, bottom, left).
    - The four values are the offsets of the clipping area from the respective sides of the containing area.
- The value "auto" represents an offset of zero.
- **Objects to which this property applies:** block-container, external-graphic, inline-container, instream-foreign-object, region-after, region-before, region-body, region-end, region-start

- color   (7.17.1; CSS; basic)

    - **Value:** *color* | inherit
    - **Initial:** depends on user agent
    - **Inherited:** yes
    - **Media:** visual
    - See Section B.2.2 on page 310 for the color functions available.
    - **Objects to which this property applies:** bidi-override, block, character, initial-property-set, inline, leader, title

- color-profile-name   (7.17.2; XSL; extended)

    - **Value:** *name* | inherit
    - **Initial:** none, a value is required
    - **Inherited:** no
    - **Media:** visual
    - **Object to which this property applies:** color-profile

- column-count   (7.25.2; XSL; extended)

    - **Value:** *number* | inherit
    - **Initial:** 1
    - **Inherited:** no
    - **Media:** visual
    - **Object to which this property applies:** region-body

- column-gap   (7.25.3; XSL; extended)

    - **Value:** *length* | *percentage* | inherit

- **Initial:** 12.0pt
- **Inherited:** no
- **Percentage:** refers to width of the region being divided into columns
- **Media:** visual
- A negative value is translated to 0pt.
- **Object to which this property applies:** region-body

● column-number (*7.26.8*; XSL; basic)

- **Value:** *number*
- **Initial:** see prose
- **Inherited:** no
- **Media:** visual
- The initial value for table-column is 1 plus the column-number of the previous table-column, or "1" for the first column.
- The initial value for table-cell is the column-number of the previous cell plus the number-columns-spanned of that previous cell.
- **Objects to which this property applies:** table-cell, table-column

● column-width (*7.26.9*; XSL; basic)

- **Value:** *length* | *percentage*
- **Initial:** see prose
- **Inherited:** no
- **Percentage:** refers to the width of the table
- **Media:** visual
- See page 166 for a discussion of column widths.
- **Object to which this property applies:** table-column

● content-height (*7.14.2*; XSL; extended)

- **Value:** auto | scale-to-fit | *length* | *percentage* | inherit
- **Initial:** auto
- **Inherited:** no
- **Percentages:** intrinsic height
- **Media:** visual

- **Objects to which this property applies:** external-graphic, instream-foreign-object

- content-type   (*7.28.1*; XSL; extended)

  - **Value:** *string* | auto
  - **Initial:** auto
  - **Inherited:** no
  - **Media:** visual
  - The string is prefixed by "namespace-prefix:" for a namespace specification.
    - A null prefix refers to the default namespace.
  - The string is prefixed by "content-type:" for a MIME type specification.
  - **Objects to which this property applies:** external-graphic, instream-foreign-object

- content-width   (*7.14.3*; XSL; extended)

  - **Value:** auto | scale-to-fit | *length* | *percentage* | inherit
  - **Initial:** auto
  - **Inherited:** no
  - **Percentage:** refers to intrinsic width
  - **Media:** visual
  - **Objects to which this property applies:** external-graphic, instream-foreign-object

- country   (*7.9.1*; XSL; extended)

  - **Value:** none | *country* | inherit
  - **Initial:** none
  - **Inherited:** yes
  - **Media:** visual
  - This property specifies the country used in language- and locale-coupled services —
    - e.g. line-justification, line-breaking, hyphenation, etc.
  - **Objects to which this property applies:** block, character, page-sequence
  - **Shorthand affecting this property:** xml:lang

- cue   (*7.29.12*; CSS; shorthand)

  - **Value:** *cue-before* || *cue-after* | inherit
  - **Initial:** not defined for shorthand properties
  - **Inherited:** no
  - **Media:** aural
  - When a single value is specified it is applied to both properties.

- cue-after   (*7.6.2*; CSS; basic)

  - **Value:** *uri-specification* | none | inherit
  - **Initial:** none
  - **Inherited:** no
  - **Media:** aural
  - This property specifies the URL of rendered information as an "auditory icon" after a construct is rendered.
  - **Objects to which this property applies:** basic-link, bidi-override, block, character, external-graphic, initial-property-set, inline, instream-foreign-object, leader, list-block, list-item, page-number, page-number-citation, table-and-caption, table, table-body, table-caption, table-cell, table-footer, table-header, table-row, title
  - **Shorthand affecting this property:** cue

- cue-before   (*7.6.3*; CSS; basic)

  - **Value:** *uri-specification* | none | inherit
  - **Initial:** none
  - **Inherited:** no
  - **Media:** aural
  - This property specifies the URL of rendered information as an "auditory icon" before a construct is rendered.
  - **Objects to which this property applies:** basic-link, bidi-override, block, character, external-graphic, initial-property-set, inline, instream-foreign-object, leader, list-block, list-item, page-number, page-number-citation, table-and-caption, table, table-body, table-caption, table-cell, table-footer, table-header, table-row, title

- **Shorthand affecting this property:** cue

- destination-placement-offset   (*7.22.5*; XSL; extended)

  - **Value:** *length*
  - **Initial:** 0pt
  - **Inherited:** no
  - **Media:** interactive
  - This property specifies where in the destination viewport or page (from the beginning) the targeted location is to be rendered.
  - **Object to which this property applies:** basic-link

- direction   (*7.27.1*; CSS; basic)

  - **Value:** ltr | rtl | inherit
  - **Initial:** ltr
  - **Inherited:** yes
  - **Media:** visual
  - This property is deprecated for all formatting objects except bidi-override;
    - if used for other objects, this property overrides the direction implied by any writing-mode property.
  - **Object to which this property applies:** bidi-override

- display-align   (*7.13.4*; XSL; extended)

  - **Value:** auto | before | center | after | inherit
  - **Initial:** auto
  - **Inherited:** yes
  - **Media:** visual
  - This property specifies the alignment, in the block-progression direction, of the areas that are the children of a reference area.
  - The value of "auto" infers either the relative-align property, if applicable, or the value "before".
  - **Objects to which this property applies:** block-container, external-graphic, inline-container, instream-foreign-object, region-after, region-before, region-body, region-end, region-start, table-cell

- dominant-baseline   (*7.13.5*; XSL; basic)

  - **Value:** auto | use-script | no-change | reset-size | ideographic | alphabetic | hanging | mathematical | central | middle | text-after-edge | text-before-edge | inherit
  - **Initial:** auto
  - **Inherited:** no
  - **Media:** visual
  - This property determines or re-determines a scaled baseline table.
  - **Objects to which this property applies:** basic-link, character, external-graphic, inline, inline-container, instream-foreign-object, leader, page-number, page-number-citation
  - **Shorthand affecting this property:** vertical-align

- elevation   (*7.6.4*; CSS; basic)

  - **Value:** *angle* | below | level | above | higher | lower | inherit
  - **Initial:** level
  - **Inherited:** yes
  - **Media:** aural
  - The angles "90deg" and "-90deg" position the sound, respectively, directly above or below the listener.
  - The values "higher" and "lower", respectively, increase and decrease the current elevation by 10 degrees.
  - **Objects to which this property applies:** basic-link, bidi-override, block, character, external-graphic, initial-property-set, inline, instream-foreign-object, leader, list-block, list-item, page-number, page-number-citation, table-and-caption, table, table-body, table-caption, table-cell, table-footer, table-header, table-row, title

- empty-cells   (*7.26.10*; CSS; extended)

  - **Value:** show | hide | inherit
  - **Initial:** show
  - **Inherited:** yes
  - **Media:** visual

- This property specifies the rendering of the borders and background of cells without visible content when using the separated borders model specified by `border-collapse`.
- If all cells in a row have a value of "`hide`", the row behaves as if it were not displayed at all.
- Visible content is everything other than XML white space (carriage return, linefeed, tab, and space characters).
- **Object to which this property applies:** `table-cell`

- `end-indent`   (*7.10.8*; XSL; basic)

  - **Value:** *length* | *percentage* | `inherit`
  - **Initial:** `0pt`
  - **Inherited:** yes
  - **Percentages:** refer to the inline-progression dimension of the containing reference area
  - **Media:** visual
  - **Objects to which this property applies:** `block, block-container, list-block, list-item, region-body, simple-page-master, table-and-caption, table`

- `ends-row`   (*7.26.11*; XSL; extended)

  - **Value:** `true` | `false`
  - **Initial:** `false`
  - **Inherited:** no
  - **Media:** visual
  - **Object to which this property applies:** `table-cell`

- `extent`   (*7.25.4*; XSL; extended)

  - **Value:** *length* | *percentage* | `inherit`
  - **Initial:** `0.0pt`
  - **Inherited:** no
  - **Percentages:** refer to the corresponding height or width of the page viewport area
  - **Media:** visual

- **Objects to which this property applies:** `region-after`, `region-before`, `region-end`, `region-start`

- external-destination   (*7.22.6*; XSL; extended)

  - **Value:** *uri-specification*
  - **Initial:** empty string
  - **Inherited:** no
  - **Media:** interactive
  - At least one of `external-destination` and `internal-destination` properties should be assigned.
  - If both are assigned, the system may either report the error, or use `internal-destination`.
  - **Object to which this property applies:** `basic-link`

- float   (*7.18.2*; CSS; extended)

  - **Value:** `before | start | end | left | right | none | inherit`
  - **Initial:** `none`
  - **Inherited:** no
  - **Media:** visual
  - Unlike CSS, this property only applies to `float` and to no other formatting object.
  - **Object to which this property applies:** `float`

- flow-name   (*7.25.5*; XSL; basic)

  - **Value:** *name*
  - **Initial:** an empty name
  - **Inherited:** no, a value is required
  - **Media:** visual
  - The value must be unique within a `page-sequence`.
  - The following names are reserved: "`xsl-region-body`", "`xsl-region-before`", "`xsl-region-after`", "`xsl-region-start`", "`xsl-region-end`", "`xsl-before-float-separator`", "`xsl-footnote-separator`".
  - **Objects to which this property applies:** `flow`, `static-content`

- font   (*7.29.13*; CSS; shorthand)

    - **Value:** `[[ `*font-style*` || `*font-variant*` || `*font-weight*` ]? `*font-size*` [ / `*line-height*` ]? `*font-family*` ] | `caption` | `icon` | `menu` | message-box | small-caption | status-bar | inherit`
    - **Initial:** see individual properties
    - **Inherited:** yes
    - **Media:** visual
    - Individual system font characteristics, such as font family, font size, etc., may be obtained by using the `system-font()` function without any arguments.

- font-family   (*7.8.2*; CSS; basic)

    - **Value:** `[[ `*family-name*` | `*generic-family*` ], ]* [ `*family-name*` | `*generic-family*` ] | inherit`
    - **Initial:** depends on user agent
    - **Inherited:** yes
    - **Media:** visual
    - Font family names with spaces should be quoted, but will otherwise be normalized.
    - Generic font family names are not quoted.
        - The generic names are "`serif`", "`sans-serif`", "`cursive`", "`fantasy`", and "`monospace`".
    - This property is a prioritized list of font family names which are tried in sequence to find an available font that matches the selection criteria specified by `font-selection-strategy`.
    - **Objects to which this property applies:** `bidi-override`, `block`, `character`, `initial-property-set`, `inline`, `leader`, `page-number`, `page-number-citation`, `title`
    - **Shorthand affecting this property:** `font`

- font-selection-strategy   (*7.8.3*; XSL; complete)

    - **Value:** `auto | character-by-character | inherit`
    - **Initial:** `auto`
    - **Inherited:** yes
    - **Media:** visual

- This property specifies if font selection is done in an implementation-defined manner or if each individual character is checked for the desired font.
- Font selection is based on `font-family`, `font-style`, `font-variant`, `font-weight`, `font-stretch`, `font-size`, and possibly one or more characters of context.
- **Objects to which this property applies:** `bidi-override`, `block`, `character`, `initial-property-set`, `inline`, `leader`, `page-number`, `page-number-citation`, `title`

- `font-size`   (*7.8.4*; CSS; basic)

  - **Value:** *absolute-size* | *relative-size* | *length* | *percentage* | `inherit`
  - **Initial:** `medium`
  - **Inherited:** yes, the computed value is inherited
  - **Percentages:** refer to parent element's font size
  - **Media:** visual
  - Possible values for *absolute-size* are: "`xx-small`", "`x-small`", "`small`", "`medium`", "`large`", "`x-large`", and "`xx-large`".
  - Possible values for *relative-size* are: "`larger`" and "`smaller`".
  - **Objects to which this property applies:** `bidi-override`, `block`, `character`, `initial-property-set`, `inline`, `leader`, `page-number`, `page-number-citation`, `title`
  - **Shorthand affecting this property:** `font`

- `font-size-adjust`   (*7.8.6*; CSS; extended)

  - **Value:** *number* | `none` | `inherit`
  - **Initial:** `none`
  - **Inherited:** yes
  - **Media:** visual
  - A number specifies the aspect (font size divided by x-height).
    - Small fonts with larger values are typically easier to read than those with smaller values.
  - Note that child elements will inherit unadjusted values because inheritance is based on computed values.

- **Objects to which this property applies:** `bidi-override`, `block`, `character`, `initial-property-set`, `inline`, `leader`, `page-number`, `page-number-citation`, `title`

- `font-stretch`   (*7.8.5*; CSS; extended)

  - **Value:** `normal` | `wider` | `narrower` | `ultra-condensed` | `extra-condensed` | `condensed` | `semi-condensed` | `semi-expanded` | `expanded` | `extra-expanded` | `ultra-expanded` | `inherit`
  - **Initial:** `normal`
  - **Inherited:** yes
  - **Media:** visual
  - This property selects a normal, condensed, or extended face from a font family.
  - Values of "`wider`" and "`narrower`" do not go beyond the values of, respectively, "`ultra-expanded`" and "`ultra-condensed`".
  - **Objects to which this property applies:** `bidi-override`, `block`, `character`, `initial-property-set`, `inline`, `leader`, `page-number`, `page-number-citation`, `title`

- `font-style`   (*7.8.7*; CSS; basic)

  - **Value:** `normal` | `italic` | `oblique` | `backslant` | `inherit`
  - **Initial:** `normal`
  - **Inherited:** yes
  - **Media:** visual
  - Note that "`italic`" will match "`oblique`" if no italic face is available in the font family.
  - **Objects to which this property applies:** `bidi-override`, `block`, `character`, `initial-property-set`, `inline`, `leader`, `page-number`, `page-number-citation`, `title`
  - **Shorthand affecting this property:** `font`

- `font-variant`   (*7.8.8*; CSS; basic)

  - **Value:** `normal` | `small-caps` | `inherit`
  - **Initial:** `normal`
  - **Inherited:** yes

- **Media:** visual
- **Objects to whlch this property applies:** bidi-override, block, character, initial-property-set, inline, leader, page-number, page-number-citation, title
- **Shorthand affecting this property:** font

- font-weight   (7.8.9; CSS; basic)

  - **Value:** normal | bold | bolder | lighter | 100 | 200 | 300 | 400 | 500 | 600 | 700 | 800 | 900 | inherit
  - **Initial:** normal
  - **Inherited:** yes
  - **Media:** visual
  - "normal" maps to a value of "400".
  - "500" will map to a medium weight value (if available for the font).
  - "bold" maps to a value of "700".
  - "lighter" and "bolder" will find the closest font whose weight is, respectively, smaller or greater than the inherited font weight.
  - **Objects to which this property applies:** bidi-override, block, character, initial-property-set, inline, leader, page-number, page-number-citation, title
  - **Shorthand affecting this property:** font

- force-page-count   (7.25.6; XSL; extended)

  - **Value:** auto | even | odd | end-on-even | end-on-odd | no-force | inherit
  - **Initial:** auto
  - **Inherited:** no
  - **Media:** visual
  - **Object to which this property applies:** page-sequence

- format   (7.24.1; XSL; basic)

  - **Value:** string
  - **Initial:** 1
  - **Inherited:** no
  - **Media:** all

- See Section D.2.3 on page 340 for details.
- **Object to which this property applies:** page-sequence

- glyph-orientation-horizontal   (*7.27.2*; XSL; extended)

  - **Value:** *angle* | inherit
  - **Initial:** 0deg
  - **Inherited:** yes
  - **Media:** visual
  - This property applies only to text written in a writing mode with a left-to-right or right-to-left inline-progression direction.
  - The only allowable angles are 0, 90, 180, and 270 degrees, counted clockwise.
  - "0deg" indicates that the top of the glyph is towards the top of the reference area.
  - **Object to which this property applies:** character

- glyph-orientation-vertical   (*7.27.3*; XSL; extended)

  - **Value:** auto | *angle* | inherit
  - **Initial:** auto
  - **Inherited:** yes
  - **Media:** visual
  - This property applies only to text written in a writing mode with a top-to-bottom or bottom-to-top inline-progression direction.
  - The only allowable angles are 0, 90, 180, and 270 degrees, counted clockwise.
  - "0deg" indicates that the top of the glyph is towards the top of the reference area.
  - This property is commonly used to differentiate between the preferred orientation of alphabetic text in vertically written Japanese documents ("auto") vs. the orientation of alphabetic text in western signage and advertising ("0deg").
  - **Object to which this property applies:** character

- grouping-separator   (*7.24.2*; XSL; extended)

  - **Value:** *character*

- **Initial:** no separator
- **Inherited:** no
- **Media:** all
- See Section D.2.3 on page 340 for details.
- **Object to which this property applies:** page-sequence

- grouping-size   (*7.24.3*; XSL; extended)

  - **Value:** *number*
  - **Initial:** no grouping
  - **Inherited:** no
  - **Media:** all
  - See Section D.2.3 on page 340 for details.
  - **Object to which this property applies:** page-sequence

- height   (*7.14.4*; CSS; basic)

  - **Value:** *length* | *percentage* | auto | inherit
  - **Initial:** auto
  - **Inherited:** no
  - **Percentage:** see prose
  - **Media:** visual
  - A percentage is based on the explicit height of the containing block and are ignored if that height is not explicit.
  - Negative values are illegal.
  - **Objects to which this property applies:** block-container, external-graphic, inline, inline-container, instream-foreign-object, table, table-caption, table-cell, table-row

- hyphenate   (*7.9.4*; XSL; extended)

  - **Value:** false | true | inherit
  - **Initial:** false
  - **Inherited:** yes
  - **Media:** visual
  - This property specifies if hyphenation may or may not be used in the line-breaking algorithm for the text in the object.
  - **Objects to which this property applies:** block, character

- hyphenation-character (*7.9.5*; XSL; extended)

  - **Value:** *character* | inherit
  - **Initial:** The Unicode hyphen character U+2010
  - **Inherited:** yes
  - **Media:** visual
  - This property specifies the hyphenation character to be used when a hyphenation break occurs.
  - **Objects to which this property applies:** block, character

- hyphenation-keep (*7.15.1*; XSL; extended)

  - **Value:** auto | column | page | inherit
  - **Initial:** auto
  - **Inherited:** yes
  - **Media:** visual
  - This property specifies whether hyphenation can be performed on the last line that fits in a given reference area.
  - **Object to which this property applies:** block

- hyphenation-ladder-count (*7.15.2*; XSL; extended)

  - **Value:** no-limit | *number* | inherit
  - **Initial:** no-limit
  - **Inherited:** yes
  - **Media:** visual
  - This property specifies a limit on the number of successive hyphenated line areas the formatter may generate in a block area.
  - **Object to which this property applies:** block

- hyphenation-push-character-count (*7.9.6*; XSL; extended)

  - **Value:** *number* | inherit
  - **Initial:** 2
  - **Inherited:** yes
  - **Media:** visual
  - This property specifies the minimum number of characters in a hyphenated word after the hyphenation character.

- **Objects to which this property applies:** block, character

- hyphenation-remain-character-count   (*7.9.7*; XSL; extended)

  - **Value:** *number* | inherit
  - **Initial:** 2
  - **Inherited:** yes
  - **Media:** visual
  - This property specifies the minimum number of characters in a hyphenated word before the hyphenation character.
  - **Objects to which this property applies:** block, character

- id   (*7.28.2*; XSL; basic)

  - **Value:** *id*
  - **Initial:** see prose
  - **Inherited:** no, see prose
  - **Media:** all
  - **Objects to which this property applies:** basic-link, bidi-override, block, block-container, character, external-graphic, initial-property-set, inline, inline-container, instream-foreign-object, leader, list-block, list-item, list-item-body, list-item-label, multi-case, multi-properties, multi-property-set, multi-switch, multi-toggle, page-number, page-number-citation, page-sequence, table-and-caption, table, table-body, table-caption, table-cell, table-footer, table-header, table-row, wrapper

- indicate-destination   (*7.22.7*; XSL; extended)

  - **Value:** true | false
  - **Initial:** false
  - **Inherited:** no
  - **Media:** interactive
  - This property specifies that areas that belong to the link target when traversed should, in a system-dependent manner, be indicated.
  - **Object to which this property applies:** basic-link

- `initial-page-number`   (*7.25.7*; XSL; basic)

  - **Value:** `auto | auto-odd | auto-even |` *number* `| inherit`
  - **Initial:** `auto`
  - **Inherited:** no
  - **Media:** visual
  - **Object to which this property applies:** `page-sequence`

- `inline-progression-dimension`   (*7.14.5*; CSS; basic)

  - **Value:** `auto |` *length* `|` *percentage* `|` *length-range* `| inherit`
  - **Initial:** `auto`
  - **Inherited:** no
  - **Percentages:** see prose
  - **Media:** visual
  - A range allows the size to be adjusted by the formatter.
  - This property does not apply when `line-height` applies to the same dimension of the areas generated by this formatting object.
  - **Objects to which this property applies:** `block-container, external-graphic, inline, inline-container, instream-foreign-object, table, table-caption, table-cell`

- `internal-destination`   (*7.22.8*; XSL; extended)

  - **Value:** `empty string |` *idref*
  - **Initial:** empty string
  - **Inherited:** no
  - **Media:** interactive
  - At least one of `external-destination` and `internal-destination` properties should be assigned.
  - If both are assigned, the system may either report the error, or use `internal-destination`.
  - **Object to which this property applies:** `basic-link`

- `intrusion-displace`   (*7.18.3*; XSL; extended)

  - **Value:** `auto | none | line | indent | block | inherit`
  - **Initial:** `auto`

- **Inherited:** yes
- **Media:** visual
- This property specifies the displacement strategy in the presence of intrusions (e.g. side floats).
- "none" allows any present intrusion to overlay the given line or block areas.
- "block" reduces the inline-progression dimension of the entire block that is in any way affected by the presence of an intrusion.
- "line" reduces the inline-progression dimension of only those line areas that are affected by the presence of an intrusion.
- "indent" will act as "line", but will also preserve for each line any indentation relative to the other lines impacted by the given intrusion.
- "auto" assumes "block" for reference areas and "line" for other areas.
- **Objects to which this property applies:** block, block-container, list-block, list-item, table-and-caption, table, table-caption

- keep-together   *(7.19.3;* XSL; extended)

  - **Value:** *keep* | inherit
  - **Initial:** .within-line=auto, .within-column=auto, .within-page=auto
  - **Inherited:** yes
  - **Media:** visual
  - **Objects to which this property applies:** basic-link, block, block-container, inline, inline-container, list-block, list-item, list-item-body, list-item-label, table-and-caption, table, table-caption, table-row
  - **Shorthand affecting this property:** page-break-inside

- keep-with-next   *(7.19.4;* XSL; basic)

  - **Value:** *keep* | inherit
  - **Initial:** .within-line=auto, .within-column=auto, .within-page=auto
  - **Inherited:** no
  - **Media:** visual
  - **Objects to which this property applies:** basic-link, block, block-container, character, external-graphic, inline, inline-container,

instream-foreign-object, leader, list-block, list-item, page-number, page-number-citation, table-and-caption, table, table row

- **Shorthands affecting this property:** page-break-after, page-break-before

- keep-with-previous   (*7.19.5*; XSL; basic)

  - **Value:** *keep* | inherit
  - **Initial:** .within-line=auto, .within-column=auto, .within-page=auto
  - **Inherited:** no
  - **Media:** visual
  - **Objects to which this property applies:** basic-link, block, block-container, character, external-graphic, inline, inline-container, instream-foreign-object, leader, list-block, list-item, page-number, page-number-citation, table-and-caption, table, table-row

- language   (*7.9.2*; XSL; extended)

  - **Value:** none | *language* | inherit
  - **Initial:** none
  - **Inherited:** yes
  - **Media:** visual
  - This property specifies the language used in language- and locale-coupled services —
    - e.g. line-justification, line-breaking, hyphenation, etc.
  - **Objects to which this property applies:** block, character, page-sequence
  - **Shorthand affecting this property:** xml:lang

- last-line-end-indent   (*7.15.3*; XSL; extended)

  - **Value:** *length* | *percentage* | inherit
  - **Initial:** 0pt
  - **Inherited:** yes
  - **Percentage:** refers to inline-progression dimension of closest ancestor block area that is not a line area
  - **Media:** visual
  - Positive values indent the end edge, negative values outdent the end edge.

- **Object to which this property applies:** block

- leader-alignment   (*7.21.1*; XSL; extended)

  - **Value:** none | reference-area | page | inherit
  - **Initial:** none
  - **Inherited:** yes
  - **Media:** visual
  - This property specifies whether all leader objects having identical content and property values shall have their patterns aligned with each other, with respect to their common reference area or page.
  - "reference-area" specifies that the pattern is aligned to the content rectangle's start edge.
  - "page" specifies that the pattern is aligned to the page's start edge.
  - **Object to which this property applies:** leader

- leader-length   (*7.21.4*; XSL; basic)

  - **Value:** *length-range* | *percentage* | inherit
  - **Initial:** leader-length.minimum=0pt, .optimum=12.0pt, .maximum=100%
  - **Inherited:** yes
  - **Percentages:** refer to the inline-progression dimension of the content rectangle of parent area
  - **Media:** visual
  - **Object to which this property applies:** leader

- leader-pattern   (*7.21.2*; XSL; basic)

  - **Value:** space | rule | dots | use-content | inherit
  - **Initial:** space
  - **Inherited:** yes
  - **Media:** visual
  - "use-content" specifies that the children of the leader comprise the repeating pattern.
  - "space", "rule", and "dots" are available in all implementations.
  - An implementation may interpret "use-content" as "space".
  - **Object to which this property applies:** leader

- `leader-pattern-width` (*7.21.3*; XSL; extended)

  - **Value:** `use-font-metrics` | *length* | *percentage* | `inherit`
  - **Initial:** `use-font-metrics`
  - **Inherited:** yes
  - **Percentages:** refer to the inline-progression dimension of the content rectangle of parent area
  - **Media:** visual
  - **Object to which this property applies:** `leader`

- `left` (*7.5.5*; CSS; extended)

  - **Value:** *length* | *percentage* | `auto` | `inherit`
  - **Initial:** `auto`
  - **Inherited:** no
  - **Percentages:** refer to the width of containing block
  - **Media:** visual
  - This property specifies the distance between the margin edge and the containing block.
  - A value other than "`auto`" overrides a `width` value of "`auto`".
  - The `end-indent` property is adjusted to correspond to any specified geometry of the content rectangle.
  - The percentage is ignored if the containing block width is not specified explicitly.
  - **Object to which this property applies:** `block-container`

- `letter-spacing` (*7.16.2*; CSS; extended)

  - **Value:** `normal` | *length* | *space* | `inherit`
  - **Initial:** `normal`
  - **Inherited:** yes
  - **Media:** visual
  - This property specifies an amount to add (may be negative) to the built-in inter-character spacing.
  - Specifying a value other than "`normal`" turns off the use of ligatures.
  - Specifying a length turns off the modifications of inter-character spacing, but not the inter-word spacing, for justifying text.

- **Objects to which this property applies:** bidi-override, character, initial-property-set, leader, page-number, page-number-citation

- letter-value   (*7.24.4*; XSL; basic)

  - **Value:** auto | alphabetic | traditional
  - **Initial:** auto
  - **Inherited:** no
  - **Media:** all
  - See Section D.2.3 on page 340 for details.
  - "auto" corresponds to an unspecified attribute in XSLT.
  - **Object to which this property applies:** page-sequence

- line-height   (*7.15.4*; CSS; basic)

  - **Value:** normal | *length* | *number* | *percentage* | *space* | inherit
  - **Initial:** normal
  - **Inherited:** yes
  - **Percentages:** refer to the font size of the element itself
  - **Media:** visual
  - This property specifies the minimal height for a block-level construct of each generated inline box.
  - This property specifies the exact height for an inline-level construct.
  - The value "normal" is implementation-specific, typically between 1.0 and 1.2.
  - **Objects to which this property applies:** basic-link, bidi-override, block, character, external-graphic, initial-property-set, inline, inline-container, instream-foreign-object, leader, page-number, page-number-citation, title
  - **Shorthand affecting this property:** font

- line-height-shift-adjustment   (*7.15.5*; XSL; extended)

  - **Value:** consider-shifts | disregard-shifts | inherit
  - **Initial:** consider-shifts
  - **Inherited:** yes
  - **Media:** visual

- This property specifies if the line height of the line is adjusted for content that has a baseline shift.
- A value of "`disregard-shifts`" will prevent superscript and subscript characters from disrupting line spacing.
- See page 94 for more details on half-leading.
- **Object to which this property applies:** `block`

- `line-stacking-strategy`   (*7.15.6*; XSL; basic)
    - **Value:** `line-height | font-height | max-height | inherit`
    - **Initial:** `max-height`
    - **Inherited:** yes
    - **Media:** visual
    - This property specifies the strategy for positioning adjacent lines relative to each other.
    - See page 93 for details.
    - "`line-height`" may be interpreted as "`max-height`".
    - **Object to which this property applies:** `block`

- `linefeed-treatment`   (*7.15.7*; XSL; extended)
    - **Value:** `ignore | preserve | treat-as-space | treat-as-zero-width-space | inherit`
    - **Initial:** `treat-as-space`
    - **Inherited:** yes
    - **Media:** visual
    - **Object to which this property applies:** `block`

- `margin`   (*7.29.14*; CSS; shorthand)
    - **Value:** *margin-width*{1,4} `| inherit`
    - **Initial:** not defined for shorthand properties
    - **Inherited:** no
    - **Percentages:** refer to the width of containing block
    - **Media:** visual
    - *margin-width* is one of *length*, *percentage*, or "`auto`".
    - Up to four individual values for margins can be specified in this shorthand.

- Four values specify the margins in the following order: `margin-top`, `margin-right`, `margin-bottom`, `margin-left`.
- Three values specify the margins in the following order: `margin-top`, `margin-right`/`margin-left`, `margin-bottom`.
- Two values specify the margins in the following order: `margin-top`/`margin-bottom`, `margin-right`/`margin-left`.
- One value specifies all four margins.

- `margin-bottom` (*7.10.2*; CSS; basic)
  - **Value:** *margin-width* | `inherit`
  - **Initial:** `0pt`
  - **Inherited:** no
  - **Percentages:** refer to the width of containing block
  - **Media:** visual
  - *margin-width* is one of *length*, *percentage*, or "`auto`"
  - **Objects to which this property applies:** `block`, `block-container`, `list-block`, `list-item`, `region-body`, `simple-page-master`, `table-and-caption`, `table`
  - **Shorthand affecting this property:** `margin`

- `margin-left` (*7.10.3*; CSS; basic)
  - **Value:** *margin-width* | `inherit`
  - **Initial:** `0pt`
  - **Inherited:** no
  - **Percentages:** refer to the width of containing block
  - **Media:** visual
  - *margin-width* is one of *length*, *percentage*, or "`auto`".
  - **Objects to which this property applies:** `block`, `block-container`, `list-block`, `list-item`, `region-body`, `simple-page-master`, `table-and-caption`, `table`
  - **Shorthand affecting this property:** `margin`

- `margin-right` (*7.10.4*; CSS; basic)
  - **Value:** *margin-width* | `inherit`
  - **Initial:** `0pt`

- **Inherited:** no
- **Percentages:** refer to the width of containing block
- **Media:** visual
- *margin-width* is one of *length*, *percentage*, or "auto".
- **Objects to which this property applies:** block, block-container, list-block, list-item, region-body, simple-page-master, table-and-caption, table
- **Shorthand affecting this property:** margin

- margin-top   (*7.10.1*; CSS; basic)

  - **Value:** *margin-width* | inherit
  - **Initial:** 0pt
  - **Inherited:** no
  - **Percentages:** refer to the width of containing block
  - **Media:** visual
  - *margin-width* is one of *length*, *percentage*, or "auto".
  - **Objects to which this property applies:** block, block-container, list-block, list-item, region-body, simple-page-master, table-and-caption, table
  - **Shorthand affecting this property:** margin

- marker-class-name   (*7.23.1*; XSL; extended)

  - **Value:** *name*
  - **Initial:** an empty name
  - **Inherited:** no, a value is required
  - **Media:** paged
  - This property identifies the marker as being in a group with others that have the same name.
  - **Object to which this property applies:** marker

- master-name   (*7.25.8*; XSL; basic)

  - **Value:** *name*
  - **Initial:** an empty name
  - **Inherited:** no, a value is required
  - **Media:** visual

- **Objects to which this property applies:** `page-sequence-master`, `simple-page-master`

- `master-reference`   (*7.25.9*; XSL; basic)

  - **Value:** *name*
  - **Initial:** an empty name
  - **Inherited:** no, a value is required
  - **Media:** visual
  - **Objects to which this property applies:** `conditional-page-master-reference`, `page-sequence`, `repeatable-page-master-reference`, `single-page-master-reference`

- `max-height`   (*7.14.6*; CSS; complete)

  - **Value:** *length* | *percentage* | none | inherit
  - **Initial:** 0pt
  - **Inherited:** no
  - **Percentages:** refer to the height of containing block
  - **Media:** visual
  - Percentages are based on the explicit height of the containing block and are ignored if that height is not explicit.

- `max-width`   (*7.14.7*; CSS; complete)

  - **Value:** *length* | *percentage* | none | inherit
  - **Initial:** none
  - **Inherited:** no
  - **Percentages:** refer to the width of containing block
  - **Media:** visual
  - This property is mapped to either the `inline-progression-dimension` or the `block-progression-dimension`, based on the applicable values of the `writing-mode` and `reference-orientation` properties.

- `maximum-repeats`   (*7.25.10*; XSL; extended)

  - **Value:** *number* | no-limit | inherit
  - **Initial:** no-limit
  - **Inherited:** no

- **Media:** visual
- **Objects to which this property applies:** `repeatable-page-master-alternatives`, `repeatable-page-master-reference`

- `media-usage`   (*7.25.11*; XSL; extended)

  - **Value:** `auto | paginate | bounded-in-one-dimension | unbounded`
  - **Initial:** `auto`
  - **Inherited:** no
  - **Media:** visual
  - This property specifies how the selected display medium is used to present the page(s) specified by the stylesheet.
  - "unbounded" generates only one page per `page-sequence` and requires that neither `page-height` nor `page-width` be specified.
  - "bounded-in-one-dimension" generates only one page per `page-sequence` and requires exactly one of either `page-height` or `page-width` to be specified on the first page master that is used.
  - **Object to which this property applies:** `root`

- `min-height`   (*7.14.8*; CSS; complete)

  - **Value:** *length* | *percentage* | `inherit`
  - **Initial:** `0pt`
  - **Inherited:** no
  - **Percentages:** refer to the height of containing block
  - **Media:** visual
  - Percentages are based on the explicit height of the containing block and are ignored if that height is not explicit.

- `min-width`   (*7.14.9*; CSS; complete)

  - **Value:** *length* | *percentage* | `inherit`
  - **Initial:** depends on UA
  - **Inherited:** no
  - **Percentages:** refer to the width of containing block
  - **Media:** visual
  - Percentages are based on the explicit height of the containing block and are ignored if that height is not explicit.

- number-columns-repeated   (*7.26.12*; XSL; basic)

  - **Value:** *number*
  - **Initial:** 1
  - **Inherited:** no
  - **Media:** visual
  - **Object to which this property applies:** table-column

- number-columns-spanned   (*7.26.13*; XSL; basic)

  - **Value:** *number*
  - **Initial:** 1
  - **Inherited:** no
  - **Media:** visual
  - **Objects to which this property applies:** table-cell, table-column

- number-rows-spanned   (*7.26.14*; XSL; basic)

  - **Value:** *number*
  - **Initial:** 1
  - **Inherited:** no
  - **Media:** visual
  - **Object to which this property applies:** table-cell

- odd-or-even   (*7.25.12*; XSL; extended)

  - **Value:** odd | even | any | inherit
  - **Initial:** any
  - **Inherited:** no
  - **Media:** visual
  - **Object to which this property applies:** conditional-page-master-reference

- orphans   (*7.19.6*; CSS; basic)

  - **Value:** *integer* | inherit
  - **Initial:** 2
  - **Inherited:** yes
  - **Media:** visual

- This property specifies the minimum number of lines of a block that must be left at the bottom of a page.
- **Object to which this property applies:** `block`

- `overflow`   (*7.20.2*; CSS; basic)

  - **Value:** `visible | hidden | scroll | error-if-overflow | auto | inherit`
  - **Initial:** `auto`
  - **Inherited:** no
  - **Media:** visual
  - "`visible`" allows overflow content to be rendered outside the box.
  - "`hidden`" clips overflow content.
  - "`scroll`" provides a scrolling region for the entire content.
  - "`error-if-overflow`" is the same as "`hidden`" but also triggers an error.
  - **Objects to which this property applies:** `block-container, external-graphic, inline-container, instream-foreign-object, region-after, region-before, region-body, region-end, region-start`

- `padding`   (*7.29.15*; CSS; shorthand)

  - **Value:** *padding-width*`{1,4} | inherit`
  - **Initial:** not defined for shorthand properties
  - **Inherited:** no
  - **Percentages:** refer to the width of containing block
  - **Media:** visual
  - *padding-width* is one of *length* or *percentage*.
  - Up to four individual values for padding values can be specified in this shorthand.
  - Four values specify each of the padding values in the following order: `padding-top, padding-right, padding-bottom, padding-left`.
  - Three values specify the padding values in the following order: `padding-top, padding-right/padding-left, padding-bottom`.
  - Two values specify the padding values in the following order: `padding-top/padding-bottom, padding-right/padding-left`.
  - One value specifies all the padding values.

- padding-after   (*7.7.32*; CSS; basic)

  - **Value:** *padding-width* | *length-conditional* | inherit
  - **Initial:** 0pt
  - **Inherited:** no
  - **Percentages:** refer to the width of containing block
  - **Media:** visual
  - *padding-width* is one of *length* or *percentage*.
  - **Objects to which this property applies:** basic-link, block, block-container, character, external-graphic, initial-property-set, inline, inline-container, instream-foreign-object, leader, list-block, list-item, page-number, page-number-citation, region-after, region-before, region-body, region-end, region-start, table-and-caption, table, table-body, table-caption, table-cell, table-column, table-footer, table-header, table-row, title

- padding-before   (*7.7.31*; CSS; basic)

  - **Value:** *padding-width* | *length-conditional* | inherit
  - **Initial:** 0pt
  - **Inherited:** no
  - **Percentages:** refer to the width of containing block
  - **Media:** visual
  - *padding-width* is one of *length* or *percentage*.
  - **Objects to which this property applies:** basic-link, block, block-container, character, external-graphic, initial-property-set, inline, inline-container, instream-foreign-object, leader, list-block, list-item, page-number, page-number-citation, region-after, region-before, region-body, region-end, region-start, table-and-caption, table, table-body, table-caption, table-cell, table-column, table-footer, table-header, table-row, title

- padding-bottom   (*7.7.36*; CSS; basic)

  - **Value:** *padding-width* | inherit
  - **Initial:** 0pt
  - **Inherited:** no
  - **Percentages:** refer to the width of containing block

- **Media:** visual
- *padding-width* is one of *length* or *percentage*.
- **Objects to which this property applies:** basic-link, block, block-container, character, external-graphic, initial-property-set, inline, inline-container, instream-foreign-object, leader, list-block, list-item, page-number, page-number-citation, region-after, region-before, region-body, region-end, region-start, table-and-caption, table, table-body, table-caption, table-cell, table-column, table-footer, table-header, table-row, title
- **Shorthand affecting this property:** padding

- padding-end   (*7.7.34*; CSS; basic)

  - **Value:** *padding-width* | *length-conditional* | inherit
  - **Initial:** 0pt
  - **Inherited:** no
  - **Percentages:** refer to the width of containing block
  - **Media:** visual
  - *padding-width* is one of *length* or *percentage*.
  - **Objects to which this property applies:** basic-link, block, block-container, character, external-graphic, initial-property-set, inline, inline-container, instream-foreign-object, leader, list-block, list-item, page-number, page-number-citation, region-after, region-before, region-body, region-end, region-start, table-and-caption, table, table-body, table-caption, table-cell, table-column, table-footer, table-header, table-row, title

- padding-left   (*7.7.37*; CSS; basic)

  - **Value:** *padding-width* | inherit
  - **Initial:** 0pt
  - **Inherited:** no
  - **Percentages:** refer to the width of containing block
  - **Media:** visual
  - *padding-width* is one of *length* or *percentage*.
  - **Objects to which this property applies:** basic-link, block, block-container, character, external-graphic, initial-property-set, inline, inline-container, instream-foreign-object, leader, list-

block, list-item, page-number, page-number-citation, region-
after, region-before, region-body, region-end, region-start,
table-and-caption, table, table-body, table-caption, table-cell,
table-column, table-footer, table-header, table-row, title

- **Shorthand affecting this property:** padding

- padding-right   (*7.7.38*; CSS; basic)

  - **Value:** *padding-width* | inherit
  - **Initial:** 0pt
  - **Inherited:** no
  - **Percentages:** refer to the width of containing block
  - **Media:** visual
  - *padding-width* is one of *length* or *percentage*.
  - **Objects to which this property applies:** basic-link, block, block-
    container, character, external-graphic, initial-property-set,
    inline, inline-container, instream-foreign-object, leader, list-
    block, list-item, page-number, page-number-citation, region-
    after, region-before, region-body, region-end, region-start,
    table-and-caption, table, table-body, table-caption, table-cell,
    table-column, table-footer, table-header, table-row, title
  - **Shorthand affecting this property:** padding

- padding-start   (*7.7.33*; CSS; basic)

  - **Value:** *padding-width* | *length-conditional* | inherit
  - **Initial:** 0pt
  - **Inherited:** no
  - **Percentages:** refer to the width of containing block
  - **Media:** visual
  - *padding-width* is one of *length* or *percentage*.
  - **Objects to which this property applies:** basic-link, block, block-
    container, character, external-graphic, initial-property-set,
    inline, inline-container, instream-foreign-object, leader, list-
    block, list-item, page-number, page-number-citation, region-
    after, region-before, region-body, region-end, region-start,
    table-and-caption, table, table-body, table-caption, table-cell,
    table-column, table-footer, table-header, table-row, title

- padding-top   (*7.7.35*; CSS; basic)

  - **Value:** *padding-width* | inherit
  - **Initial:** 0pt
  - **Inherited:** no
  - **Percentages:** refer to the width of containing block
  - **Media:** visual
  - *padding-width* is one of *length* or *percentage*.
  - **Objects to which this property applies:** basic-link, block, block-container, character, external-graphic, initial-property-set, inline, inline-container, instream-foreign-object, leader, list-block, list-item, page-number, page-number-citation, region-after, region-before, region-body, region-end, region-start, table-and-caption, table, table-body, table-caption, table-cell, table-column, table-footer, table-header, table-row, title
  - **Shorthand affecting this property:** padding

- page-break-after   (*7.29.16*; CSS; shorthand)

  - **Value:** auto | always | avoid | left | right | inherit
  - **Initial:** auto
  - **Inherited:** no
  - **Media:** visual

Value	break-after	keep-with-next
"auto"	"auto"	"auto"
"always"	"page"	"auto"
"avoid"	"auto"	"always"
"left"	"even-page"	"auto"
"right"	"odd-page"	"auto"

- page-break-before   (*7.29.17*; CSS; shorthand)

  - **Value:** auto | always | avoid | left | right | inherit
  - **Initial:** auto
  - **Inherited:** no
  - **Media:** visual

Value	break-before	keep-with-previous
"auto"	"auto"	"auto"
"always"	"page"	"auto"
"avoid"	"auto"	"always"
"left"	"even-page"	"auto"
"right"	"odd-page"	"auto"

- page-break-inside   (*7.29.18*; CSS; shorthand)

  - **Value:** avoid | auto | inherit
  - **Initial:** auto
  - **Inherited:** yes
  - **Media:** visual
  - "auto" infers keep-together of "auto".
  - "avoid" infers keep-together of "always".

- page-height   (*7.25.13*; XSL; basic)

  - **Value:** auto | indefinite | *length* | inherit
  - **Initial:** auto
  - **Inherited:** no
  - **Media:** visual
  - "auto" determines the value from the window (for continues media) or the size of the page.
  - "indefinite" determines the value from the laid-out content.
    - It overrides a value of "indefinite" for page-width to be "auto".
  - **Object to which this property applies:** simple-page-master
  - **Shorthand affecting this property:** size

- page-position   (*7.25.14*; XSL; extended)

  - **Value:** first | last | rest | any | inherit
  - **Initial:** any
  - **Inherited:** no
  - **Media:** visual

- **Object to which this property applies:** `conditional-page-master-reference`

- `page-width`   (*7.25.15*; XSL; basic)

  - **Value:** `auto` | `indefinite` | *`length`* | `inherit`
  - **Initial:** `auto`
  - **Inherited:** no
  - **Media:** visual
  - "`auto`" determines the value from the window (for continues media) or the size of the page.
  - "`indefinite`" determines the value from the laid-out content.
    - It is overridden to be "`auto`" by a value of "`indefinite`" for `page-height`.
  - **Object to which this property applies:** `simple-page-master`
  - **Shorthand affecting this property:** `size`

- `pause`   (*7.29.19*; CSS; shorthand)

  - **Value:** [*`time`* | *`percentage`*]{1,2} | `inherit`
  - **Initial:** depends on user agent
  - **Inherited:** no
  - **Percentages:** see descriptions of `pause-before` and `pause-after`
  - **Media:** aural
  - This propetry is a shorthand specifying, in order, `pause-before` and `pause-after`.
    - This property specifying one value applies to both properties.

- `pause-after`   (*7.6.5*; CSS; basic)

  - **Value:** *`time`* | *`percentage`* | `inherit`
  - **Initial:** depends on user agent
  - **Inherited:** no
  - **Percentages:** see prose
  - **Media:** aural
  - This property specifies the pause to be observed after speaking an object's content.
  - **Objects to which this property applies:** `basic-link, bidi-override, block, character, external-graphic, initial-property-set, inline,`

instream-foreign-object, leader, list-block, list-item, page-number, page-number-citation, table-and-caption, table, table-body, table-caption, table-cell, table-footer, table-header, table-row, title

- **Shorthand affecting this property:** pause

- pause-before   (*7.6.6*; CSS; basic)

  - **Value:** *time* | *percentage* | inherit
  - **Initial:** depends on user agent
  - **Inherited:** no
  - **Percentages:** see prose
  - **Media:** aural
  - This property specifies the pause to be observed before speaking an object's content.
  - **Objects to which this property applies:** basic-link, bidi-override, block, character, external-graphic, initial-property-set, inline, instream-foreign-object, leader, list-block, list-item, page-number, page-number-citation, table-and-caption, table, table-body, table-caption, table-cell, table-footer, table-header, table-row, title
  - **Shorthand affecting this property:** pause

- pitch   (*7.6.7*; CSS; basic)

  - **Value:** *frequency* | x-low | low | medium | high | x-high | inherit
  - **Initial:** medium
  - **Inherited:** yes
  - **Media:** aural
  - This property specifies the average pitch (frequency) of the speaking voice.
  - **Objects to which this property applies:** basic-link, bidi-override, block, character, external-graphic, initial-property-set, inline, instream-foreign-object, leader, list-block, list-item, page-number, page-number-citation, table-and-caption, table, table-body, table-caption, table-cell, table-footer, table-header, table-row, title

- pitch-range   (*7.6.8*; CSS; basic)

  - **Value:** *number* | inherit
  - **Initial:** 50
  - **Inherited:** yes
  - **Media:** aural
  - This property specifies variation in average pitch.
  - A highly animated voice, i.e. one that is heavily inflected, displays a high pitch range.
  - **Objects to which this property applies:** basic-link, bidi-override, block, character, external-graphic, initial-property-set, inline, instream-foreign-object, leader, list-block, list-item, page-number, page-number-citation, table-and-caption, table, table-body, table-caption, table-cell, table-footer, table-header, table-row, title

- play-during   (*7.6.9*; CSS; basic)

  - **Value:** *uri-specification* mix? repeat? | auto | none | inherit
  - **Initial:** auto
  - **Inherited:** no
  - **Media:** aural
  - *uri-specification* specifies the sound played as a background while the object's content is spoken.
  - "mix" specifies that the sound inherited from the parent object is mixed with the object's background *uri-specification*.
  - "repeat" specifies a short background to be repeated while the object's content is being spoken.
  - "auto" specifies that the sound of the parent's background is to be continued.
  - "none" specifies silence for the background of the object being spoken.
  - **Objects to which this property applies:** basic-link, bidi-override, block, character, external-graphic, initial-property-set, inline, instream-foreign-object, leader, list-block, list-item, page-number, page-number-citation, table-and-caption, table, table-body, table-caption, table-cell, table-footer, table-header, table-row, title

- position   (*7.29.20*; CSS; shorthand)

  - **Value:** static | relative | absolute | fixed | inherit
  - **Initial:** static
  - **Inherited:** no
  - **Media:** visual

Value	relative-position	absolute-position
"static"	"static"	"auto"
"relative"	"relative"	"auto"
"absolute"	"static"	"absolute"
"fixed"	"static"	"fixed"

- precedence   (*7.25.16*; XSL; extended)

  - **Value:** true | false | inherit
  - **Initial:** false
  - **Inherited:** no
  - **Media:** visual
  - This property specifies whether the inline-progression dimension of the region extends to content rectangle of the page reference area ("true") or only to the edges incurred by the adjacent regions ("false").
  - **Objects to which this property applies:** region-after, region-before

- provisional-distance-between-starts   (*7.28.4*; XSL; basic)

  - **Value:** *length* | *percentage* | inherit
  - **Initial:** 24.0pt
  - **Inherited:** yes
  - **Percentages:** refer to the inline-progression dimension of the closest ancestor's block area that is not a line area
  - **Media:** visual
  - See page 129 for a discussion of this property.
  - **Object to which this property applies:** list-block

- provisional-label-separation   (*7.28.3*; XSL; basic)

  - **Value:** *length* | *percentage* | inherit
  - **Initial:** 6.0pt
  - **Inherited:** yes
  - **Percentages:** refer to the inline-progression dimension of the closest ancestor's block area that is not a line area
  - **Media:** visual
  - See page 129 for a discussion of this property.
  - **Object to which this property applies:** list-block

- ref-id   (*7.28.5*; XSL; extended)

  - **Value:** *idref* | inherit
  - **Initial:** none, value required
  - **Inherited:** no
  - **Media:** all
  - **Object to which this property applies:** page-number-citation

- reference-orientation   (*7.20.3*; XSL; extended)

  - **Value:** 0 | 90 | 180 | 270 | -90 | -180 | -270 | inherit
  - **Initial:** 0
  - **Inherited:** yes (see prose)
  - **Media:** visual
  - Degree values are counted clockwise from "0" degrees at the top.
    - Note this is a simple integer and not an angle data type value.
  - **Objects to which this property applies:** block-container, inline-container, region-after, region-before, region-body, region-end, region-start, simple-page-master

- region-name   (*7.25.17*; XSL; basic)

  - **Value:** xsl-region-body | xsl-region-start | xsl-region-end | xsl-region-before | xsl-region-after | xsl-before-float-separator | xsl-footnote-separator | *name*
  - **Initial:** see prose
  - **Inherited:** no, a value is required
  - **Media:** visual

- **Objects to which this property applies:** region-after, region-before, region-body, region-end, region-start

- relative-align   (*7.13.6*; XSL; extended)

  - **Value:** before | baseline | inherit
  - **Initial:** before
  - **Inherited:** yes
  - **Media:** visual
  - This property specifies the alignment, in the block-progression direction, between two or more areas.
  - **Objects to which this property applies:** list-item, table-cell

- relative-position   (*7.12.1*; CSS; extended)

  - **Value:** static | relative | inherit
  - **Initial:** static
  - **Inherited:** no
  - **Media:** visual
  - "static" stacks the area normally.
  - "relative" positions an area as if it were stacked, but the area does not affect the position of any other area.
    - Any such area that breaks over a page boundary is clipped to the page and the remainder is discarded.
  - **Objects to which this property applies:** basic-link, bidi-override, block, character, external-graphic, initial-property-set, inline, inline-container, instream-foreign-object, leader, list-block, list-item, page-number, page-number-citation, table-and-caption, table, table-body, table-caption, table-cell, table-footer, table-header, table-row
  - **Shorthand affecting this property:** position

- rendering-intent   (*7.17.3*; XSL; extended)

  - **Value:** auto | perceptual | relative-colorimetric | saturation | absolute-colorimetric | inherit
  - **Initial:** auto
  - **Inherited:** no
  - **Media:** visual

- This property is applicable primarily to color profiles corresponding to the CMYK color space.
- The different values cause different methods to be used for translating colors to the color gamut of the target rendering device.
- **Object to which this property applies:** color-profile

- retrieve-boundary   (*7.23.4*; XSL; extended)

  - **Value:** page | page-sequence | document
  - **Initial:** page-sequence
  - **Inherited:** no
  - **Media:** paged
  - This property specifies how far "back" in the flow the formatter will look for a marker, starting with the current page.
  - **Object to which this property applies:** retrieve-marker

- retrieve-class-name   (*7.23.2*; XSL; extended)

  - **Value:** *name*
  - **Initial:** an empty name
  - **Inherited:** no, a value is required
  - **Media:** paged
  - This property specifies that the marker whose children are retrieved by the retrieve-marker must have a marker-class-name property value that is the same as the value of this property.
  - **Object to which this property applies:** retrieve-marker

- retrieve-position   (*7.23.3*; XSL; extended)

  - **Value:** first-starting-within-page | first-including-carryover | last-starting-within-page | last-ending-within-page
  - **Initial:** first-starting-within-page
  - **Inherited:** no
  - **Media:** paged
  - This property specifies the preference for which marker children shall be retrieved by a retrieve-marker.
  - **Object to which this property applies:** retrieve-marker

- richness   (*7.6.10*; CSS; basic)

  - **Value:** *number* | inherit
  - **Initial:** 50
  - **Inherited:** yes
  - **Media:** aural
  - This property specifies the richness, or brightness, of the speaking voice.
  - A rich voice will "carry" in a large room; a smooth voice will not.
    - The term "smooth" refers to how the waveform looks when drawn.
  - **Objects to which this property applies:** basic-link, bidi-override, block, character, external-graphic, initial-property-set, inline, instream-foreign-object, leader, list-block, list-item, page-number, page-number-citation, table-and-caption, table, table-body, table-caption, table-cell, table-footer, table-header, table-row, title

- right   (*7.5.3*; CSS; extended)

  - **Value:** *length* | *percentage* | auto | inherit
  - **Initial:** auto
  - **Inherited:** no
  - **Percentages:** refer to width of containing block
  - **Media:** visual
  - See left for details.
  - **Object to which this property applies:** block-container

- role   (*7.4.2*; XSL; basic)

  - **Value:** *string* | *uri-specification* | none | inherit
  - **Initial:** none
  - **Inherited:** no
  - **Media:** all
  - This property provides a hint for alternate rendering agents (aural readers, etc.) regarding the role of the XML element or elements that were used to construct this formatting object.
  - *uri-specification* specifies an RDF resource.
  - **Objects to which this property applies:** basic-link, block, external-graphic, footnote, footnote-body, initial-property-set, inline,

instream-foreign-object, leader, list-block, list-item, list-item-body, list-item-label, multi-case, multi-properties, multi-switch, multi-toggle, page-number, page-number-citation, table-and-caption, table, table-body, table-caption, table-cell, table-footer, table-header, table-row, title

- rule-style   (*7.21.5*; XSL; basic)

  - **Value:** none | dotted | dashed | solid | double | groove | ridge | inherit
  - **Initial:** solid
  - **Inherited:** yes
  - **Media:** visual
  - "none" and "solid" are always supported.
  - Other values may be interpreted as "solid".
  - **Object to which this property applies:** leader

- rule-thickness   (*7.21.6*; XSL; basic)

  - **Value:** *length*
  - **Initial:** 1.0pt
  - **Inherited:** yes
  - **Media:** visual
  - This property only applies if the leader-pattern is "rule".
  - **Object to which this property applies:** leader

- scaling   (*7.14.10*; XSL; extended)

  - **Value:** uniform | non-uniform | inherit
  - **Initial:** uniform
  - **Inherited:** no
  - **Media:** visual
  - This property specifies whether scaling is to preserve the intrinsic aspect ratio.
  - **Objects to which this property applies:** external-graphic, instream-foreign-object

- scaling-method   (*7.14.11*; XSL; extended)
  - **Value:** auto | integer-pixels | resample-any-method | inherit
  - **Initial:** auto
  - **Inherited:** no
  - **Media:** visual
  - This property indicates the preference in the scaling/sizing tradeoff to be used when formatting bitmapped graphics.
  - **Objects to which this property applies:** external-graphic, instream-foreign-object

- score-spaces   (*7.28.6*; XSL; extended)
  - **Value:** true | false | inherit
  - **Initial:** true
  - **Inherited:** yes
  - **Media:** visual
  - This property specifies whether the text-decoration property is to be applied to spaces.
  - **Objects to which this property applies:** bidi-override, character, initial-property-set, page-number, page-number-citation

- script   (*7.9.3*; XSL; extended)
  - **Value:** none | auto | *script* | inherit
  - **Initial:** auto
  - **Inherited:** yes
  - **Media:** visual
  - This property specifies the script used in language- and locale-coupled services —
    - e.g. line-justification, line-breaking, hyphenation, etc.
  - **Objects to which this property applies:** block, character

- show-destination   (*7.22.9*; XSL; extended)
  - **Value:** replace | new
  - **Initial:** replace
  - **Inherited:** no
  - **Media:** interactive

- This property specifies whether the destination resource should replace the current document view or open a new document view.
- **Object to which this property applies:** basic-link

- size   (*7.29.21*; CSS; shorthand)

  - **Value:** *length*{1,2} | auto | landscape | portrait | inherit
  - **Initial:** auto
  - **Inherited:** N/A [XSL: no, is optional]
  - **Media:** visual
  - This is a shorthand specifying, in order, page-height and page-width.
    - Specifying one value applies to both properties.

- source-document   (*7.4.1*; XSL; basic)

  - **Value:** *uri-specification* [*uri-specification*]* | none | inherit
  - **Initial:** none
  - **Inherited:** no
  - **Media:** all
  - This property provides a pointer back to the original XML document used to create the XSL-FO input.
  - W3C Accessibility guidelines strongly encourage the use of this property either on root or on the first formatting object from each source document.
  - **Objects to which this property applies:** basic-link, block, external-graphic, footnote, footnote-body, initial-property-set, inline, instream-foreign-object, leader, list-block, list-item, list-item-body, list-item-label, multi-case, multi-properties, multi-switch, multi-toggle, page-number, page-number-citation, table-and-caption, table, table-body, table-caption, table-cell, table-footer, table-header, table-row, title

- space-after   (*7.10.6*; XSL; basic)

  - **Value:** *space* | inherit
  - **Initial:** space.minimum=0pt, .optimum=0pt, .maximum=0pt, .conditionality=discard, .precedence=0
  - **Inherited:** no
  - **Percentages:** N/A (differs from margin-bottom in CSS)

- **Media:** visual
- **Objects to which this property applies:** block, block-container, list-block, list-item, region-body, simple-page-master, table-and-caption, table

- space-before   (*7.10.5*; XSL; basic)

  - **Value:** *space* | inherit
  - **Initial:** space.minimum=0pt, .optimum=0pt, .maximum=0pt, .conditionality=discard, .precedence=0
  - **Inherited:** no
  - **Percentages:** N/A (differs from margin-top in CSS)
  - **Media:** visual
  - **Objects to which this property applies:** block, block-container, list-block, list-item, region-body, simple-page-master, table-and-caption, table

- space-end   (*7.11.1*; XSL; basic)

  - **Value:** *space* | *percentage* | inherit
  - **Initial:** space.minimum=0pt, .optimum=0pt, .maximum=0pt, .conditionality=discard, .precedence=0
  - **Inherited:** no
  - **Percentages:** refer to inline-progression dimension of the closest ancestor's block area that is not a line area
  - **Media:** visual
  - **Objects to which this property applies:** basic-link, character, external-graphic, inline, inline-container, instream-foreign-object, leader, page-number, page-number-citation, title

- space-start   (*7.11.2*; XSL; basic)

  - **Value:** *space* | *percentage* | inherit
  - **Initial:** space.minimum=0pt, .optimum=0pt, .maximum=0pt, .conditionality=discard, .precedence=0
  - **Inherited:** no
  - **Percentages:** refer to inline-progression dimension of the closest ancestor's block area that is not a line area

- **Media:** visual
- **Objects to which this property applies:** basic-link, character, external-graphic, inline, inline-container, instream-foreign-object, leader, page-number, page-number-citation, title

- span   (*7.20.4*; XSL; extended)

  - **Value:** none | all | inherit
  - **Initial:** none
  - **Inherited:** no
  - **Media:** visual
  - **Objects to which this property applies:** block, block-container

- speak   (*7.6.11*; CSS; basic)

  - **Value:** normal | none | spell-out | inherit
  - **Initial:** normal
  - **Inherited:** yes
  - **Media:** aural
  - This property specifies the manner by which text will be rendered aurally.
  - "none" suppresses the aural rendering to zero time (unlike setting the volume to zero).
  - **Objects to which this property applies:** basic-link, bidi-override, block, character, external-graphic, initial-property-set, inline, instream-foreign-object, leader, list-block, list-item, page-number, page-number-citation, table-and-caption, table, table-body, table-caption, table-cell, table-footer, table-header, table-row, title

- speak-header   (*7.6.12*; CSS; basic)

  - **Value:** once | always | inherit
  - **Initial:** once
  - **Inherited:** yes
  - **Media:** aural

- This property specifies whether table headers are to be spoken before every cell, or only before a cell when that cell is associated with a different header than the previous cell.
- **Objects to which this property applies:** basic-link, bidi-override, block, character, external-graphic, initial-property-set, inline, instream-foreign-object, leader, list-block, list-item, page-number, page-number-citation, table-and-caption, table, table-body, table-caption, table-cell, table-footer, table-header, table-row, title

- speak-numeral   (*7.6.13*; CSS; basic)

  - **Value:** digits | continuous | inherit
  - **Initial:** continuous
  - **Inherited:** yes
  - **Media:** aural
  - This property specifies how numerals are spoken.
  - **Objects to which this property applies:** basic-link, bidi-override, block, character, external-graphic, initial-property-set, inline, instream-foreign-object, leader, list-block, list-item, page-number, page-number-citation, table-and-caption, table, table-body, table-caption, table-cell, table-footer, table-header, table-row, title

- speak-punctuation   (*7.6.14*; CSS; basic)

  - **Value:** code | none | inherit
  - **Initial:** none
  - **Inherited:** yes
  - **Media:** aural
  - This property specifies how punctuation is spoken.
  - Note that "borge" is not an available option.
  - **Objects to which this property applies:** basic-link, bidi-override, block, character, external-graphic, initial-property-set, inline, instream-foreign-object, leader, list-block, list-item, page-number, page-number-citation, table-and-caption, table, table-body, table-caption, table-cell, table-footer, table-header, table-row, title

- speech-rate   (*7.6.15*; CSS; basic)

  - **Value:** *number* | x-slow | slow | medium | fast | x-fast | faster | slower | inherit
  - **Initial:** medium
  - **Inherited:** yes
  - **Media:** aural
  - *number* specifies the speaking rate in words per minute (varying somewhat by language).
  - **Objects to which this property applies:** basic-link, bidi-override, block, character, external-graphic, initial-property-set, inline, instream-foreign-object, leader, list-block, list-item, page-number, page-number-citation, table-and-caption, table, table-body, table-caption, table-cell, table-footer, table-header, table-row, title

- src   (*7.28.7*; XSL; basic)

  - **Value:** *uri-specification* | inherit
  - **Initial:** none, value required
  - **Inherited:** no
  - **Media:** visual
  - **Objects to which this property applies:** color-profile, external-graphic

- start-indent   (*7.10.7*; XSL; basic)

  - **Value:** *length* | *percentage* | inherit
  - **Initial:** 0pt
  - **Inherited:** yes
  - **Percentages:** refer to inline-progression dimension of the containing reference area
  - **Media:** visual
  - **Objects to which this property applies:** block, block-container, list-block, list-item, region-body, simple-page-master, table-and-caption, table

- starting-state   (*7.22.10*; XSL; extended)

  - **Value:** show | hide
  - **Initial:** show
  - **Inherited:** no
  - **Media:** interactive
  - This property specifies the multi-case that can be initially displayed.
  - **Object to which this property applies:** multi-case

- starts-row   (*7.26.15*; XSL; extended)

  - **Value:** true | false
  - **Initial:** false
  - **Inherited:** no
  - **Media:** visual
  - **Object to which this property applies:** table-cell

- stress   (*7.6.16*; CSS; basic)

  - **Value:** *number* | inherit
  - **Initial:** 50
  - **Inherited:** yes
  - **Media:** aural
  - This property specifies the height of "local peaks" in the intonation contour of a voice.
  - **Objects to which this property applies:** basic-link, bidi-override, block, character, external-graphic, initial-property-set, inline, instream-foreign-object, leader, list-block, list-item, page-number, page-number-citation, table-and-caption, table, table-body, table-caption, table-cell, table-footer, table-header, table-row, title

- suppress-at-line-break   (*7.16.3*; XSL; extended)

  - **Value:** auto | suppress | retain | inherit
  - **Initial:** auto
  - **Inherited:** no
  - **Media:** visual

- "auto" will suppress a U+0020 space character if it is the first or last in a line.
- "suppress" and "retain" will act accordingly with the given character.
- **Object to which this property applies:** character

- switch-to   (*7.22.11*; XSL; extended)

  - **Value:** xsl-preceding | xsl-following | xsl-any | *name* [*name*]*
  - **Initial:** xsl-any
  - **Inherited:** no
  - **Media:** interactive
  - This property specifies which multi-case object this multi-toggle will switch to when evoked.
  - **Object to which this property applies:** multi-toggle

- table-layout   (*7.26.16*; CSS; extended)

  - **Value:** auto | fixed | inherit
  - **Initial:** auto
  - **Inherited:** no
  - **Media:** visual
  - **Object to which this property applies:** table

- table-omit-footer-at-break   (*7.26.17*; XSL; extended)

  - **Value:** true | false
  - **Initial:** false
  - **Inherited:** no
  - **Media:** visual
  - This property specifies if a table whose last area is not at the end of an area produced by the table should end with the content of the table-footer formatting object or not.
  - **Object to which this property applies:** table

- table-omit-header-at-break   (*7.26.18*; XSL; extended)

  - **Value:** true | false
  - **Initial:** false
  - **Inherited:** no

- **Media:** visual
- This property specifies if a table whose first area is not at the beginning of an area produced by the table should start with the content of the `table-header` formatting object or not.
- **Object to which this property applies:** `table`

- `target-presentation-context`   (*7.22.12*; XSL; extended)

  - **Value:** `use-target-processing-context` | *uri-specification*
  - **Initial:** `use-target-processing-context`
  - **Inherited:** no
  - **Media:** interactive
  - This property specifies the limited context in which the resource should be presented if the external destination is a resource of a processed structured media type for which a limited presentational context makes sense.
  - **Object to which this property applies:** `basic-link`

- `target-processing-context`   (*7.22.13*; XSL; extended)

  - **Value:** `document-root` | *uri-specification*
  - **Initial:** `document-root`
  - **Inherited:** no
  - **Media:** interactive
  - This property specifies the root of a virtual document that the processor preparing the new presentation should process if the external destination is a resource of a processed structured media type.
  - **Object to which this property applies:** `basic-link`

- `target-stylesheet`   (*7.22.14*; XSL; extended)

  - **Value:** `use-normal-stylesheet` | *uri-specification*
  - **Initial:** `use-normal-stylesheet`
  - **Inherited:** no
  - **Media:** interactive
  - This property specifies the stylesheet to be used for processing the target resource.
  - **Object to which this property applies:** `basic-link`

- text-align   (*7.15.9*; CSS; basic)
  - **Value:** start | center | end | justify | inside | outside | left | right | *string* | inherit
  - **Initial:** start
  - **Inherited:** yes
  - **Media:** visual
  - *string* applies only to table-cell and specifies which cells in a table column will align.
  - "left" and "right" are interpreted respectively as "start" and "end".
  - **Objects to which this property applies:** block, external-graphic, instream-foreign-object, table-and-caption

- text-align-last   (*7.15.10*; XSL; extended)
  - **Value:** relative | start | center | end | justify | inside | outside | left | right | inherit
  - **Initial:** relative
  - **Inherited:** yes
  - **Media:** visual
  - "left" and "right" are interpreted respectively as "start" and "end".
  - **Object to which this property applies:** block

- text-altitude   (*7.27.4*; XSL; extended)
  - **Value:** use-font-metrics | *length* | *percentage* | inherit
  - **Initial:** use-font-metrics
  - **Inherited:** no
  - **Percentages:** refer to font's em-height
  - **Media:** visual
  - This property specifies the "height" to be used for the ascent above the dominant baseline.
  - **Objects to which this property applies:** block, character, leader, page-number, page-number-citation

- text-decoration   (*7.16.4*; CSS; extended)

  - **Value:** none | [[underline | no-underline] || [overline | no-overline] || [line-through | no-line-through] || [blink | no-blink]] | inherit
  - **Initial:** none
  - **Inherited:** no, but see prose
  - **Media:** visual
  - This property is not inherited, but descendant boxes are formatted with the same decoration.
  - The color of the decoration remains the same even if descendant elements use different colors.
  - **Objects to which this property applies:** character, initial-property-set, inline, page-number, page-number-citation

- text-depth   (*7.27.5*; XSL; extended)

  - **Value:** use-font-metrics | *length* | *percentage* | inherit
  - **Initial:** use-font-metrics
  - **Inherited:** no
  - **Percentages:** refer to the font's em-height
  - **Media:** visual
  - This property specifies the "depth" to be used for the descent below the dominant baseline.
  - **Objects to which this property applies:** block, character, leader, page-number, page-number-citation

- text-indent   (*7.15.11*; CSS; basic)

  - **Value:** *length* | *percentage* | inherit
  - **Initial:** 0pt
  - **Inherited:** yes
  - **Percentages:** refer to the width of containing block
  - **Media:** visual
  - Positive values indent the start edge, negative values outdent the start edge with a hanging indent.
  - **Object to which this property applies:** block

- text-shadow   (*7.16.5*; CSS; extended)

  - **Value:** none | [*color* || *length length length*? ,]* [*color* || *length length length*?] | inherit
  - **Initial:** none
  - **Inherited:** no, see prose
  - **Media:** visual
  - This property specifies a comma-separated list of shadow effects to be applied to the text of the element.
  - Each shadow effect is specified as the color used as a basis of the effect, the horizontal distance to the right (positive) or left (negative) of the text, the vertical distance below (positive) or above (negative) the text, and optionally a blur radius.
  - **Objects to which this property applies:** character, initial-property-set, leader, page-number, page-number-citation

- text-transform   (*7.16.6*; CSS; extended)

  - **Value:** capitalize | uppercase | lowercase | none | inherit
  - **Initial:** none
  - **Inherited:** yes
  - **Media:** visual
  - This property is deprecated in XSL-FO due to "severe internationalization issues."
  - **Objects to which this property applies:** character, initial-property-set, page-number, page-number-citation

- top   (*7.5.2*; CSS; extended)

  - **Value:** *length* | *percentage* | auto | inherit
  - **Initial:** auto
  - **Inherited:** no
  - **Percentages:** refer to the height of containing block
  - **Media:** visual
  - See bottom for details.
  - **Object to which this property applies:** block-container

- `treat-as-word-space`   (*7.16.7*; XSL; extended)
  - **Value:** `auto | true | false | inherit`
  - **Initial:** `auto`
  - **Inherited:** no
  - **Media:** visual
  - This property specifies if the character shall be treated as a word space ("`true`") or as a normal letter ("`false`").
  - **Object to which this property applies:** `character`

- `unicode-bidi`   (*7.27.6*; CSS; extended)
  - **Value:** `normal | embed | bidi-override | inherit`
  - **Initial:** `normal`
  - **Inherited:** no
  - **Media:** visual
  - This property specifies the opening of an additional level of embedding of bidirectional characters.
  - **Object to which this property applies:** `bidi-override`

- `vertical-align`   (*7.29.22*; CSS; shorthand)
  - **Value:** `baseline | middle | sub | super | text-top | text-bottom | `*`percentage`*` | `*`length`*` | top | bottom | inherit`
  - **Initial:** `baseline`
  - **Inherited:** no
  - **Percentages:** refer to the "`line-height`" of the element itself
  - **Media:** visual
  - Values specify the vertical positioning of inline-level constructs.

Value	alignment-baseline	alignment-adjust	baseline-shift	dominant-baseline
"baseline"	"baseline"	"auto"	"baseline"	"auto"
"top"	"before-edge"	"auto"	"baseline"	"auto"
"text-top"	"text-before-edge"	"auto"	"baseline"	"auto"
"middle"	"middle"	"auto"	"baseline"	"auto"
"bottom"	"after-edge"	"auto"	"baseline"	"auto"
"text-bottom"	"text-after-edge"	"auto"	"baseline"	"auto"
"sub"	"baseline"	"auto"	"sub"	"auto"
"super"	"baseline"	"auto"	"super"	"auto"
percentage	"baseline"	*percentage*	"baseline"	"auto"
length	"baseline"	*length*	"baseline"	"auto"

- visibility   (*7.28.8*; CSS; extended)

  - **Value:** visible | hidden | collapse | inherit
  - **Initial:** visible
  - **Inherited:** yes
  - **Media:** visual
  - This property specifies whether the boxes generated by an element are rendered even while affecting layout.
  - **Objects to which this property applies:** block, character, inline, leader, page-number, page-number-citation, table-body, table-column, table-footer, table-header, table-row, title

- voice-family   (*7.6.17*; CSS; basic)

  - **Value:** [[*specific-voice* | *generic-voice*],]* [*specific-voice* | *generic-voice*] | inherit
  - **Initial:** depends on user agent
  - **Inherited:** yes
  - **Media:** aural
  - *generic-voice* values are voice families from the set "male", "female", and "child".

- *specific-voice* values are specific instances that may be recognized by the rendering agent —
  - e.g. "comedian", "romeo", "juliet", etc.
- **Objects to which this property applies:** basic-link, bidi-override, block, character, external-graphic, initial-property-set, inline, instream-foreign-object, leader, list-block, list-item, page-number, page-number-citation, table-and-caption, table, table-body, table-caption, table-cell, table-footer, table-header, table-row, title

- volume   (*7.6.18*; CSS; basic)

  - **Value:** *number* | *percentage* | silent | x-soft | soft | medium | loud | x-loud | inherit
  - **Initial:** medium
  - **Inherited:** yes
  - **Percentages:** refer to the inherited value
  - **Media:** aural
  - This property specifies the median volume of the waveform.
  - **Objects to which this property applies:** basic-link, bidi-override, block, character, external-graphic, initial-property-set, inline, instream-foreign-object, leader, list-block, list-item, page-number, page-number-citation, table-and-caption, table, table-body, table-caption, table-cell, table-footer, table-header, table-row, title

- white-space   (*7.29.23*; CSS; shorthand)

  - **Value:** normal | pre | nowrap | inherit
  - **Initial:** normal
  - **Inherited:** yes
  - **Media:** visual
  - This property specifies a set of properties that would otherwise be individually specified.

Value	linefeed-treatment	white-space-collapse	white-space-treatment	wrap-option
"normal"	"treat-as-space"	"true"	"ignore-if-surrounding-linefeed"	"wrap"
"pre"	"preserve"	"false"	"preserve"	"no-wrap"
"nowrap"	"treat-as-space"	"true"	"ignore-if-surrounding-linefeed"	"no-wrap"

- white-space-collapse   (*7.15.12*; XSL; extended)

  - **Value:** false | true | inherit
  - **Initial:** true
  - **Inherited:** yes
  - **Media:** visual
  - This property specifies that a space, tab, or carriage return character is ignored if it follows another such character or immediately precedes a linefeed character.
  - **Object to which this property applies:** block

- white-space-treatment   (*7.15.8*; XSL; extended)

  - **Value:** ignore | preserve | ignore-if-before-linefeed | ignore-if-after-linefeed | ignore-if-surrounding-linefeed | inherit
  - **Initial:** ignore-if-surrounding-linefeed
  - **Inherited:** yes
  - **Media:** visual
  - This property specifies the behavior of space, tab, and carriage return characters.
  - **Object to which this property applies:** block

- widows   (*7.19.7*; CSS; basic)

  - **Value:** *integer* | inherit
  - **Initial:** 2
  - **Inherited:** yes
  - **Media:** visual

- This property specifies the minimum number of lines of a block that must be at the top of a page.
- **Object to which this property applies:** `block`

- `width`   (*7.14.12*; CSS; basic)

  - **Value:** `length` | `percentage` | `auto` | `inherit`
  - **Initial:** `auto`
  - **Inherited:** no
  - **Percentages:** refer to the width of containing block
  - **Media:** visual
  - Negative values are illegal.
  - This property does not apply to non-replaced inline-level elements.
  - **Objects to which this property applies:** `block-container`, `external-graphic`, `inline`, `inline-container`, `instream-foreign-object`, `table`, `table-caption`, `table-cell`

- `word-spacing`   (*7.16.8*; CSS; extended)

  - **Value:** `normal` | `length` | `space` | `inherit`
  - **Initial:** `normal`
  - **Inherited:** yes
  - **Media:** visual
  - This property specifies inter-word spacing behavior in addition to the default space between words.
  - Negative values are allowed.
  - **Objects to which this property applies:** `bidi-override`, `character`, `initial-property-set`, `leader`, `page-number`, `page-number-citation`

- `wrap-option`   (*7.15.13*; XSL; basic)

  - **Value:** `no-wrap` | `wrap` | `inherit`
  - **Initial:** `wrap`
  - **Inherited:** yes
  - **Media:** visual
  - This property specifies how line-breaking of the content is to be handled.

- "no-wrap" will cause lines longer than the width of the content rectangle to be considered an overflow condition on the reference area.
- **Objects to which this property applies:** block, inline, page-number, page-number-citation

- writing-mode   (*7.27.7*; XSL; basic)
  - **Value:** lr-tb | rl-tb | tb-rl | lr | rl | tb | inherit
  - **Initial:** lr-tb
  - **Inherited:** yes (see prose)
  - **Media:** visual
  - "lr" is a shorthand for "lr-tb".
  - "rl" is a shorthand for "rl-tb".
  - "tb" is a shorthand for "tb-rl".
  - **Objects to which this property applies:** block-container, inline-container, region-after, region-before, region-body, region-end, region-start, simple-page-master, table

- xml:lang   (*7.29.24*; XSL; shorthand)
  - **Value:** *country-language* | inherit
  - **Initial:** not defined for shorthand properties
  - **Inherited:** yes
  - **Media:** visual
  - *country-language* is a language and/or country value in conformance with RFC 3066.
  - This property is recognized as a shorthand for country and language.

- z-index   (*7.28.9*; CSS; extended)
  - **Value:** auto | *integer* | inherit
  - **Initial:** auto
  - **Inherited:** no
  - **Media:** visual
  - Constructs with higher z-index numbers are "in front" of those with lower z-index numbers and obscure the constructs that are "behind".
  - **Object to which this property applies:** block-container

E

Choosing
XSL-FO
products

E Choosing XSL-FO products

Answers to the following questions may prove useful when trying to better understand an XSL-FO product offering from a vendor. The specific questions are grouped under topical questions. These by no means make up a complete list of questions, as you may have your own criteria to add; nonetheless, they do cover the aspects of XSLT that may affect the stylesheets and transformation specifications you write.

- How is the product identified?
  - What is the name of the XSL-FO processor in product literature?
  - Which version of XSL-FO is supported?
  - To what email address or URL are questions forwarded for more information in general?
  - To what email address or URL are questions forwarded for more information specific to the answers to these technical questions?
- What are the details of the implementation and invocation of the XSL-FO processor?
  - What hardware/operating system platforms does the processor support?
  - What character sets are supported for the input file encoding?
  - What is the XSLT processor used?
    - Can it be replaced with another XSLT processor?

- What is the XML processor used?
  - Can it be replaced with another XML processor?
  - Does the XML processor support minimally declared internal DTD subsets with only attribute list declarations for ID-typed attributes?
  - Does the XML processor support XML Inclusions (Xinclude)?
  - Does the XML processor support catalogues for public identifiers?
  - Does the XML processor validate the source file?
    - Can this be turned on and off?
- Can the processor be embedded in other applications?
  - Can the processor be configured as a servlet in a web server?
- Is the source code of the processor available?
  - In what language is it written?
- For Windows-based environments, the following questions are relevant.
  - Can the processor be invoked from the MS DOS command prompt?
  - Can the processor be invoked from a GUI interface?
  - What other methods of invocation can be triggered (DLL, RPC, etc.)?
  - Can error messages be explicitly redirected to a file using an invocation parameter (since, for example, Windows 95 does not support redirection of the standard error stream to a file)?

- What features of XSL-FO are supported?
  - What constructs are absent or only partially supported?
  - What graphics formats does the product support?
    - Does the formatter support relative URIs for external graphic resources?
    - Does the formatter require a protocol specification in the URI?
    - Are vector-based formats rendered at device resolution?
  - What color schemes are supported?

- How are specific features implemented?
  - At what conformance level is each feature implemented?
  - What is the thickness of each of the border width named values?
  - Which writing directions are supported?
  - What fonts are supported and how are fonts supported?
  - What ligatures are recognized for adjacent characters?
  - Which properties and states of `<basic-link>` are supported and how?
    - Does the user interface have a "back" function to retrace steps?

- What convenience features are implemented?
  - Can the resulting file be fragmented for ease of management or transmission?
  - Can the result be packaged in groups of different page sizes (to support fold-outs)?
  - Can different hoppers be specified for the printer for different paper selections?

- What extension formatting objects and properties are implemented?
    - Are there any vendor-defined extensions to the vocabulary?
    - What namespace URI is used to identify the vocabulary?
- What output formats are supported?
    - PDF?
        - Are internal links supported?
        - Are external links supported?
        - Is there an extension for turning on the PDF security bit in the result?
        - Is there an extension for defining the "General Info" fields for title, subject, author, etc.?
    - PostScript?
    - Windows GDI?
    - PCL?
    - T$_{\mathrm{E}}$X?
    - RTF?
    - Other?
- What instream foreign object vocabulary namespaces are supported?
    - SVG?
    - MathML?
    - Other?

Index

leader-length, property
  defined, 388
  referenced, 153, 342
leader-pattern, property
  defined, 388
  referenced, 153, 342, 411
leader-pattern-width, property
  defined, 389
  referenced, 153, 342
leaders, 146–152
  distance between, 151
  multiple, 150–151
left, property
  defined, 389
  referenced, 86, 326, 410
length, data type
  defined, 335
  referenced, 336, 346, 349–352,
    362, 366, 369–371, 373, 375,
    378, 382, 385, 387, 389–395,
    397–403, 406–407, 410–411,
    413, 417, 421–425, 428
length-bp-ip-direction, data type
  defined, 336
  referenced, 362
length-conditional, data type
  defined, 336
  referenced, 353, 355, 358, 363,
    398–400
length-range, data type
  defined, 336
  referenced, 352, 385, 388
lengths
  percentages in, 87, 309–310
  units in, 86, 309–310
letter-spacing, property
  defined, 389
  referenced, 103, 106, 153, 204,
    294–295, 342
letter-value, property
  defined, 390
  referenced, 66
ligatures, 82
line-height, property
  defined, 390

  referenced, 61, 81, 94, 96, 101,
    103–104, 106, 108, 118, 140,
    142, 146, 153, 204, 294–295,
    342, 377, 385
line-height-shift-adjustment,
  property
  defined, 390
  referenced, 101, 342
line-stacking-strategy, property
  defined, 391
  referenced, 93–94, 101, 342
linefeed-treatment, property
  defined, 391
  referenced, 101–102, 342, 427
lines, 80, 83, 88, 93–94, 284
  breaks in, 107, 244
  first in a block, 98, 149
  last in a block, 98, 149
  minimum number of, 246
  orphans, 246–247
  stacking of, 83, 93–94
  widows, 246–247
links see hyperlinks
list-block, formatting object
  defined, 131–132
  referenced, 69, 81, 124, 130–133,
    137, 318, 320, 326, 328, 330,
    332, 334, 347–365, 367, 372,
    374–375, 384, 386–387,
    392–393, 398–401, 404–408,
    410–411, 413–418, 426
list-item, formatting object
  defined, 133–134
  referenced, 124, 131–132,
    134–136, 318, 320, 326, 328,
    330, 332, 334, 347–356,
    358–365, 367, 372, 374–375,
    384, 386–387, 392–393,
    398–401, 404–405, 408,
    410–411, 413–418, 426
list-item-body, formatting object
  defined, 136–137
  referenced, 124, 130, 133, 137,
    318, 320, 326, 384, 386, 411,
    413
list-item-label, formatting object
  defined, 134–135